"Frank, well written . . . [it] raises provocative questions." —*Elle*

"One of those rare books that has the potential to create shock waves and revolutions within a profession. An inspiring, lofty statement from a very courageous physician." —Larry Dossey, M.D.

"Orloff tried to stave her intuitions off during medical school until she found herself 'trapped' in a profession that was itself dependent on dispensing drugs to silence the spirit. . . . To listen only to the mind and not the soul is, Orloff believes, a form of insanity." —*San Francisco Chronicle*

"Truly special . . . [Orloff is] a physician to the heart, mind, and soul." —*Philadelphia Daily News*

"If anyone can bridge the gap between the paranormal and the world of Sigmund Freud it's Dr. Judith Orloff." —*New York Post*

"[Dr. Judith Orloff] sensitively merges the spiritual and material worlds and brings the reader in touch with the deeper mysteries of life." —Deepak Chopra

"Fascinating . . . Dr. Orloff writes with wisdom and humility about her emergence as a physician with extraordinary abilities. Highly recommended." —Dean Ornish, M.D.

"You must open this book and your mind. It is a book full of courage and enlightenment. I speak from experience when I say *Second Sight* is a wise teacher." —Bernie Siegel, M.D.

"We are far more than we have allowed ourselves to be. Judith Orloff is to be commended for helping us to understand this simple truth." —Louise Hay

"An intensely personal spiritual odyssey. Dr. Orloff's self-portrait as an intuitive psychiatrist is filled with love and a truth born of an extraordinary gift." —Norman Lear

Also by Judith Orloff, M.D.

Positive Energy
Dr. Judith Orloff's Guide to Intuitive Healing
Emotional Freedom

SECOND SIGHT

An Intuitive Psychiatrist
Tells Her Extraordinary Story and
Shows You How to
Tap Your Own Inner Wisdom

Judith Orloff, M.D.

Three Rivers Press   New York

All the stories in this book are true. As a physician, however, I've sought
to protect the privacy of my patients by not using their real names.
I've also changed certain identifying details to be absolutely sure
not to violate confidentiality.

Copyright © 1996, 2010 by Judith Orloff, M.D.

Published in the United States by Three Rivers Press, an imprint of
the Crown Publishing Group, a division of Random House, Inc., New York.
www.crownpublishing.com

Three Rivers Press and the Tugboat design are registered trademarks
of Random House, Inc.

Originally published in hardcover in the United States by Warner Books, Inc.,
New York, in 1996.

Library of Congress Cataloging-in-Publication Data

Orloff, Judith
Second Sight/Judith Orloff.
p. cm.
1. Orloff, Judith.   2. Clairvoyants—United States—Biography.
3. Psychiatrists—United States—Biography.   I. Title.
BF12383.075A3   1996
133.8'4'092 - dc20
[B]   95-46444
CIP

ISBN 978-0-307-58758-9

Printed in the United States of America

3 5 7 9 10 8 6 4 2

Revised Edition

To the memory of my mother and father

For the first few days which followed this vision experience I was sick with shock. . . . My Irish background made me wonder if this might not be what the country people called *second sight*. I did not dare mention the vision to anybody. . . . Fear overwhelmed me when I realized that I had something unusual in my makeup which made it possible for events to register themselves vividly in some part of my being, whether I wished it or not. Furthermore, I began to realize that the event could be happening either close to me or at a distance, could be occurring in the present, or could have occurred in the past, or might even be about to happen in the future. . . .

—Eileen Garrett (1893–1970), *My Life*

Contents

New Introduction

As a physician, I combine intuition with mainstream medicine, a mix still considered heresy by some statistics-equals-reality-oriented physicians. What I do isn't just my job. It's my life's passion. With my patients and with those who attend my workshops, I listen and diagnose with my intellect and my intuition, a potent inner wisdom that goes beyond the linear mind. I experience intuition as a flash of insight, a gut feeling, a hunch, or a dream. I always wait for the goose bumps, those marvelous tingles that tell me "Yes! I'm on center." I don't act unless they are there. I use my intuitive abilities to complement hard science and my medical background to develop a diagnosis and treatment plan. Blending my intuition with conventional medical knowledge, I can offer my patients the best of both worlds.

In *Second Sight,* I share with you my struggles and triumphs as I came to terms with intuition in my personal life and as a physician. Although listening to intuition is sacred to me and my intuitive voice is loud, clear, and unafraid, it hasn't always been so. The only child of two physician parents, with another twenty-five physicians in my extended family, I come from a lineage of hard-core scientific thinkers. As a child, I had dreams and intuitions that came true. At first my parents wrote these off as coincidences, but Mother and Dad soon became so unnerved I was forbidden to speak about them at home. I grew up ashamed of my abilities, convinced there was something wrong with me.

I was moved to write *Second Sight* because I yearned to free my intuitive voice and help others do the same. As a board-certified psychiatrist in private practice and an Assistant Clinical Professor of Psychiatry at UCLA, I work in a mainstream medical system which too often worships the intellect at the expense of intuition. *Second Sight* took me seven years to write because I had to steadily confront my fears about what my physician colleagues would think. Was it appropriate to bring intuition into clinical practice? Was it trustworthy? Would I be criticized by the medical community to which I felt so honored to belong? Ultimately, my passion for writing this book carried me through because I believed, and continue to believe, that favoring science over intuition is a deplorable disservice to patients. We don't have to choose the intellect over intuition; true healing embodies these dual forms of knowledge.

A huge gift that came from publishing *Second Sight* was that it allowed me to come out of the "intuitive closet." I was no longer able to take refuge in anonymity, wary of being condemned by a hyper-cerebral world that has forgotten how to see. I had to take a stand on the value of intuition in healing. True, there are risks whenever you stretch yourself. But once I grew certain of the power and goodness of the message—and saw how much listening to intuition could help others heal—this overrode my fears. The rewards of following my calling, and not letting fear stop me, continue to be transformative and sustaining. You can see why I, myself, owe *Second Sight* a great debt, and why it will always be so special to me.

Since the original release of *Second Sight*, it's been beautiful to watch a renaissance in numerous aspects of society with regard to integrating intuition, from the way we manage our health, to our finances and business opportunities, to our relationships. Today, all kinds of people are validating the usefulness of listening to our inner voice: the perception that it is "woo-woo" is fading. Minds and hearts are opening. Nearly half of Americans use complementary medical modalities such as acupuncture or homeopathy, either on their own or to augment mainstream medical treatments. The National Institutes of Health funds numerous research projects on holistic therapies, from how yoga can relieve insomnia to how qigong can be an adjunct to cancer care. Brain-mapping studies have shown our brains are wired for spiritual experiences—over one hundred medical schools now teach spirituality courses. "The Science of Meditation" has graced the cover of *Time* magazine.

At the same time, conventional Western medicine is waking up. Cutting-edge science associates intuition with a separate "brain" in the gut called the enteric nervous system, a neuronal network that learns and stores information. In addition, Harvard researchers have linked the overall capacity for intuition with the basal ganglia, a part of the brain that informs us something isn't right and we'd better act on it. *Science* magazine reports that when we sleep on a decision, this "unconscious thought" results in smarter choices than overthinking, particularly with larger issues. In my medical practice and life, I passionately subscribe to the "sleep on it" school of decision making. As I share in *Second Sight,* there is tremendous insight to be gained by tapping the wild creativity of dreams and the subconscious mind.

In recent years, the worth of intuition has also been ever more recognized in business and leadership. The *Harvard Business Review* indicates that nearly half of corporate executives now rely on instinct instead of just facts and figures to run their companies. *Forbes* magazine calls intuition "the golden gut." Luminaries from Conrad Hilton to Bill Gates to Oprah have declared it essential for success. In fact, Donald Trump stated, "I've built a multibillion-dollar empire by using my intuition."

Since the original publication of *Second Sight,* I've also experienced miraculous changes to my own relationship with intuition. Until then, I'd been in private practice for thirteen years, seeing patients five days a week, and had rarely done any public speaking. I'm quiet and shy, basically an introvert who requires much alone time. But *Second Sight* catapulted me into a larger sphere, allowed me to fully own who I am and convey my message more openly. I've been delighted to address audiences worldwide about claiming their intuition. I've spoken to wonderfully diverse groups in churches, prisons, synagogues, hospitals, universities, alcohol-recovery centers, corporations, human rights forums, and hospices. I'm pleased to report that I was the first "intuitive psychiatrist" invited to speak at the American Psychiatric Association Convention, where the bigwigs of our profession go, the most conservative of the conservative. I've mentored UCLA medical students and psychiatry residents as well as offered intuition training seminars for health care professionals. It is critical that healers develop confidence in their intuition and use it in service of others. Intuition is our universal legacy, a language that everyone can learn.

Nonetheless, despite the widespread positive changes I've seen in medicine, I still encounter resistance to intuition among some mainstream physicians. My style, though, isn't to try to convince anyone of anything. I've found that what makes sense to skeptics is simply stating how intuition can be applied clinically—for instance, teaching patients to listen to their gut feeling to choose healthy relationships. I've also seen that often when these physicians or their loved ones suffer a health crisis, they become more receptive to alternatives as they encounter the limitations of conventional treatments. Though crisis can be a potent awakener, what I advocate in *Second Sight* is that we need not—and should not—wait for one to open up to the power of intuitive healing.

Each and every day, my own understanding of intuition continues to evolve. I've seen how its vibrant intelligence keeps teaching us new ways to be—how to stay more aware, more sensual, and more receptive to the range of reliable signals available to us when making all decisions. I consider myself a lifelong student of intuition. I always teach it in conjunction with expanding the heart—a process of spiritual growth and finding compassion without limits. It's not just an extrasensory skill to gain access to information, such as picking lottery numbers. That holds no interest for me. Rather, my intention is to use intuition for health and healing. Years ago, I was most dazzled by the high-voltage intuitive moments, the big-time synchronicities, déjà vus, and premonitions—all truly thrilling occurrences I discuss in this book. As time has passed, however, I've become equally besotted with the smaller moments that intuition brings—tuning in and knowing what to say to a friend in pain; how to handle a difficult situation at work; what will soothe your partner during hard times. These heartfelt interactions are extremely meaningful.

I continue to be touched by how *Second Sight* has deeply affected my readers' lives. Since writing candidly about my journey of embracing intuition, I've become a safe harbor for others to share similar experiences. I've heard from people all over the world who've said about their intuitions, "I can't tell my spouse, my friends, or my therapist!" They were afraid of being criticized, mocked, of being called illogical or crazy. Those who contacted me were hungry to express themselves to someone accepting, someone who would understand. *Second Sight* gives them permission to nurture and take pride in this precious, intimate aspect of themselves. I hope it will help you to do the same.

This book provides a road map for everyone who is drawn to intuition and describes how to make it a seamless, inspired part of your life. In Part 1, "Initiations," you'll read about my story growing up as an intuitive child and how later I began to integrate these abilities in medicine. In Part 2, "Teachings," I share practical techniques to develop intuition, dreams, and a connection with your own spiritual path. Our overintellectualized society doesn't support intuition nearly enough. But the quest to develop it is forever relevant, not only in terms of trusting yourself but also in deepening insight and compassion toward others. The message of *Second Sight* is timeless.

In the past decade, I've grown from someone fighting to find my intuitive voice to feeling a great comfort with this essential aspect of myself. It's wondrous, really, to develop confidence in the power within—to feel the harmony and peace of aspects of the Self converging. This ongoing process continues to hold an intense attraction for me, a coming together of all that is and could be. This is what the adventure of developing intuition can offer.

These days, no matter what I'm going through, especially when my heart is torn in a million pieces or I feel isolated and alone, my intuition and spiritual connection have strengthened me. Whether a situation appears promising or downright dismal, I now have the resources to look beyond the obvious, to achieve a deeper grasp of the picture. I always strive to hear the larger message—not acting hastily out of fear but driven by a sounder sense of truth. The blessing of intuition is that it allows us to tune into an authentic inner authority, offering an alternative to yet again acting out the negative scripts in our heads.

I hope you are inspired by my story in *Second Sight,* that my journey with intuition can help you trust yourself, too. We're all traveling this spiritual path. Of one thing I am certain: if you follow your intuitive voice, you can't go wrong—it's the best friend you'll ever have. Stay true to it. Intuition is about empowerment, not having to conform to someone else's notion of who you should be. It's about becoming attuned to yourself, and all the grace that comes from that.

—Judith Orloff, M.D.
Marina del Rey, California

Foreword
by Thomas Moore, author of *Care of the Soul*

For several centuries now, we have been creating a modern culture that offers many advantages and conveniences and appears to be a natural evolution of human ingenuity. We don't hesitate to tout it as the supreme achievement of human creativity. Its philosophical values—rational, mechanistic, secularistic—touch every area of life from education to medicine to politics, giving the sense, perhaps the illusion, that we understand nature and the human body and mind, and that we can now control them for the good of all.

There must be something profoundly attractive in this philosophy of modernism, because it continues to spread across the globe, drawing into its gaping mouth people who have long maintained ancient traditions of intuitive, enchanted, magical, religious, and erotic responses to life—values generally anathema to modern tastes. Few seem to be aware of modernism's dangers, of the severe limits it places on what is categorized as "normal" human experience and understanding. We have become expert in the materialistic dimensions of nature and culture, and at the same time inarticulate about many experiences that are meaningful and deeply felt in the life of the ordinary person.

In the context of this incredibly shrinking vision of human life, Judith Orloff's *Second Sight* offers profound relief. Her story is both moving and enlightening, revealing how difficult and yet how rewarding it is to be open to forms of knowledge and empathy excluded by the modern idea of what is normal. Her honesty about her own experiences and her insight into the cultivation of intuition, dreams, intuitive impressions, healing, and community might give some halting readers the courage to embrace their own gifts, their individuality, and their unconditional compassion.

Dr. Orloff demonstrates in her own life story how we all, including the most gifted and aware, internalize the limiting vision of the modern world as we hesitate to trust our intuitions and worry about acting on our more subtle perceptions and knowledge. In poignant stories of lovers, parents, and patients, she gives important lessons in the deep ties that link intuition and community, intimate knowledge and love. Through her own example, she teaches us to trust the less rational certainties of the heart, demonstrating how we might draw unexpectedly closer to the people around us and live with a heightened, less defensive ethical sensitivity by living from a deeper source of knowledge and reflection.

Second Sight is not a defensive book. It doesn't shield or bolster the tender subject of intuitive knowledge with technical jargon but instead presents transparent, inviting stories laced with valuable lessons in cultivating intuitive capacities. We can't stretch the edges of modernism's values unless we also break out of its modes of expression. I am much more moved and convinced by the stories she tells—intimate, honest and captivating—than I would be by experiments, studies, and statistics.

Some days I allow myself to imagine a time when we will have jettisoned our superior attitudes toward past and traditional cultures, where intuition has been practiced with intelligence and style. I believe that once we expand our ways of knowing and responding to life, we will discover solutions to personal and social problems, which, in the high-tech world of modern medicine and philosophy, are elusive. We can't find answers to our problems because we have closed our minds to appropriate methods and approaches.

Surprisingly in some ways, *Second Sight* is a book characterized by heart rather than mind. Its purpose is clearly not to convince the world of a point of view or to display powers and achievements. Because of its good heart, I trust it and have learned from it. I invite the reader to bring a matching openness of heart to it, and perhaps discover in our own lives the deep soul that lies beneath layers of modern assumptions and expectations. That soul, with its own unusual, highly individual, often inexplicable powers, can make any life vibrant, heartening, and profoundly meaningful.

Prologue

Early one Saturday morning the telephone rang. My patient Christine's boyfriend had found her unconscious on the floor in her apartment. After taking an overdose of pills, some of which I had prescribed, she was in a coma in the intensive-care unit at a nearby hospital in Los Angeles.

I was stunned. For a few minutes I just sat there immobilized. How could this be? Nothing in my sessions with Christine had pointed to a suicide attempt. That is, nothing my medical education had prepared me for. Still, I agonized, filled with self-reproach. Then, suddenly, I realized that a part of me had been expecting it all along. A premonition had warned me, but I hadn't trusted it; I hadn't listened.

When I first met Christine I had been in practice as a psychiatrist for just six months. From the start she wasn't an easy person to work with. There was an invisible barrier between us that I found both frustrating and aggravating. Even my most tactful inquiries seemed to irritate her, as though I were violating her privacy. When I needed to get her to open up, the requisite mental calisthenics drained me. I got the impression that she wanted to finish each session and get out of my office as quickly as possible.

For years, Christine had gone from psychiatrist to psychiatrist, seeking relief from her depression. She'd been given a gamut of antidepressants, but either they'd had no effect or the side effects outweighed the benefits. When I told her about a new medication that had worked well with other patients, she agreed reluctantly to try it. Over the next few months, I carefully monitored her progress.

Before Christine's regular appointment one morning, I was caught in a traffic jam on the freeway. Sitting in a sea of bumper-to-bumper cars, I began to remember dream fragments from the night before. I had seen Christine wandering down a maze of streets in downtown Manhattan, late at night. The sounds of the city enveloped her, and for moments she would disappear from my sight, swallowed up by the darkness. As I watched her from a distance, she looked alone and lost, searching for something. I called out, but she was too far away to hear my voice.

The dream took me by surprise. In medical school I had stopped dreaming completely. Or at least I couldn't remember my dreams anymore. It was years since I had been able to recall them in such detail. It seemed particularly odd that my dream was about Christine, because we hadn't made much of an emotional connection: I rarely thought about her outside of appointments.

Later in the day, escorting Christine from the waiting room into my office, I apologized for being a few minutes late. She didn't seem bothered, however, which was unusual for her. She was typically annoyed if I wasn't on time. Now, as we sat down opposite each other, she looked tanned and cheerful.

"For the first time in years," she told me, "my depression seems to be lifting. The medication has helped a lot. I don't feel so cut off or afraid of everything anymore."

Observing Christine, I recalled how she'd looked on previous visits: slump-shouldered, eyes dull and downcast, monotone voice, wearing heavy makeup. Today she sat up straight, her eyes animated and alive, her voice strong, her face bright and natural. Over the past six months I had noticed other such positive signs, slow but steady improvement, a good indication that the antidepressant had taken effect. I listened while she described the beginnings of a new romantic relationship. I knew she had also reconciled with her estranged daughter recently, and they were talking about taking a vacation together. I was pleased: Christine was emerging from a cocoon, determined to get well, making plans for the future.

As she spoke, I glanced out the window and noticed a billowy white cloud formation. I stopped hearing Christine, momentarily, lost in watching the changing shape across the sky. Her voice sounded miles away, her words reaching me in slow motion, yet my mind was perfectly lucid. I felt peaceful, as if I were surrounded by freshly fallen snow. Everything was cool, still, silent. I breathed easily, and my body relaxed. I don't know how long this lapse lasted, but in a state of deep quiet and despite everything she was saying, all at once it hit me: Christine was about to make a suicide attempt.

This sudden knowledge felt like an arrow hitting the bull's-eye or a chord ringing clear and pure. But to be aware of a premonition in the context of being a physician felt alien, threatening. A part of me wanted to deny it, to block it out. I felt unsteady, almost faint. My stomach tightened into a knot.

Christine was my last patient that day. It was Friday, and I was exhausted. I left my office late, having signed out to another psychiatrist who would take my calls for the weekend. But the possibility of Christine making a suicide attempt kept gnawing at me.

That evening, I took a walk with a girlfriend in Santa Monica Canyon, a wooded section of Los Angeles, far from the smog and congestion of the inner city. The air was crisp and fragrant, unseasonably warm, like a spring day. As we passed through a quiet tree-lined neighborhood, admiring fields of wildflowers in bloom, I finally began to unwind, but the image of Christine's face kept appearing in my mind.

I saw her as she had been in the dream, directionless and alone, with me chasing her through the streets of Manhattan. Of course, I had no hard evidence that Christine would try to end her life. In fact, everything I knew logically pointed in exactly the opposite direction.

Reminding myself of this, I tried to rationalize my fear, to explain it away. Only at the end of the walk, when my friend observed how edgy I seemed, did I tell her about my premonition. A practical woman, she didn't make too much of it but suggested that the following week I could gently bring up the subject with Christine, just to lessen my own anxiety. I agreed. If Christine's response warranted it, we would then explore her feelings further. For now, since she was doing so well, there was no urgency.

But Christine never made it to her appointment; the next time I saw her she was hooked up to life support in a stark, airless ICU. On the surface I strained to remain professional, but my mind was reeling. By discounting my premonition, I had betrayed both Christine and myself. I couldn't think straight. I felt like Alice when she stepped through the looking glass; suddenly there were no safe landmarks, nothing familiar.

For nearly a decade I had worked night and day. I knew the medical literature backward and forward. I knew all the signs of improvement, all the danger signals, too. Over and over again I asked myself what I had missed. My entire professional foundation was crumbling beneath me.

After poring over my library of medical books, I finally called David, a friend and colleague who had finished his residency a few years before.

He tried to reassure me that I hadn't missed anything, but I wasn't convinced. Medically, he was right. But it wasn't my medical competence that concerned me. I was shocked by my blatant disregard of intuitive information that could have benefited Christine, that might have made the difference between her life and death. Because the source of my impressions hadn't fit the traditional model, I had ignored them.

During my medical training I had opted to trust the scientific method above my intuition, which seemed inexact and undependable in comparison. When making critical decisions that affected other people's lives, I had chosen a system that was more concrete and absolute. I had lost track of the fact that such a system, whatever its virtues, rarely tells the whole story.

All that month I made daily visits to the hospital, checking Christine's medical charts, watching the shallowly breathing form on the white bed, the almost unwrinkled sheets pulled over her body. I listened to the wheeze and chug of the respirator beside her; I watched the drip of the IV. Christine looked like a ghost of herself, pale and gray. I longed to hear her voice, to witness some signs of life so that my guilt would be assuaged. But there was only a deathly quiet.

Many days I pulled the curtains around Christine's bed and sat beside her, reviewing her case in my mind from every conceivable angle, thinking of all the ways I might have broached the subject of suicide with her. In the course of my medical education, I had been taught guidelines to follow, rules to rely on. To act on a premonition in making clinical decisions would have been sacrilege. We had been taught that many people don't consider suicide on a conscious level until the last moment. Such thoughts may churn in their minds, unnoticed and unheeded, breaking through only when they are alone, beyond the reach of a therapist. And so it was in dealing with the unconscious that my premonition could have best served Christine.

The only mention of premonitions or other intuitive abilities I ever found during my medical education was in textbooks labeling such claims a sign of profound psychological dysfunction. I took great pride in my status as an active member of the American Psychiatric Association, in being an attending staff physician at prestigious hospitals, in the respect of my peers. Sitting there at Christine's side, however, I suddenly felt as if two distinct parts of me had collided. I could see my face as a young girl in the early 1960s overlaid on the outline of my face now: two disjointed images, positioned on top of each other, about to merge. What had I been running from for so long? I felt a fluttering in my chest, a cold, still tension. I became rigid inside, afraid that if I moved I would shatter into a million pieces of broken glass.

The truth of my premonition both validated and terrified me. But I had to acknowledge the facts of Christine's case. If I could draw on both intuitive and medical knowledge, I had the tools to stay one step ahead of a patient, keeping tabs on thoughts and feelings before they became irreversible actions. Used with care, my intuitive abilities would do no harm and, more important, might prevent suffering.

As I looked at Christine's face on the pillow, plastic tubes protruding from her nose and mouth, I realized that as a responsible physician I could no longer dismiss information simply because it came to me in forms traditional medicine had not yet accepted. There had to be a way to integrate intuition into mainstream medicine. When brought together, each could enhance the other and become more powerful than either was alone.

After several long weeks, during which I wasn't sure if she would live or die, Christine came out of her coma. I had tried to prepare myself for the possibility that she wouldn't survive, but deep down I knew her death would have devastated me. I would always have felt in some way responsible for not having acted on my premonition. Thus, despite the long nightmare of her coma, I was relieved and grateful. We had both been given a reprieve.

When we resumed our therapy together, my approach as a psychiatrist changed. I took a vow that became part of my own Hippocratic Oath: not only to do no harm, but also to seek a therapeutic relationship in which I could give my all. I wasn't sure how I was going to accomplish this, but one thing—which Christine had taught me—was certain: The penalty for my not trying was too high.

My struggle with Christine played a pivotal role for me both personally and in my practice. From this experience, I understood that I had to reopen a part of myself that long ago had shut down—no matter how much it frightened me. In truth, I was a child when I started down the path to this critical crossroads. For years, though I fought it, I knew that something set me apart from others, as if I were guided by a different rhythm, a different truth. Now, looking back on my life, I could see that a series of unusual and, to me, unexplainable events had set the stage.

PART 1

Initiations

CHAPTER ONE

The Beginnings of Wisdom

I am large . . . I contain multitudes.
—WALT WHITMAN

It was 3:00 A.M., the summer of 1968. A magical southern California night. I was sixteen years old and had spent the weekend partying at a friend's house in Santa Monica, oblivious to my exhaustion. The soft, warm Santa Anas whipped through the eucalyptus trees, blowing tumbleweeds down deserted city streets. These winds were seductive, unsettling, conveying a slight edge of danger.

The scene was Second Street, two blocks from the beach, in a one-bedroom white clapboard bungalow where my friends and I hung out. We were like animals huddled together for a kind of safety, apart from what we saw as a menacing outside world. Brightly painted madras bedspreads hung from the ceiling, and candles in empty Red Mountain wine bottles flickered on the floor. Barefoot and stretched out on the couch, I was listening to Bob Dylan's "Girl from North Country." I was restless; I wanted something to do.

A young blond man I'd met only an hour before invited me to go for a ride up into the hills. He was a James Dean type, cool and sexy, dressed in a brown leather jacket and cowboy boots, a pack of Camels sticking out of the back pocket of his faded jeans: the kind of guy I always fell for but who never paid much attention to me. I wouldn't have missed this opportunity for anything.

The two of us headed out, stepping over couples who were making out on a few bare mattresses placed strategically on the living room carpet. We jumped into my green Austin Mini Cooper, my companion at the wheel, and took off for Tuna Canyon, one of the darkest, most desolate spots in the Santa Monica range, a remote place the Chumash Indians had consecrated, made sacred.

The road snaked up into the mountains to an elevation of about 1,500 feet; we could see the entire Malibu coastline laid out before us in a crescent of lights all the way from Point Dume down to the southernmost tip of the Palos Verdes Peninsula. The balmy night air blew through my hair, filling my nostrils with the scent of pungent sage and fresh earth. A few lone coyotes howled to one another in the distance.

For a moment, the man I was with glanced over at me and I felt something inside me stir. The softness of his voice, the easy way he moved his body excited me, but I did my best not to show it, determined to play the game of acting as if I didn't care. The heat of his arm extended across my body, his hand now on my leg. I reached my hand over to meet his, slowly stroking each fingertip, one by one. I felt intoxicated: He was a stranger, completely unknown to me. It was the ultimate risk. The closer our destination became, the more my excitement grew. I was anticipating what would happen when we reached the breathtaking view at the top.

The higher we climbed, the more treacherous the curves in the road became. But we were paying little attention, talking nonstop, high on a potent amphetamine we'd taken an hour before at the house. On the last curve before the top, he didn't respond quickly enough and the right front tire plowed into the soft gravel along the shoulder. The car lurched wildly as he wrestled with the steering wheel in a frantic effort to regain control. He slammed on the brakes. I heard the tires shriek and then we were skidding off the pavement and hurtling over the edge of the cliff, plunging down into the darkness below.

I recall only fragments of what happened next. I do know that time slowed down and I began to notice things. The night sky was swirling beneath my feet instead of above me. I could hear peculiar sounds, as though amusement park bumper cars were crashing into one another. I made the emotionless observation that something was distinctly odd, but couldn't quite pinpoint what it was. The horror of my predicament—my imminent death—never really registered. Instead, something shifted; I found myself standing in a sort of tunnel, feeling safe and secure. It didn't occur to me to question where I was or how I got there. Although far in the distance I could hear the wind rushing past the open windows of the car, I was now suspended in this peaceful sanctuary while we fell through space toward the canyon floor hundreds of feet below.

With no impulse to move or to be anywhere other than where I found myself, I looked around the tunnel now surrounding me. It was an amazingly still, long, cylindrical space, its gray color gleaming as if illuminated from behind by a subtle, shimmering source. Though the tunnel did not seem solid, as in ordinary reality, its translucent walls appeared to extend endlessly in both directions, comprised of a swirling, vaporous material resembling billions of orbiting atoms moving at enormous speeds. Other than enclosing me, this surreal world was completely empty, but comfortable and soothing: There were no harsh edges, and the whole tunnel seemed to be vibrating gently. In fact, my body now also looked translucent and was vibrating, as if it had changed form to suit this new environment. I felt utterly at peace, contained, and self-contained, in a place that seemed to be without limits, going on forever.

Suddenly I remembered being a little girl, looking up into space while sitting on my rooftop, fascinated by the sky and the planets, sensing an invisible presence. For hours I'd stare at what I couldn't see but could feel more strongly than anything material. From my earliest memory, I always believed in God. Not so much the God of the Jewish religion in which I was raised, or any other religion for that matter, but a formless, ever-present being that twinkled through all things and lovingly watched over me. That same presence was now with me in the tunnel, more familiar and closer than it ever had been when I was a child. Enveloped by it, as if wrapped in a warm cashmere blanket on a cold winter's night, I was in perfect balance, impervious to harm, protected by an invisible but somehow tangible, sustaining life force.

Time had stopped, each moment stretching out into eternity. From what felt like a great distance away, I gazed through the shattered windshield, noticing soft moonlight streaming through the canyon. The car bounced off huge boulders, turning end over end through the air as we plummeted down the mountainside. And yet I never perceived that I was in the slightest danger; I experienced not a single moment of fear. With the coolness of a detached observer, I counted the times the car somersaulted: once, twice, three, four, all the way up to eight. Protected by the shelter of the tunnel, I remained in a void, suspended in free fall, not knowing if this was life or death.

As abruptly as I'd been pulled into it, I was jolted out of the tunnel and back into the present, just as the car crashed down on solid ground. With a high, shuddering bounce and a grating sound of steel against rock, we careened to a grinding halt, the front wheels of the car projecting over a narrow ledge. We were precariously balanced, actually teetering on the precipice.

Thrown by the impact of our landing, my companion and I had both ended up in the backseat. Fragments of broken glass were scattered all over the inside of the car, but miraculously, neither of us was hurt. We quickly realized, though, that we were still in danger: At any moment the car might slide forward and tumble into a large ravine below. We had to get out of there fast.

A live oak tree trying to crawl in through the window appeared to be our only available support. Without looking back I grabbed on to its branches and managed to pull myself out of the mangled car. My companion close behind, we scrambled up the side of the cliff, pushing through thickets of manzanita and wild mustard, barely penetrable scrub brush and wild chaparral. Trying to avoid the loose, unstable mounds of dirt and slippery leaves beneath our feet, we used shrubs as ropes to pull ourselves up the sheer hillside. Yet even as we inched our way to the top, I kept asking myself, Why were our lives spared? We should have been killed. Instead, we were walking away with hardly a scratch. And already the image of the tunnel haunted me.

Very relieved to be on solid ground again, we were soon able to hitchhike a ride down the winding canyon roads back into the city. Faint rays of pink dawn light were beginning to illuminate the hills. I don't think either of us said a single word the entire time, but I'm not certain. I have little recall of the trip. Staring off into space, I replayed the accident over and over in my mind, unable to account for how we could still be alive. Only a miracle could have saved us.

For many days, I blanked out the details of the actual fall but retained a few disjointed images. I could distinctly remember the car rolling over the cliff and the giddy, weightless, out-of-control sensations during the drop. It was like going over the first big dip on a gigantic roller coaster. I also recalled how every cell in my body had screamed in protest in the instant of the screeching, bone-jarring landing. As for the tunnel, I had no idea what to make of it. It was an enigma, a mystery I would continue to try to unravel for a long time to come.

For my parents, what happened that night was only the latest in a series of drug-related calamities in my life. I was their only child and they were frantic. It wasn't so long before that my mother had sung me to sleep with lullabies, that my father and I had played miniature golf on the weekends. I looked up to my parents, and I knew they both wanted my life to be easy, to shelter me, but the tighter their hold, the more I rebelled. When I began to take drugs, I could see I was breaking their hearts. I knew they feared for my safety, saw our relationship slipping away. But I felt I had no choice. I had to break free. During the past years, they'd watched me change from being a quiet, sensitive girl into a stranger—unreachable, out of control.

Before the Tuna Canyon wreck, my parents had done all they could to get me some help. My mother, a strong-willed family practitioner, and my father, a soft-spoken radiologist, were both prominent physicians in Beverly Hills; they had the resources of the community behind them. A practical man, with a root integrity, successful but satisfied with the simplest pleasures, my father would look at me with his large oval, blue-green eyes as if trying to see where I'd gone. And my mother, powerful, gregarious, afraid I wouldn't fit in, seemed to be determined with all her intensity and faith to straighten me out, even at the risk of being overbearing. But I was stubborn and rebellious. I just wouldn't listen, was convinced my parents were incapable of truly understanding my inner struggles, perhaps because I didn't understand them myself.

Among other things, I was fed up with being so sensitive. I felt no one could understand me anyway—how I sometimes knew things about people before they said a word. Or how I made accurate predictions about the future, often unhappy ones. My father never gave these predictions much credence or even said anything about them. Loyal, a man of few words, he was a strong, steady presence; his chief concern was keeping peace in the family. His mind sought the concrete, was most comfortable with the world in which he'd succeeded so well. The strange, the unusual—well, if it created problems, he was against it. But for my mother, my predictions seemed to touch a raw nerve. She never encouraged them; they made her uneasy, fearful that such talk would keep me from being normal. Much honored, my mother took enormous pride in being part of the Jewish community, the medical community, having a celebrity practice in Beverly Hills, many friends, a phone that never stopped ringing. But my predictions made me no more comfortable than they made her. In fact, I would have done anything to shut them off. And drugs could do that for me. They provided a way out and I took it.

After the accident, my parents did their best to protect me. The next morning, they packed up my things from our Westwood home and sent me to stay with some of their close friends in Malibu Colony, a well-guarded and affluent section of Malibu Beach. While they were deciding how best to help me, they insisted I remain there, isolated from my own friends, and most important, away from drugs. I knew their motives were good, but still I went grudgingly.

Nonetheless, I'd reached a turning point. My close brush with death had shaken me, but more than that, I'd undergone a passage, had in some strange way come back to myself. I couldn't stop thinking about the tunnel, its utter tranquillity, and the miracle that somehow, in defiance of the laws of physics, it allowed me to survive a catastrophic wreck.

When my parents dropped me off at the Malibu beach house, a dense fog was beginning to burn off as the sun lit up the coast. Disgruntled and moody, I settled in as best I could. Refusing to talk to anyone, I installed myself on the living room sofa and turned on the TV. There I lay, in a pink tie-dyed tank top and bell-bottom jeans with flowers embroidered on the pockets, mindlessly watching a *Star Trek* episode. Soon, however, my parents' friends barged in and introduced me to a neighbor. Viewing any interruption as an intrusion, I was hostile when I looked up at him, but I quickly did a double take.

Jim was a tall, lean man in his midforties, with full, curly white hair and a white beard. He also happened to be standing in front of a backdrop of golden rays being reflected off the ocean, creating a halo effect. He looked like a storybook version of God. I wanted to burst out laughing, but I stopped myself. On sheer principle, I refused to cooperate, and laughing might be misconstrued as my "coming around." But in the celestial light of Jim's presence, this whole mess suddenly took on a comic twist. Here I was, exiled in Malibu, very much alive for no apparent reason, and now a man who looked like God was towering over me.

Almost before I knew it, Jim was sitting on the couch beside me and gently asking me questions about myself. Annoyed by how forward he was, I wondered, Who is this man anyway? I wanted to dislike him, but somehow I couldn't. His large brown eyes and kind, unassuming manner soothed me. His presence gave me a feeling of acceptance, something I seldom experienced around adults. The quality of his voice and the tender way he looked at me seemed familiar, as if we'd sat together a thousand times before, though in fact no one in my life remotely resembled him.

I instantly connected with Jim, felt some sort of magical alliance between us. But there was no way in the world I was going to admit that to anybody. I'd programmed myself to be miserable, and nothing would change my stance. Adamant about refusing to give in to my parents' demands, I hardly spoke to him that first day. Eventually he said good-bye, got up, and left. I made a point of not watching him, kept my gaze fixed on the television.

The next morning my parents issued me an ultimatum. As usual, my mother did most of the talking while my father quietly sat back, giving her his silent but strong support. Either I had to agree to go into psychotherapy now, or they'd send me to live with relatives on the East Coast. My only exposure to psychotherapy had been the few instances when my parents dragged me to family counseling sessions that always ended up in yelling matches, after which we all went home in frustration. As a result, I viewed therapy as a farce, punishment for the inept who couldn't work out their own problems. But since I wanted to stay in Los Angeles at any cost, I reluctantly consented.

Late that August afternoon in 1968, two months after my high-school graduation, the three of us headed for Beverly Hills in the family Lincoln. I sat in the backseat, watching my father's somber but kind face in the rearview mirror. My mother's eyes were unflinching, but whenever she glanced at me, they were sad. To stay numb and pretend I didn't care, I kept silently repeating the words to "Purple Haze," a Jimi Hendrix song.

Our destination was a modest, four-story office building with two cramped elevators and long, windowless halls. While sitting in the waiting room before the appointment, our tension mounted. It was all I could do to keep my mouth shut and not fly out the door.

Not a moment too soon, a familiar figure greeted us: Jim, our friend's neighbor in Malibu, the man I'd met the day before. He was the pyschiatrist we were scheduled to see. I was furious; I felt I'd been tricked and set up. At the same time, I was strangely attracted to him, intrigued by my sense of our intangible rapport. Against my will, it seemed I shared an unspoken camaraderie with him, almost a kinship. Whirling with feelings, I nodded at Jim and grumbled a guarded hello. Then my parents and I followed him into his office.

For the first session, Jim met with us all together. He sat in a black leather swivel chair and motioned for me to sit beside him on an oversized rust-colored ottoman. My parents stiffly sat opposite us on a green-and-beige-striped couch. Soon my mother started sobbing and told Jim how worried she was about me. I pulled my knees up to my chest and rolled into a tight ball. I felt suffocated by the intensity of my mother's love. Her attention always seemed to be on me. I knew how much she cared, but was afraid that if I let her in too close I'd be devoured. She was so dominant a personality that the only way I could be real, I felt, was to oppose her. Given her intensity and persistence, to do so took every ounce of strength I possessed.

Jim listened patiently to both my parents. Then he listened to me. I felt unusually timid around him, paying attention to his opinions, sneaking looks at his clothes, noticing his wedding ring, how he held his hands. I never once intentionally provoked him or cut him off, as I did so often with other adults, particularly authority figures. At the end of the hour, I surprised myself by agreeing to come back again, to try whatever "therapy" was supposed to be.

Relieved that I was at last cooperating with them, my parents allowed me to move back into their home. But after a few months, Jim suggested that I stay in what he called a "halfway house." He knew of two therapists, Pat and Ray, who rented rooms to people like me, people who were in transition and needed support. They lived on the premises with their two young daughters, a cat, and two dogs. Jim thought the move would give me a chance to grow up and begin to separate from my mother and father. I was all for it; I couldn't wait to be on my own. My parents were wary but they'd made a decision to trust Jim and so reluctantly agreed.

I fell in love with the house the moment I saw it. It was a two-story, weathered pink Victorian A-frame on the corner of Park Avenue and the Speedway, an alley that runs along the entire stretch of Venice Beach. The boardwalk and the sand, separated from us by an empty dirt lot, were less than a half block away. At night, I could hear waves breaking on the shore as I fell asleep. I quickly became fast friends with Pat and Ray, good-hearted hippies in their midthirties with degrees in social work who now devoted their lives to helping others. They welcomed me into their home.

The big surprise was the other residents: Pete, a schizophrenic in his early twenties who mostly kept to himself, and Dolly, a wired manic-depressive woman. My God, I thought, Jim put me here with the mentally ill! Pat and Ray agreed: That was exactly what Jim had done. And yet, somehow, it didn't matter to me. What mattered was that I felt free. Still, the first time I opened the medicine cabinet and placed my toothbrush beside Pete's Thorazine and Dolly's Lithium, it did give me the creeps. But besides the times when Pete was hearing voices or Dolly had her bouts of insomnia, we all got along just fine and life was pretty uneventful.

I continued my therapy with Jim. Yet despite the bond I felt I had with him, I didn't open up immediately. Nor did my initial timidity last: I was a hard case, fighting him at every turn, testing and probing to see how far I could go. For several months I missed appointments, challenged him, threatened never to come back again.

Then, one day, after being in therapy about a year, I told Jim about a troubling dream I'd had when I was nine years old. The dream was similar to a wakeful state, vivid, not at all like a regular dream. I'd never discussed it before with anyone except my parents. In fact, I'd purposely kept it a secret. Recalling it now as part of my therapy, I described it in my journal:

> *My nightgown is drenched in sweat as I bolt awake, knowing that my grandfather, who lives three thousand miles away, had just died. I can hear his voice saying good-bye to me over and over again as I struggle to get my bearings. It's the middle of the night. My bedroom is pitch black. I can't tell if I'm dreaming or if this is really happening. Almost too frightened to move, I drag myself from bed and run as fast as I can into my parents' room to give them this message.*
>
> *Instead of being upset by my announcement, my mother smiles and assures me, "You were having a nightmare. Grandpop's fine." The absolute certainty in her voice makes me doubt myself. Of course Grandpop's all right. I've simply overreacted, I'm told. So I head back to my own room again, comforted by the notion that my panic was unfounded, and drift off to sleep.*
>
> *A few hours later, my aunt calls from Philadelphia, to tell us that my grandfather has died of a heart attack.*

As I recounted the dream to Jim, he listened intently without flinching or recoiling as I expected he would. Instead, showing genuine interest, he asked me to speak more about it. I first told him my mother's reaction to the dream, which had confused me. She'd been intrigued and quite tender, yet at the same time seemed to be holding something back, as if she was purposely trying not to make too much of it. Even after she learned of my grandfather's death, she seemed to write off my dream as coincidence. But something in her eyes said she didn't fully believe what she was telling me. And neither did I. I was certain my grandfather had come to say good-bye. The way he looked and the sound of his voice had been too alive, too real, to be mere imagination. Unable to resolve this puzzle, I'd wondered if somehow I was to blame for my grandfather's death.

Grandpop and I had always been close. Years before, he would hoist me up on his shoulders and promise that even after he died we'd never be apart. All I'd have to do was look up at the brightest star in the sky to find him. Our love ran deep, and it was unbearable that I might have hurt my grandfather.

My capacity to bring up these feelings was enhanced by a growing romantic relationship I was developing with Terry, an artist I eventually moved in with for two years. He lived across the street from the halfway house in an old two-story converted brick Laundromat with enormous clear glass pyramidal skylights in practically every room, including the bathroom. As the sun shone through them, the light was pristine. Terry also used the space as his studio. A few inches taller than I, and twenty-five, Terry had a short, blond ponytail and piercing blue eyes. He habitually wore a pair of paint-splattered jeans that mimicked the colorful brush strokes of a Sam Francis canvas.

Terry was one of a four-member group of male muralists who were futurists of a sort. They painted visionary disaster scenes such as earthquakes, snowstorms, and floods. Their murals so closely resembled some of my own premonitions that it seemed they'd been painting my inner life. The group called themselves the Los Angeles Fine Arts Squad and did their artwork on huge bare walls of commercial and residential buildings all over the city. A first of their kind, they were a central part of the Venice art scene.

Terry and I related to each other through the world of images and dreams. I used to speak a lot to him about the dreams that I'd written down for years. I dreamed voraciously, and relished waking up in the morning and retrieving my dreams. On the days when I couldn't hold on to them, I felt empty and vacant, as if I'd missed out on something important. When the images lingered, their richness filled me up like the finest food. They were sacred to me.

Terry and I used to take long walks at night in front of the deserted amusement park—Pacific Ocean Park—where he shared his artistic visions and I shared my dreams. With our faces eerily lit up by the blue mercury lights lining the boardwalk, Terry said that sometimes he could see the images shining right through me. He believed that my ability to generate them indirectly influenced the quality of his art.

Terry's only desire since he was a little boy was to be an artist, to create. As I watched him, so calm and directed, sketching at his rough-hewn pine drawing table late into the nights, lost in the world of art, I prayed I too might find a calling that could give me so much joy.

When at the last minute I decided to forgo college in favor of living with a struggling, long-haired artist eight years my senior who wasn't even Jewish, my parents were exasperated. Having already paid thousands of dollars for my tuition at Pitzer College in Claremont, where I was supposed to begin the following semester, they forfeited the money and refused ever to meet Terry. Convinced that at seventeen I was throwing away my future, they couldn't support that. Not knowing what else to do, my parents decided to withdraw all financial help except the fees for my therapy sessions.

To help earn living expenses, I got my first job as a salesgirl in the towel department at the May Company, earning seventy-five dollars a week. It was located on Fairfax and Wilshire, less than half a mile away from the Climax nightclub, where Terry had been commissioned to paint an outdoor mural. From our studio in Venice, he would drive me to work each morning on his BMW motorcycle. On the coldest, rainiest days, our eyes tearing from the cold, bundled up in our army jackets, I would hold tightly on to his waist as we sped through the city streets. I had never felt happier or more free.

It was through Terry's love and insight that I slowly began to accept myself and my images. Whether or not they were intuitive, they were an intimate part of who I was, and Terry recognized that. He understood and valued their importance as no one had ever done. Terry was the first man I'd been with who I felt could truly "see" me. By encouraging me to explore my intuitive life, he also helped me to start trusting Jim.

In the course of my therapy, I slowly recalled other premonitions I'd had as a child. For instance, one day when I was nine, my parents introduced me to Evan, a longtime friend of theirs from London who took frequent business trips to the States. An impressive man, he was an extraordinarily successful entrepreneur who appeared to have it all: a beautiful wife and family, good health, and the means to maintain an elegant lifestyle, complete with servants, a Rolls-Royce with chauffeur, and a country estate in Surrey.

Within minutes of first being introduced to Evan, however, a sense of dread overtook me, a sinking feeling in my stomach, a certainty that something bad was about to happen to him. My feelings alarmed me because I could see no apparent reason for them. Here was this successful friend of my parents, but I couldn't wait to escape his presence. When I told my mother, she said, "How can you feel that? You've barely met him." I couldn't explain my feelings; there was nothing to back them up, and I felt terrible about myself for having them. We both gladly dropped the subject. Nonetheless, I couldn't help my response. It was automatic, instinctive. I was reminded of how my dog once reacted to a friend of mine, barking and growling at her whenever she came to the house. That was annoying to me, so I had a sense of how my mother felt.

But then, three weeks later, my parents received a call from mutual friends. To the surprise and shock of everyone who knew him, Evan had committed suicide. This time my mother didn't call it a coincidence. Rather, she acknowledged that I must have sensed something: "You were right about Evan. I can't figure it out, but somehow you knew." It was also clear, however, that she was unsettled, reluctant to have further discussion. There was an unusual resignation in her voice, a heaviness, a mix of awkwardness and sadness. She seemed not to know what to do with me— I was odd, a curiosity, something from another planet. My mother had validated what I'd said, but in the end she left me more mixed up than ever. She dropped the subject and life went on as if all this had never happened. Once again, I felt alone, tainted, fearing I'd colluded in something awful, as if stranded with my own thoughts on a deserted island in the middle of the ocean. So I tried to act normal, didn't talk about my feelings.

Jim's attitude toward these incidents was enormously comforting. What I appreciated the most was that he didn't seem judgmental or afraid. A psychiatrist, trained of course in conventional medicine, he could very well have pigeonholed me as a "nut" and dismissed my experiences. Worse, he could have analyzed and interpreted them, searching for hidden meaning rather than taking them on their own terms. Or he could have prescribed antipsychotic medications to squash my abilities. But he didn't. Nor did he hide his bewilderment. It was an odd situation: He was confused; I was confused. But we were trying to sort out our confusion together, which in a roundabout way, allowed me to feel safe.

One day, Jim recounted an intuitive experience of his own, which occurred when he was a psychiatric resident at the Meninger Institute in Kansas. During a snowstorm, his car had a flat tire on a remote country road. When it was clear that he wouldn't be able to return home on time, he knew that his wife would be worried. He really wanted her to know he was okay, but there were no phones. During what they later established had been the same period, his wife had a dream in which she saw Jim's car having tire trouble but that he was unharmed. Not surprisingly, this unusual communication between them had stirred Jim's interest in intuition.

I was touched by Jim's story as well as incredibly relieved to be in the company of an educated person with advanced academic credentials who'd also had such experiences. At least I wasn't the only oddball running around! This gave me solace. Also, I'd taken a risk in trusting Jim, and he didn't let me down. Far from condemning me, he'd shown a profound respect for what I was going through. So when Jim encouraged me to go further and remember other such events, I felt safe enough to do so.

My mother had a close friend, Harry, a Superior Court judge in Philadelphia. She thought of Harry as her mentor, loved him dearly, credited him with inspiring her to attend medical school in an era when few woman were being accepted. When I was ten, Harry ran for reelection to the post he'd held for the past thirty years. Few things in life meant more to him than being a judge. A week before the election, I had the following dream:

> I'm in a huge, well-lit room jammed with people. Harry is up on the podium giving a speech. It's so crowded I can barely breathe. My head pounds. I'm afraid of something but I don't know what it is. A man's voice comes in over a loudspeaker and announces that Harry has lost to his opponent. Harry lowers his head, walks into the crowd, and is about to leave the room when suddenly a woman whose face I can't see rushes toward him and bites his hand. From Harry's expression, I know he recognizes the woman and is crushed.

I didn't want to alarm my mother, especially after her reaction to my premonition about Evan. But I was upset and wanted her support, so I took a chance and told her. Anticipating the success of her friend, she of course found my dream the last news she wanted to hear. She sighed and put her arm around me. "Why do you say such negative things?" she asked, exasperated. After my predictions of her father's death and her friend's suicide, this was just too much. I sat there and wished I could take it back, but the damage was already done.

The night of the election, I sat with my parents in Los Angeles, anxiously awaiting the outcome. Nightmarishly, it was as my dream had predicted: Harry lost by a landslide. If it had only been his defeat, the dream would have seemed less significant. But there was more. At the polls that night, Harry's daughter-in-law, a manic-depressive under psychiatric care, had an acute psychotic break and rushed up to him, viciously biting his hand. Immediately following this attack, she fled into the crowd to hide. Later, she was found and admitted to a hospital for treatment.

Of course, the lives of Harry, his son, and his daughter-in-law were radically disrupted that evening. Over the next few months I heard a lot about their suffering, and couldn't help but question what role my dream had played. Although my parents never suggested that my prediction was in any way responsible, I had my doubts, especially when in a moment of frustration my mother told me never again to mention another dream to her. I knew she was disconcerted by what had happened; I knew she hadn't meant to hurt me. She was simply on overload, and I backed off. But it was also true that she could be overbearing, that she was a woman of great force, and that I couldn't help reacting to her. From that day on, in any case, I kept to myself what I'd come to regard as a shameful secret.

With Jim's support, I was able to feel my tremendous sense of guilt about having made these catastrophic predictions. It seemed, in fact, that I could easily foresee death, illness, and earthquakes, but rarely picked up anything on a happier note. I'd grown up believing there was something malign in me, that somehow I was causing the negative events I was able to predict. Could I have contributed to Harry's defeat, triggered his daughter-in-law's psychotic break? I wondered. None of my friends ever spoke of such experiences. Increasingly, I felt like an outsider, never quite fitting in anywhere.

Then, I told Jim, in 1967, my junior year of high school, I discovered drugs. Although I attended University High, affectionately known as "Uni," in nearby West Los Angeles, most of my friends were seniors at Palisades High in the Pacific Palisades, a more prestigious part of Los Angeles some ten miles away. After school my "Pali" friends would pick me up and we'd go get stoned. I found that most drugs, with the exception of hallucinogens, dulled my intuitive abilities, giving me the illusion that I fit in with my friends. My yearning to feel a sense of belonging would temporarily be satisfied. But no matter how many friends I thought I had, a part of me knew I was living a lie. Then came the night of the accident.

Was the tunnel I encountered as I plunged downward over the cliff related to my premonitions? Neither Jim nor I was sure, but he taught me to trust the authenticity of my experiences. Most important, he helped me see how irrational it was to believe I was causing the events I predicted. He conveyed how children with these gifts who were not educated about them were prone to making preposterous assumptions about themselves. Jim showed me that the real issue was not my abilities, but my misunderstanding of them.

Jim's only concern about helping me explore this aspect of myself was that I'd get so absorbed in it I'd let go of the rest of my life. He had watched people become obsessed with extrasensory experiences and lose track of reality. Even so, he felt I had enough strength to straddle both worlds.

When I first opened up to Jim about my intuitive abilities, he had to accept whatever I told him on faith. For all he knew I might be fabricating grandiose stories to manipulate him. There was no proof because, out of fear, I'd suppressed my gifts, and they didn't come back right away. But Jim trusted me, in part because he believed that everybody had such sensitivities but discounted or rejected them. They just got crushed by parents, teachers, or therapists along the way. But Jim didn't think these abilities ever really disappeared—they kept trying to reemerge, and that scared people. He said it took immense energy to keep anything so powerful sealed up within, resulting in depletion and depression, but added that he'd get little support for these beliefs from his peers.

Though everything Jim told me made sense, I'd lived with isolation for many years, and still resisted his authority. It was a long time before I could really let him in. Over a year after the car wreck, I was in one of Jim's group-therapy sessions. Six of us met in his Beverly Hills office each Tuesday afternoon. I was the youngest and by far the most angry, combative, and disagreeable. It wasn't that I really wanted to pick fights; I just wanted to keep others at a distance. Everyone else in the group had been in therapy long enough to understand that I would either work through my anger and settle down, or leave. I had little doubt that most of them were hoping for the latter.

Toward the end of one of our meetings, John, a businessman in his late fifties, and our newest member, started talking about his depression. Though I was listening to him, my attention began to drift: I must have been either daydreaming or in a light trance when suddenly I saw a car catch on fire with a woman and child trapped inside. I gasped, and everyone fell silent, their attention focused on me.

When, as Jim asked, I recounted the vision, John's depression turned to anguish. Through his tears, he revealed to us for the first time that his wife and young daughter had recently been killed in a tragic explosion when their car collided on the freeway with a gasoline truck.

Even though I logically knew I couldn't have been linked to his family's fate, at that moment I felt responsible for John's sorrow. Every childhood fear I'd ever associated with my intuitive abilities erupted; the self-accusatory voices in my head took over, full of blame.

After the session ended, Jim took me aside. It had been one thing for him to sit in a plush Beverly Hills office and listen to my far-out stories week after week, but it was something else to witness a living demonstration. I remembered when I was a child, my mother, in her desire for me to have a normal, happy life, had warned, "Don't tell anyone about your predictions. They'll think you're strange." I'd believed her. Now I was really worried that Jim wouldn't want to see me anymore, that he'd decided I was too much to handle.

It turned out that my apprehensions were unwarranted. Reassuring me, Jim said I wasn't crazy; my suffering and confusion had been caused by the suppression of my "gifts." Rather than being gotten rid of, they needed to be developed with proper guidance. He suggested I meet Dr. Thelma Moss, a psychologist and researcher at the UCLA Neuropsychiatric Institute who specialized in the study of paranormal phenomena. I was astonished that such a person actually existed. In the past, she'd referred numerous people to Jim who were having difficulty coping with their intuitive experiences. Jim was certain that if anyone could appreciate my experiences and support me in learning more about them, it would be Dr. Moss. For the first time, I felt a glimmer of hope.

CHAPTER TWO

Validating the Voice

Come to the edge. / We might fall.
Come to the edge. / It's too high!
Come to the edge. / And they came
and he pushed / and they flew . . .
—CHRISTOPHER LOGUE

I stood in front of my closet in turmoil. I had no idea what would be appropriate to wear to the meeting. It didn't occur to me that I could just be myself, wear whatever I liked. Instead, I saw my mother's eyes checking me out from head to foot. "It's such a shame," I could hear her saying. "You're so beautiful and you don't show it off." I always battled with my mother over clothes. She was an impeccable dresser in her sleek silk Chanel suits and luxurious Armani coats. She always wanted me to wear dresses. But I liked jeans, especially one particular pair with a big hole in the left knee. I used to put them on day after day, and it drove her crazy. Some nights I even slept in them, as an act of rebellion.

I stared blankly at my wardrobe. I wanted to be comfortable but more important, I wanted to fit in. So a few hours later, wearing a red-and-white-plaid sleeveless dress that I'd bought with my mother at Saks, beige nylon stockings, and black Capezio pumps, I walked past a row of purple jacaranda trees into the B-floor lobby of the Neuropsychiatric Institute. Having tied my shoulder-length brown hair into a ponytail to make it seem less wild, I looked like I'd just stepped out of *Mademoiselle* magazine and couldn't have felt more awkward. Since at that time my stereotype of an intuitive was a carnival Gypsy in a colorful dress reading a crystal ball, or a man dressed in white wearing a turban, I was well disguised.

When Jim first suggested I see Dr. Moss, I lay awake for hours that night, listening to the unusual downpour of summer rain against the bedroom windows. I couldn't stop thinking. Not only was Jim taking me seriously, there was actually an expert at a reputable university who studied intuitive occurrences. I wondered how it would feel to get some real help. Even to contemplate such a possibility was to turn on a very bright light in a room that had been dark my entire life, a light that was now chasing away my worst fears. At last I saw the possibility of breathing easily, of finally being myself.

The following day I'd called Jim and agreed to meet with Dr. Moss, although a week passed before I actually saw her. In the interim, I rode a roller coaster of emotions. Jim sent me a copy of an article from the *Los Angeles Times* that presented Dr. Moss as a forerunner in her field, a maverick scientist willing to investigate areas that more traditional psychologists shunned. But after reading the article, I got a sinking feeling in my stomach. Why would such a respected researcher be interested in meeting with me? I became paralyzed with self-doubt. Maybe I should just forget the whole thing. But I couldn't. I was too intrigued, too curious, too hungry for guidance. Still, I felt split: excited by the prospect that she might understand me, and also desperately afraid of being let down.

I'd awakened on the day of our meeting with a sense of optimism that was new for me, but by the time I reached UCLA, my confidence once again was shaken. It was ten in the morning and already in the nineties. With the previous night's rains, the city had turned into a gigantic steam bath. The building that housed

Dr. Moss's office, the Neuropsychiatric Institute (NPI), was a huge, coldly impersonal eight-story medical center surrounded by the college campus. As I wandered through the long, sterile halls feeling alone and frightened, I doubted I'd ever find the answers I needed.

Dr. Moss, who met me at the door, was a commanding presence. Looking to be in her midforties, about five foot three, with short dark hair and deep brown eyes, she conveyed a strong will and passionate belief, a capacity for being totally present in the moment, and a sense of focused attention and dedication. Dressed like a cover girl, I felt like a naive kid next to this professional in her white lab coat, but she welcomed me into her office with an inviting smile. My heart was racing and I was very much on edge as she asked me to sit and then did her best to put me at ease. She obviously recognized how self-conscious and tense I was, so we chatted for a few minutes until I began to calm down.

"Thanks for coming," she said. "I've spoken with Jim on the phone and I'd like to test your intuitive abilities with a technique known as psychometry. Do you know what that is?"

"No," I answered.

"It's the capacity to hold a physical object and receive specific information about people, places, and events to which it's related," she said, handing me a set of keys. "Hold on to these and relax," she continued in a quiet, comforting voice. "Just stay open to any impressions that might enter your mind."

I'd never done anything like this before, but I followed her directions.

"Close your eyes and concentrate on the keys," she said. "Describe whatever comes to you, no matter how unusual it might seem. I'll be taking notes but try to think of me only as an impartial observer. I won't react or give you any feedback until the end."

As she spoke, the stillness around Dr. Moss became more profound. My body, following her lead, relaxed, and my anxiety began to fade.

I hesitated at first, and then I heard myself say, "These are house keys. Your house keys." Her facial expression was impossible to read. My attention wavered and I found it difficult to keep my mind on the keys. Then, gradually, a distinct image came to me. I saw a colonial-style house in a hilly neighborhood, perhaps a canyon. I was about to relate this to her when my critical mind quickly censored the image, telling me that I was just picturing a house I'd noticed somewhere in the past—there were many of this type scattered throughout L.A. What I observed could easily have been no more than a random memory.

"I'm not getting much of anything," I told Dr. Moss, convinced it was safer to say nothing rather than to risk making a mistake.

"That's okay. Just say the first thing that comes into your awareness. Don't worry about being right."

"I'm not sure," I replied hesitantly, deciding to risk it. "I just see a house with pillars in front of it. Faded white or maybe beige." While I didn't know if I was imagining the house or if it was real, my uncertainty was chipping away at my enthusiasm.

"Stay with it," she said, in the same neutral tone. "Pretend I'm not even here."

I desperately wanted a sign that I was on the right track, at least a little support or validation, yet none was forthcoming. I closed my eyes, about to give up, but what then came to mind was a memory I hadn't thought about for years. As a teenager, whenever life became difficult, I climbed to the top of the largest pine tree on our block. From the highest branches, I had a panoramic view of Westwood. Safely hidden from sight, I'd observe the city all the way from the high-rise Wilshire Boulevard condos in the east to the tall Bruin movie theater tower at the center of Westwood Village. Thus, when I wanted to be alone, to get away from everything, I often retreated to this protected place in my daydreams.

As I remembered this special spot, my tension seemed to disappear and my body softened. Then, slowly, the images began to shift, one flowing effortlessly into the next. Within moments I was standing once more in front of what I was sure was Dr. Moss's home. I knew I was awake, yet unlike a daydream, the scene was startlingly realistic. The strangest part was that I was acutely aware of being at both her home and her office at the same time, equally present in each. It was as though two separate realities were being superimposed one upon the other, a notion that intellectually seemed impossible yet at some deep level felt almost like second nature.

As I moved closer to the entryway, I was astounded by the detail I was able to pick up. "I see a front door with a small window in it." I focused on the façade of the house, and more images appeared, as if I were watching a slow-motion movie. With my eyes shut, the darkness provided a backdrop upon which each image was projected. But it was a very different experience from ordinary sight. A picture would appear upon the backdrop, frozen for a second or two as I viewed it. Then another would follow. I examined each of them closely, noticing subtle variations that in real life I would have missed. I was awestruck by how rich these images were; they seemed to have a life of their own, like images in a brightly painted landscape or portrait.

Soon my senses began to get overloaded: What I was seeing became almost too much to absorb. Abruptly, my logical mind took over and I started to analyze the images self-consciously rather than letting them flow, and the more I analyzed them, the fewer new impressions I got. Finally, they all faded and I fell silent, opening my eyes and glancing around the room. Dr. Moss asked me what had happened.

"The house disappeared," I conceded in frustration. I wanted to stop, to admit I wasn't capable of doing what she asked.

"Don't worry," she said, gently urging me to go on. "Take a moment to relax. Breathe deeply. Quiet your thoughts and then visualize yourself back at the house again, as if you're really there. Stay aware of any smells, sights, sounds, or images you pick up. But don't force them. Notice what they are and then let them go."

Once back in the silence, I found myself on a porch. "There are beautiful shrubs everywhere. The scent of jasmine is filling the air, and I can hear the sound of a lawn mower in the distance."

Dr. Moss motioned for me to go on. Now I could hardly contain myself. Finding that I could reenter the scene at will, smell fragrances, and observe the landscape, design, and architecture of a house I'd never seen was like discovering that I could fly. The limits of my capabilities seemed endless. For the first time I knew there wasn't any reason to be afraid. I felt restored, vindicated, determined never to allow this experience to slip away. Eager to go on, I opened the front door and stepped forward into the living room.

"The house is nicely furnished but not lavish by any means. It isn't occupied," I continued. "I hope I don't run into anyone. I don't want to intrude." There were no signs of people, but I knew they were present. Dr. Moss didn't live alone. She had children, one or maybe two, and I had a feeling that other close relatives visited her a lot. There was a warmth, a family atmosphere. This surprised me; I guess I thought she worked all the time. It wasn't how I imagined her life to be, but I related it to her anyway, trying hard not to confuse my preconceptions with what I was actually seeing.

It had never occurred to me previously that I could consciously direct or focus my premonitions, looking at details the way I did in real life. Usually my visions had appeared unpredictably, in a flash, giving a general overview of a situation, then vanishing. The possibility that I might be able to turn my head left or right to explore various aspects of a room, for instance, or even choose to float above it, seemed incredible. I had entered an entirely new world.

I then found myself standing in the center of a large bedroom. "I'm now on the other side of the house but I haven't walked a single step to get there," I told Dr. Moss, trying to convey my delight as I continued to look around. "I see a wide, double bed with a wooden headboard and a light-colored bedspread. On both sides of the bed are identical wooden tables.

"The right one has a single drawer where you've put some notes you've written to yourself. On the wall opposite the bed are two large windows. Between them is a long dresser that stands about waist high. There's an old faded photo on the top— it looks like you with your arm around a bright-faced teenage girl. Off to the right of that wall is a closet with your clothes in it. You left the door open."

Now immersed in the reading, I forgot where I was. My only reality was the house, its rooms and hallways, scents and colors. All my previous concerns had been replaced by an intense curiosity to absorb each moment of this experience, as if I'd been starving for it my entire life.

When, finally, Dr. Moss told me it was time to stop, I felt incredibly invigorated. Whatever I'd been doing seemed natural—preferable, in fact, to my ordinary life. So preferable, actually, I suddenly realized that a part of me didn't want to come back, wished I could stay there forever. I began to feel a wrenching sensation in my stomach, a sense of loss, a sadness, as though I'd been taken from my home.

Perhaps because she sensed what I was experiencing, to reorient me Dr. Moss asked that I take a few deep breaths, begin to feel my arms, my legs, my toes, and then prepare to leave the house and return to her office. This gave me some time to catch up and get my bearings. Finally I opened my eyes and looked around. Dr. Moss sat quietly at her desk, smiling warmly. Even so, it took a few minutes to acclimate myself. It was like the lingering sensations of an extraordinary dream as you wake up, having part of yourself in both realities but being fully present in neither.

"How did I do?" I inquired cautiously at last, scared to hear Dr. Moss's response.

Leaning closer, she answered, "I think you did remarkably well. For the most part, your reading of my home was quite accurate."

Her words caught me off guard. I could hardly speak. In effect I heard her saying, "You're all right. In fact, you've always been all right. There's never been anything to worry about." I felt liberated, light, as if I'd won a race when nobody believed in me. But no one could dispute it; I had won, even when I hadn't believed in myself.

"You mean I'm psychic?" I asked.

"Well, that's often used as another word for 'intuitive,'" she said. "So yes, you are."

I tried not to look too excited. I didn't dare reveal any of my insecurities to Dr. Moss, but I'm certain she was aware of them. Wisely, she didn't press me to open up. I guess she knew I needed time for everything to sink in. In a scholarly tone, she proceeded to give me feedback on the reading, minimizing how phenomenal the whole situation was. In this, Dr. Moss was similar to many other scientists, striving to be objective by putting emotions on hold. To hear her discuss what had occurred, I could just as well have been sitting in algebra class listening to a teacher review the principles of a new theorem.

As she went on, Dr. Moss validated every significant specific I had described in her home. "It's quite common for intuitives to pick up an exceptional amount of detail," she informed me. "In fact, many intuitives have told me that in this highly receptive state, colors appear more vibrant and objects seem more defined and compelling than they do in everyday life. Nuances we wouldn't ordinarily attend to stand out with a crispness that isn't otherwise present."

I listened intently, transfixed. Despite my youth and inexperience, Dr. Moss was treating me as a colleague, an equal, never using her credentials or expertise to place herself above me. Not once, however, did I mistake her understated supportiveness as a lack of enthusiasm or interest. Rather, I saw it as a sign of her professionalism. It was clear that she had a deep respect for abilities such as mine, yet at the same time refused to glorify them or present them as anything but perfectly natural.

I could easily have spent the entire afternoon with her. There was so much I longed to know. Questions arose from my childhood: What do these abilities mean? Was I responsible for the dire events I was able to predict? Also, new questions arose from our meeting: Can I direct my abilities? Is it possible to look into another person's life whenever I like? How lucky I felt as I listened to her responses, the intelligence of this quite human but tough-minded researcher. With practice, she explained, I could learn to direct my abilities, which were now in an unformed, immature state, and happened spontaneously without conscious control. But, she continued, when intuitive abilities are fine-tuned, one can look into a person's life if the person is open. When someone is closed off and private, she continued, it's much harder to pick up information about them. The key now was for me to practice and get feedback on my readings. Though all people had some degree of intuitive ability, she felt I had a talent.

And then, as it was clear she had to proceed with her workday, she asked, "How would you like to come work as a volunteer research assistant and intuitive here at the lab?"

Dumbfounded for an instant, I doubted that I'd heard her correctly. But there was no mistake. She wanted me to join her UCLA staff! I accepted immediately and we agreed to meet at the lab the next day.

At exactly eleven, there I stood, facing the NPI, a towering red brick giant looming above me. Two large automatic doors swung open; I walked through a large central lobby and stepped into the elevator. For the past twenty-four hours I'd been fantasizing how the lab would look. I'd envisioned it as a huge place that took up an entire floor, with phones constantly ringing off the hook. I imagined a staff of scientists, both men and women, all wearing horn-rimmed black glasses and white lab coats like Dr. Moss's, and wondered what they'd think of me.

I exited the elevator on the seventh floor, took a right turn, and headed down a long beige-tiled corridor until I reached

Room 23-189. I stood still for a moment, inhaled deeply, and then slowly pushed open the door.

At first I thought I must be in the wrong place. I panicked. The lab was not at all what I'd pictured. Off balance, I tried to steady myself. Then I saw Dr. Moss waving for me to come in. I was so relieved that for an instant I had an impulse to jump into her arms and ask her to hold me—an appalling thought for somebody who was trying so hard to appear mature.

The lab was one big room, slightly larger than a good-sized bedroom. There were no high-powered scientists in white coats, nor were there any experiments going on. There were just two guys in jeans, roughly my age, organizing piles of loose black-and-white photographs on narrow Formica desks lining the far left wall. They smiled and said hello.

The lab centered around a huge rectangular metallic structure about ten feet square called a sensory-deprivation chamber. This is where they did the Kirlian photography, a technique by which energy fields around the body could be photographed and documented. The chamber, which had one tiny window that filtered out all audible sound and most of the light, was artificially lit from the inside and could comfortably fit about four people. It reminded me of a giant refrigerator and was sealed as tightly as a vault. I poked my head through the entrance and saw photographic equipment inside. Even though the air reeked of the potent smell of film developer, I liked this space. It felt mysterious, as if something secret were going on. The rest of the lab was basically functional with a few desks, lots of files, and two telephones. When I looked out the window to the left, I could see Westwood Village in the distance, and to the right were fringes of the UCLA athletic field in the northern part of the campus.

Dr. Moss was extraordinarily warm. She insisted that I call her Thelma, and I couldn't help but feel at home. One of the men, Barry, poured me a cup of coffee and invited me to sit down. A psychophysiologist and intuitive responsible for many of the research projects, Barry was short and slight, spoke in rapid bursts, and gave the sense that he was tuned in to realms others didn't perceive. He was offbeat, energetic, and smart. I took to him immediately. Indirectly, Dr. Moss assigned me to him that day. For the next few weeks I dutifully followed him around and watched everything he did.

The lab soon became a wonderland for me. It was a gathering place for scientists, scholars, healers, and specialists in parapsychology to share their research and theories. For the first time I had the opportunity to meet other people who were intuitive. They were not aging crystal-ball readers wearing turbans with smudged red lipstick and rouge, but real men and women with real jobs who dressed and acted—most of the time!—just like everybody else. I felt like I'd awakened on a different planet, a saner one, where I wasn't a freak or a crazy person. It was as if I'd been initiated into a secret society only a few people knew about, camouflaged and protected by the conservative exterior of the NPI.

I was a kid at the most spectacular carnival I ever could have imagined; each ride was better than the next. Nobody there cared what I wore or who my parents were. And, most important, I was encouraged to become intuitive, as outrageously intuitive as I could be, without any restrictions or rules. Besides what I'd felt with Jim and Terry, I'd never experienced such unconditional acceptance before. Everyone I met, everything I saw, including healings, Kirlian photographs of energy fields, and intuitive spoon-bending demonstrations, brought me one step closer to myself and everything that had been untapped in my own heart.

Though it had now been years since my parents and I discussed my premonitions, it seemed that this aspect of my life, under the auspices of the UCLA Neuropsychiatric Institute, wasn't as untenable to them. Their change of attitude was gradual, but universities were a familiar world they respected. Although I was studying phenomena conventional scientists didn't condone, if both Jim and UCLA approved of what I was doing maybe it had some merit. Since even my childhood premonitions were now being defined in an academic context, they became more acceptable: My mother began to speak about them once again and my father actually showed a visible interest. Compared to my being on drugs or drifting from job to job or dropping out of college, of course, they thought this was an improvement. As for Thelma, though my parents were skeptics, they were willing to keep an open mind about her work, mostly because she was a clinical psychologist.

Overall, I was relieved by their reaction, though still cautious. We took it slow, but my parents and I were beginning to trust each other. Nonetheless, my mother's response continued to possess a spin that made it less credible for me. She'd say that my childhood intuitive experiences were "something I don't understand," and she would again and again convey her fear that they would preclude me from fitting in, that others would deem me crazy. My mother believed in the importance of observing social norms, and she valued the opinion of the medical community. I knew that. Even so, I sensed that some other truth was being withheld. In any case, now I was a "research assistant" at NPI, something, it seemed, we could all live with.

Despite this validation, I didn't approach being at the lab with an attitude of deadly seriousness. I viewed the whole thing more with a sense of play. I didn't scrutinize the events I witnessed nor was I overly critical of them. After all, when someone is released from prison after many years they don't question their own freedom. For me, the lab was a wondrous gift, plain and simple.

Before drugs and the accident, I used to dance alone in my bedroom at sunset. With my arms spread wide, I would imagine myself flying like an eagle high above the canyon floor or twirling wildly like a whirling dervish, uncontrollable and free. Then, when life got painful and complicated, I shut down. I'd now begun to open up again. Sometimes after a day at the lab, I would come home and turn on Miles Davis, Vivaldi, or the Stones, depending on my mood, and let my body move in whatever way it liked. With nobody watching, as the sun set over the ocean, I'd once again extend my arms and begin to dance.

I was being born, but birth is seldom easy. I needed all the help I could get. Thank goodness for Barry; he nudged me along. If it had not been for him I might have put off going to his special group forever. I really wanted to check it out, but the mere thought terrified me. Once a week, members of this group got together to develop their intuitive abilities—it wasn't a lecture course where I could hide in the back row and just listen. If I attended, I'd have to participate and practice my readings out loud in front of everyone. What if I couldn't do it? Suppose I wasn't able to perform on command? Though I'd been successful with Thelma, I was afraid my reading was a fluke. It had just spilled out of me, but I didn't have a clue what I did to make it happen or how to repeat it.

"You don't even need to open your mouth," Barry assured me. "You can just sit there and observe." His promise of no expectations and no pressure eased my fears. I was hooked.

On a Wednesday night at eight, there I sat on a green vinyl chair in a large conference room on the C-floor of the NPI. At age eighteen, I stared at five strangers sitting across from me, and to my surprise they were all cute men, and even friendly. This was an angle I'd never considered—that I might like the other members of the group, or that it would be fun. I still generally viewed others as "the enemy" during this period of my life, especially when it came to dealing with my intuitive abilities, and I was slow to believe that I wouldn't be mocked or shot down.

These guys were paying a lot of attention to me. It felt good and I began to relax. Barry introduced them: Jim, an ex-cop, who looked more like a male model; Kerry, Barry's colleague, who was wearing a pooka shell necklace and flowered Hawaiian shirt; Steve, a television writer; Dick, an astronomer; and Peter, a chemist. They all knew one another. I was the new kid on the block and they were treating me like a queen. It was amazing how much confidence the attention helped me muster; my silence lasted all of about thirty seconds and they even convinced me to be the first "sender."

Barry shut off the light to begin, and the room became so dark I could barely see the outline of my arm. Then we all held hands. In the center of the circle were a microphone and a tape recorder to document our responses. Barry was the first to speak, softly leading us through a visualization to help us relax. I must have dozed off, because after five minutes passed, I jumped at the sound of Barry's voice.

"Send a name, Judith," he instructed. "Choose someone you know very well, and hold that person in your awareness."

He went on to say that the others would spontaneously relate any impressions they received about the person, no matter how ridiculous.

I followed the directions and spoke aloud the name "Geordie," a close family friend I'd known for years. Then I sat back and waited.

There was a long silence that seemed to last forever. Predictably, my first thought was that I was doing something wrong. Then there was an outbreak of laughter.

Barry giggled. "I can't believe what I'm picking up. I see a can of Bacobits sitting on a kitchen shelf. I can almost taste them. Food. Food. All I can think of is food."

Everybody laughed. For a moment, I tensed up, afraid they were laughing at me.

"I see an image of a big house," Steve continued. "It looks like the Palisades or Brentwood. Not bad. I wouldn't mind living there myself."

I began to let go, feeling less self-conscious, already blown away by the accuracy of their comments.

Jim spoke next. "I keep hearing a word repeating over and over in my head. It sounds like 'Hummel' or 'Himmel,' but I have no idea what it means."

"I can see a picture of Geordie," Peter offered. "He's a thin man in his midforties with straight brown hair down to his waist."

For ten minutes they took turns giving their impressions until everybody was finished. Then we went on to the next phase: feedback.

Barry turned to me. "Rewind the tape, Judith, and play it back so that everyone can hear it. Please stop it only when the statements are correct." This was a method of positively reinforcing the "receivers" whenever they had an accurate "hit."

It had been hard for me to keep quiet during the reading. I kept stopping the tape during the feedback phase, because I could hardly believe how many "hits" there had been. Peter had seen Geordie pretty much the way he was: in his forties, with a thin build and long, straight, brown hair he often tied back in a ponytail. Steve had described his estate, which was in fact located in the Pacific Palisades. The word Jim had been struggling with was "Hormel," Geordie's last name. But the most striking hit of the session came from Barry. Although Geordie was an avid vegetarian, his family owned a well-known company named Hormel Meats. They were responsible for producing canned products like Spam and other prepackaged meats. The Bacobits Barry had seen were right on target!

After this evening, I continued to meet with the group. Each round, we would trade off: one person sending, the others receiving. Week after week, we came to the NPI to practice, and those of us who stuck with it noticed tremendous improvements in our intuitive abilities. Initially, during my first times with the group, I'd draw a blank when we did readings, though everyone else was getting images and impressions. Perhaps it was performance anxiety, or the high expectations I had after the psychometry reading with Thelma. Nonetheless, I kept attending and finally the images started to come, perhaps one or two at each session, and I would share them with the group. Sometimes they were accurate, sometimes not, but the important thing for me was that I got them out and that the group was supportive.

Over the next few months, I was able to intuitively read names that were sent in the group and received feedback when I was correct. Deep inside, I continued to worry I might self-destruct if the intuitive part of me emerged. But as it did, and as I saw I was still in one piece, and even feeling better than before, the flow of impressions increased. Occasionally, though, I'd hold back if an image seemed too weird, like the strange plexiglass-figurine maker I once saw, which I later learned stood in the middle of a carnival location Steve was sending. Such specific and unusual images, I was finding, turned out to be the most accurate, the ones I shouldn't censor. During this period, I also started having intuitive dreams, my readings in the group became more accurate, both Thelma and Barry asked me to do readings as part of my work in the lab, and I began to sense information about friends that they'd confirm was correct.

One day, a man carrying a leather suitcase joined us for about fifteen minutes of a session and then left. He slipped in when the lights were out and, although we knew he was there, nobody wanted to interrupt the reading. We hadn't been quick enough to find out how he'd gotten in or who he was, and then he was gone. Later, we discovered he was an escaped inpatient from one of the locked psychiatric wards upstairs. That same night, he jumped in front of a car. While he was in the emergency room, he told the psychiatric resident that what had happened in the group made him feel unbalanced, hence his suicide attempt.

In fact he was a paranoid schizophrenic, unbalanced to begin with. While we were all trying to listen more closely to the voices in our heads, he was being overwhelmed by his own voices. Focusing on what we were saying was the worst thing he could have done; it only fed into his psychosis. He wasn't stable enough emotionally to enter into this work. We learned a hard lesson from this event. From then on, we'd carefully screen all participants, and no one with serious psychiatric problems would be allowed to attend the sessions.

A regular member of the group further confirmed our stance. Dottie, an editor at a film-production company, made some stunning predictions: her mother's heart attack several weeks before it happened, a friend's car crash, a big Los Angeles earth-quake. Unfortunately, she became seduced by her intuitive pow-ers, saw herself as someone uniquely gifted, even chosen. Then she became afraid, obsessed with needing to know where these abilities came from. She wanted answers, but didn't like the ones we gave her. Although we believed there was a spiritual compo-nent to our work, we also held to the idea that prescience was a human capacity that everyone had and could develop.

Dottie listened, but was still convinced that her abilities sug-gested a special relationship with God. She saw herself as being like the prophets in the Bible. After speaking with a priest, she became so convinced she was hearing the voice of God that she turned into a zealot. Seemingly overnight she gave up her job, renounced her earthly possessions, and became a nun. The last I heard of Dottie, she was living in a secluded nunnery on the New England coast.

All these experiences, positive and negative, opened my eyes to the world of intuition. Like other worlds, this one was im-perfect, with a variety of difficulties and rewards. The more deeply I became involved, the more I was forced to release my romantic illusions about being intuitive. Only then could I see these abilities for what they really were: a gift as well as a re-sponsibility that could complicate life. When I watched people go off the deep end—growing too enamored of themselves, emotionally unstable, or spiritually obsessed—it became clear which roads had to be avoided. Intuitives, I was learning, weren't perfect: They had the same problems as everyone else, and maybe some extras, too. Trying to integrate intuition into one's life and maintain balance was no mean feat. If when I first came to the lab I tended to idealize the intuitives I met, making them larger than life, then I slowly learned to avoid those who had big egos. In fact, most of the intuitives I met dealt with their abilities humbly and with respect. The gift itself demanded such respect. Knowing things about others gave you no right to mis-use the knowledge. When properly applied, however, intuitive ability added richness, color, depth, and new dimensions to life.

It also allowed me to know myself better, to appreciate others by seeing them—seeing into them—with greater clarity.

As I proceeded, the hardest part was to practice continually with a group and to have them witness my failures. I hated making mistakes in front of other people, but I did it along with everyone else. It was the only way I could expand my capacity. At least in the lab it was all done with laughter and love, which made it much easier. Our group setting was ideal. The real test, however, would be putting intuition to use in the outside world.

The more I practiced, the more my childhood came into perspective. My confusion and unanswered questions surfaced from what felt like a murky brown sludge hidden within me. Little by little, I dealt with it all. In the end, it was as if I were bathing in warm healing waters and finally emerging, cleansed and purified from the inside out.

I'd never thought much about ghosts one way or the other except for bad horror movies on TV. Although I clearly felt that the spirit of my grandfather was sometimes with me, his spirit had no physical shape, no human aspect. Every once in a while I would wake up in the middle of the night sensing his presence, but I was never frightened. I felt only love for him. On the other hand, ghosts in my mind were something to be afraid of—or a cliché epitomized by Casper—if I believed in them at all. I had to get beyond this stereotype, especially since one of my first assignments in the lab was to work with Barry investigating calls from people reporting "ghosts" in their homes.

The lab would get anywhere from about thirty to sixty such calls a year. Typically, someone would phone, beat around the bush, and then say that strange things were happening around them. They would describe electronic machinery going on and off uncontrollably, objects flying around the room, or noises they were unable to account for—voices or footsteps—apparitions, and lights. Interesting . . . not like their grandfather at all. But what was this? I couldn't wait to see.

One day, we received a frantic call from a divorced mother in her midthirties. She swore she had been assaulted by a number of different spirits in her Culver City home. Her sixteen-year-old son, in fact, said he walked in one day and witnessed his mother being bounced around like a rag doll by a force he couldn't see. Afterward they both noticed extensive bruises on her body that hadn't been there before. They were at their wits' end. When we privately interviewed her daughter and other sons, each said they had seen two apparitions inside the house. The entire family emphatically insisted that the figures had been too vivid to be anything but real.

After Barry first described the case, I didn't believe a word of it. It seemed hokey; I thought these people were either hallucinating or lying. In my mind it wasn't even worth investigating; they obviously needed some professional help. I suggested that we give them a referral to a psychiatrist and be done with it. My reaction was so negative, in fact, that I finally had to ask myself just what was bothering me so much. After all, I had been in the tunnel and had felt my grandfather's presence. Try as I might I couldn't articulate my mistrust clearly, but I did know that at the heart of my experiences was a component of love. The utter absence of love in this family's account made it distasteful to me.

Barry, on the other hand, agreed that it all seemed far-fetched, but he wanted to check it out. Though he and Kerry, another researcher at the lab, suspected that the mother was emotionally disturbed, they decided to pay one quick visit to her house in Culver City. When they went inside, they later told me, cabinet doors in the kitchen appeared to open and shut of their own accord. And although their visit was on an extremely hot autumn day, the bedroom where the alleged attacks had occurred was as cold as the inside of a refrigerator.

During a ten-week investigation, Barry and other members of the research team found cold spots in various places in the house and an overpowering stench in one of the bedrooms. On several occasions, as many as twenty separate observers from the lab saw whirling balls of bright light flying through the bedroom. To eliminate outside influences, they hung heavy quilts and bed-spreads over the windows, but these precautions only increased the brilliance of the light show in the darkened surroundings. Simultaneously, the register on a Geiger counter, which previously had been constant, suddenly dropped to zero.

At one point, the lights actually began to take shape, forming a partial three-dimensional image of a man. Unfortunately, although a battery of cameras flashed pictures of the form, no images were picked up on film. At a later time, though, after a particularly elaborate display, Barry photographed one of the cold spots in the bedroom. When the film was developed, in the center of the photo he found a ball of light about a foot in diameter.

Midway into the investigations Barry invited Frank DeFelita, who had previously done a television special for NBC on ghosts, to visit the house. DeFelita brought in equipment for documentation, and was lucky enough to witness many of the phenomena. (He went on to write a novel about this extraordinary situation, *The Entity,* which was later made into a feature film.)

My job on the project was to relate the impressions I received while in the house. The greatest challenge was to distinguish my emotional reactions from a definite influence that existed outside myself. As an intuitive, I was discovering how to separate the fine points. True, everyone present was tense and on edge. But also, apart from this, I sensed a buzzing and swirling energy, chaotic and disturbing, pushing in on me. Physically, it was a dull pressure, a tightening band around my head, fading in and out. The odd part was that within moments of leaving the house, I would feel this oppressive sensation lifting. Other intuitives had similar responses. Unfortunately, though I'd been excited to encounter the lights and faces that many researchers had observed, I wasn't there for these occurrences. Barry and the others were staked out at the house, whereas I was only able to visit a few times. I learned that this type of phenomenon doesn't happen on command. You have to be there at the right time to catch it.

Aside from the question of what team members saw or did not see, many of our energetic perceptions were consistent. Furthermore, there was the house itself—dilapidated, twice condemned by the city—and the family, terrified by events they couldn't explain. Although they didn't complain, it must have been a burden, all these strangers in their home lugging around massive amounts of equipment. I barely spoke in a personal way with them; I simply conducted an interview about the facts. Actually, I was afraid to get too close, lest what was happening there might somehow rub off on me.

Barry believed that in the vast majority of ghost cases, even if the manifestations were authentic, they were misinterpreted. The unexplained activity, he felt, generally had little to do with a specific house. Rather, it was an outgrowth of the anger or frustration within a family, an unconscious by-product of human emotions that created physical manifestations (psychokinesis), such as objects flying around the room and lights going on and off. Just as the mind can affect our bodies, so too can it affect our environment. It was Barry's opinion that, for the most part, people are haunted, not houses. His theory was supported by the fact that when this family moved out of their home, the phenomena followed them. They, however—and others in similar situations—tend to be unwilling to accept the problem as a psychokinetic product of their own minds. If they did, they would be forced to take responsibility, to make the necessary steps to change. Most people who experience such disturbances, not surprisingly, would rather remain victims.

The experiences in this house, and others like it, were invaluable. They forced me to sift through and identify the true authenticity in circumstances that I would normally write off as sensationalized. Most convincing was the information I intuitively perceived. I didn't know if the energy I picked up in Culver City was a ghost, but I was sure it was real—there was a presence there. Even so, as Barry suggested, it might have simply been an extension of the family's angst. Imagine what anxiety would be like if it was magnified a thousandfold and took on an external life of its own. This is what I was sensing. Still, as an intuitive, I was in virgin territory, feeling my way. Visually I never saw much as I worked with Barry, but I was beginning to discern presences. Step by step, I was being primed to accept that many different kinds of beings exist—spirits included—a reality I came to embrace fully later on. For the time being, I wanted to keep an open mind, to view new situations without prejudging, to leave room for all possibilities.

This didn't mean that I was going to walk around with blinders on or ignore common sense. It's just that previously my intuitive abilities had been discounted by well-meaning parents, teachers, and friends who were unwilling to accept what they couldn't understand. This had really hurt me. I was now determined not to repeat the same mistakes. I'd become so sensitive to people not listening to me while growing up, that I now made a special attempt to listen to others. There was nothing wrong with healthy skepticism, but I also sought to maintain a healthy sense of awe, and the humility to remember that there was much I did not know.

Complete silence. I could easily have been in a space capsule orbiting a million miles away from earth. If I listened hard enough, I could almost hear the faint sound of blood pulsing through my body. I was glad I'd brought my sweater. The maintenance people had once again turned the air-conditioning on way too high. It was getting chilly in here; I had goose bumps on my legs.

Every Tuesday at four o'clock I would lock myself in the sensory-deprivation chamber and develop my Kirlian photographs. I've always had a touch of claustrophobia, so simply getting myself in there was a major accomplishment. The handle on the outside of the door, a big circular steel wheel that looked as if it belonged on a meat locker, had to be slammed shut with such force I was afraid it would never open up again. When the rubber lining inside the door hit the surrounding metallic frame, there was a horrible sucking sound. It felt frighteningly final. What if I were locked in there forever? Over time, I got used to it; the magic available within the place far outweighed my fears.

Thelma had assigned me a plant experiment in which I would use Kirlian photography to monitor the seasonal changes of five specific plants over a period of a year. I had been attracted to plants as long as I could remember, and I surrounded myself with them at home. My boardwalk apartment in Venice was a one-room jungle with flowerpots everywhere; plants were hanging from ceiling hooks, draped over the bathtub's rim, and took up every inch of floor and window space. I did more than talk to them and touch them; I communed with them, actually felt their spirits. Nobody taught me how. I just started doing it on my own, a private habit that felt completely natural. Not surprisingly, I relished this chance to work with plants more closely. From my abundance of plants at home, I carefully chose a few to use for the project: a creeping Charley, a geranium, a ficus, an African violet, and a Wandering Jew. I got to know each of these plants so well that I began to think of them as friends.

The first time I saw a Kirlian photograph of a plant, I was touched by its fragile beauty. It was even more beautiful than the human corona, which, in a black-and-white photo, shoots off the edge of a fingertip like the flame of a magnificent white fire. A Kirlian photograph of a single leaf reveals the details of its entire inner structure, each vein outlined by a border of tiny gray bubbles with a white speck in the middle, similar to the nucleus of a cell. When shot in color, these bubbles light up like a string of brilliant Christmas lights stretched out over the branches of a tree. The image is two-dimensional but appears to be in constant motion, contracting and expanding as though taking a breath. Filtering off the outer edges of the leaf is a radiant, purplish blue discharge, the intensity varying according to species and season.

The theory behind Kirlian photography is that it records a subtle energy field that surrounds all forms of life as well as inanimate objects, energy not detectable by ordinary means. This field extends as far as a few feet or more beyond the body and is as much a part of us as our arms or our legs. Some intuitives can see it or feel it but most people can't.

The notion of energy fields sparked my interest and put into words something I had intuited for a long time. It explained why, as a child, within seconds of meeting someone I knew whether or not I liked them. This "knowing" wasn't about how nice a person was acting or what they looked like. Rather, it was a clear impression in my gut. At times I could almost sense invisible tendrils reaching out to me from a person that conveyed information about them. It would happen before we'd even exchanged a word. Some people just felt good; others didn't. I did not think to question myself until it bothered my mother when I made what she called "snap judgments" about her friends. She felt I wasn't giving them a chance, but I couldn't help it: What I felt was perfectly obvious to me. And later on, my initial impressions were often shown to be accurate.

At the lab, wanting to prove myself to Thelma, I set to work determined that the plant project be perfect. The photographic technique I used was simple. Once inside the chamber, I would place a single leaf directly on top of a one-foot-square photographic plate and press a button. That was all there was to it. Once the picture was developed, it was done. I would take about ten separate photos of the front and back of each leaf, compare the results, then mount them in a notebook. My recordkeeping was meticulous. I never missed a week. At two o'clock on Tuesdays, I would carefully collect fresh leaves from my plants at home, seal them in envelopes, and bring them to UCLA. I would then organize them according to day and month, with each species having its own separate section. Kirlian photographs in color are breathtaking, but they were far too expensive for the lab's budget, so my plant notebook was primarily done in black-and-white.

Doting on my plants, I felt like a mother watching her children grow, noticing every little thing. The days passed. I saw shifts. The leaves seemed to be bonded in some way, responding in unison to seasonal changes. During fall and winter, the energy fields around the leaves began to shrink, as though they were pulling into themselves. By April, a few tentacles of light would gradually extend beyond the body of each leaf, stretching out like the arms of someone who was awakening from a deep sleep. June produced the most dramatic changes when, suddenly, each leaf would burst open into a full bushy halo, remaining that way until September.

Plants, I noticed, reacted not only to seasons but also to people, their energy fields showing observable changes. One day a well-known psychiatrist from Johns Hopkins University in Baltimore visited the lab. He was an unpleasant man, arrogant and loud. It was clear to us that he was closed to our experience: The purpose of his visit was to put down our research, not to learn from it. Thus we decided to play a little trick on him. First we photographed a species of ivy and measured the diameter of its field. Then, with a pretty good idea of what would ensue, we asked him to place his index finger beside the plant. Surprised, he watched as the corona of the ivy shrank to about half its original size and recoiled. Our sentiments about this psychiatrist matched the ivy's: At the end of the day we were all relieved to see him go.

As I became absorbed in the plant project, I also became frustrated with my inability to duplicate the "phantom-leaf effect" that Thelma had reported in her research. The phantom leaf was the ghost of the whole leaf or "energy imprint" that stayed intact, even though part of it was cut away. It was similar to "phantom pain," which many amputees describe soon after the surgical removal of a limb. The arm or leg is gone, but they still feel pain in the place where it used to be. Month after month, I photographed at least ten different varieties of leaves but never captured the outline of the missing portion on film. Thelma said that some people just had a knack for it, that the phantom leaf had less to do with the photographic apparatus or the actual leaf than it did with some aspect of the photographer. There was a college student named Ron from UC Santa Barbara who was great at getting the phantom-leaf effect. He used to come down on weekends to work in the lab. Many of us had a chance to observe him—there were no tricks. Thelma said he had a gift; there seemed no other way to account for it. I agreed that Ron took some stunning pictures.

The longer I worked with Kirlian photography, the more I wanted to find out about it. For over a year, I would spend hour after hour locked inside the sensory-deprivation chamber. No human voices. No telephones. Just the distant buzzing of the fluorescent lamp above my head. Only the plants and me. I developed a rapport with them. When I placed my hand just over the leaves, I could feel an energy current running through them, palpable waves of heat, an increased pressure and mass, a buzzing vibration that made my palm tingle even when I raised it as much as a foot in the air. Eyes open or shut, it was all the same. Eventually, with practice, I learned to sense these fields intuitively, without having to use my hand at all. By simply looking at them, I could accurately trace the location of the leaves' extended borders. At times I would see a golden glow around the leaves and correlate that with the feeling in my palm. But more often, the extent of the field simply registered in my body, a quite physical sensation.

There was no scientific explanation for Kirlian photography that parapsychological researchers agreed upon. It might have been true that energy fields were not photographed at all, that the beautiful pictures we were seeing were only the artifacts of something as mundane as the moisture content of the object on film. This, however, was less important to me than the intuitive impressions I picked up during the Kirlian work. There lay its greatest value. Photographs or not, I was beginning to trust my own experience.

It was during this time that many things I couldn't previously explain started to become clear, like the afternoon in the airport when I was picking up so much sadness from the man sitting beside me that I couldn't concentrate on the magazine I was reading. I thought to myself, You're crazy. You're just imagining it. But when I moved to the other side of the room, the sadness disappeared. I'd always wondered why plants and certain people were so healing to be around. It wasn't anything that they did or said: It was how it felt to be with them. Through my plant research, I realized that when I was younger I hadn't been making things up, nor had I been trying to be "purposely disagreeable." I was simply noticing qualities about people that others couldn't perceive. To an intuitive, a person's energy field is as real as the scent of her perfume, her smile, or the warm red color of her hair.

This work had validated what I'd felt for a long time: There was more to human beings than their physical qualities. A palpable essence extended outward. Before, I had no way to confirm what I sensed to be true. But now another missing piece of the puzzle was falling into place.

A lot of talk was circulating inside the NPI. A well-known Israeli intuitive, Uri Geller, had agreed to take part in an experiment at the lab. He was coming in a few weeks, and even the receptionist at the front desk had been grilling me to get the full scoop. Uri had made some incredible claims: that he could bend thick metal rods without touching them, that he could fix broken clocks with his mind. Uri was controversial; he stirred people up. Everyone had a strong opinion about him, all equally convinced they were right. Nancy, a clerk in Medical Records and a fundamentalist Christian, accused Uri of doing the "devil's work." Jean, an intuitive herself, was adamant that he was authentic. Stan, a skeptical pharmacologist down the hall, swore that Uri was a fake, nothing more than an expert magician who wanted to put something over on us. I didn't know what to think.

The day of Uri's visit the lab was buzzing, our small space packed with researchers, students, scientists, and other intuitives who'd come to witness Uri's feats. It had gotten so crowded that we had to turn away anyone who hadn't specifically been invited. A friend of Barry's, the West Coast editor of *Popular Photography,* was there to document the event on film. The atmosphere in the lab was electric; we were preparing for a celebrity.

Uri arrived with the fanfare of a true star. He was a handsome man in his twenties with wavy black hair and large sparkling eyes, and he walked as if he owned the place, strutting around the room like a prize rooster at a county fair. He was charismatic in the most obvious way. Like a little kid starved for attention, he craved the spotlight and wouldn't be satisfied until it was his. Uri had a boyishness, and a seductive air; although I tried to resist, I was taken by his charm.

Uri started his career as an entertainer for the Israeli armed forces, touring the country performing intuitive readings and doing metal bending. Andrija Puharich, a well-respected parapsychologist, saw him at a club in Tel Aviv and was so struck by Uri's ability to bend rings from a distance that he brought him to the United States. From what I understood, Uri's act had begun as a mixture of magic and true intuitive prowess, but few could discern which was which.

After his stagy entrance at the lab, Uri settled into a chair beside Thelma in the far corner with a crowd of observers huddled around him. The experiment was scheduled to begin at one o'clock. Although I was riveted by his presence, his self-confidence disconcerted me. I was content to stand back and watch at a distance. But Barry grabbed my hand and led me up to the front to make sure I could see. As I stood there staring at Uri, I remembered having heard that his act in Israel included an intuitive attempt at randomly guessing the color of a woman's underwear. It was a gimmick, I suppose, a way to get laughs. But I certainly didn't want him to choose me!

To my relief, the experiment started with a metal-bending demonstration. Thelma handed him an ordinary kitchen fork. He took the fork and, with great tenderness, stroked it with one finger, as lovingly as he might have petted a favorite cat or dog. Then, holding the fork high for everyone to view, he spoke to it in a loud, assertive voice.

"Bend!" he commanded.

For a moment, I thought he was joking. He was addressing the utensil as though it could understand him.

"Bend! Bend!" he yelled, perhaps five more times, repeating it like a mantra with sacred powers. Then, without emotion, he set the fork on the table. All eyes were glued to it, but nothing happened. Not at first. But then, suddenly, the prongs began curling inward until the fork had rolled itself into a tiny metal ball.

"I can't believe it," I almost blurted out, but caught myself. I didn't want to create a stir by letting on how startled I was; I did my best to appear adult about the whole thing. The fork, however, was only a beginning. A consummate showman, Uri proceeded to bend the contents of a large desk, including a complete table setting of matching forks, knives, and spoons. Within an hour, the desktop was strewn with an array of demolished metal utensils that looked like they'd been crushed by a steamroller.

What do you say when your concept of reality has been seriously altered, especially by somebody as self-absorbed and attention seeking as Uri Geller appeared to be? Uri had defied both our expectations of the physical world and our skepticism about the authenticity of performers. I simply stood there speechless, my throat dry. Barry, on the other hand, seemed elated; he was talking up a storm. Stan, the pharmacologist, left as soon as the demonstration was over, declaring that we had all been tricked. He felt that despite the precautions we had taken to ensure the experiment's authenticity, Uri had used magic to deceive us. I knew that Uri had many critics—magicians, parapsychologists, traditional scientists—who would agree. Some went as far as to call him an illusionist with a panoply of tricks, ranging from chemicals, magnets, and presoftened metal to the purposeful misdirection of an audience's attention.

It was difficult to sort through the emotional uproar Uri created to evaluate him fairly. The general consensus among lab members was that Uri's talents were genuine. Ordinarily, I would have been put off by someone like Uri, but I ended up liking him. Despite all the hype, though he might well be a trickster, clearly he had a real talent, and there was a sweetness about the man. Although he went overboard to show off, I found it easy to forgive him. I guess I empathized with his need to feel special and be understood. Only a very short time before, I had been too frightened to express my intuitive abilities at all, and so Uri's fearlessness and need to prove to the world what he could do struck a special chord in me.

After Uri left, Thelma gave me a bent spoon as a souvenir. I carefully placed it on the front seat of my green Volkswagen bus and headed for Venice, my head swimming with the day's events. I felt as though I had just swallowed several cups of strong coffee: wired, yet at the same time drained. But I had to shift gears and reenter my day-to-day life. My refrigerator was bare and my laundry had been piling up for days.

Bent spoon in hand, still a bit giddy, I trudged up the stairs that led to my second-floor apartment. Reconciled to an evening of chores, I reached into my pocket for my house key. I placed the key in the lock as I'd done hundreds of times before and tried to turn it, but it jammed. Something was odd. I flipped on the porch light and pulled out the key. It was the correct one, but, incredibly, the entire metallic body of the key was bent backward. It was useless.

My God, I thought. Uri must've done that. I shook my head in disbelief. Laughing out loud, I reached under the mat and pulled out another key, grateful that I'd hidden a spare.

Touching someone with the goal of helping or healing can do so much more than I ever imagined. I was familiar with traditional medicine; my parents were both doctors. Whenever I got sick, I would go to my internist, he would listen to my heart and lungs, ask me a lot of questions, and then write out a prescription. But he rarely touched me. No doctor ever placed his hands on my body the way Jack Gray, a hypnotist and healer at the lab, touched his patients.

I was told that Jack had performed a miracle. A young man named Mitchell had been in a near-fatal accident. A car collided with his van head on, demolishing it and shattering his leg in forty places. The ligaments and bones were so badly damaged that a team of orthopedic, vascular, and plastic surgeons concluded the leg would never heal. Infection was threatening his life; they recommended amputation. Unwilling to accept this outcome, though he understood the doctors were doing their best, Mitchell took an enormous risk. Through a combination of prayer, laying on of hands, and hypnosis, Jack effected a regeneration of the bone, nerve, and muscle tissue that the surgeons had deemed impossible.

I still had stereotypes in my mind of what intuitive healers should look like, and Jack didn't fit the part. Short, thin— almost gaunt—and in his sixties, Jack always wore inexpensive-looking blue suits and a white shirt, sometimes with a handkerchief in the coat pocket, never dressed more casually, and appeared to be a conservative retired businessman. Something about him seemed rural, simple, newly arrived in the city. He was kind and friendly, apparently quite ordinary. In fact, there was nothing notable about him except for his clear, steel-gray eyes and a face that vaguely resembled Fred Astaire's.

Jack came to the lab to conduct some healing experiments a few times a month, and his healings were the most loving acts I had ever witnessed. Working in the sensory-deprivation chamber, he saw patients with illnesses ranging from cancer to heart attacks to broken bones, and he allowed some of us to observe. One day, a woman came in with a painful tumor in her stomach.

She lay down on the thin leather bench in the chamber and closed her eyes, her head propped up on a small hospital pillow. Jack's hands took on a translucent quality as he waved them about six inches above her body. He was performing what he called "magnetic passes." After a few sweeping passes up and down and across the entire span of her body, he placed his palms directly on her skin, resting them for a few minutes at various locations, starting at the heart. Then he moved to the top of her head, her throat, her abdomen, and finally the soles of her feet. Jack was matter-of-fact about the whole thing, even cracking jokes, but the tenderness with which he touched this woman made me think of a mother with her newborn infant.

Whenever Jack worked, his patients would become so relaxed I could barely see their chest walls moving up and down. They looked so peaceful, in fact, that I often wondered if they were still alive. Faces wracked with pain at the onset of the session would appear angelic as their suffering dissipated. Jack's healing sessions were contagious; I often felt better simply from being there, even when I hadn't felt bad to begin with. It was as though someone had tapped me on the head with an invisible wand, awakening me from a deep rejuvenating sleep.

One of Jack's patients was a young housewife, Claire, with debilitating lower back pain from an automobile accident. She had a medicine cabinet stocked with medications for pain, but they made her feel so listless and disconnected she couldn't function. And then, when the pills wore off, the pain always returned. Conventional doctors had pretty much given up on Claire, and she was getting beaten down. Jack was her last resort.

It was hard for me to be around Claire. Within minutes of seeing her, my lower back would develop a nagging, dull ache, which alternated with an annoying burning sensation. It disturbed me so much I'd fidget in my chair, unable to find a comfortable position. At first I wrote off my reaction to being "overly suggestible" and decided not to mention it to anyone. I didn't like complaining, and I didn't want anyone in the lab to think I was being difficult. So I dreaded the days when Claire would show up. Then, once while suffering through another of her healing sessions, I remembered I'd been through this kind of thing before.

Growing up, if I was around someone in pain, occasionally, within seconds, I would develop the same discomfort. Once in junior high, for instance, I was eating lunch with a friend on the lawn and suddenly started getting stomach cramps. When I mentioned this to my friend, she said she wasn't feeling well either, having started the day with nausea and stomach pain. I saw nothing strange in this until, several minutes after she left, my symptoms disappeared completely. The times I told my mother about such incidents, she would be concerned that I wasn't feeling well, but neither of us ever made the connection that I might be picking up another person's pain.

That afternoon in the lab, I took a risk. I mentioned my reaction to Jack, and he didn't seem at all surprised. Quite the contrary. To my great relief, his eyes lit up and he winked at me. Always the perfect gentleman, he patiently took the time to explain that intuitives often perceive many of the physical symptoms in the people around them. He called it a powerful form of empathy, which if unrecognized could be overwhelming. He said that the resistance and fear I associated with pain or unpleasant sensations was what caused them to persist. He suggested that whenever I picked up symptoms, instead of fighting them I could relax and let them flow right through me. It would involve some practice, but he was sure that I would get the hang of it.

I never saw Jack reverse cancer or perform any such miraculous cures, but his patients did improve. Naively, I had hoped he could relieve them of all their symptoms, but I soon discovered that healing didn't work that way. What Jack gave his patients was a second wind, a jump-start of powerful energy. With the added boost, they could continue their own healing processes. Jack was not a magician; he was an ordinary man with extraordinary abilities, which made him all the more credible to me. At a time when his patients were about to give up out of sheer desperation, he offered them hope. He handed them their power back and they took it, an interchange that ultimately inspires the most profound healing of all.

What I relished about Jack and other healers who came to the lab was that they talked about forbidden subjects such as death, a tremendously compelling topic for me. One afternoon when I was thirteen years old, coming out of a movie theater with a girlfriend, I suddenly realized that my time on earth was limited. For no apparent reason, I was faced with my own mortality; for the first time I realized that someday I would die. Since then, I have thought a great deal about death, though it has never been a morbid topic for me. Rather, this kind of contemplation has helped bring an immediacy to my life, a sense of impermanence that has kept its specifics in a clearer perspective. The healers didn't think it strange that I found graveyards to be peaceful places where I could sit, meditate, and connect with myself when I wanted to be alone. Most of the healers I met at the lab had a strong set of spiritual values underlying their practices, and we would often have conversations about an afterlife.

As a child, I always believed in an afterlife. This wasn't something that anyone taught me. I had just never thought to question it. To me, the spirit felt different from the body, stronger, more resilient. That it would ever die seemed impossible. Yet in Hebrew school and on the high holidays, the subject of an afterlife was rarely mentioned. The rabbi's sermons focused more on politics and ethics than on spiritual truths. In the Reform Jewish faith I was raised in, there were no intuitive role models to train children. My experiences never seemed to fit into the mold. Now as a young adult, I found the lab a safe place to express my spiritual beliefs. I had finally found other people who thought as I did and understood.

A healer named Caroline told me a story that struck close to home. While undergoing heart-valve replacement surgery, a client's heart stopped beating and her EKG went flat. An emergency code was called and a team of doctors and nurses rushed in to resuscitate her. The client later reported having been aware of everything happening around her, but from a different vantage point. She said she had been transported to a tunnel, a long, cylindrical passage with no end, filled with golden light. Exhilarated, she began walking through the passageway, while the commotion in the operating room slipped farther and farther away. The intensity of the light kept drawing her forward with a movement so exquisite in its gentleness that she didn't think to resist. She felt complete tranquillity and had no interest in turning back. Then abruptly, in one swift motion, she was pulled out of this place and thrust back to the hospital again. Her life had been saved. The tunnel was gone.

According to her doctor, she had been hallucinating, the result of a shortage of oxygen to the brain. He also reassured her that there had been no irreparable damage. But this woman knew he was mistaken; her experience was too real to have been a hallucination. Caroline agreed. She had spoken to numerous people who were explicit in their descriptions of these near-death experiences. Many of them had described the same things.

When I heard about this, I was transfixed. The tunnel I had visited during the Tuna Canyon accident suddenly made sense. Although Jim had been open-minded, the experience of the tunnel was novel for him, too. He had never been sure what it meant. I couldn't wait to tell Caroline my story. It matched her client's description so closely that I blurted out every detail. I felt as if I had just confessed a sin and been absolved. Caroline laughed and assured me that I hadn't done anything wrong. She went on to say that although there were small discrepancies in our perceptions, her client and I had basically visited the same place. She felt I had come closer to death than I'd imagined: The tunnel saved me; it had provided a perfect sanctuary.

I was astonished by the similarity of our experiences, and by the fact that others in life-threatening situations had been to the tunnel. I had always been fascinated by the bridge between life and death, the geography of the spirit moving between worlds. Now the tunnel also appeared to be a two-way passage: Even when physical life was over, in certain cases the spirit might return to the body.

I believed I had stumbled on a great secret: Having met death head on and survived, I had glimpsed what the other side looked and felt like. I now had a sense of myself as a pioneer, bearing testimony to the tangible link between life and death. Such validation of my personal experience brought me closer to my true voice, to self-respect, to the person I felt I was meant to be. And, finally, the discovery that I had gone through a near-death experience reinforced what I already suspected: Death was not an end but simply a transition into another form. A circle had been completed. I began to look at life with a broader viewpoint. I saw that human beings were blessed with gifts that I never dreamed possible. Intuitive ability was only one of them. I no longer was willing to limit myself or to buy into other people's notions of my capabilities. The sky had no ceiling. It was boundless. And so was the spirit within us. It needed room to fly high and dive deep without restraint or restrictions.

CHAPTER THREE

Loss of Innocence

You can't always get what you want,
But you get what you need.
　　　—THE ROLLING STONES

I am standing in a huge open space, listening to an anonymous voice giving me instructions. It is telling me that I am about to go to medical school and become a psychiatrist. With an M.D., I will have the credibility to continue my intuitive work. I feel like a secret agent who has just been given a special assignment. How can I refuse? The words seem so right, I never once think to question them.

I woke at dawn, puzzled, remembering this dream in detail. Although I had accepted it with ease, the message made no sense to me now. My head was spinning. There must have been some mistake. Me, a psychiatrist? Unbelievable. I just wasn't the type. I might as well have heard that I was going to be shot out of a cannon into another galaxy. I felt like the object of some bad practical joke, that any minute someone was going to jump out from behind the curtains and burst out laughing.

As the daughter of two physicians, it might have seemed logical that I would consider following in their footsteps, but I had never shown the slightest interest. My parents, wanting to point me in a reasonable direction while I was still in high school, had sent me to a private psychologist in Beverly Hills for career counseling. She handed me a pile of tests filled with questions, each one more meaningless than the next: Do you like gardening? Do you get along with other people? Do you like working with your hands?

I took the questionnaires home and labored over them for eight hours. After they were scored, the psychologist and I went over the results. "Whatever you do," she advised, "don't ever go into medicine, counseling, or any of the helping professions. Your aptitude in these areas is far too low. You'd be happier and more successful in a career in the arts."

I wasn't surprised. At that time in my life, the thought of dealing with illness or listening to somebody else's problems all day long held no appeal for me. I had enough problems of my own. Furthermore, most of my parents' friends were doctors, so I'd been around them all my life. They'd never really interested me; I had little in common with them. My friends were artists; the more eccentric and far out the better. And I too wanted to become an artist of some kind.

But while I lay in bed, the dream gnawed at me. I couldn't go back to sleep. Throwing on my favorite green sweater and an old pair of sweatpants, I took off for a coffee shop on the Venice boardwalk. Except for a waitress who was cleaning up behind the counter, the place was still empty. I slid into a corner booth. Watching the joggers and street people pass by, I let the dream sink in. I'd learned enough at the lab to know better than to ignore such a clear message, even though it seemed so far-fetched.

Listening to old fifties songs on the juke box and sipping strong coffee, I sat there for hours, thinking. Even if I wanted to, would I be able to follow the guidance in the dream? I wasn't sure. Finally, after much deliberation, I reached an agreement with myself that I thought I could live with: I would enroll in Santa Monica City College, take one class, and see how it went. That was the most I could promise. I hadn't been to school for almost three years, and although I'd always done well with a minimum of work, I didn't miss it. No matter how absurd this new plan sounded to me, I was now committed to giving it a try.

The fall semester, which began in mid-September, happened to be a few weeks away. But I was registering late, so most of the classes were already full. One of the last choices was meteorology. Totally uninterested in the subject, I enrolled anyway, certain my experiment was doomed.

I couldn't have been more wrong. I quickly found that I was moved by the beauty of how rain was made, how clouds were formed, the way weather happened. Something inside me responded, and in this unlikely setting I discovered that school wasn't so alien after all. When it was over, I registered in more classes. And so the cycle began.

Nine months after the first meteorology class, as I sat on my living room floor typing up an English term paper, the rightness of the dream hit me. It hadn't even been on my mind, but I couldn't argue with this feeling. I knew for certain my dream was true. At that moment, I made a clear choice to begin premed. I picked up the telephone.

"Mother, I have something to tell you. I want to go to medical school." There was a long silence; I thought the phone had gone dead. "Mother, are you there?"

"Of course, dear. I'm just surprised. This is so sudden. Why didn't you ever mention it before?"

I opened up and told her about the dream. She had become more tolerant of such things since I began working with Thelma. When I had finished, there was another long pause.

"So what do you think?" I finally asked.

My mother seemed to be choosing her words carefully. "I'm sure you'd make a wonderful doctor. If that's what you want to do, I'm completely behind you. But this is a big decision. I don't believe in dreams the way you do, so I wouldn't start a career on the basis of one. Why don't you give it some time to sink in? Remember, you never liked high school. Medical school and residency are a long haul."

When I hung up, doubt overtook me. My mother had sounded extremely cautious. I could see that she wasn't against my becoming a doctor. She'd be thrilled if I did something "positive" with my life, and of course valued the status and service of the medical profession. But understanding my past as she did, she was genuinely concerned for me. Maybe she was right. Medical school had to be a crazy idea. Why would I choose to upset the balance in my life to pursue so demanding a path? But finally, all the considerations she raised didn't make any difference. Logic had nothing to do with what I seemed impelled to do.

During the months following this dream, problems with the lab that I hadn't noticed before became more evident. When I began, I had felt a purity of purpose in the research we conducted. But in the past year, some of that had changed. Because of increasing involvement with the media, our work was gradually getting polluted. Films based on the lab were sensationalizing and misrepresenting intuition. TV magazine shows were the worst, viewing the paranormal with obvious disbelief, presenting many factual inaccuracies, using our work as hype to improve their ratings.

Perhaps this was the reason I was being directed to become a doctor. Intuitive experiences were so easily misunderstood, they needed to be legitimized. Although Thelma's Ph.D. was helpful, it didn't carry enough clout in a medical center comprised primarily of physicians who often considered themselves a step above such a degree. For some of the more conservative doctors at the NPI, our lab was an embarrassment to science. If they had the power, I'm sure they would have forced us to leave. Although the director, Dr. Jollyn West, was a skeptic about parapsychology, still he provided Thelma's lab space and defended her right to do research. But since she seemed always to paste together the lab's finances from gifts and her teaching income, or relied on volunteers, the lab was never really secure.

My only hope of turning such attitudes around, I was convinced, was to become part of the medical community, no matter how much I disliked the idea. If I had ever really sat down and mapped out what I was getting myself into, I probably wouldn't have chosen medical school. But luckily, I didn't think too far into the future. I was riding an invisible wave. I tried to let go and trust it.

My work with Thelma had given me a strong foundation in intuitive research and a structure from which to grow, but I was ready to move on. One final factor was that Kirlian photography was falling out of favor among parapsychologists: There was increasing data indicating that the effect was due only to moisture. Although Thelma never believed this, my own enthusiasm for working with it waned: I wanted to find other methods of establishing the validity of phenomena I knew to be authentic. Gradually, then, the lab was getting less of my attention as my life became consumed with school. It took every available ounce of energy and discipline to stay focused on my classes. With a single-mindedness that was new for me, I forged ahead, concentrating on getting through one subject at a time. I barely stopped long enough to take a breath. Years flew by—until it was time for the MCATs.

I was never good at taking computerized multiple-choice tests, particularly when my future depended upon them. The pressure surrounding the MCATs, the equivalent of college SATs, was enormous. I would have to score extremely high in order to be accepted into medical school. Packed into the UCLA student union with a thousand other students, I spent eight grueling hours taking the test. By the time it was over, I'd lost faith in myself. On that same night, certain that I'd failed, I returned to my grammar school, climbed the steps, and sat down.

Alone, my legs drawn up to my chest in fetal position, I rocked back and forth, wishing I were a child again, trying to put this harrowing day behind me. I gazed across the street at the house I used to live in as a child. The lights were on, making it look warm and inviting, and I wanted to run inside. Remembering the tiny vegetable garden I'd planted with my father in the front yard, I broke down and wept cleansing tears that had been bottled up for a long time. Huddled on the steps, engulfed in memories and caressed by them, I felt calm again. As I got up and walked away, my strength had been renewed.

My fears turned out to be unjustified. I was accepted at Hahnemann Medical School in Philadelphia, the alma mater of both my parents. For them, this was almost too good to be true. I had turned my life around. They not only paid for my school tuition and housing but also offered emotional support. So in late August of 1975, I packed up my van and my black Labrador retriever, and we drove to the East Coast.

My new home was a studio apartment in an old converted 1920s brownstone with art deco trim. It was directly adjacent to the Philadelphia Art Museum and across the street from a two-story Catholic convent. My window looked directly into the convent's front garden, giving me an unobstructed view of a pure white life-size statue of Jesus. In the winter, the statue would often be half buried in snow. I liked to think it was watching over me.

The first few months of medical school elicited great resistance. Nothing in my life looked familiar; I felt I had been swallowed by a black hole. My days were regimented, planned down to the last minute, so much more rigid than pre-med had ever been. In the early mornings, my only time for myself, my dog and I would walk through Fairmount Park and watch the crew teams rowing past the banks of dogwoods and azaleas down the Schuylkill River.

During this period, I was afraid that a part of me was dying. The more I struggled to hold on to my once crystal-clear intuitive images, the further away they seemed to be. At the lab, I had fought hard to reclaim them; they had become a lifeline. But the rigid discipline of medical school seemed to be undoing the progress I'd made. I was caught in a bind, so conflicted that the countless facts I needed to memorize for class wouldn't stick in my mind. The more anxious I became, the tighter I clamped down. Then I failed my first biochemistry test. I was floundering and needed some help.

Angels come in the most unlikely packages. Daniel was an Orson Welles look-alike with a laugh that shook his entire body. The lab assistant in my anatomy class, Daniel supervised the dissection of our cadavers. Soon after we met, we started dating. Once again, a strong man had shown up to be the bridge from one phase of my life into another. Daniel had a wild sense of humor, and I trusted him far more than the medical school philosophy in which we were both immersed.

From the start, I despised anatomy. I was furious that the school hadn't better prepared us to cut open a human body. We were simply handed a scalpel and instructed to slice. There was no mention made of the inherent sacredness of this act or of the emotions we might be having. It wasn't that Daniel didn't sympathize with my dilemma; he just wouldn't coddle me or allow me to wallow in despair. One night he locked us both in the anatomy lab and refused to let me leave until I allowed him to teach me the basics of this class. I railed and complained but when I saw it would do no good, I gave in. With a Bruce Springsteen tape blasting in the background, I learned the technique of dissection. By the time Daniel unlocked the door, it was midnight and an enormous obstacle had been removed from my path.

It was Daniel's energy and unshakable belief in me that got me through my first year of medical school. Every night we would review the class notes together. Then he would test me. If I made excuses why I couldn't do it, he shot them down. When I felt I was losing myself, he gave me books to read that kept my inner life alive. Daniel introduced me to the lush intricacies of *One Hundred Years of Solitude* by Gabriel García Márquez, and the irreverent humor of Tom Robbins's *Even Cowgirls Get the Blues*, works of fiction that fueled my own imagery and dreams. Reading became my touchstone to intuition, a well I could dip into to fill myself before I went to sleep each night.

Daniel wasn't worried that I would lose my gift. He was more certain than I that it was strong enough to outlast four years of medical school and another four years of psychiatric residency. He believed that my abilities had an inherent integrity. In the long run, it wouldn't matter if I placed them on hold. When the time was right, Daniel was convinced, they would return. How he came to this view, I did not know. But because of my profound respect for his opinions, I chose to believe him.

When, after two years in Philadelphia, I transferred back to USC to complete medical school, I struggled to hold on to Daniel's words, but it became more and more difficult. I threw myself into my studies, living and breathing the rational, the linear, the provable. There was no room for anything else.

I remember dragging myself home late one night after a grueling day of classes. Eager for some fresh air, I took my dog for a walk to a grassy park right by Santa Monica beach. There before me in the parking lot a string of billowing circus tents had popped up overnight. I'd stepped into an enchanted land. In the pale moonlight, a tall man dressed in blue sequined tights suddenly appeared, leading four elephants down to the water's edge. Then, after a wave of his hands, one by one they started to run across the sand, making wild trumpeting cries that sounded like pure bliss to me. I was breathless; I envied these gorgeous creatures. A surge of sadness rushed through me. I realized that my intuitive voice was fading; the sweet freedom I'd tasted while finding it was slipping away.

As a third- and fourth-year medical student, I was on call every third night at L.A. County USC Medical Center, a massive thirteen-story beige monolith hovering over the slums of East L.A. I slept there on a bunk bed in a room I shared with at least four other doctors. Our beepers were constantly going off; I would consider myself lucky if I got one or two hours of uninterrupted sleep. When I did sleep, it was leaden.

One night, at the peak of this sustained exhaustion, I was invited to a Rod Stewart concert at the Forum in Inglewood. I had been on call the previous night, but the tickets had been so hard to get I didn't want to cancel. Surrounded by 40,000 screaming people thunderously clapping in rhythm to a blaring set of rock and roll songs, I placed my head on my date's shoulder for a moment. And fell sound asleep.

As a senior medical student, I did my first psychiatric rotation on Ward 4A, the locked unit that housed the most severely mentally disturbed. We got the patients who had either tried to kill themselves or hurt somebody else. They were usually psychotic and couldn't function. Late one evening, when I was standing in the hallway across from the day room where the patients watched TV and smoked, I heard a woman cry out. It was a piercing scream; it went right up my spine and through my nervous system. Four orderlies dressed in white coats and a cop with a billy club and gun were wheeling a patient on a gurney toward our ward. As she came closer, I could see that she was a beautiful girl, quite thin, about twenty years old, fighting for her life.

The front door to 4A slammed open. She let out a howl. Although her arms and legs were strapped with hard leather restraints that were buckled and locked, she was still writhing violently, her back arched like a wildcat's. With all their combined strength, five muscular men could barely contain her. I had seen other patients on the unit who had been restrained, but I could hardly watch the tortured expression on this girl's face.

Suddenly, the gurney crashed against the wall, all four orderlies momentarily off balance, in danger of losing their grip on the metallic sidebars, and I was afraid that the whole thing was going to tip over. The patients in the day room were wide-eyed. Nobody uttered a word. I stepped away, back up against a corner wall. I didn't offer to help: The situation looked too dangerous.

Then one of the psychiatric residents, who couldn't have been more than twenty-three, came running down the hall, yelling, "Bring me five milligrams of Haldol stat!" Janet, the head nurse, quickly filled a syringe with brightly colored pink liquid and flicked it with her index finger to get rid of any air bubbles. Utterly cool and collected, she handed the syringe to the flustered resident. Janet had been working on 4A for over twenty years, and it seemed that emergencies like this no longer fazed her. I carefully moved closer.

"What in the world is going on with this patient?" I asked Janet.

"She's psychotic. She thinks she can predict the future."

I swallowed hard.

"Her name is Rae," Janet continued. "She's schizophrenic. She's a frequent visitor here. We all know her."

My thoughts exploded. Psychotic? Predict the future? Why was Janet connecting one to the other? The resident plunged the pink liquid into Rae's left buttock, and Rae quietly moaned. A few minutes later, she lay limp on the gurney, which had now been moved into the isolation room. Her struggling had ceased as the Haldol, a strong antipsychotic medication, took effect. The orderlies then transferred her from the metal gurney onto a small, single bed and strapped her down in the same leather restraints, hooked securely to all four corners of the frame. She was lying on her back, her arms and legs spread open as wide as they could reach.

As things returned to "normal," I took a look at Rae through the isolation room's tiny rectangular window. Now completely knocked out by the Haldol, she was snoring under the blankets. The darkened cubicle reminded me of a prison cell. Since bright colors or lights would overstimulate a person in her condition, all four walls were painted the same dingy shade of green as you might find in the bathroom of a run-down gas station. The intention was to create a calming effect.

The young resident who had administered the shot looked exhausted. He walked over to me. "Rae is your patient," he announced. "I want you to follow her."

I reluctantly agreed. I had no choice: Each medical student on the ward was allotted a certain number of patients and it was my turn to pick one up.

It had been my choice to work on 4A, the toughest psychiatric unit in the county hospital. Determined to become a psychiatrist, I was sure I could handle it. But Rae's case horrified me. I strongly identified with her. Rae claimed to be intuitive and had ended up in a straitjacket. I recalled the old adage,

There but for the grace of God go I. Why wasn't I the one strapped down in the isolation room? Rae was young, pretty, had her whole life in front of her. What made me different from her? I understood that she was schizophrenic. But what else was different? I needed to find out.

The next morning I visited Rae. The nurses reported that during the night she'd been given two more Haldol injections. Trying to pretend I knew what I was doing, I walked in wearing my white coat, her chart securely under my arm. "I'm Dr. Orloff, a medical student here. I'll be coming to talk to you."

Rae grinned, and didn't seem to mind. She was cooperative, even pleasant. Nonetheless, during the interview I stayed a few inches away from the doorway. I didn't want to risk getting too close to her in case she lashed out: A crazed lunge, even of a patient bound ankle and foot with cloth restraints, could be terrifying.

Over the next few weeks, I got to know Rae well, but she talked about her premonitions with such ferocious intensity it scared me. She clung to them with the resolve of a wild-eyed prophet speaking the word of God. Rae heard voices. They gave her messages. She listened to them. Her voices were mostly wrong, but not always. Her mother, a reliable source, volunteered that Rae's predictions sometimes came true. Rae had recently predicted the death of the family dog, but no one had listened. The next day, in a freak accident, he was run over by a car. But such valid predictions were lost in the endless flow of Rae's psychotic verbal ramblings.

In medical school, my training focused on the biological aspects of psychiatry. This meant that many disorders—schizophrenia, anxiety, mania, and severe depression—were considered biochemical imbalances, treatable with medications (Haldol, Valium, Lithium, or antidepressants). Every morning on Ward 4A, I attended an hour-long psychopathology lecture intended to teach medical students how to diagnose and treat psychiatric patients. During these lectures, I was bombarded by a belief system that associated clairvoyance with psychosis. I learned, for instance, that Rae's insistence on being intuitive was a "symptom of schizophrenia," a serious mental "disease." If Rae stayed on the Haldol, our teachers said, her predictions would go away. And that was the goal. I was floored!

The ward chief on our unit was a soft-spoken man in his early sixties who had been a psychiatrist at the county hospital his entire professional career. Over the years, he had seen every kind of patient, and I trusted his expertise. One morning, I asked him if he thought Rae was intuitive. No, he responded, that was inconceivable to him. Along with most other physicians, he simply didn't believe in the existence of intuitive abilities. My concern struck him as odd, but understanding that this was my first psychiatry rotation, he gave me the benefit of the doubt. He assured me that Rae's accurate prediction of her dog's death was merely coincidence.

I didn't tell Rae that I was an intuitive or share with her my experiences in Thelma's lab. Instead I withdrew, became increasingly detached, and started to question myself. I figured I wouldn't be much help if I fed into her delusions. I would just make things worse, so I kept quiet. I felt conflicted, confused. I couldn't decide if a vital part of her was being crushed or if she was the victim of a terrible illness. What swayed me, finally, was seeing Rae's dramatic transformation on the Haldol. Rational and calm, she was no longer preoccupied with her predictions, nor did she miss them. I was reminded of how relieved I was as a teenager when I used drugs to squelch my intuitive abilities. I was so disturbed by them I was glad they were gone. Although Rae didn't articulate it, maybe on some level she felt the same way. She certainly looked better following treatment. Two weeks after she was admitted, Rae was ready to go home.

Through my work in the lab, I had come to terms with the fact that intuitive abilities were real. But suddenly new questions had arisen. Were they dangerous to develop? What were the risks? The lab had been an isolated little bubble. In Barry's group, we treated our intuitive abilities nonchalantly, almost as if they were a game. Now, as a medical student, I was skeptical about the practical applications of such research. It was true that I had met a handful of well-adjusted intuitives in Thelma's lab. But maybe they were the exception. Now I was in the real world. During my medical training, I was to see far more examples of the unbalanced type.

Look at what happened to Rae. She might very well have been a gifted intuitive, but so what? She was psychotic. The price Rae paid for her prescience was much too high. I was beginning to feel that it was neither safe nor appropriate to encourage people in this pursuit. Even if they were mentally sound, could exploring this part of themselves destabilize them? The cost suddenly seemed monumental. What I had previously considered so precious was now tainted by the horror of the reality I witnessed each day.

Later, as an intern and psychiatric resident at UCLA, I worked in the emergency room every third night for two years. Such a regimen didn't leave much time to philosophize. The few days when I wasn't on duty at the hospital, I was at home asleep. I was basically running on adrenaline. During my nights on call, I watched many psychotics like Rae pass through UCLA: The locked inpatient psychiatric wards were packed with them. And always the drill was the same. The police delivered them in restraints. Then I had the nurses shoot them up with Haldol, and their intuitive claims would gradually disappear. I soon lost sight of the implications of what I was doing. It became a matter of economy. Seduced by the rationality of conventional medicine, and scared by the horrors I'd observed, I was adopting an attitude that deemed intuitive abilities a sign of psychological dysfunction.

Meanwhile, being a doctor agreed with me. It grounded me, and gave me a feeling of being in control. My intuitive experiences had mostly stopped and, since medical school at USC, I had been able to recall very few of my dreams. The flow of images that used to fill me was almost entirely cut off. They were a distant memory, and strange as it may seem, I didn't give them much thought. I was worn down and inundated. My life was moving in fast motion; every moment was full. The intuitive part of me was on hold. I had no time or support from others to nurture that aspect of myself. It had been replaced by my new identity as an M.D.

The emergencies kept coming, and I got used to thinking on my feet. During my psychiatric residency, so much happened so fast that I was forced into a bunker mentality. The other residents and I might just as well have been fighting a war—we stuck together that closely.

One Saturday night when I was on call at the Brentwood Veterans Administration emergency room, a Vietnam vet walked in. Six foot four with a shaved head, covered with tattoos, he had a tightly knotted noose clutched under his arm. I was aghast. The man declared he wanted to die because his girlfriend had just left him. Looking me straight in the eye, he threatened to hang himself if I didn't admit him to an inpatient ward. All right, I thought, anyone who'd go to such lengths to get into a hospital had to be taken seriously. I reserved a bed for him at once.

A few weeks later, I was in session at the Veterans Administration with a schizophrenic outpatient I was treating with large doses of Thorazine. Nicknamed Jackknife, and as always carrying a set of headphones to drown out the voices in his head, he wore a sleeveless white T-shirt and a silver cross around his neck. That particular afternoon, something set him off. Without warning, he lunged across the desk, his right fist aimed squarely at my face. Although he wasn't much taller than I, he was a bodybuilder with sculpted arm muscles. Fortunately, I had good instincts whenever I thought I was in danger: I tore out of my office and ran. We were on the ground floor, and with Jackknife trailing close behind I fled past a potted palm into the reception area. Then the security guard rushed in and restrained him as I stood trembling a few feet away. Swearing and threatening revenge, he was hauled off to the locked ward and placed on a seventy-two-hour hold for being a "danger to others."

The wards and locked units where I worked were indisputably war zones. We didn't have the luxury of penetrating the intricate layers of a person's psyche slowly. Time was precious. We had to get people better, and fast. Continual close calls propelled me into looking for quick and easy answers. This was where drugs such as antidepressants and Lithium came in. I grew to like the idea of a quick fix, especially when someone was in great pain. It was hard for me to watch people suffer; I just didn't see the point. With medication, I had the tools to effect rapid change.

In the Mood Disorders Clinic, where I was assigned during my senior year of psychiatric residency, I met a manic-depressive named Arnie who was as handsome as a soap-opera star. He had been sent to us straight from L.A. County Jail, having spent the previous night in a drunk tank. According to the police report, Arnie, stark naked, had jumped into the fountain in front of the Century Plaza Hotel. A bottle of champagne in one hand and a huge container of bubble bath in the other, he'd emptied them both into the water. Bubbles were everywhere; the parking lot was a mess. The parking attendant just wanted him out, but when he refused to leave the manager had called the cops.

Arnie hadn't come to the clinic willingly. His wife, who knew we specialized in the treatment of depression and mood swings, had bailed him out of jail and then dragged him to us. She was frantic and wanted him to get help. When I first met Arnie, he was dressed in a wrinkled business suit, furiously smoking a cigarette. He paced around my office, talking so fast that I couldn't get a word in edgewise. Without pausing for breath, he was ranting about some stock options and a financial scheme that was going to make him millions. He reminded me of a wind-up doll that couldn't be turned off. A typical manic, he had big ideas but nothing to back them up.

I immediately started Arnie on Lithium. Like many manics in the midst of a high, he didn't want to be put on medication. But his wife threatened to commit him to a mental institution unless he agreed. Under duress, Arnie took his Lithium capsules religiously, three times a day for over two weeks. The next time I saw him, the medication had already taken effect and he was a completely different person: calm, intelligent, charming. Since our clinic didn't offer psychotherapy or family counseling, I continued to see Arnie only once a month for fifteen minutes to renew his Lithium prescription. Much improved, he was able to return to his job as a stockbroker at a prestigious downtown firm.

Time and again, I witnessed how medications could transform lives. People who had been miserable for years were suddenly able to hold jobs, develop human relationships, become productive and functional. Prescribing medications and watching patients come alive made me feel powerful. I liked being in charge. Before this, much of psychiatry had seemed vague and inexact. There were so many different therapeutic approaches to choose from. Now, with medications, the solutions seemed clear-cut. Instead of seeing that they could be useful only in certain situations, I went overboard and became convinced that I'd found the ultimate answer.

I had fallen into the trap of believing that I'd stumbled upon a cosmic truth that stood above all others. Why should anybody waste time and money if they could be cured by a pill? With the unswerving conviction of the newly converted, buying into the prevalent attitudes that were supported throughout the clinic, I started to get cocky. I viewed my patients as being the "sick" ones and thought it my job to fix them. And many times I did. But while I was being romanced by the science of psychiatry and the position of authority that went along with it, I discovered that I was losing a treasured part of myself.

My best friend, Kathleen, lived alone on the top of Mount Baldy. I used to take my dog and visit her there, where her small cabin was perched on the edge of a wooded hillside overlooking a riverbed about thirty feet below. After the winter rains, the water would rise so high that it sounded like thunder flowing beneath her living room. In the early mornings, dressed in heavy wool parkas and thick, knitted gloves, we would take long walks along the river's edge and scavenge for unusual stones.

Before I went to medical school these walks were easy. Kathleen and I, often in silence, would follow the course of the river downstream. We would notice the textures of stones and pebbles beneath our feet, and we always returned with at least two or three remarkable ones. But since I'd become an M.D., all the stones had started to look alike and it had become harder for me to spot them. It wasn't that my vision had changed, it was just that the subtle differences between the stones became invisible to me. Finally, I had to use Kathleen's eyes to select them. When we got home and laid them out to admire on her kitchen table, neither of us spoke about my change of sight. But in my heart, I knew a part of me had gone blind.

At the same time, with my spiritual and intuitive abilities seemingly on hold, only events relating to death were evoking them. During my internship—mainly medical with a three-month rotation in psychiatry—I was on call in the hospice unit of the Wadsworth VA Hospital in Westwood. This was a separated ward where terminal patients, many without families, were sent to die. One of my main jobs, I was informed, was to pronounce people dead. No one could have adequately prepared me for this task, and I will never forget the first night I spent at the hospice.

I stayed in a tiny room, a tiled cubicle on the third floor, where I passed the first part of the evening reading a science fiction novel, trying hard to lose myself in the pages or occasionally napping, if you can call it that—attempting to sleep while guarding against the shock of my beeper going off. I prayed that things would stay quiet so that the nursing staff would leave me alone. Not a chance. At two in the morning the phone rang. I groped in the dark for the receiver. The nurse on duty spoke in a bored voice. "Dr. Orloff, Bill has just expired. Could you please come down to write a note in the chart and sign the death certificate?" Her tone was so impersonal she might as well have told me my parking meter had run out of time.

The blood drained from my hands and feet. I sat up and vigorously rubbed my palms together to work up some heat. It never dawned on me that I would confront death so soon: I had done my best not to think about it. Also, I knew Bill; he was a retired bus driver in his late seventies with metastatic lung cancer. I forced myself out of bed, put on a fresh pair of socks, slapped some cold water on my face, ran a brush through my hair.

The hospital was an eerie place at night. The corridors were practically deserted, but they teemed with the lingering presence of people who had died there. Dressed in my surgical greens and a worn pair of white Reeboks, I headed down hall after hall toward the hospice, hearing the loud squeaking of my rubber soles, my stethoscope thudding against my chest.

The nurse working the graveyard shift, leisurely sipping a can of Diet Coke, handed me Bill's chart and led me to his bed. An old checkered sports coat he had proudly worn when his daughter came to visit was draped over the chair in the corner. Bill's body was covered by a newly laundered, starched white sheet and on it I could see the impression of his form. Truly, the last thing I wanted to do was uncover him. But I couldn't just stand there forever. Finally, my arm reached down to turn back the sheet. His face! I kept staring at it. Except for the cadavers we had dissected in anatomy class, I had never viewed a dead body. Bill looked stiff and smooth, more like a wax statue than a human being. I slowly reached out and touched his cheek. It was still warm.

What next? I blanked out. How to tell if someone's actually dead? I knew there were specific signs to look for, but what if I made a mistake?

I had to do something, so I placed my index finger over Bill's carotid pulse. Nothing. But maybe it was so weak that I missed it. I looked over anxiously to the nurse for help, but she was busy chatting on the phone. I fumbled for my flashlight, then shined it into Bill's eyes. His pupils were fixed and dilated. What a relief: That meant he really was dead. Even so, I continued the protocol. I pricked the skin on the sole of his foot with a pin I used to test for a pain response during neurological exams. Nothing. Then I sat on a chair beside Bill and waited. I really had to get myself together. This was going to take a little time. I didn't want the nurse to see that I was shaken and badly needed to think things through.

I had always imagined that when people died they would look much the same as in life, only more peaceful. In part, that was true, but there was a factor I hadn't accounted for. On the surface, Bill's features hadn't changed, but I became acutely aware that now only the body remained, plastic and hollow, a mere shell. But there was something else going on that I couldn't ignore, even though I might have liked to: I sensed Bill's spirit nearby, watching what was taking place in the room. Had it tapped me on the shoulder, I wouldn't have been surprised. In fact, it felt as real to me as the nurses and orderlies on the ward. And then I became conscious of another feeling. As the minutes passed, I understood more and more clearly that Bill's torment had ended: What remained I could only describe as love. There was the unmistakable presence of a human spirit, distilled to its purest form. Body now obsolete, it had survived death with a life of its own. I was filled with awe.

Working in the hospice was always difficult; some nights I received as many as two or three calls. But each opportunity to witness a death deeply moved me. I began to seek it out, waiting and watching for that moment when the spirit leaves the body. In my months on this ward I was privileged to be present with several patients at the time of their death. In each case, the instant death took hold, there was an incredible silence. Not that the normal hospital activities stopped or that the staff passing by were any quieter. This was a silence surpassing all sound, penetrating every pore of my being, as if the silence knew it well, was in fact part of my substance. The sensation wasn't creepy or cold; it was warm, soothing, and kind, radiating peace.

Intuitively, my impression was that an alchemical reaction had occurred: The body died, the silence graced and entered it, and after a pause of seconds or even minutes, its essence was transformed into love. Always, I sensed I was standing at the threshold of a great mystery, the point when life as we know it is completed and the spirit takes hold. The nights I spent at the hospice strengthened my conviction that although the body is temporary, the spirit lives on.

I didn't share my observations with my fellow UCLA interns. Convinced that they wouldn't understand, I didn't want to jeopardize my position in our tight-knit group. I was afraid of being ostracized, of seeming weird, untrustworthy. It meant more to me than anything to be taken seriously. We had been taught about the physiology and mechanics of death from the standpoint of medical science. Spiritual theories were never discussed. That was for rabbis, ministers, and priests. We were just struggling to make it through a day, trying to get all the IVs done, the blood drawn, our rounds completed to get home for a few hours' sleep. For whatever reason, we kept our distance from the issues that surrounded dying. Wanting to fit in, I tried to repress the terrible conflict I felt in not openly acknowledging what I knew to be true. No matter what the cost, however, I wasn't going to be the one to bring up such taboo topics.

My thoughts and feelings about death, however, gave me some comfort; they provided the main link to my intuitive life. As for my spiritual life, these thoughts and feelings solidified my connection with a compassionate, transcendent intelligence permeating every aspect of the physical world . . . and beyond. For now, I chose not to speak about this part of my being. And though it may have seemed remote from me, it wasn't gone. Still alive, my spirituality was in a secret place that no one else could touch.

CHAPTER FOUR

Healing the Split

*The really valuable method of thought to arrive at a
logically coherent system is intuition.*
—ALBERT EINSTEIN

The view from the eighteenth floor of the Century City Medical
Plaza was spectacular. In the distance I could see the sun setting
over a deep blue strip of ocean lining the horizon, cradled by the
rugged Santa Monica Mountains in the north. Now thirty-two,
I felt I had arrived.

I was beginning my own private psychotherapy practice in
one of the most prestigious areas of the city: Four blocks south
on Pico was the Fox studio lot, the offices of ABC television
were five minutes away, and directly across the street on Century
Park East were the twin tower buildings, identical forty-eight-
story triangular metallic and glass obelisks packed with the
densest concentration of high-powered attorneys in Los Angeles.

With financial help from my parents, I had leased an elegant
penthouse suite in a top medical building, and I was determined that everything be first class. My mother hired a decora-
tor to pick out the finest fabrics, wallpapers, and paints to
color-coordinate the office. The wall beside my desk was covered

with my laminated degrees from college, USC medical school, Wadsworth VA internship, and psychiatric residency at UCLA—proof that I was now a full-fledged M.D. The stage was set. The external trappings were perfect.

But opening a private practice was a risky business. The Westside was already overrun with therapists: Entire office buildings were packed with them, and there were probably more therapists per square foot in Beverly Hills, Century City, and West L.A. than anywhere else in the country except Manhattan. It was also true that I had never been very good at selling myself. With such stiff competition, the odds against my practice succeeding were high. But I tried hard to look the role, to project a professional image to the world.

Sparing no expense, my mother bought me an entire new wardrobe and a car. On a resident's salary there was no way I could have afforded this. Each morning I would dress in a tailored two-piece business suit, a pressed linen or silk blouse, and a pair of one-inch Ferragamo heels and drive to work in my beige '77 Mercedes sedan.

Ushering me into their world, my parents were offering me all the advantages. Medicine was a comfortable language that they understood, and we now had a common bond. When I talked to them about patients or doctors we both knew, they could relate. Our relationship grew closer: They were proud of me and I was proud of myself.

But I wasn't doing this just to please them. I relished my authority and responsibilities, the respect of nurses and staff, the power to help people. I was getting an enormous amount of positive reinforcement from teachers and patients alike. Still, in my quiet moments, I knew something was missing. I had left a part of me behind, though in no conscious way had I intended it. To survive the manic pace of my medical training, a kind of protective amnesia had taken over. It was similar to what happens when the body goes into shock, closing down sensation and memory, cutting off my intuitive experiences, nor did I have the energy or desire to backtrack to find them. Though I wasn't oblivious to what had happened, it was easiest not to look back. I became programmed to think more than to feel, and this became habit as I resigned myself to the loss and focused on the present. But there was a price: vague melancholy, a sense of absence, nagging emptiness—all covered up by the incessant pressure and motion of my practice.

Also, twelve years had passed since I'd worked in Thelma's lab. During most of that period I had been a teenager, with part-time jobs, often financially dependent on my parents, without a sense of calling. Now, at last, I had one. Finding medicine, I had been indoctrinated into the scientific method. Compared to the rigors of conventional psychiatry, the intuitive research I had done seemed vague, less exhaustive than I was currently comfortable with. I'd come to value what could be systematically proved and gave little attention to anything else.

I intended to open a traditional psychiatric practice. I would see patients all day in my office and then in the evenings make hospital rounds, a typical routine for many psychiatrists. Since I would be on call twenty-four hours a day and weekends, my life would revolve around work. I subscribed to the system I had learned, matching symptoms to treatments, using medication and psychotherapy as my primary tools.

At UCLA, despite an emphasis on the biochemical components of psychiatric illness, we were also given supervisors, physicians from the community, to teach us psychotherapy. In my case, the supervisors were classical Freudian psychoanalysts. For them, it was essential to be caring, but to convey as little as possible about themselves. The goal was to remain a blank screen on which patients projected their own behavior. The theory is that removed from personal interaction, therapists are better able to help. Thus some psychoanalysts would seldom speak during a session, giving only occasional interpretations, mostly taking notes, sometimes not even sitting where the patient could see them. Generally, psychoanalysts also made a point of dressing conservatively, accentuating a neutral professionalism.

Not surprisingly, with this in mind, though searching for a style that felt natural, I was afraid of polluting the psychotherapy process. Determined to maintain a cool therapeutic distance, I was careful never to reveal any personal information. Stiff, I conveyed little emotion, keeping the boundaries between doctor and patient well defined.

I also had the medical role models of my parents to draw on, but my father was a radiologist, having little direct contact with patients. My mother, on the other hand, socialized with patients, even vacationed with them, none of which undercut her authority as a physician. But she was a family practitioner, not a psychiatrist. The same degree of emotional objectivity and neutrality required of a therapist wasn't as critical for someone in her specialty.

My first patient, Cindy, was a young makeup artist who was going through a divorce. Cindy worked in a well-established beauty salon on Rodeo Drive in Beverly Hills. The referral had come from the salon owner, a very successful businesswoman and close personal friend of my parents. There was a great deal of pressure on me. I wanted Cindy to like me, and I wanted to show my family I could succeed. I anticipated this first appointment with the apprehensiveness of a teenager awaiting her first date.

When Cindy walked into my office, I was relieved to see that she was more anxious than I was. Redheaded and pixyish, in her midtwenties, Cindy was so distraught over the messy breakup of her marriage that she cried through the session, using up a whole box of Kleenex. I was off the hook, and barely opened my mouth: All she needed was a sympathetic listener. Fifty minutes flew by. When it was time to leave, Cindy thanked me profusely and scheduled a regular weekly appointment.

The salon where Cindy worked was the same place I went once a month to have my legs waxed. I figured it was such a busy, sprawling place that she and I were unlikely to meet, and assured her that in any case our relationship was confidential. She didn't seem concerned, however: It was my own uneasiness I had to contend with. Cindy was my first patient, and I wanted to hold on to her.

One afternoon, I was in a secluded back room of the salon getting my legs waxed when there was a knock on the door. I heard the sound of a familiar voice and then the door opened. It was Cindy, looking for a client, not knowing that the room was occupied by me. Our eyes locked and my face turned beet red. There I lay on the leather massage table, flat on my back, legs spread wide, covered with hot yellow wax, wearing only underwear from the waist down. Also embarrassed, Cindy nervously apologized for the intrusion and backed out of the room.

I was humiliated, sure that by psychoanalytic standards any hope of maintaining a professional relationship with Cindy had been compromised. But I learned that, now seeing me as more vulnerable, Cindy felt closer to me, and our therapy took off, though this was a response I certainly hadn't anticipated. I soon came to see the waxing incident as a wake-up call, a message telling me, "Lighten up. It's okay to be human."

In any case, however hard I tried to keep a wall between my patients and me, it always seemed to get broken down. I would run into my patients everywhere: jogging on the beach, in movie lines, even at friends' parties. Since we lived in the same general vicinity, our paths naturally crossed. And though these meetings often unsettled me, it was my patients' sense of ease that gradually taught me to relax and be myself. I kept trying to play out a role, but the specifics of life were teaching me something else entirely, showing me the distance between theory and the complex reality of human lives.

Early in my practice, I began treating Eve, a ninety-year-old widow struggling with anxiety because her daughter had cancer. Some months later, when her daughter finally died in the Cedars-Sinai hospice, Eve called me to be by her side. As I came down the hall, I could hear the sound of Eve's wailing: She was making such a ruckus that the nurses were concerned. Not knowing what to expect, I braced myself as I walked into the room.

The sight of this frail, gray-haired woman pacing back and forth, moaning and crying, scared me. I was afraid she might have a heart attack or collapse. I wasn't sure what to say or how to console her. I just stood there, trying to be calm, not wanting to reveal how unprepared I felt.

But if Eve noticed, she didn't let on. Overcome with grief, she rushed toward me, weeping, and threw her birdlike arms around my shoulders. These were not controlled, guarded tears, but sobs. Her tiny chest heaved against mine, convulsing with each breath. It all happened so fast that my body stiffened in response: I wasn't used to such an uncensored outpouring. It blasted all my circuits; for a moment everything turned black. I was threatened by Eve's intensity, overwhelmed by her need. I had an impulse to rip her away from me, to tear out of the room and never look back. I believed that patients weren't supposed to touch their therapists, much less curl up in the fetal position in their laps, as Eve was now doing. That was a job for family members. But now that her daughter was gone, Eve had no family left. I was the closest connection she had.

Craving the warmth that comes only from physical affection, Eve clung to me like a heartbroken child. A few times I attempted to shift position, to loosen Eve's grasp, but she had no intention of letting go. So there I sat, on the unmade hospital bed, cradling Eve, her daughter stone cold on a gurney less than a foot away. Once I realized there was no escape, I gave up trying so hard to be the "appropriate" psychiatrist and began to relax. There was no more pressure; I was able to feel a tenderness for Eve that my contrived notion of professionalism had blocked off. Not drawing back, I allowed myself to care for her, woman to woman. She could have been my own grandmother, the love I felt for her was so great.

For more than an hour I held Eve close. We didn't say much to each other; I just let her cry. When she was finished, we walked to the cafeteria arm in arm for coffee, and talked. But this was no formal session; rather, it was an exchange of anecdotes about her daughter, a time of remembrance. I had known her daughter from family meetings that the three of us had had at the hospital after she became ill. Now, surrounded by clanging trays and the smell of cigarette smoke, we brought her memory alive and honored it. To do this, however, was not how I was trained to conduct therapy in school. But it was what was needed, and I knew it was right. Something essential had happened. Eve had been given the freedom to express her grief, and I had learned how vital it was to be loving and authentic.

As I continued my practice, I found that I attracted the kind of patient who insisted on intimacy. They didn't want me to sit back quietly and nod my head while they endlessly talked. It wasn't enough for me simply to ask, "What are you feeling?" and then take notes. I was called upon to react, to be engaged emotionally and to offer my opinions. My patients also wanted me to reveal more of myself, and when I did, a chemistry was established, an energetic interplay that led to change. I followed my patients' leads and learned from them. A detached style might have worked for other therapists, but I was coming to see that it was not appropriate for me.

For six months, I played the role of the traditional doctor. Friends who were physicians in the community referred patients to me. My practice filled up fast. I enjoyed the intensity of the work, the hectic schedule, and the adrenaline rush of being called into the emergency room to see suicidal patients in the middle of the night. It was a challenge to face new problems each day, a privilege to help people change and better their lives. I began to feel confident, certain I'd found my niche.

And then I met Christine. As I recounted in the Prologue, it was at this point that my experience with her—when I ignored my premonition of her suicide attempt—pulled me up short. For the first time I realized how I'd lost track of my original goal in getting medical training. Instead of working to bridge the parallel worlds of intuition and science, I had become as skeptical—of even my own abilities—as my colleagues.

But keeping that long vigil by Christine's bedside made me reclaim those feelings and focus on incorporating intuition into my practice. I would never risk endangering another patient the way I had Christine. But although this was absolutely clear to me, I still did not know what my next step should be.

Occasionally, I went back to the Neuropsychiatric Institute to visit; returning to the familiar hallways and clinics was always comforting. One afternoon, shortly after Christine came out of her coma, I fortuitously ran into Scott, who was working on a postgraduate fellowship. I hadn't seen him for over a year. Scott was the only doctor I knew who had been connected to Thelma's lab. A conventionally trained child psychiatrist, he also had an appreciation of unorthodox healing approaches and was the one person at UCLA I felt safe enough with to discuss Christine. The timing of our meeting was perfect. Drinking tea in the cafeteria, I told him what had happened.

When I finished, he enthusiastically said, "There's someone you have to meet. Brugh—pronounced B-r-e-w—Joy. His real name," Scott added, smiling. "Brugh was a successful internist in Beverly Hills. Then, when he came down with a severe pancreatic disease, his doctors wrote him off. Incredibly, through a process of meditation and self-healing, the disease disappeared. This inspired Brugh to give up his practice and begin conducting workshops on intuitive and spiritual development. Why don't you do a retreat with him? It might really help you understand what happened with Christine."

It was a big step even to consider attending one of Brugh's workshops. They were two weeks long, tucked away in the high desert, two hours' drive from L.A., and during that time I would be asked to cut off all communication with the outside world. If I attended, this would be the first time since opening my practice nine months before that I would leave my patients in the care of another psychiatrist.

Aside from such considerations, however, my reticence went deeper. After my premonition about Christine, I didn't know where to go next. I wanted to open up and yet I was conflicted.

My medical training had taken me so far away from the intuitive realm that the idea of reexamining that part of my life felt dangerous. I was afraid to begin, wary that I might jeopardize everything I had worked so hard for. I held on for dear life to the identity I had carved out for myself: as a traditionally trained medical doctor. The arguments in my head wouldn't shut off. The difficulty was that for so long I had come to view my dilemma in all-or-nothing terms. Every scenario I constructed was the same: The intuitive and medical worlds could never mix.

I was driving myself crazy. I had to do something. Finally, I followed Scott's advice. Three weeks after our conversation I called Brugh Joy's office in Lucerne Valley and scheduled a retreat in early September. This gave me a month to mull over my decision, and I changed my mind many times, but whenever I picked up the phone to cancel, I stopped myself. Remembering Christine, I just couldn't let myself back out.

At seven o'clock the evening before the retreat, I decided to take an aerobics class and do my packing afterward. Leaving home a little bit later than I'd intended, I quickly parked my car on a side street, tossed my duffel bag over my shoulder, and rushed down the street toward the gym. The sun was nearly down, the horizon dimly lit with a pale pink glow. I flew past an alley not looking where I was going—and ran into a moving car. Going perhaps twenty-five or thirty miles an hour, an aging Oldsmobile driven by an elderly man hit me with such force that I was hurled up and back against the windshield twice, each time crashing with a horrible thud.

Suddenly I was transported to a tunnel identical to the one from the Tuna Canyon accident. Watching safely from inside, I saw my body bounce off the hood of the car and then slam against a brick wall alongside the alleyway. Two teenage boys sitting on their front porch witnessed the accident and rushed over to help me. I could have been an acrobat in a black leotard and tights, performing a death-defying stunt. After rebounding from the impact against the wall, I landed upright and on my feet, almost as if waiting for the audience to applaud and the judges to score my performance.

A crowd gathered around me. The driver, extremely feeble and confused, his vision not good, was shocked. He wanted very much to help me, as did the teenagers. But feeling all right, and perhaps foolishly independent—in this period of my life I found it hard to ask for help—I drove myself to the UCLA emergency room. Except for a painful whiplash, there were no broken bones or other injuries. Having been to the tunnel before, I recognized what had taken place, but it had never occurred to me that this might be a repeating pattern that would protect me a second time when my life was in jeopardy. I found this notion extraordinarily consoling, realizing that the tunnel was a great blessing. People were severely injured and killed in accidents every day. But both times I had been in grave danger, the tunnel had saved me. Now, thinking it over, taking stock of what had happened, I knew I would be all right. Against medical advice, I prepared for my trip. And in the morning, I threw the suitcases in the backseat of my car and headed for the Institute of Mental Physics in Joshua Tree.

The temperature was over 110 degrees when I arrived. Visible waves of heat rose from the asphalt driveway that led up to the entrance. The desert surrounding the conference center was a vast expanse of sand with pale green barrel cacti dotting the landscape. Brugh's personal secretary, a robust middle-aged woman, directed me down a winding stone path lined with blooming oleander bushes to my room. Hot and weary from the drive, I took a shower and settled in.

After dinner that evening, forty men and women of various ages gathered in a circle in a large conference room. Brugh himself was a lithe, pale, androgynous-looking man in his midforties. Trained at Johns Hopkins and the Mayo Clinic, he was a member of Alpha Omega Alpha, the medical honor society. Wearing jeans and a pullover sweater, he appeared reserved but unflinchingly blunt and confident as he spoke in a calm, evenly articulated voice, outlining the rules. Stay off the phone.

Stay on the grounds. No drugs or sex. No outside distractions. Brugh wanted us to remain focused on the present. The purpose of the conference was to shift us out of our ordinary, conditioned habits of viewing the world and to open to a different reality. With group dream discussion, meditation, periods of silence, fasting, and other techniques, we could shift into a more intuitive state.

At six o'clock the next morning the group reconvened, with Brugh leading, and we were to discuss our dreams. To get up so early was appalling to me, but I set my alarm for 5:30 and showed up on time. Sitting cross-legged on a meditation pillow, I planned not to participate, but inevitably, that first morning Brugh started with me.

The only dream I could summon up was a recent one I chose because I could remember it, not because I thought it particularly significant. For some time I hadn't been dreaming much; it was a special occasion when I could remember one at all. In this dream, I was walking through a residential neighborhood on a bright and sunny day, an area much like where I grew up, with manicured lawns and large houses. Suddenly, I came upon a huge, dusty, empty lot in the middle of the block. I paused, hesitating to enter: The lot obviously didn't belong in that setting—it had a suggestion of menace. At the same time, though, it had a strange appeal and evoked a kind of longing. I kept staring from my safe distance, feeling something in its emptiness that I couldn't quite understand.

That was all. Short, few frills, no real plot. The dream had left me unsettled, however. Brugh responded with an extended discourse about what it meant. He seemed to be making too big a production, and the language he used sounded like it had been taken straight out of Guru 101, a mix of intellectualism, spiritual jargon, and a know-it-all attitude. "Dream states are far closer to our natural Beingness than even our most highly intensified external reality. The empty lot represents the great mystery of consciousness, your spiritual and intuitive potential.

You've created an artificial partition within yourself that keeps you from experiencing total awareness."

Brugh went on to say that I had fixed ideas about many things. Unless I let go of my rigidity, he argued, it would get in the way of any spiritual progress I hoped for. By the time he finished, I was mortified. It was unnerving to have him be so direct with me in front of everyone, as if trying to confront me so that I would react. The more he spoke, the more irritated I became: Who gave him the right to pass judgment on me?

I ate lunch that day with Michael, a writer and director from Malibu who was to become a good friend. Michael Crichton, a towering six-foot-nine Harvard-educated M.D., had given up medicine to write novels, many of which were later made into feature films. He reminded me of a huge, magnificient bird with outstretched wings flying high above the earth. Cynical and smart, he wouldn't easily be won over by spiritual mumbo jumbo. Having traveled all over the world, Michael had met intuitives of many different cultures. As Michael now saw it, Brugh had given me a reading, and his interpretation of my dream was based less on content than on his deeper impressions.

"Did it fit?" Michael asked.

I knew Brugh had me pegged, but still I wanted to deny his words: Although Christine's suicide attempt had left me intellectually prepared to explore my intuitive life, an enormous part of me remained frightened. Sensing this, Brugh had used the dream to break through that fear, and I had responded by fighting back, tightening, protecting myself.

The evening session began with high-intensity sound, a technique for stimulating the intuitive process by listening to loud music and paying attention to the images evoked. Brugh described it as a powerful tool that could bypass our minds and help us to open up. He told us to relax, have no expectations, and to remain receptive to whatever took place. All forty of us lay down on pillows, side by side with our heads pointed toward the center of the circle. Brugh dimmed the lights and then, at full blast, he played the sound track from *Chariots of Fire*.

Instantly, I felt the vibration of the bass pulsing through the floor and into my body. I was terrified that my eardrums would explode, the noise was so deafening. The music assaulted me; I cringed and I fought it. But after ten agonizing minutes, something shifted. I forgot my discomfort, swept away by the beauty of what I was hearing. My mind became lit up by a fireworks display of mesmerizing images. Wild horses galloping through a lush, grassy meadow. A fierce electrical storm exploding over the ocean. The face of my grandfather when he was a young man. A troop of traveling mimes. All were disjointed pictures that flashed one after the other as the music built into crescendo after crescendo.

A floodgate had opened. I was being transported to a time when I was much younger. I was again able to see clearly, sometimes into the future. But I wasn't scared. The walls I had built around me were gone. Anything was possible. I felt courageous and free. I ached to recapture that innocence and freshness; I had lost so much. The sadness rushed through me, leaving me disoriented and drained.

When the music was done, Brugh turned on the lights and I was jolted out of the session. The room was spinning so fast I felt nauseated. I struggled to gain my balance, overwhelmed by the lavish outpouring of images and memories from the past. It was a shock to my system to have them resurface so precipitously after being buried for so many years. I felt wobbly, as if someone had taken a plumber's snake to my unconscious and dislodged a gigantic plug. When we went around the circle and shared our responses, I could barely concentrate. Afterward, I returned to my room and went straight to bed.

I woke up the next morning in a fury. I didn't know why, but everything made me angry. The whiplash from my accident had worsened and the muscles in my neck had condensed into a stiff, knotted rock. I couldn't move my head in either direction. I wanted to go home, but something kept me from leaving. At breakfast, I decided to tell Brugh about my symptoms.

"How wonderful!" he said. "You're finally waking up."

"Waking up?" I snapped. "I feel miserable."

Brugh shot me a knowing look that made me seethe. He seemed so smug and sure of himself that I wanted to deck him.

Unfazed by my hostility, he continued. "The music was just a catalyst. It heightens your senses, opens you up quickly and makes you more aware. Last night you remembered something important about yourself and got frightened. Fighting it only creates tension. When you shut down, your body tightens and reacts with symptoms. The secret is to let go. . . . Trust your images instead of trying to censor them. Then tell me how you feel."

"What does letting go have to do with it?" I pleaded. "I'm in enough pain. Why make it worse by purposely bringing up all that sadness?"

Brugh was soft-spoken but adamant. "The sadness is a key to your pain. You can't keep running from it forever."

That was the last thing I wanted to hear. Preferring to believe that my problems were physical, I was outraged. What kind of doctor was Brugh, anyway? He didn't seem sympathetic at all. And I had no intention of reliving the images of the previous night. Maybe some other time, when I was in better shape. But not when I felt so awful. Exasperated, I got up from the table and left in a huff.

My dizziness and nausea continued to get worse. I was ready to give up. In the middle of the afternoon, tired of battling Brugh and myself, I collapsed in the desert beside a juniper bush and fell into a deep sleep. I slept there for hours, curled up on my orange beach towel. When I awoke in the twilight, something inside me had released. From that point on, my attitude changed.

Watching a half moon rise in the violet desert sky, I felt refreshed, unusually clear. I lay stretched out and tranquil, cushioned by the softness of the sand. I had reached a breaking point. Like a child who'd worn herself out after a tantrum, the fight in me was totally gone. I hadn't intended to let go. It happened in spite of myself. An unsuspected wisdom took hold, an organic impulse to bend and survive under pressure instead of getting blown apart. Whether an activation of a wiser aspect of myself or divine intervention, the result was that my resistance had melted. I was lifted over a chasm uncrossable by will alone. I'd gotten through medical school and residency on sheer will and perseverance. Whatever the obstacle, I'd just bear down, concentrate harder, and push through it. This style had worked a long time for me. But it hadn't succeeded here. I couldn't have forced myself to change. It was an act of grace, totally beyond my conscious intent.

I had never known the great relief that came from surrender. Thus far in my life, I'd always equated surrender with "giving in" or failing. But now I was bursting with energy, radiant. A thick, rigid band within me had dissolved, and my body felt unconstricted and agile. Within hours, my nausea disappeared and my neck muscles loosened. The tension drained from me; I was a different person, laughing and talking with the others, no longer pushing them away.

In this receptive state, I was primed to reexperience the intuitive side of myself. To do that, I had two weeks of dream groups, meditation, introduction to the use of healing rituals, energy work (the laying on of hands), and two days of silence and fasting. Far from the stresses of my ordinary life, I had a chance to acclimate to the renewed flow of my images and dreams. It was like learning to ride a bicycle all over again. I was awkward at first, hesitant to experiment. But with the encouragement of Brugh and the rest of the group, I slowly opened up.

Working with Brugh, I also got a firsthand demonstration of how intuition and medicine could be blended in a positive way. One day, Brugh arranged for a cancer patient, referred by a person who had previously attended his conferences, to come for what he termed a "healing session." Debbie, a thin, very attractive brunette in her late thirties, hair cut short in a pageboy, wearing designer jeans, polished cowboy boots, and a T-shirt, came to our morning group and sat down on a pillow next to Brugh. Except that her hair was thinning, which I recognized as a sign that she was taking chemotherapy, there was nothing to suggest she was ill. She said she'd been looking forward to this session for weeks. A flight attendant and mother of a five-year-old daughter, Debbie had been diagnosed with leukemia three years before. Despite treatment with Interferon, an experimental drug, her white blood counts were still abnormal, indicating that the illness hadn't improved. Now Debbie was facing a bone-marrow transplant, a risky surgical procedure that had a chance of saving her life. Traditional medicine could offer no more. This was where Brugh came in.

Brugh interviewed Debbie in front of the entire group. I couldn't get over how brave she was, revealing intimate details of her life with great candor. Though I was impressed with Debbie, what had the most impact on me was the thoroughness of Brugh's approach. Starting with a complete medical history, he went on to an appraisal of her psychological makeup far more sophisticated and subtle than any I had seen in medical school. Guided by his intuition, he uncovered areas in Debbie that might have taken years to emerge in traditional psychotherapy.

Remarkably, I saw Brugh pose questions that weren't based on information Debbie provided. Rather, they came from his intuition. The most stunning example took place about halfway through the interview. While Debbie was talking about the progression of the leukemia, Brugh abruptly asked, "Have you ever lost a child?" Debbie turned pale and, in a whisper, answered "Yes." She'd given birth to a stillborn infant twenty years before, when she was eighteen. The incident had been so painful that she had blocked it out for years.

Brugh saw in this the essence of a mind-body link, that there was a strong emotional component to Debbie's illness. Over the next hour, I watched him deftly uncover a lifelong pattern of losses for which she had never grieved: the grandmother who raised Debbie dying when she was fourteen; the death of a good friend a few years later; her two divorces; and the death of her son. Debbie's pattern had been to check out and not deal with her feelings. She'd pop a quaalude, snort cocaine, or, as a flight attendant, hop on a plane to escape. Although she had finally left drugs behind after enrolling in a hospital recovery program, she had never dealt with her unresolved feelings of guilt, self-blame, and unworthiness. And all of these, Brugh felt, contributed to the subsequent development of her leukemia. More so he believed that by dealing with the losses she could positively alter the course of the disease.

A master navigator, Brugh cut through Debbie's resistance and identified her blind spots. I studied his every move, noting how he incorporated intuition with his medical and therapeutic expertise, the art with which he wove these approaches together.

Watching Brugh, I was given a template for how I might have handled Christine. He showed me that it was possible to listen intuitively while at the same time remaining medically astute. There were other doctors at the conference who, like me, wanted to use intuition in their work. In this I was not alone, and I planned to keep up contact with them to pursue this new course after we left.

Before heading back to Los Angeles, I had seen that Brugh's eclectic philosophy incorporated the essence of many religions, above all the concept of unconditional love. This was the underpinning of what he had done with Debbie, the spirit with which he approached her life. For Brugh, intuitive experiences weren't an end in themselves, but rather an extension of a compassionate spiritual awareness. Through meditation, that awareness could be nurtured and trained. No intellectual construct, unconditional love was a way of being in the world, a great gift Brugh was able to transmit in words and through his hands. I'd met many healers, like Jack and others in Thelma's lab, but no one who could so powerfully generate this force and bring it to bear with such impact on others.

I had received a taste of unconditional love, the spiritual link I had been missing for so long. During the conference I got glimpses of what it meant to be openhearted, to see the best in others, and to help reach to their truest needs. It was such a relief, suddenly, not to judge or criticize everyone I met. I'd gotten so used to focusing on people's faults, I developed a kind of blindness, rooted in fear, that I engaged in automatically.

I'd no idea how long it would take to move beyond my self-centeredness, the number of surrenders it would entail to allow that love in. Unconditional love is something achieved after very dedicated spiritual work, and I was just beginning. Nonetheless, I'd found the promise of what I was looking for, and in Brugh I had a new kind of role model. Returning home, ready to continue the integration of intuition into my life, I couldn't foresee that the glow of the love I felt would soon dim in the ordinary world, without Brugh and the others to generate and reinforce it. My greatest challenge would be to learn how to renew and sustain such love in myself.

Three weeks after my return was the anniversary of my grandfather's death. On Friday night, after lighting a Yahrzeit candle in his memory, I wanted to do something special to commemorate the occasion. I had never been particularly observant of my religion, with the exception of attending services with my parents on the Jewish holidays. But shortly before sunset, I decided to take a walk to an Orthodox synagogue in Venice Beach. I was greeted at the doorway by a short, studious-looking man in his midthirties who seemed to be in a position of authority. He had bushy auburn hair and was wearing wire-rimmed glasses, a yarmulke, and a blue and white silk tallis draped over his shoulders. Directing me to an empty seat in the women's section, he then went to sit down on the opposite side with the other men. After the service, he approached me, introduced himself as Richard, and invited me to his home for a Shabbat dinner.

We soon became romantically involved. Richard was a successful entertainment attorney and had recently divorced. He was also a devout Jew, trying to balance his religious beliefs with his busy career. I quickly fell in love, and every Friday for the next three months I returned to the synagogue to pray with the group, a scarf covering my head as was the Orthodox custom. Afterward, since Richard didn't drive on Shabbat, we'd walk to one of the congregants' homes nearby for dinner.

I knew little about the Orthodox Jewish community, never having been exposed to it before. One Friday evening, Richard started asking me questions about my family, and the conversation made its way to my grandfather. Having recently returned from Brugh's retreat, I felt quite open about discussing almost anything, so I told Richard about the dream I'd had that predicted my grandfather's death. When I recounted this, however, I could see Richard's expression change; he then too politely inquired if I had had any other such experiences. Undaunted, I enthusiastically shared them with him, overlooking his obvious discomfort, trusting that he would understand. He didn't. When the night ended and he left, a wall stood between us.

A long letter arrived from Richard the next week, saying he couldn't see me anymore. Heartbroken, I called and asked him why. He said I was a psychiatrist and he didn't want to be in a relationship with a woman who had such a demanding career, but I didn't believe him; I knew there was another reason. Ruth, my friend and a member of the same synagogue, had appeared open-minded, so I asked her if she knew what had happened. It was just as I suspected. Ruth told me Richard had been so disturbed about my premonitions that he had consulted his rabbi. An elderly man of European descent, the rabbi told Richard that I was a witch and that he should cut off all contact with me. I continued going to the synagogue for a little while, but word had gotten around. People who had previously been friendly now became distant. I stopped getting invitations to attend Shabbat dinners. For all practical purposes, I'd been blackballed.

Before Brugh's workshop, such a humiliation would have dissuaded me from my pursuit of intuition. But now I was more resilient. Though wounded by Richard's withdrawal and the synagogue's response, I didn't use this as an excuse to reject my abilities.

An opportunity to test my new resolve presented itself almost immediately. Anna, one of my patients, was a receptionist who worked for a cardiologist in my office building. Divorced, she'd lived alone for years in a small house in Culver City. She was in her early sixties, short, with sleek gray hair and clear blue eyes. Born and raised in Orange County, she had lived a quiet life, had never traveled, and followed a daily routine of work and coming home to watch TV.

Anna entered therapy to sort through a tumultuous relationship with her son. While seeing me, however, she developed a particularly aggressive type of lung cancer that rapidly metastasized to her brain. Even after massive doses of radiation and chemotherapy, the cancer didn't respond. Over a period of six months, she went from being a healthy, vital woman to being bedridden. Shortly after one of the chemotherapy treatments, she suffered a partial stroke, which rendered her unable to walk.

Following her stroke, Anna found it too strenuous to come to my office, but we stayed in phone contact. Despite her recent setbacks, the oncologist hadn't given up hope that she might still go into remission. One evening I visited Anna at her home. Prior to this meeting, we hadn't spoken much about the possibility of her death; the focus had always been on her recovery. But it didn't matter that her physical condition was more stable than it had been for months. Early that morning, she had had a premonition that she was going to die. This was not a vague impression or merely a fear. As we spoke together that evening, it was clear that Anna knew without a shred of doubt that within twenty-four hours her life would be over. And this absolute knowing horrified her.

In the past, I would have reassured Anna that her anxiety about dying was natural, considering the severity of her illness. After she had vented her feelings, I would then have emphasized recent gains. But I had a strong instinct that Anna's premonition was right: It rang as true as what I had felt six months before about Christine. Now, instead of questioning it, I made the choice to trust both Anna and myself. I didn't listen to the part of me that warned, "Don't risk it. You're going to make a big mistake." I had followed that voice before and paid too high a price. This time, rather than trying to diffuse or ignore the premonition, I allowed it to guide me. Once that decision was made, I heard a voice in my head that instructed, "Direct Anna toward her own death."

At first I didn't understand, but then an idea came to me. If I did a guided meditation with Anna to help her approach her death, if I brought her face to face with it, I knew she would somehow be consoled. I had only been meditating a few months, though, and had never tried this before. Even so, I felt strangely confident, certain I was taking the right tack, as if I were being directed by an intelligent force and shown what to do.

As for Anna, she was so distraught that she hesitantly consented to go along with me. I asked her to lie down on her bed and close her eyes. Then I began by leading her through some breathing exercises to help relieve her stress. When she seemed more at ease, as gently as I could I said, "Picture your own death. Tell me what it looks like."

Anna flinched. I knew this would be hard for her. Anna didn't consider death to be peaceful; rather, she saw it as a painfully final separation from her loved ones. "I'm afraid to even imagine it," she said. "What if there isn't anything there?" I tried to reassure her, and then, eyes still closed, she went on. "All I see is darkness. An empty void. Nothing. A dreadful silence. I'm cold, numb. I don't like it here." Tears rolled down her cheeks. She squeezed my hand. "I want to stop," she said.

I quietly urged her to go on, to keep focusing on her vision. Even though it was uncomfortable, I believed something important was there for her. I hoped she would stay with it and not give up. For some time, Anna remained alone in the darkness. I sat without speaking, sensing she was okay but not wanting to interrupt her. Five or ten minutes passed.

Then, abruptly, Anna began to speak. "It's very strange," she said. "I can see a faint golden light, a glow like embers in a fire coming from behind the darkness. It's exquisite, I can't keep my eyes off of it. It keeps getting brighter and brighter, pulling me in." As Anna continued to watch the light approach, a great tranquillity overtook her. Her breathing slowed; her body was still and calm. She remained like this for about a half hour. By the time the meditation had ended, her fear was gone.

"You're right," she whispered and cracked open her eyes for a few seconds. "If this is death, it's nothing to be afraid of." Then she drifted off into a deep sleep.

I found this striking, not only because of what Anna had said, but also because she wasn't a religious person and was unfamiliar with metaphysical literature and had no belief in an afterlife. Still, she'd had an instant recognition of her death as radiant light, could feel its brilliance and serenity. Without any prompting from me, she'd confirmed both my own direct experience and accounts of healers who had been with the dying.

That was the last time I saw Anna. Her son called my office the following day to inform me that his mother had died. Anna's death had been a peaceful one, he said. The whole family had been by her side. I hung up the phone and let the news sink in slowly. Anna and I had been working together for over a year. We were close and I would miss her. It was hard for me when anyone I cared for died. I would always be expecting to run into them, to see them smile or hear their voice. I knew that I would feel Anna's absence for a long while. I was sad that she was gone but, at the same time, relieved. Remembering the acceptance on

Anna's face as we said good-bye, I realized that I had done the right thing.

For the first time in years, I had acknowledged the validity of my internal voice, had listened to it, and doing so had brought Anna solace. Even though I knew I had taken a huge chance, I felt giddy, almost euphoric: Since I had done it once, the next time would be easier. I couldn't have asked for a more positive affirmation.

On my way home that evening, I rolled down the windows in my car and took in the night. The stars seemed brighter, the air fresher, my hearing more acute. With a cool breeze blowing through my hair, singing along to a Willie Nelson song on the radio, I headed west on Olympic Boulevard toward the beach. As Anna had found peace in her death, so I was finding a new clarity in my life.

CHAPTER FIVE

Mixing Medicine

Because science expands one type of knowledge, it need not denigrate another. All great scientists have understood this.

—MARGARET MEAD

Goose bumps shot up my arms. I was looking at a full-color picture of a man on the cover of *L.A. Weekly.* I had never seen him before, had never even heard of him. Still, the cells of my body were registering the familiarity. I quickly flipped to the inside story.

His name was Stephan Schwartz, I read, a parapsychologist, founder and director of the Mobius Group, an organization in the Los Feliz area that conducted intuitive research. Assisted by a staff of intuitives, he had worked in association with police departments, insurance companies, and private individuals to help solve crimes and unearth lost archaeological relics, some of them underwater. I immediately wrote him a letter describing my own experiences and dropped it in the mail. I figured that he would be swamped by responses to the story, so I didn't expect to hear back right away, if at all. But the next week, I received a phone call from Stephan himself. We talked for a few minutes and then arranged to meet at his home.

The moment I saw him, there was instant recognition between us; it was as if we had known each other for years. Immediately I knew Stephan would be a pivotal influence in my life. As we spoke, he reminded me of a blue-blooded New Englander who could have stepped straight out of a country club in Connecticut. I fell in love with his preppy looks, his intelligence, and his full-spectrum ability to blend with scientists as well as intuitives. It soon became obvious that Stephan's deep-seated belief in spirituality made him one of those rare people who gracefully straddle many different worlds simultaneously.

I told Stephan that my abilities had been dormant for a long time, but it didn't seem to matter to him at all. He said the rebirth of images triggered at Brugh Joy's conference a few months earlier would be further quickened by my meditation practice. The next step for me was to put them to practical use by participating in what he called a "remote-viewing experiment." He agreed to teach me this technique, used to visualize past, present, and future events about which the viewer had no previous knowledge. He said that by going into a meditative state, and having an interviewer specifically guide me, I could be trained to engage my intuitive abilities consciously. Stephan was about to take over where Thelma Moss had left off. He enlisted me to join his staff of intuitive respondents. I jumped at the chance, and he put me to work.

The remote-viewing experiments were done as a team effort: A composite of the viewers' independent responses was analyzed for areas of concurrence. Stephan had selected this group on the basis that each individual intuitive had a specialty in which he or she was most proficient, typically related to their careers. The central core of respondents consisted of Jack, an engineer; Hella, a fine arts photographer; Andre, a musician; Ben, a film producer and documentarian; Alan, a parapsychologist; John, a newspaper photographer; and Rosalyn, an educator and healer.

Stephan felt that I would bring to their work a piece that had been missing.

I continued to conduct a busy private practice during the day. Then, after office hours a few evenings a month, I would take part in remote-viewing experiments at Mobius as an outlet for my intuitive expression. In the past, I'd always felt that I needed to sacrifice one part of myself for the sake of the other. There had never been enough space inside of me to include both. Although initially I was careful to maintain a separation between these two major aspects of my life, I had begun a new phase, fully active in both the medical and the intuitive worlds.

One day, at the end of a stiflingly hot Thursday afternoon, Stephan called me in for a remote viewing. It was one of those suffocating Indian summer days in Los Angeles when people lie listlessly by their swimming pools trying to steal some precious oxygen from the air. On my way to the Mobius offices, I was in my car, windows rolled down, inching through the rush-hour traffic, heading for Los Feliz. Perspiration dripped down my neck; I was wiped out from having seen clients back to back since nine A.M. The cool softness of my bed was the only vision I felt capable of having.

I usually felt like this at the close of a long day's work when I was heading to the Mobius offices. My life had become so demanding. My beeper would go off at all hours of the day or night. Most of the time I was drained from making hospital rounds, battling with insurance companies, and answering panic calls from patients and their families. There were constant emergencies and little space for anything else. These evenings were the only times I set aside for myself. The whole trip, from office to office, took about fifty minutes. As much as I might feel like turning back, no matter how burned out or irritable I might be, by the time I pulled onto Hyperion Avenue and parked my car, most of my energy would be back. I knew this, and it kept me going. I also knew I needed to be at Mobius more than I needed sleep.

I pulled my car into the lot. I looked gratefully at the modest two-story fifties-style building. Slowly, I felt my stomach releasing, my jaw letting go, my mind clearing. For much of my life, when I tried so diligently to squash my visions, ever present and hammering to get through, I felt imprisoned in a tiny little box. Working as an intuitive at Mobius, the walls of that box began to soften and then melt away. Suddenly I'd find myself in a reality so huge that the boundaries disappeared and I knew that anything was possible. It was there I was privy to a myriad of images, sensations, and sounds outside the realms of my ordinary perceptions. It was there I could drop the claustrophobic persona of "psychiatrist," a role that seemed too small to fit who I was anymore. It was there I could release all defining and confining concepts of self and become something more.

And then there was Stephan. On Mullholland Drive late one night after dinner while we were watching the city lights sparkle and entice, I told him one of my dreams. Already I trusted him enough to risk it. For me, dreams are the most personal part of myself that I can share. Immediately he clicked in, following what I recounted, beat by beat, reading aspects of it that I couldn't see myself. Stephan has the uncanny ability to travel those realms with me and I with him. Since then we've sustained a friendship that has remained easy, smooth, and strong.

The evening of the remote viewing, Stephan greeted me as I walked through the door to his office. I watched him with amusement, phone plastered to his right ear, papers piled high on his desk, his computer screen wildly flashing. There he was, business as usual, trying to do several things at the same time. His life was a three-ring circus, and he was a master juggler. When I had first met him in his office, I had an intuitive vision of Stephan, encircled by books and manuscripts, which were strewn all over the floor. He was fully clothed, taking a shower in the middle of his living room. But instead of water, pure white light was pouring out of the faucet. He was worried that his papers would become wet and damaged, but I assured him that in the light they would be safe.

Stephan hung up the phone, looked at me, and smiled. The remote viewings always took place in this office, a small conference room looking out onto a lush, beautifully planted garden. The only wall hanging was a five-foot-square framed map of Alexandria, Egypt, where precious artifacts had been located through the intuitive work of the Mobius Group in 1980, five years before. Adjacent to the map were floor-to-ceiling shelves filled with books spanning the hard sciences, parapsychology, and the arts. One section was devoted entirely to translations of sacred religious poetry and prose. The pile of papers on Stephan's desk were letters from the farthest reaches of the world, people looking for validation of their intuitive experiences. Apparently disorganized but impeccably thorough, Stephan would eventually answer each one of them personally.

As we began, Stephan told me that tonight we were doing an experiment to locate possible shipwrecks, but, in order not to bias me, gave no further details. He then shut off the phones and informed the other staff members that we weren't to be disturbed. I had grown familiar with our routine, having participated in a number of other remote viewings. On the basis of past performance, I had been selected as a respondent for this project. After Stephan and I took our usual places in comfortable chairs at opposite sides of the table, he placed in front of me an audiotape player to record the session, pencils and pens, a blank 8 1/2-by-11-inch piece of drawing paper, and four different nautical charts.

Once we were settled, I closed my eyes and quieted myself. Silence filled the room, and the heat and various stresses of the day dropped away as I started to slip into a meditative state. I emptied my mind of all thoughts. The traditional mind had no role there. No more analyzing. Complete receptivity. Nonthinking. I sought the Zen-Buddhist state of becoming an empty rice bowl so the Universe could fill it. I was that rice bowl. I was empty. I was ready. I heard a sound, a voice from far away. It was

Stephan's. He instructed me to turn the unmarked chart right-side-up and begin to indicate the various locations of sunken ships. He asked me to focus particularly on a missing sixteenth-century Spanish galleon. Besides the location of the wrecks, I was to tell him what the sites looked like in terms of any geographical markers, and to explain what would be found there.

As I perused the charts and drifted into a light trance, I watched to see where my hand was drawn. Nothing. I waited. I was patient, knowing that impressions don't always come right away. Still nothing. A minute passed, maybe two. I couldn't judge time. Then my body seemed to come alive. I became more alert, aware, open. Not focusing on images or thinking at all, I began to buzz with feelings: My hand was a direction finder. As I glided it over the map, some areas felt hotter than others; there was a tingling, a heightened intensity, a palpable swirling sensation like millions of atoms vibrating in sync. A burst of invigorating heat rushed through the entire length of my body as my hand continued to scan the chart. I felt like I'd been plugged into an electrical socket; I broke out in a sweat. My hand was magnetized, pulled to specific spots. I was merging with the land and water in an unconscious communion with them.

"This area is very rich, high energy," I said. "My hand is burning up."

"What does it look like?" Stephan asked.

"These are land masses." I pointed to a place on the chart. "There's a high frequency, like a sound wave, going up and down the land masses."

With Stephan's encouragement, I watched, slightly detached, while my hand, still tingling with heat, marked circles on the chart around three one-mile-square areas.

"Keep going, Judith," Stephan said. "Draw a picture of whatever objects you think might be found there."

I had no idea whether or not my drawings would make sense or simply be an incoherent mass of scribbles. I was just a witness to these circular motions and long, sweeping lines connecting themselves together at their own pace. Watching the blank paper, I saw my hand begin to sketch first an anchor, then a cross-shaped medallion, and then some medicine vials.

When these images were completed, the motion in my hand stopped. I knew not to force it. I'd learned it was pointless to draw what my mind thought should be there rather than allowing myself to be guided. Setting down my pencil accordingly, I stopped. For the remainder of the session Stephan asked me more detailed questions about the location of the ships and their contents. After about an hour we finished, and Stephan coded the chart and the tape of the session with the date and my name, then filed them.

As Stephan subsequently explained, we had started the first stage of the *Seaview* project. A local businessman had approached him with a proposition: Along with traditional magnetometer readings—which measured metallic content—and aerial surveys, he wanted Mobius to utilize remote viewing to scan a 1,500-kilometer stretch of the Great Bahama Bank for lost ships and buried treasure. Stephan was interested but knew that the cost of such an undertaking could be prohibitive. Through sheer determination, Stephan and some associates had raised over $1 million to subsidize the project. This was practically unheard of, since in the past parapsychology as a field was notoriously underfunded. But Stephan was able to pull things off that seemed close to impossible; he was unquestionably a pioneer.

In August 1985, after extensive historical research, our staff defined an area where there was some likelihood of finding Caribbean shipwrecks. Stephan then obtained a license from the Bahamian government to conduct a search in that vicinity. Subsequently, he compiled charts of the designated locales and gave them to me and the eleven other intuitive respondents, interviewing us individually numerous times over the two-year period we were involved in the project. To prevent bias, we agreed as usual not to discuss our sessions or anything else about the experiment with one another.

When all the initial remote viewings were complete, each of the respondents' maps was analyzed for areas of agreement. Independently and with no prompting from our interviewers—and avoiding even body-language cues—we had all individually chosen a number of identical sites. These six "consensus areas" provided us with the direction of where to begin the fieldwork.

That first interview I had with Stephan, for instance, I had identified, among other areas, Beak's Cay, an island, as a site where a ship would be located. As I later learned, six of the other intuitives had also identified this site. Our descriptions were astonishingly similar: "It's like the top of this uninhabited mountain, a sand mountain, stands out and extends beyond the water," I had said, giving Stephan as much detail as I could summon. "A set of low-lying inlets," Andre had related "not proper islands though they are almost a mile long." And Hella had told Stephan, "They're like low reefs that have rocks stuck up above their surfaces, uninhabited, with a little vegetation."

Once these consensus sites were determined, we were ready to leave for Miami, to set sail. Incredibly enough, the expedition had come together. Not only was this the adventure of a lifetime, but the other intuitives and I were having all expenses paid as well as a share of whatever treasure we found. My parents could hardly believe it. Their attitudes toward my involvement with Mobius were mixed. Whatever came of the voyage, my father still considered things like remote viewing to be "different." Nonetheless, pleased by the success of my practice—I had more referrals than I could handle—and seeing that my beliefs weren't harming me, he kept an open mind. Above all, he had faith in my decisions. Even if my father didn't believe in intuition, he did believe in me.

My mother was intrigued by Mobius, despite her reservations. She was openly supportive of the group, though still warning me not to get "too far out" with it. As always, she was concerned about what other doctors would think, about the risk of compromising my practice. But as I became more secure as a woman, doctor, and intuitive, my mother's incessantly adamant opinions became less threatening. Over the years we had worked at being closer, talked through our difficulties. Both of us were strong women, and we had come to respect each others' needs. With my professional success, many of her fears were eased. My identity as an intuitive, though still hard for her to accept, posed less of an obstacle. My mother wanted to be actively involved with my life, in which Mobius now played a large part. So cautiously, but with real interest, she followed my Mobius work, eager to know the details of each of our projects.

In September 1987, having said good-bye to my parents and friends, I flew from Los Angeles to Miami to meet Stephan, Hella, Alan, and the rest of the crew at the *Seaview*. I had heard rave reviews about this 110-foot vessel: It slept twenty-two, was equipped with a state-of-the-art navigational system and full welding and diving shops.

Stephan picked me up at the airport and drove me straight to the shipyard where the *Seaview* was docked. My expectations had been completely off; this was no luxury liner. It was a bare-bones utility vessel originally designed to service oil rigs off the Gulf of Mexico. Now it had been converted for research purposes. I took one look and wanted to run, but I controlled myself and followed Stephan on board.

The top deck resembled a machinery salvage yard, strewn with tools and noisy equipment. Above the ship's twin propellers was a pair of huge metallic blowers that could dig holes in the sea floor in the event that we uncovered a wreck. The living quarters, just below, consisted of several rows of thin wooden bunk beds only a few feet apart. This meant that the crew, divers, and intuitives all would be crammed right next to one another without so much as a single partition to separate the beds. There were only three showers for everyone, and limited hot water. We were instructed to flush the toilets only when they were completely full. If all this wasn't enough, there was the incessant background drone of the ship's engine. I wondered how I'd ever get a moment's sleep.

There was a hurricane warning in Miami, and so with *Seaview* in dry dock I checked into the local Holiday Inn. I needed time to adjust to the idea of living on a ship. I have never been the type of person who enjoyed camping or rugged living conditions. I treasured my privacy and relished hot baths. But after a few days, when the weather improved, I warily moved onto *Seaview* with the others. We hung curtains around each bunk to ensure a small degree of privacy and set sail at five A.M.

Aimed for Bimini and the Great Bahama Bank, I watched Miami Harbor become dwarfed in the distance as a wave of exhilaration quelled my fears. Later that day, sitting up at the bow at dusk, watching bolts of heat lightning streak across the sky, I reflected on how far I had come. Lying with my bare feet dangling over the rim of the boat, dressed in a pair of cotton shorts and a sleeveless white T-shirt, I felt free for the first time in years.

Seaview was a miniature city, bursting with activity, driven by a special sense of collective mission. Those of us on board melded into what Stephan described as "a working unit of combined minds, bodies, and spirit united with Spirit." We had a concrete goal, but the whole project was shaped by a spiritual, though not overtly religious, impulse. Each of us, hired by Stephan, had in common a belief in a divine intelligence and the interconnectedness of all things. The intent of *Seaview* was to form both a spiritual and a scientific community. Every day we began by meditating as a group, asking to be guided toward right action in accordance with a divine plan.

Our work started at eight in the morning and sometimes continued on long past dark. We were all in constant motion, working hand in hand planning our schedules, conducting remote viewings, and sharing our discoveries about science and intuition. The excitement was contagious; one of us always had a new theory, hope, or dream. By the end of each day I was happily spent; despite the constant roar of the engine, which vibrated the sides of my bunk, I slept more soundly than I ever had in my life.

When we reached the first southern consensus zone, each of the intuitives did a more exact remote viewing to narrow down the location of possible ships to an area small enough for the divers to search. We were taken out individually and asked to sense intuitively where the wreck was situated. Buoys would be dropped where we chose, and divers would then explore the terrain below. While some of us were doing this, the other respondents would be engaged in remote viewing at other locations.

Shortly past dawn one morning, the sea was a deep shade of turquoise, so transparent that schools of iridescent fish and turtles could be seen swimming beneath the surface. One of the divers and I boarded a small rubber boat equipped with a radar reflector. We sat in silence in the middle of the ocean, twenty miles from the southernmost coast of Bimini. With my eyes closed, listening to the solitary sound of small waves gently slapping against the bow, I focused on the work at hand. Within seconds, an image of a location came to me. It was so much easier to do the viewings while floating on these warm, amniotic waters; the images flowed more naturally than they ever had on land, taking on a certain rhythm, a seamlessness, that had been missing in the city. Just by listening to and watching the water I was being told things. As the pictures took form in my mind, I saw an underwater shelf adjacent to a warm current of bubbles, situated in an area marked, on the grid we were using, 41 degrees north by 47 degrees east, which happened to be nearby. I rarely picked up numbers, so the clarity of my perception surprised me.

Fifteen minutes later, we'd found the spot, threw out a Styrofoam marker buoy, and logged its location on a work chart. The diver then went underwater to check out the area, leaving me completely alone on the deck of our small boat. *Seaview* was now out of sight; in every direction I was surrounded by a great expanse of water. I sat with the warmth of the sun beating down on my shoulders, the sea glistening like a brilliant jewel. Then, seemingly from out of nowhere, a group of seven blue-gray dolphins appeared. They all surfaced at once and encircled my boat, flapping their fins in unison, singing in high-pitched chirping tones that reminded me of a haunting sound I once had heard long before in a dream. For a few precious moments I was certain I'd arrived in heaven, not wanting for a single thing.

Suddenly, the diver's head popped up out of the water and he yelled, "I found a ship!" I was jubilant, thrilled that my reading had been accurate. He climbed back on board, telling me that a forty-foot sailboat, which appeared to be about ten years old, was resting on an elevated sandy shelf. Although the sailboat was of no archaeological significance, it was a heartening sign that on the very first day of fieldwork, we were already on the right track. The only mistake I'd made was that my goal during the remote viewing had been too general. I had concentrated on finding a sunken ship but hadn't specified the type.

Throughout the voyage, our team of intuitives would work for four hours, take a break, and then work another four hours, either studying and reading charts or going out with the divers. Always we were a collective. As Stephan described it, we had formed a macromind, an extraordinary energy circuit: the remote viewers as the intuitive part of the mind; the scientific researchers as the analytical mind; the crew as the physical mind; and Stephan functioning as coordinator. Together, we were invisibly but powerfully bound, united by our shared goal and intense physical proximity.

The intuitives were all experienced at remote viewing, but each of us also had special abilities complementing the others. That is, the skills we had in our normal lives tended to carry over to and shape our intuitive impressions. Hella, artist and photographer, had a gift for description, for seeing simple geometric forms, colors, shadows, and ornaments. Of one wreck site we later discovered, Hella described "cylindrical timbers extending upward into the light, comprising the mast of the ship. Below deck, enveloped in darkness are rectangular planks which make up the floor." Jack, an engineer who was drawn to technical details, saw "metallic joints which connect portions of the ship's rigging at the tension points, forming a right angle, to allow for a full range of motion and maximum mechanical flexibility." Michael, the writer-director I'd met at Brugh's conference, had a flair for visualizing spatial relationships and he saw this same wreck's "moth-eaten rectangular beams piled on top of one another like pick-up sticks, forming a pyramid." Ben, a television director, was skilled at forming a general master shot, a description of the broader picture, as if looking through the lens of a camera at a complete scene: "I see a two-story ship. The sleeping quarters are below deck, there's a small cooking area above, with storage sections on the starboard side. The top deck is huge, maybe a hundred feet or more." And I, as a trained listener, as a psychiatrist tuned to emotions, honed in on the remnants of a slaver, the intensity of the slaves' misery inexorably drawing me to pinpoint the site of the wreck. I could feel the torment of these captives, see them shackled, starved, ill, in nightmarish despair.

Toward the end of the week, *Seaview* headed due north to investigate the consensus zone extending 11.5 miles around Beak's Cay. On a rainy evening with threatening storm clouds looming above us, we threw out three orange buoys onto the ocean a few hundred yards from a small, uninhabited limestone island looking very much as our team of intuitives had described it in Los Angeles. Stephan had been reluctant to investigate this location because it was a favorite spot for sports divers and one of the most heavily scavenged areas of the Bahama Bank for hundreds of years. In addition, the magnetometer readings hadn't been strong enough to indicate the underwater presence of a large ship. Nor were we sure the weather would cooperate. Logically, there was every reason to skip this location. But what made our expedition special was that it was not dictated solely by logic.

At dinner, Hella, Alan, and I urged Stephan to remain at this site. When he took us aside individually to get our independent impressions, each of us said we sensed that something of value might be found the next day. Despite the weather and lack of significant magnetometer readings, our instincts told us not to leave. Stephan listened to us. He considered the remote viewers to be his radar, his sensors, and agreed to stay at Beak's Cay another twenty-four hours.

According to the readings done both in Los Angeles and on site, a vessel of salvageable worth lay concealed nearby. The divers thoroughly scanned the sandy bottom but came up empty-handed. Just as they were about to give up and return to the *Seaview*, however, one of them noticed a line of fire coral that lay below some thick eel grass. Though there was no evidence of a ship, acting on intuition he broke apart the coral with a hammer, revealing a row of metal spikes, the kind once used to fasten a ship's ribs to its keel. Surfacing, the divers enthusiastically waved the small pieces of metal in the air. Thrilled, we all gathered on deck to greet them, the heroes returning from war. The atmosphere was truly explosive.

Unfortunately, it was hurricane season in the Bahamas. A big storm was approaching from off the coast of South America and was about to hit at any time. After twelve days at sea, Hella, Alan, and I were picked up by a private schooner to begin our journey home. With a very careful eye on the weather, the *Seaview* stayed out another week while Stephan and the other divers collected additional samples of metal, wood, and nails. Then the *Seaview* was returned to dry dock in Miami, where alterations and additions were made. Six weeks later, without the intuitives, the crew revisited the Beak's Cay site and uncovered an intact ship, over 100 feet in length, beneath a dense blanket of eel grass and sand. It was later ascertained to be an armed American merchantman, the brig *Leander*, which had been lost at sea near Beak's Cay in 1834.

Locating this vessel, after 150 years and much searching by others, was a valuable archaeological and historical find, as the *Leander* was one of the most well-preserved remains discovered in the Bahama Banks area. It had lain undisturbed, buried under the sea floor, for well over a century. Imagine unearthing an entire ship beneath the sand, looking very much like it did before it sank. Not only did it provide knowledge of how sailing vessels were constructed in the early 1800s, but it gave us a firsthand record of personal artifacts of the period. Very specific objects belonging to the passengers were recovered from the wreckage that our group of intuitives had described: a pearl-handled razor, parts of a drafting set, a pewter cruet. Of special interest were several small bottles on board, because glass rarely manages to remain intact due to the constant shifting of the current and sand on the treacherous limestone banks.

The search for other wrecks continued, and a total of eighteen sunken ships were found, most of recent origin, many foreseen by the remote viewers and confirmed by magnetometer readings. What's striking to me is that these sites had been pinpointed by our remote viewings two years before any of us had even traveled to the Bahamas. Time and space didn't stand in our way. The information was there to perceive intuitively.

Later in the expedition, using blowers, our crew uncovered a lengthy dyewood trail lining the ocean floor. Used to create the rich reds and blacks of Renaissance painting, dyewood was transported to Spain from the New World. So valuable was dyewood that only galleons and rich merchant ships transported it. The dyewood trail, therefore, suggested a high probability that we were close to discovering a Spanish galleon from between the fifteenth and seventeenth centuries.

It was all the more exciting because dyewood has no metallic content—no technological device could have located it. This was an exceptional example of how the intuitive functioned as an essential part of our project. Other members of our team, the historians and archaeologists, then dated the dyewood and established its significance. Always the intuitive, the analytical, and the technological collaborated. (I didn't know it then, but the project's funding would soon run out, though now the search for the Spanish galleon has resumed. A wreck has been found at the dyewood site that contained several dozen emeralds. The work is ongoing.)

The day I left the Bahamas to return to Los Angeles, I felt I was leaving a part of myself behind. Taking off from Bimini in a twin-engine white seaplane, I sadly watched the golden silhouettes of the islands recede behind me. And yet I felt triumphant, filled with the adventurous spirit of the project, the close camaraderie that had developed among us, the knowledge of how beautifully science and intuition had mixed. Aboard *Seaview*, I had been a valued member of an intuitive family. This was a reversal of my childhood, a vindication. I'd been deeply influenced by the unity—the community—of our incredible voyage. Born of a dream, *Seaview* had been made real.

Heading home, we all viewed our experiment with enormous elation. Our aim had been to conduct an intuitive archaeology project. We had succeeded in this, confirming the practical uses of remote viewing by intuitively locating eighteen ships. Yet our expedition had meant so much more. Our voyage on the *Seaview* had been a spiritual pilgrimage, a mission into which we all threw ourselves heart and soul. The energy that comes from such an inspired group undertaking is dazzling. We learned that intuition is an efficient technical skill, sometimes exceeding the capacity of radar, sonar, and magnetometers. But most important, the intuitive was telling us something vital about human nature: that we're all part of an interconnected network, privy to information that exists beyond the confines of the rational mind. By exploring the intuitive aspect of ourselves, we discover that we're linked to a greater whole, a wisdom that allows us to know the grandeur and the possibilities humans can achieve.

Having glimpsed a great mystery, I came away in awe of how much we still didn't know. I realized that we were just at the first stages of learning how to work with our intuitive side. Questions filled my mind: Where does this information really come from? How is it stored? Can we have more consistent access to it? Even more intriguing, How could I put remote viewing to use in my psychiatric practice? Until now, I had been cautious about incorporating intuition into sessions with my patients. If I had a clear-cut premonition, I would listen to it, but this happened only infrequently. I had no formal routine to integrate the more subtle aspects of intuition. It had taken a few years at Mobius before I became confident of my own abilities. My practice was precious to me. I didn't want to experiment with any technique until I was first comfortable with it. But my experience aboard *Seaview* had instilled certainty in me: I was now ready to begin a new phase in my work.

It followed that if I could accurately describe a distant person, place, or event before it ever happened during a remote viewing, the same principle could be applied to obtaining information about my patients, particularly new ones. I decided, accordingly, that before I met a patient I would try tuning in. Then I could compare my reading with actual information they gave me once we met. This initial screening would be the ideal opportunity to test out the reliability of remote viewing as it pertained to my psychiatric work.

One morning, after doing remote viewings on patients for several months and finding them accurate, I received a call on my answering service from a woman named Robin. She told the operator that she was looking for a new therapist and she wanted to set up an appointment with me. There had been no referral— it was a cold call—nor had she explained why she wanted to come in. She simply left her first name and a San Fernando Valley phone number.

I scribbled this information on a notepad and put it on my desk. At lunchtime, my first uninterrupted break in a full morning, I set aside ten minutes to read Robin. Turning off the phone, I lay down on the couch and closed my eyes. I passively focused only on her name. Shifting my awareness from the sounds, smells, and sights of my physical environment, I emptied my mind. I had no specific questions; I simply remained open to any impressions I might perceive.

Within seconds I became restless, antsy. I was oddly repelled by Robin. I had the sensation of being pushed and pulled in opposite directions. There was something about her I didn't trust; I found myself questioning her motives for coming to see me. Although I suspected she had a hidden agenda, I couldn't say what it was. All I could see was a clear image of a bottle of scotch on a kitchen table, and I smelled alcohol permeating the air.

I jotted down all of this in my notebook, initially intending to compare it with what Robin told me about herself. But the reading had made me so uneasy I was wary of scheduling an appointment for her. This was rare: Even my most difficult patients didn't trigger such loud alarm signals. The fact that my past remote viewings had been so much on target added to my decision to postpone contacting Robin. Instead, I waited.

A few hours later, I received a call from a Mr. Young of the Los Angeles County District Attorney's Office. He told me that he'd been assigned to a suit filed against Robin.

"Robin is under a court order to receive psychotherapy and treatment for drug addiction and alcoholism," he explained. "You should also know the district attorney is processing a complaint against her by two of her former psychotherapists, both women. It seems she became obsessed with them. They're charging her with harassment."

Mr. Young went on to describe how Robin would show up at the therapists' offices unscheduled and call them at all hours of the day and night. A restraining order was finally issued by the Superior Court. Now, learning from Robin that she was planning to start treatment with me, Mr. Young advised that I not take her on, suggesting that she would do better with a male therapist.

I agreed and thanked him, not mentioning anything about my intuitive impressions. I was relieved to have been let off the hook. Robin sounded like a therapist's nightmare. The scenario could have gone an entirely different way. But thanks to my remote viewing and Mr. Young's fortuitous call, I was spared unnecessary grief.

Later, I phoned Robin to let her know why I couldn't see her. I informed her that Mr. Young and I had talked, and that we both recommended she seek out a male therapist. Although she angrily balked at the suggestion, I later learned from Mr. Young that she did take it. He and I were both hopeful that with this man's help Robin would progress.

From then on, I made it a policy to "read" every new patient prior to our initial appointment. It provided me with a quick and easy breakdown of their basic issues, both physical and emotional, and acted as a signpost that set the course their psychotherapy would take. Remote viewing turned out to be a godsend. It helped me to sort quickly through the many calls I received each day. If, during a reading, I determined that a patient and I were not well matched, I would decline to take them on. In each case, however, I tried to refer the caller to a therapist I instinctively felt would be better suited to them. This not only eliminated unnecessary expense for them, but was a time-saver for both of us. From the feedback I later received, I learned I was a pretty good matchmaker: The therapeutic relationships I instigated tended to work out.

Slowly, between experiments at Mobius and using remote viewing to screen patients, I became more secure with my intuitive abilities. By constantly engaging them, I fueled the flame that kept them alive. As I increasingly included them in my work, they felt less alien. In the beginning, I treated my intuitive impressions suspiciously, like strangers, vigilantly scrutinizing their every move. But as time passed and I saw that they weren't going to turn on me, that the quality of my work was improving, I let down my guard and relaxed. If anything, I was overly cautious, but I had witnessed time and again the benefits of remote viewing. More confident, I was ready to take it one step further.

Remote viewing had proved an invaluable tool prior to meeting a patient. Why couldn't I also use it to read someone when they were in therapy with me? Just as I had done with Robin, I selectively tuned in to a few of my patients' names. But now I gave myself more room to experiment. Rather than restricting myself to my office, I tried this in any quiet place where I felt at ease: at home sitting in front of my altar, by the ocean, and in my bathtub in the dark, surrounded by flickering candles. First

I would aim for total emptiness, without thoughts or goals. Then, with my mind stilled, I'd direct my attention to a name and allow impressions to come. It was like opening a door and waiting for someone to enter. No expectations. No judgments. I was a witness watching scenes unfold before me. Passively concentrating on a name set a tone, created an open-ended atmosphere conducive to receiving rich imagery and sensations.

As a result of meeting Brugh, and subsequently studying for many years with an Eastern meditation teacher in Los Angeles, I came to believe that by meditating in this way a divine connection is established. From this, our intuitive awareness expands and we're able to see into people more clearly. Thus I approached every remote viewing with an attitude of reverence, holding the name I was reading sacred.

Cynthia had been in therapy with me for a year. A twenty-six-year-old Harvard graduate, a vivacious journalist, she came in because of difficulties with her boyfriend, a managing editor at the same newspaper where she worked. They'd had a volatile five-year relationship: He wanted them to spend more time together and for Cynthia to cut down her workload. Ten years her senior, he was anxious to start a family, but she defended her right to have a high-powered job, wanting to rethink the question in a few years. Infuriated, he'd argue that nothing would change. But then he'd back down and they would passionately make up. For a few weeks he'd stay away from these charged subjects, but inevitably there would be yet another blowup.

One evening, after a particularly agonizing argument, Cynthia's boyfriend announced that he was leaving her. The next week he moved his things out of their home. He refused to answer her calls or to talk to her at work. Cynthia felt betrayed, abandoned. Despite their disagreements, she loved this man and clung to the hope that they would work out their differences. But he wasn't willing to try. Devastated, she mourned for months.

I knew that it was important for Cynthia to grieve. She was increasingly depressed, fixated on a reconciliation that seemed

unlikely. Struggling with how to help her, I needed more information, and decided to turn to a remote viewing for guidance.
Sitting in front of my altar at home, I went into meditation, focusing on Cynthia's name. After a few minutes, a distinct image
of her boyfriend came to me. (I had met him once when he came
in for a couple's session with Cynthia.) He appeared happy, his
arm around the shoulders of another woman. They seemed very
much in love. And the woman was pregnant!

I took a second look, wondering if somehow I'd gotten my
wires crossed. Cynthia's boyfriend in another relationship with a
baby on the way? My critical mind wanted to explain away what
I was seeing. But I stopped myself from overanalyzing the
image, not wanting to break concentration, trying to remain
neutral. I kept waiting for the image to fade, to change form, or
to explain itself better. But it held strong—sharp, clear, unmistakable.

In meditation, eyes closed, as I watched the image hovering
before me, I realized that Cynthia's boyfriend sincerely wanted
me to understand his situation so I could assist Cynthia. Contrary to my expectations, which derived in part from Cynthia's
stories about him, he exuded no malice, was filled with goodwill
for her. Such love was a tip-off of the image's authenticity. Yet
his stand was also firm, conveying, "This is my life now; nothing
is going to change."

I had to trust the message and let it shape the course of Cynthia's therapy. Following the remote viewing, I could no longer
convey the possibility that they might get back together. However, although Cynthia believed in intuition and knew I utilized
it in my work, I decided not to share the impression at this
point. The timing wasn't right. She was despondent, vulnerable;
such knowledge would have been hurtful and without benefit.

The issue of when to tell someone about intuitive information
is always tricky. I am well aware of the ethical obligations of dis-
closure—that is, to tell a patient the truth as I understand it.
But, even more essential, I am never going to intentionally do
anything that harms the patient. Often I'm faced with hard

choices. In the end, I am always guided by whether or not I believe it will serve a patient to know, and I'm careful never to present myself as an absolute authority or intuition as infallible. For instance, if I'm working with someone who gives the intuitive no credence, it is seldom useful to broach it with them. Rather, I rely on my impressions as backup material that helps me pose certain questions or fill in gaps. If a person is open, however, I may be more direct. In each case, this has to be a judgment call.

What I learned from the remote viewing altered my perspective as Cynthia's therapist. Making a subtle shift in attitude and emphasis, I encouraged her to give up hope of reigniting the old relationship. This enabled Cynthia to move on in a positive direction. A few months later, more self-assured, Cynthia said that she had heard her boyfriend was getting married and that his wife-to-be was pregnant. Flabbergasted, Cynthia reexperienced the old hurt, but she was now better able to confront it. Sensing that the moment was right, I told Cynthia about my vision, not to make a point of how prescient I was, but to validate the truth of what she had heard. When I explained why I had waited, she didn't feel I had wrongly withheld information. Rather, she was relieved that I hadn't told her before. It would only have added to her troubles. Cynthia's response was enormously important to me, confirming that I had made the right choice.

With practice, I also became able to read patients while I was with them in my office. I grew agile at shifting states of awareness at will without always having to set aside a special time to meditate: Intuition became a vital part of how I listened to someone. It was a gradual process, but I became adept at staying attuned to many different levels at once. Intuitive impressions would often spontaneously pop up in the middle of a session. Sometimes there would be only a single image, sometimes many. I discovered that it wasn't the number or complexity that mattered—simple, straightforward impressions can be the most potent.

Over the next few years, I grew comfortable with remote viewing and used it with many patients, realizing that it had something substantial to offer medicine. In part this was because of the impressive research being done by respected scientists in both the United States and the Soviet Union. (For a list of books on intuitive research, see the Guide for Further Reading at the back of this book.) I was especially drawn to the work of physicists Russell Targ and Harold Putoff at the Stanford Research Institute in the 1970s. Funded by the U.S. government, they conducted remote-viewing experiments, and showed that in a controlled laboratory setting even novices could learn to be intuitive. The import of this went well beyond academia: Targ and Putoff also taught subjects how to obtain material about the past, present, and future through remote viewing, and to incorporate this technique into their lives.

I was further impressed by Albert Einstein's introduction to Upton Sinclair's *Mental Radio* (1930), in which Sinclair documented his wife's intuitive abilities and experiments, forerunners of remote viewing. As Einstein wrote, "The results of the telepathic experiments . . . set forth in this book stand surely far beyond those which a mature investigator holds to be thinkable." I was particularly impressed that a genius like Einstein— whose theories ultimately had to be confirmed in the practical world—would go on record supporting inquiry into the nature of intuition. I was moved by his vision that reality might extend beyond what science thought possible.

Through remote viewing, I found that I could get all kinds of information about my patients—their health, relationships, careers, childhood—to discern stumbling blocks that were not obvious on the surface but that became clear when looked at intuitively. If a patient was stuck in her life, if therapy wasn't progressing, I could reevaluate the situation through remote viewing. Where the intellect could spin endlessly in circles formulating theories, intuition could zero in like a laser, penetrating to the heart of the problem. It provided a powerful magnifying glass, illuminating a universe of information unavailable to me before. I blended intuition with my clinical work, drawing on the best from both worlds.

An enormous energy boost and sense of freedom came from dissolving the barriers that had previously kept intuition so walled off. Increasingly, I felt like the conductor of a magnificent orchestra, musicians and instruments finely tuned, utilizing their full range. The music I was creating, the harmony I felt inside, instilled faith that I'd chosen the right path. I had been searching for so long, and finally I was home.

As I became less divided, I began to change. For instance, for many years I had a fear of darkness. Not the darkness that comes from turning off the bedroom light at night, but the darkness that resides in the recesses of canyons, on the edge of cliffs, or deep in the woods. I never liked taking night hikes, even with friends when the moon was full. I was afraid that the power of the night in remote, shadowy places would somehow swallow me and make me invisible.

While I worked at Mobius, and as I allowed intuition to filter slowly into my practice, my fear of dark places abruptly faded. I recall an evening when a friend had made a special request for his fortieth birthday that I take a walk with him in Topanga State Park. While sitting with him on a ridge overlooking a deep abyss, I noticed that my fear was gone. I had discovered in myself what Joseph Campbell called an "inner compass" that went with me everywhere. The night took on new dimensions; I no longer became lost in it. Instead, I now found that it had a special brilliance all its own.

About six months after returning from the *Seaview* expedition in 1987, I had a series of five consecutive dreams that I couldn't explain. In each one, a man in his early thirties with chin-length blond hair and glasses visited me. He closely resembled Terry, my old boyfriend, and we talked intimately in my living room. Like Terry, this was an enormously creative man with a career in the arts. The dreams were baffling: It had been over five years since I'd seen or heard from Terry.

Then Josh, a new patient, walked into my office, and the dreams stopped. When I first saw Josh in my waiting room, dressed in a smartly pressed white shirt and rust-colored corduroy jacket, I did a double-take. He could have been Terry's identical twin. The dream had anticipated his coming.

Josh was a film producer and artist. He had come to me depressed, unsatisfied with the direction of his career. Trying to please his agent and family, wanting to be a dependable wage earner, he often took projects he didn't believe in. Josh had dreamed of excelling as a filmmaker, yet he felt he was doing only mediocre work. He lacked confidence in his choices, succumbing to outside pressure at the expense of listening to himself. He believed that he had sold out, lost track of his artistic vision, and, as a result, had paid a huge price both in his relationships and in his career. His intuition, which had once guided him, had grown distant, inaccessible. He wanted me to help him find it again.

Josh was one of those people who, having decided to enter therapy, makes enormous strides in a very short time. Ripe for change, he was willing to look into his past, to reveal where he had lost track of his priorities and why. With his wife's support, he gave himself permission to turn down projects if they didn't feel right and to wait for ones that inspired him. He started listening to his body—the subtle headaches he got when a decision was wrong, the surge of energy he felt whenever he stuck to what he believed in. Over the next few months, Josh became more sensitive to his own needs. Finally, a script came along that he loved, and he agreed to produce the movie.

I hadn't shared my *Seaview* experiences with many of my patients, fearing that they wouldn't understand. But since Josh was clearly well grounded and wanted to cultivate his intuition, I decided to tell him. He was intrigued by my descriptions of remote viewing. His film was scheduled to begin shooting the following month in South Carolina. After interviewing a variety of directors, he still hadn't found the right one. Time was running out; he had to make up his mind. He wanted to see if, by focusing on the three final candidates' names, he could use remote viewing to narrow down the search.

This was a new twist. I had never taught a patient how to do a remote viewing. What did this have to do with psychiatry? And if I tried it, would it work? I didn't want to use my patients as guinea pigs. I knew caution was important, yet I also trusted the integrity of my experiences at Mobius. Carefully, I continued to evaluate the situation. If Josh had been the slightest bit unstable, I would have immediately refused his request. But he was a strong, emotionally balanced man, so I decided that we could test it out. We agreed to view our venture as an experiment, a joint effort to explore a new technique. If we failed, there would be no negative repercussions.

Josh was a quick study. As an artist, he was accustomed to picking up rich images, so remote viewing came naturally to him. Josh was open-minded, a seeker, attracted to the unusual. He wasn't afraid of intuition as I had once been. In a single session, I taught him the basics of what Stephan had taught me.

"In any remote viewing," I explained, "the first step is always to shift out of a thinking mode into a calm, meditative state, remaining receptive, allowing visual images, bodily sensations, or any other impressions to surface."

To put Josh in touch with his intuition, I had already introduced him to meditation. Gradually, he found it easier to quiet his mind. Its constant dialogue was still distracting, but by concentrating on his breath he was paying less attention to it—a challenge not only for Josh but for everyone who embarks upon a meditation practice.

"The next step," I went on, "is for you to succinctly formulate the question you want answered, so you can receive as direct a response as possible. Close your eyes, take a few deep breaths, and begin meditating." He took his shoes off, sitting cross-legged in the chair and settling into a comfortable position. Continuing, I said, "When you're ready, let me know what your question is. Be as specific as you can. This helps to focus the remote viewing and put it in context."

Josh was silent for a moment, then asked, "Which director would be best for this project?"

I told him to say the first name aloud and then notice whatever impressions he received, no matter how unusual. At first Josh found this difficult. Instead of picturing only one of the candidates, he saw them all grouped together on a stage.

"Is it okay if all three are there?" Josh asked.

"It would be much easier to look at each person separately," I said. "As a general rule, it's better to have clear divisions between the people you're reading. Otherwise their characteristics may blend, which is confusing."

After a long silence, Josh began. On his own, he isolated one candidate by visually graying out the two others, as if lights were dimmed on them on stage. I was fascinated by Josh's creative solution. Without any cueing, he instinctively used his artistic talents of daily life to solve this logistical problem, as the intuitives had done in the *Seaview* project.

Josh then said, "Keith," this director's name. I told him to spend no more than a few minutes on each person. If a time limit is set, images can be programmed to come quickly, and there is more of an immediacy to them.

"What should I expect?" Josh asked. "Will a picture just appear by itself? Do I have to do anything?"

"The most important thing is to relax and wait," I said. He waited, but nothing came. Finally, he saw a small lake. Keith was standing onshore, afraid to go in the water—he couldn't swim.

"Wow!" Josh exclaimed. "I guess this doesn't bode well for us working together."

"Try not to analyze the images right now. That will engage the analytical mind. Go on to the second person."

Without pausing, Josh said, "Diana." Immediately he smiled and sighed. He felt a warmth for her, an affinity. He sensed that she was creative, smart, an ideal partner for this film.

"Good," I said. "Now let Diana go, shift gears, and read the final person."

The third name was "Cheryl." Josh liked her too, sensed they could get along. But as he focused more closely on her face, he saw an unsettling image of her whacking a man's head off with a sword. He laughed. "I guess I need to be more careful than I thought."

Josh was thrilled. Like an excited schoolboy first learning to read, he had gone through each name, struck by how different each person felt, how distinct their characteristics were. He felt the intimacy that comes with remote viewing, the revitalizing energy of connecting with another person at this level. By the time we were finished, he knew his first choice was Diana.

The following week, Josh and a group of studio executives scheduled meetings with Keith, Diana, and Cheryl. He'd be able to see if his intuitive impressions were confirmed. That day, Josh felt that Keith lacked confidence. Cheryl's résumé was impressive, but Josh sensed an angry edge beneath her personable façade. In the end, he chose Diana both because of her qualifications and because of the compatibility he had felt with her during the remote viewing.

A few weeks into the shoot, Josh phoned. "Hi, Judith," he said. "I just wanted to thank you. The director I picked is a perfect match. Filming is right on schedule and the dailies look great. I thought you'd want to know our experiment worked."

Once again, my instincts had proven right. Instead of being plagued by the usual onslaught of questions and confusion, I had received direct validation for what I believed. The feeling evoked a long road trip to Yosemite when I was nine. After hours in the car, my parents finally let me out next to a large, grassy field. Like a wild, unbroken horse, I galloped back and forth, exuberant in my freedom, until all the tension in my body was relieved.

Josh's success gave me this same sense of liberation. Though remote viewing wasn't taught to me in medical school, it was helping me to create a style of my own. Having gone through a period of learning, I was making a transition from student to teacher. Now I could share what I knew with my patients. The painful disconnection of my inner and outer worlds was ending; they were beginning to merge. I had tried something new, it had benefited Josh, and I had gained another therapeutic tool. I hung up the phone, relaxed back in my chair, and smiled.

After Josh, I began to teach many of my patients remote viewing. I realized that it could help them in all aspects of their lives. One difficulty for an intuitive therapist is that others disempower themselves by believing that they can't be intuitive as well. Or they see someone like me as unique. For such patients, remote viewing is the perfect vehicle. It can be used by everyone. The possibilities are endless. Let's say you're hiring an employee, or thinking of taking a new job, or dating a new person, or are at a crossroads in your life and need to make a decision. Remote viewing can fill in the blanks, convey a fuller perspective, or shed light on nuances you never considered before. This is not meant to trivialize remote viewing but to expand its scope. When done with sincerity and integrity, extra information becomes available, facilitating more informed choices about your life.

Because I see intuition as a direct extension of spiritual connectedness, I have never taught remote viewing as an isolated skill. Even though people can improve their intuition without a spiritual reference point, the power that comes from this can be seductive, and their egos often get out of control. Thus the importance of ethical values, of using intuition for service, not for power plays or to take advantage of others, and of remembering its divine source. This is the foundation of my beliefs.

Rosalyn Bruyere was the first healer I ever saw who conducted her sessions in a jogging suit. With perfectly manicured red fingernails, impeccable makeup and color-coordinated sweats, she looked like a mix between a glamorous housewife and an aerobics instructor. Once quite heavy, she had recently lost a lot of weight, disproving the popular myth that intuitives, to remain grounded, must be obese. Rosalyn, one of the remote viewers at Mobius, had founded the Healing Light Center, an outreach clinic and school for healing in Glendale. When she heard about Mobius's latest project, she offered us the use of her facility.

I was already familiar with Rosalyn's work: She'd been treating me for stomach problems the past few months. When she placed her hands on my body, directing energy into my stomach, she would chat about her kids, her work, or anything else that came to mind. Healing was so second nature to her that she didn't have to keep up any pretenses. My physical symptoms markedly improved during these treatments. Not only did Rosalyn rid me of the annoying tight knot in the pit of my stomach, but her sessions left me with a sense of extreme well-being that would last for hours.

Our current project at Mobius concerned the chemical alteration of water molecules in a healing situation. Based on the research of biologist Bernard Grad at McGill University in Canada, healers "treated" jars of water and reportedly increased the vitality in cell colonies, enzymes, and seedlings. We sought to design an experiment to expand on Dr. Grad's initial work. The idea was to see if water, when placed in the hands of a healer during treatment sessions, would be altered significantly. By actually measuring the changes in the treated water with infrared spectrophotometry, we wanted to prove that healing was more than a placebo.

Stephan opted to employ a wide variety of techniques: therapeutic touch (typically used in a nonreligious context such as medical and nursing settings); laying on of hands (also known as faith healing); evangelical Christianity; and channeling (trance-induced healing). Some of the practitioners were experienced; others, like me, were intuitive but hadn't been specifically trained to heal. Getting used to the idea that I could do such work was not easy. I thought it was for the elite few, the gifted ones. As yet, I didn't understand that, like remote viewing, this was an expression of intuitive ability, an art that could be learned.

The afternoon of the experiment, I showed up early at the Healing Light Center. I wanted to observe the other healers closely and, hopefully, discover their secrets. Although I couldn't sit in on their therapeutic sessions, I waited in the reception area and took mental notes as they arrived. None appeared as flamboyant as Rosalyn; their ordinariness was outstanding. Both men and women were dressed simply and conservatively, as if straight out of the fifties, and they mostly kept to themselves. Ranging all the way from thirty to sixty years of age, they seemed a bunch who could have easily belonged to an Orange County bridge club.

My only experience with direct hands-on healing since Brugh's conference had been when a girlfriend and I practiced on each other a few times at home. We'd both found it pleasant, but I wasn't sure how much difference we had made. We felt like kids, awkwardly playing with something we really didn't know anything about. It seemed too easy to heal someone simply through a loving touch. I knew that's how people said it worked, but it was hard to believe that it wasn't more complicated than that.

When my turn arrived, I followed Stephan into a small back office, hoping I could do some good. Hanging on the wall in front of me was a picture of the Buddha in the lotus position. I listened closely to Stephan's directions. "Allow yourself to slip into a calm state, similar to that of a remote viewing," he said. "Focus your awareness on a pure intention to heal."

My patient was George, a burly man in his late fifties. A truck-driver type, he had a raspy smoker's cough, a stubbly gray beard, and was wearing a faded purple-and-gold Lakers T-shirt. George had been suffering from persistent lower-back pain caused by a bulging lumbar disc at the base of his spine. For a period of forty-five minutes, I was to touch his body wherever I felt it would relieve his distress. Simple enough, I supposed, but I was nervous. I felt like a fraud since I had so little direct experience, but I tried not to let that fear consume me. I was quickly swept away by the challenge of the experiment.

Before I began, Stephan strapped a vial of sterile water with a special glove to my right palm. At intervals of five, ten, and fifteen minutes, the vials would be changed and analyzed. I recalled the instructions I had received to still my mind; it was better that I wasn't supposed to think too much about what I was doing.

I had George lie down on his stomach on the examining table and propped a small cushion beneath his head. Then I tentatively placed my palm on his lower back. I didn't notice anything unusual happening, but I kept my hand there. A few minutes passed.

"George, are you okay?" I asked, wanting to hear something from him. He sighed and finally replied, "Your hand feels good. Whatever you're doing, just keep it up."

As I let my hand drift to different parts of George's body, I remembered that when I was a little girl my mother used to sing lullabies and stroke my hair before I went to sleep. The tenderness of her fingertips and the warmth of her presence on the quilt beside me wrapped me in a safe, protected cocoon. I lingered in that image, and the sweetness of the love I had felt back then started flowing through my hands into George. In that moment, a tangible current passed between us, a heat like the rays of the sun on a summer's day. It drew us closer to each other, spirit to spirit. We developed a rapport neither of us expected, but which seemed to stem directly from the healing process itself.

George left the session looking brighter. The stress had lifted from his face, his back pain eased. Though I'd always believed there was something special about touching another person, working on George had deepened my appreciation. It was extraordinary to know that I could convey love through my hands. It seemed so basic, so human, to affect another person positively in this way. I now realized that we can help each other more than we know. Such healing doesn't take years of schooling to master. Rather, it requires our compassion, that we temporarily set our fears aside and extend our love to someone else. How many of us go through our lives consumed by work, insulated in protective bubbles, without being touched even once during the day? We walk around starved, deprived of a sweetness that could so easily replenish us.

I came away that afternoon renewed, as if a fresh rain had just fallen. My desire had been to do something for George, but I hadn't anticipated that he would give me something in return. The healing had been mutual. Rather than feeling depleted, as I often did after a long day with patients, I was exuberant. The love I had given George was regenerative, and flowed directly back to me. There wasn't a finite supply: The more I gave, the more there seemed to be.

Over the next month, Stephan analyzed the results of the experiment and found that when the atomic structure of the water was measured for changes, there was a marked difference between the untreated and treated vials. The most dramatic results occurred in the first five minutes of the session, indicating that healing wasn't constant and its effects didn't increase with time. As expected, skilled practitioners did better than novices. However, those who were untrained still produced substantial effects. This suggested that it was possible to alter the composition of water simply if the therapeutic intent was present. The intuitive healer in me had been validated by working with George, but now the physician in me was heartened as well.

In psychiatry, touching a patient is considered taboo. Yet the healing experiment had aroused my curiosity about how the therapeutic use of touch could be applied to my work. I had been deeply moved when I observed Jack's sessions in the UCLA lab years before. But in my own practice I was afraid that the act of touching might be misconstrued. If it hadn't been for Lilly, a young woman I met through Mobius, I would probably never have experimented. But she specifically requested that hands-on healing be part of her therapy.

The cousin of a researcher on staff, Lilly was beautiful enough to have been a high-fashion model. Unfortunately, she was in constant pain from debilitating rheumatoid arthritis, and be-

cause of extensive joint damage in both legs she had to walk with
a cane.

During our second appointment, Lilly had a full-blown panic
attack in my office. Hyperventilating and riddled with fear, her
face a ghostly white, she was convinced that the disease was ruin-
ing her life. This was not the first time she'd had such an attack.
Doctors had prescribed Valium to quell her anxiety temporarily,
but it always returned. As I watched Lilly unable to sit still, pacing around my office, wringing her hands, I tried to console her.
Despite my reassurances, however, her panic escalated.

The difficulty is that medication and talk therapy may only
take one so far. Deep-seated panic can be an earthquake rocking
the foundation of one's being. It doesn't listen to reason; it feeds
on itself, cycles relentlessly, sometimes for months or years unless the underlying cause is healed. For Lilly, Valium was not a
solution but rather a tiny Band-Aid covering a gaping wound.
She needed something more; I had to act fast. I persuaded her to
take off her sandals and lie down on the couch. I remembered
the relief in George's eyes. Why couldn't transmitting love
through my hands work as well for anxiety?

Lilly's body looked thin and frail; she was quivering like a
frightened bird. Panic can be contagious. I tried not to get swept
away by its intensity. I set one of my hands over her heart, about
two inches above her diaphragm, and the other directly on her
stomach. I felt her pulse racing erratically beneath my fingers.
Centering myself, I became incredibly lucid and directed, my
palms growing warm. I simply sat on the couch, hands steady on
her body, allowing myself to be a vehicle through which love could
flow. To be successful, healing requires a transparency, a passive receptivity, rather than any purposeful effort. Just as in remote viewing, I cleared my mind of all thoughts. Instead of receiving intuitive
information, however, the sweetest feeling of love came through.

At first Lilly didn't respond. But a voice inside me said,
"Don't give up. Keep your hands still and be patient." I paid attention and waited. Slowly, I felt the love pulsing through me
and into Lilly. Not strongly at first, but then building, the lux-

urious, almost blissful feeling mounted. Within minutes, Lilly's body went limp, her breathing became heavier, and her tension began to melt. A half hour later, when I lifted my hands from her body, I saw a wonderful clear light in Lilly's eyes.

She told me that, during the session, she'd drifted into a daydream. In it, she had been walking down a mountain trail on a bright spring morning. A balmy breeze was filtering through the branches of the trees. With each new breath she took, the breeze gently lifted her anxiety. By the time we finished, it had completely gone. I had never witnessed such a rapid turnabout of a panic attack without the use of Valium or similar antianxiety medication. Neither of us had expected the results to be so dramatic, but Lilly most definitely left my office more at peace than when she first walked in. Had Lilly just been extremely suggestible? I wasn't sure, but for the moment she was better, and I was satisfied.

In subsequent meetings we would spend about thirty minutes talking, and for the rest of the hour I would work on her with my hands. Often, while she rested quietly, that same tranquil breeze would return. As Lilly became more accustomed to the feeling, she was able to re-create it on her own whenever she was in anxiety or pain. This served as a built-in biofeedback device she could call on whenever she was in need. By learning how to draw on her memory of our sessions, she eventually was able to translate them into real-life situations. After six months, our therapy came to a close. Lilly had begun to heal herself.

For me, Lilly's success offered several special rewards. To begin with, I received verification of an added dimension that healing could lend to traditional psychiatry, and this contributed to my own sense of competence. At the same time, I was able to offer my patients a new kind of self-empowerment.

Since working with Lilly, I've come to realize how many ways such healing can be applied, not just in the context of psychiatry but in everyday life. The comfort it creates can benefit us all. If we become upset for any reason, simply placing our hands over our heart, with a calming intent, will settle us down. We can transmit love to ourselves, as well as be able to communicate it to another person. Doing so, we generate tranquillity during stressful times. Love is the universal balancer. It has the power to soothe us like nothing else. By consciously calling on it to help us, we gain strength and a belief in our capacity to heal. The truth is, we can all do this, though many of us don't realize it. We too easily reach out for physicians, nurses, therapists; we forget to look within. Being able to heal with our hands is a great gift, a natural asset. Once we gain access to it, a long-buried potential becomes realized.

My aim is to teach patients to care for themselves and others, to find their own resources to heal. Contacting this love, discovering how to be compassionate, is the essence, an attitude about life that can be conveyed through touch. If we can all generate and communicate this love, we can create a more cohesive, more supportive community, even a better world. But, always, we first have to find that love in ourselves.

Shortly after Lilly's last session, my alarm clock awakened me from a familiar dream. It had recurred many times since 1983, when I began my practice, but had never before come to a conclusion. That morning I knew I would never again have that dream.

It always started out the same. I would be standing in my office at twilight, gazing out a window that faced the ocean. A pale sliver of a moon graced the western sky. When the dream first occurred, the water on the horizon next to the Santa Monica skyline appeared as it really was: a few miles away. Over the years, with the repetition of the dream, the waves gradually drew closer and with them came a flock of seagulls. I watched them glide through the air, riding the early evening updrafts, eighteen stories up. But this last time the dream occurred, any separation between myself and the sea was gone. There was water shimmering on all sides, but it didn't pose a threat. I was as comfortable with it as I had finally become with my inner union of medicine and intuition. My office building and the ocean had finally merged.

CHAPTER SIX

Female Lineage

Around the ancient tower, I have been circling for a thousand years.

—RAINER MARIA RILKE

Mothers and daughters. I was now forty years old. Over the last decade, I'd been a practicing psychiatrist, a member of the faculty at UCLA Medical Center, Saint John's Hospital, and Cedars-Sinai Medical Center. That I was devoted to a profession my mother understood and respected meant a great deal to her. It had taken compromise by us both, but we initially had found safe terrain by talking about medicine. My mother referred patients to me, and we discussed their treatment. It was easier to stay away from more personal subjects like our relationship or my boyfriends. In her eyes, no one was ever good enough for me: They were too old, too young, not Jewish, not financially secure enough. . . . Otherwise we'd argue—get defensive, take strong opposing positions, and then a blowup would inevitably follow. So we learned to use our discussions of medical issues as neutral ground where there was mutual trust.

As time passed, when I'd go to my parents' home for weekly Shabbat dinners, my mother and I grew able to talk about everything. We had found a more tender way of relating. Increasingly, she became my close friend, my confidante. Now more sure of myself, I no longer felt overshadowed by my mother's strength. I could be giving, express my feelings, and listen without always being on guard. Realizing how important my parents were to me, I was determined to savor the love we had for each other. As for my mother, she had been afraid of my anger, how fiercely I could lash out and wound her when we disagreed, and she had learned perhaps too well to avoid these clashes. Over the years, sensing that our time together was finite, she risked reaching out to me.

In the winter of 1990, my mother became ill with cancer. Twenty years before, she had been diagnosed with a slow-growing type of lymphoma, but her symptoms—small lumps in her neck—had been treated with minimal doses of radiation. Recently, however, she had been having low-grade fevers, indicating that the disease had progressed.

One February evening while my mother and I were drinking tea on the living room couch, chatting, feeling particularly close, she began to talk to me about her mother, Rose Ostrum. Though my mother had in the past spoken of Grandmom as a free spirit and ardent feminist, Rose lived most of her life in Philadelphia, and my parents and I moved to Los Angeles when I was six, so I never really knew her until her later years.

"I want to tell you something about Grandmom," my mother began. "You know, she was always flamboyant. A whirlwind of energy, wildly opinionated. She walked with her head high. She managed the family pharmacy. And at a time when women didn't go to college, she sent two daughters to medical school."

I suddenly noticed an undertone of urgency in my mother's voice, as she paused before going on, seeming to compose herself for what she was about to say.

"Judith, I don't know how to put this." Several moments passed. "The point is . . . your grandmother had an unusual reputation in the neighborhood, a reputation for . . . for being a healer."

"What?" I blurted out. I couldn't believe my ears. "You must be kidding."

My mother pushed on with what she was determined to say. "Grandmom also had a knack for predicting events that came true. She was raised Jewish and kept a kosher home, but she believed that her abilities to heal and see into the future were separate from religion. These talents were passed down through the generations, from woman to woman. It was during the Depression. Many of her neighbors couldn't afford doctors. They would come to Grandmom when they were sick. She would take them back to a tiny, unheated wooden shed behind our home, would lay them down on a wooden table and place her hands on their body. Warmth would radiate from her hands, going deeper than the skin. When they sat up, my mother would give them herbal tea concocted from medicinal plants she grew herself. These were recipes that had been passed down from her mother."

I felt dizzy, an intense heat rising into my face. My grandmother an intuitive and a healer? "Mother," I exclaimed bitterly, "why didn't you tell me this before?"

My mother's terrible look of anguish stopped me short. "Try to understand. I only wanted the best for you. Your grandmother was eccentric. Though she was beloved by most of our neighbors, some people thought she was weird. I was afraid for you."

"But couldn't you see it would have helped me to feel that I wasn't alone?"

She noticed the struggle in my eyes, reached over to touch my hand. "Oh, Judith. When you were a young girl and I found out that you were intuitive, I didn't want to encourage it. I didn't want you to be ridiculed like my mother sometimes was."

I was overwhelmed by conflicting emotions. I was flabbergasted and hurt. I felt cheated out of the closeness we could have had. How much difference this would have made to me as a child. To learn it now seemed far too late.

"Maybe I made a mistake," my mother went on. "I was only concerned about your happiness. I was torn, so I downplayed your abilities to protect you."

"So what made you bring this up tonight? What changed?"

"Judith, dear, please hear me out. Our lives are so different now. You stuck to your beliefs, carved out your own path, even though it's not the one I would have picked for you. But I respect your choice. We're not at war anymore. And I have so little left to risk."

I was reeling. An old emptiness was being unearthed, a terribly familiar unnerving sensation that I had lived and breathed so often as a child. As these dark thoughts coursed through my mind, I fought back my tears. My greatest fear was that my rage would cause my mother to stop talking. I realized what an extraordinary moment this was, that my mother finally felt compelled to place my intuitive abilities in context, to show me my true lineage—also that she wanted to clarify her own position, to set the record straight. Finally, of course, she had done everything but make explicit that she was really ill, with all that might imply.

My mother and I quietly watched the brilliant flames of the fire cast long shadows on the corner walls. I tried to collect myself. Looking over at my mother, now so tiny and frail, I felt my anger undercut, replaced by compassion. I would gain nothing from lashing out or blaming her. As she lay her head back and rested in front of the fire, I made a decision: I refused to allow my anger to poison whatever time we had left to be together.

By now, in my spiritual search, I had learned that everything in life has a time and a purpose. It was no mistake that I hadn't known about my grandmother before. I had had to struggle, to grow, to gain strength, in order to become the woman I was now. I began to comprehend that my battle to make intuition my own had been crucial to my growth. It had been arduous, a fight I could have lost. To win, I had been pushed to my limits and then beyond. It was also true that my mother had been one of my greatest teachers. Her uncompromising dedication to her convictions had over and over again forced me to take a stand. Nonetheless, I had waited a lifetime to hear these words.

My mother leaned toward me, love radiating from her face. I had paid a price for her decisions, but I knew in this moment that none of them had been based on malice. She had done her best. As difficult as it was to accept this, as angry as I wanted to be, I couldn't deny that I also was experiencing a profound sense of relief. She was finally telling me the truth. I appreciated, too, that she'd taken an enormous chance that I wouldn't understand. She was, I saw, counting on the resilience of our love, on the intimacy we had worked so hard to establish.

As my mother and I sat there, silent, I remembered a recurring dream I'd had about my grandmother. Naked, her body soft and fleshy like a Renaissance nude, she would lead me through a labyrinth of dark underground tunnels. We proceeded down blind passageways without so much as a candle to light our path. I held on to her hand, trusting that she knew her way. There was a quality of yearning and timelessness in our closeness. I could now see that we were linked by an invisible cord. As long as I'd been having that dream, she had served as my guide.

"You know," my mother said, bringing me back to the present, "when I was a child my mother would lay me down on a couch, and with a sweeping motion run her hand over me three times from head to foot. Then she would shake my feet up and down, making me giggle and squirm. And while she did this she'd repeat in Yiddish, *'Grace, Grubb, Gizunt.'* Through her hands she was imparting, as the words said, greatness, hardiness, and good health. She wanted to help me grow. She would only do this for children, to give them long life and make them beautiful. It was an extension of the healing work she used in the shed room with her patients."

I was amazed. Suddenly I remembered my mother doing just this to me when I was a child. How I loved her to hold me then, the subtle scent of her perfume, the warmth of her touch, the tranquillity afterward. It was hard for me to take in, but my mother had known she was transmitting energy, although she refused to speak of it that way.

I realized that many parents are able to send love through their hands, but see it matter-of-factly, as a natural expression of their affection. They don't think of this as healing, but it is. When a mother holds her newborn in her arms, her joy and acceptance are directly communicated through touch. If our child is hurt, we rush to embrace her, to stay close and soothe her pain. Our impulse to comfort, our need for physical contact, is predicated on an instinctual desire to give and receive love. This is the essence of being human: to share our hearts, to exchange warmth and be nurtured by one another.

When I was a child, sometimes just before I went to sleep, and always when I was ill, my mother would sit beside my bed and gently pat my stomach, creating a subtle rocking motion, until I either fell asleep or felt better. I found this sensation of love flowing into my body very soothing.

"Yes," my mother said. "I learned this from your grandmother. I knew it was a form of healing, but I didn't want to fill your head with strange ideas."

I breathed deeply and thought of Grandmom's death. At eighty, she had gotten Alzheimer's disease, losing her memory and regressing to a childlike state. Having moved to Los Angeles, she spent her last few years in a retirement home in the Pico-Fairfax district, a few miles from us. The night she died, I was the one they called, because my parents were traveling in Europe and couldn't be contacted. I was told that Rose had been sitting in her favorite rocking chair, eating a vanilla ice-cream cone. When she finished, she mentioned to her companion how delicious it was, and then quietly slumped over. No fanfare, no fuss. A perfect departure. Beyond this image of my grandmother, however, I barely knew her. I had missed so much.

Throughout that winter, my mother gradually opened up more about my intuitive heritage. She told me that my cousin Sindy went into labor at midnight, with her second daughter. Melissa, her four-year-old, was sound asleep and unaware that her parents had rushed out to the hospital, leaving her in the care of Sindy's mother, Phyllis. At two A.M. Melissa woke up, crying hysterically, "Something happened to Mommy!" No amount of reassurance would quiet her. The truth was that at exactly that moment Sindy's labor became complicated. The anesthetic had been too strong, she wasn't taking in enough oxygen, and a tube had to be inserted down her trachea in order for her to breathe. Although Sindy suffered no ill effects and the baby was healthy, Melissa had picked up the danger they were in. Because Sindy was herself somewhat intuitive, she wasn't alarmed by Melissa's premonition. She recognized that Melissa might be intuitive, too.

These conversations about the family became an after-dinner ritual. On Friday nights, after office hours, I would drive over to my parents' condo. When dinner was finished, my father, delighted that my mother and I were getting along and relieved that our fighting was over, would conveniently disappear into the den to watch a Lakers game. With cups of mint tea in our hands, my mother and I would move into the living room.

Though my mother had always spoken her mind, it had been a huge step for her to divulge that Rose was a healer. I soon found out that as bold as these admissions had been, she had been holding back something even more intimate. It was about her own life: her most well-guarded secret.

"When I first opened my medical practice," she said during one of our Friday nights, "I realized that I had some intuitive and healing abilities, too. They weren't as strong as in you or your grandmother, but they were definitely there."

My mother an intuitive healer? I stared at this thin, determined woman beside me and wondered who she was. She had kept this part of herself hidden just as I had tried to do when I began my practice.

"I knew that modern medicine didn't have all the answers," she went on. "From the beginning, twenty years ago, my oncologist recommended that I take intravenous doses of chemotherapy to treat the lymphoma. But I decided to keep the disease in check with my mind. I never told anyone, but every morning when I woke up, I would hypnotize myself into being well. I would place my hands over my body and send positive thoughts through them while I visualized the tumors shrinking. I believe that I kept myself healthy: According to statistics, I shouldn't be alive today."

"Why didn't you confide in me?" I asked. "I would have understood."

My mother shot me a look of disbelief. "If you recall, when I was first diagnosed back in nineteen seventy, you and I were arguing so much that it didn't feel safe to talk to you. You were withdrawn and unreachable. I didn't consider you a support. My healing was private. Talking about it with anyone would have taken away the power."

Pictures of our many fights came hurtling into my mind: doors slamming, bitter words exchanged, running out of the house, threats never to return. We were both stubborn. It had been a battle of wills. I could see why she had been reluctant to trust me.

"I learned privacy the hard way," she continued. "While I was growing up, your grandmother talked a lot about her gifts. And her premonitions were really far-fetched. Rose predicted the jet age, rapid transit, the use of laser beams in medicine. But in the twenties, nobody believed her. I loved her very much, but I was a kid. She embarrassed me. I wanted to be normal. Rose couldn't understand that."

Mothers and daughters. I could see that we had both engaged in our own forms of rebellion. She had reacted to her mother by becoming conservative, denying her gift; I had fought to express my intuitive abilities and let them shine.

The more my mother spoke, the bluer her eyes seemed to become. "When I was ten," she went on, "I had a premonition that I was going to be a doctor. Nothing would stop me. But there I was, in a society that looked down on anyone who was different. My mother didn't care what people thought about her, but I did.

I didn't want to repeat her mistakes, so I decided to keep my abilities to myself."

I knew her position was well founded. In 1942, when she was accepted into Hahnemann Medical College in Philadelphia, the field of medicine was male dominated. Only a small quota of women was admitted, as compared to the fifty percent today. And of course during my own residency, over three decades later, I still didn't feel I could discuss intuition with my peers for fear of being judged and ostracized. (When my mother was at Hahnemann, the unusual curriculum covered both traditional and homeopathic medicine. Though she was able to study legitimately what her mother had done in her practice with herbs, homeopathy was already well out of mainstream contemporary medicine.)

For the past thirty years, after our move to Los Angeles, my mother had been a traditional Beverly Hills family practitioner with an office on Bedford Drive. Her patients became an extended family, and she was the mother hen. Being a doctor was everything to her; she would do nothing to jeopardize that. But unbeknownst to her patients, she would consciously direct loving energy through her hands. This had become so routine that she barely gave it a second thought. I felt it was a shame that she couldn't have been more open about her gifts, but I respected her decision to heal in the context of mainstream medicine. Just as the persona of "psychiatrist" was one I had to make fit, my mother could never come to terms with that of "healer." Still, I was sad that she had felt she needed to wall off so much of herself, to deprive herself of such precious talents.

"I sometimes knew things about my patients before they even told me," she continued. "There's a little voice in my head that I listen to. It's never wrong. My patient Rita is a good example. She once came to see me with a terrible cold. When I was taking her temperature, the voice told me to examine her breasts. I didn't usually do that for a cold, but I followed my instincts. Her right breast was fine, but in the left one I found a small, hard, pea-sized nodule. I knew it hadn't been there before, so I sent her for a mammogram and a biopsy."

"What happened?" I was spellbound.

"The lump was malignant. In a week, she had it surgically removed and started radiation and chemotherapy. That was two years ago. Rita's been cancer-free ever since. If I hadn't picked up the lump so early, there's a good chance that the cancer might have spread. I believe that by listening to the voice in my head, I saved Rita's life."

I was now completely reappraising my mother. The effort I had made to incorporate intuition into my medical practice was a task she had already accomplished! Without knowing it, I was following in her footsteps, carrying on a family tradition. I had always searched for a feeling of rightness about my life, and now I was getting validation for the direction I'd instinctively chosen to pursue.

I later found out that my mother's younger sister, Phyllis, a doctor in Philadelphia specializing in internal medicine, was also an intuitive. Despite their mutual affection, there had always been a certain amount of competition between them. Yet intuition was a common bond: When they couldn't talk to anyone else, they became confidantes in late-night long-distance phone conversations, discussing their intuitive experiences with each other.

"In nineteen sixty-three," my mother told me, "Phyllis's husband had his first heart attack. While he was still in the hospital, she had a dream that she was making medical rounds with a group of physicians. After they all reviewed the current treatments for heart conditions, she came away knowing that subcutaneous heparin was the right medication for her husband."

"What made that dream intuitive?" I asked. "Heparin is routinely given to cardiac patients to prevent blood clots."

"But in the early sixties," my mother replied, "heparin wasn't used for that. There was no clinical documentation to indicate that heparin would help in postcoronary care. It didn't become

standard practice until much later. When Phyllis told the cardiologist to give her husband heparin, he refused. So she decided
that she'd administer it on her own. Phyllis didn't have many
dreams, but when she did, they almost always were right."

"Did she ever tell anyone about her dream?"

My mother shook her head. "She once mentioned it to another
doctor, but he gave her such a strange look that she never
brought it up again. He wanted scientific proof, but of course
she didn't have any."

Phyllis's husband, a gynecologist, had no interest in intuition
when they married. At first, when her predictions came true, she
felt that he was threatened. He had been raised believing in traditional male roles, and she was convinced it challenged his need
for control. But over the course of fifteen years, she watched him
become more comfortable with her predictions. When enough
of them had proven accurate, he no longer viewed them as untenable. He had come to appreciate their value in time for her to
save his life.

Since 1942, there had been twenty-five physicians in our family: five women and twenty men. The healing instinct had been
there for all of us. But as far as my mother knew, none of the
males had ever been intuitive. She couldn't explain why. Maybe
there was something inherent in being female that made it easier
to tap into this information, or perhaps it was genetic. Maybe
some of the men were intuitive also, but had even less cultural permission to express it than the women had. Neither of us was sure.

What was sure for me was that with each conversation I had
with my mother, the inner fabric of my being was being woven
more tightly. After years of floating above myself, disconnected
from my body, I felt as if a gigantic magnet were pulling me
back down to earth. The ground seemed more solid beneath my
feet. I now began to pamper myself in ways that I'd previously
dreaded or considered an inconvenience. I went shopping for
new clothes, permed my hair so that it was wild and curly, had
regular facials, and, when I was especially brave, darkened my
eyelashes with black mascara.

In my freshman year of high school, I'd had my first heart-break, which undermined my confidence. I was fourteen. Without any warning, my boyfriend left me for a gorgeous blond-haired, blue-eyed cheerleader who drove a red Camaro. I blamed myself; I decided that I hadn't been pretty or popular enough to keep him. It took me months to get over the breakup, and my insecurities stayed with me for years, churning below the surface. After I learned about my family history, these beliefs changed. Looking in the mirror at my Modigliani face, olive skin, and hazel eyes that peered into people for a little bit too long, I now liked what I saw. Discovering intuition's link among the women in my family had strengthened me; I was allowing the richness of my womanhood to emerge.

In the spring of 1990, I had a dream.

> I'm standing in a bombed-out deserted chapel in a desert wilderness. Above me there is a four-story cathedral ceiling with huge triangular-shaped windows on each wall with sunlight flooding through them. The remnants of a small altar stand toward the front of the room. The atmosphere is peaceful and comforting. Although I can see no one, I am aware of the presence of a group of ancient invisible beings, but I don't know who they are.
>
> All at once, I am overcome with shame about my anger and rebellion at being on earth. There has always been a part of me that never felt I belonged here, and so I didn't feel obliged to cooperate fully. I never gave my all; I hid in my mother's shadow, not speaking up about what I knew. She was the star and I remained anonymous. I am ashamed of my lack of courage.
>
> Gently and with care, the group of invisible beings lift me high into the air, showering me with a feeling of pure forgiveness. I see my life with sudden clarity, and I understand that none of my concerns about the past matter. Everything is exactly how it was meant to be. I have been

forgiven. Now is the time to share what I know with others.

This dream led me back to my past. While I was growing up, I kept notebooks filled with poems I'd written. They were intimate accounts of my first love affair, feelings about my mother, about my LSD trips I took in high school, all laced with a thread of the separateness that pervaded my life at the time. When I was fourteen, my mother told me she wanted to publish these poems. She was obviously extremely proud of my writings and wanted to share them. Hungry for her approval, I reluctantly gave my consent, a decision I hadn't fully thought out. She published the poems in a small hardcover book, and before I knew it she had given copies to all of our family, friends, and her patients. One of her friends, a music teacher at Julliard, even set a few of my poems to music and sent us the tape. I was mortified; my inner life was on public display. Embarrassed and exposed, I wanted to curl up into a tiny ball and become invisible. I didn't write another word for years.

The forgiveness dream brought with it great freedom. It was as if a restrictive mantle had finally been removed, one I hadn't even known was covering me. That very morning, I grabbed a yellow legal pad from my desk and began writing. Ideas flowed out of me like a torrent of water breaking through a dam. The voice that had been stifled for decades was released. The dream had given me permission to take chances, think in new directions, let my daydreams take form.

While my strength was mounting, my mother was gradually beginning to fade. She lived through the next two years propelled solely by her ferocious passion for life. Her body was gradually weakening, but she put on a convincing front. No one besides my father and a few close friends knew the seriousness of her illness. Her medical practice continued to flourish, and she didn't miss a single day of work. Each morning, outfitted in designer dresses, her hair perfectly groomed, her makeup flawless, she'd see patients nonstop for eight hours. No one suspected that there was anything wrong.

Although I was aware that the cancer had grown and I could see that she was wilted with fatigue each evening, I refused to acknowledge how sick my mother really was. I didn't want to know. I had expected her to live forever. My mother had always been vivacious and outgoing. She loved nothing better than attending extravagant black-tie parties and lavish high-profile political events. Wherever she went, she had always been the center of attention, commanding the respect due to a matriarch. Now that the years of struggle were behind us, I clung fiercely to my mother; I had no intention of letting her go. The possibility of her death was unthinkable. I simply blocked it out.

Early in October of 1992, my mother visited me at my condo in Marina del Rey. We laid a madras blanket on the beach and sat down to talk. She had noticed that I was short tempered and burned out, that I hadn't had a vacation for eight months. I had never been very good at carving out time for myself, so together we went over my appointment book and blocked out a week at the end of the month. I agreed to take that time to rest and regenerate.

The night before my vacation, I had a dream:

> *I'm a child practicing T'ai Chi movements on the grass in a freshly mowed public park. A compassionate older Asian man is guiding me. I recognize him; he has been my teacher in earlier dreams. He shows me that by moving my body in a certain way, I can learn how to cross the bridge between life and death at will. I try the exercise, and I am ecstatic at the ease with which I can traverse both realms. My teacher says that to ready myself for what is to come, I must remember that I possess this ability, and I must have faith that death is not the end.*

I stayed curled up under the covers half asleep, luxuriating in the triumph of my accomplishment in traveling between two worlds. But my hands and feet turned cold as I came more fully awake and the meaning of the dream began to sink in. It was a clear sign predicting my mother's death, and I didn't want to see it. Grief welled up in my chest, a virtual tsunami that threatened to swallow me up. But I had to protect myself. This was my first day off in many months. I was too tired and depleted to dwell on the implications right then. With as much emotional control as I could muster, I suppressed my feelings before they had a chance to gather momentum. I would reexamine the dream after I rebuilt my strength.

For the entire week I rested. I soaked up the sun, read Anne Rice's *Interview with the Vampire,* an escape into the world of the preternatural, and meditated for an hour a day, slowing myself down to a saner pace. When my vacation was over, I was reenergized and my mind was fresh. I was eager to resume work. On the evening of my first day back, however, my worst fears were realized: I received an urgent phone call from my father. His voice was faint; he could have been a million miles away.

"Judith, your mother collapsed on the floor with a fever of a hundred and four. She's in the intensive-care unit at Cedars-Sinai."

I strained to hear him, to take in the news. The words sounded long, drawn out, and deep, as if he were speaking in slow motion. Then I went numb. All was deadly silent. In one swift movement, the earth had been ripped out from beneath my feet. Unsupported, I was falling through space. Alone. Spinning out of control.

I don't know how I managed to drive myself to Cedars. I can't recall much of the trip. I do remember being dazed, wandering down the long hospital corridors past a blur of modern artwork on the wall. I took the elevator up to the third-floor intensive-care unit, where I joined my father. Although I had treated many terminally ill patients in the very same ICU, some comatose, some on the edge of death, I was unprepared for what

I saw. There was my own mother, hooked up to a life-support system. Not a stranger or a patient. The woman who'd given birth to me lay in bed, tubes in every orifice, an arterial catheter in her neck, restraints tied to her wrists and ankles to prevent her from pulling out the IV. She was ranting, delirious from the fever, didn't even recognize me. I was seized by the horror of the scene, my helplessness, and the love I felt for both her and my father.

It was long after midnight when I got home. I went straight to bed but couldn't sleep. Getting up, I turned on the lights and rummaged through my closet shelves until I found the old stuffed white rabbit I'd slept with as a child. Then, again wrapped up in the covers, sheets quickly soaked with sweat, I rocked back and forth clutching the rabbit in my arms. The pain was too great; I didn't know how I'd ever get through it. I was terrified of the loss of my mother, of the hollow pit of aloneness that had lodged itself in my gut. My mind was racing; it was impossible to calm down. I got up and knelt at my meditation altar in my study, praying harder than I had ever prayed before. I made my bed beside the altar that night, and slept under a thick, pale blue down comforter. It felt safer there than in my bedroom. Finally, at three o'clock, I drifted into a dream:

> *I am in God's reception room waiting to be seen. God is late and I am impatient. His secretary, a radiant brunette woman, about thirty with a pageboy haircut, tells me that God has been delayed but has sent a message for me. He apologizes for his lateness, but he's very busy today. He hopes I won't get angry with him and leave in a huff. When he comes back, he promises that he'll meet with me for as long as I like.*

When morning came, I arose still shaken, but I had regained my bearings. I had reached out for help and received it. The innocent sweetness of the dream, the acknowledgment that God was with me even though it didn't always feel that way, was tremendously reassuring. My mother's circumstances were no less distressing, but my panic and despair had lifted.

Within twenty-four hours, my mother's fever broke. I visited her in the hospital late that afternoon. She was limp with exhaustion and could barely talk. In one brief, lucid moment, she said, "Judith, I've passed the power on to you. It's yours, and you're ready to take it."

"Stop being so melodramatic," I said. But I understood. I saw an image of my mother handing me a priceless golden serving platter piled with luscious fruit that would remain perpetually ripe. The generational gift in our family—our intuitive heritage—had been transmitted.

For me, the most difficult part of this time was watching the intensity of my mother's anger about being sick and out of control. She didn't want to die. She held on to life with the tenacity of a prizefighter, bloody and knocked down, but continuing to drag herself back into the ring. Sometimes, when I arrived at the hospital after a long day's work, my mother looked like a wild-eyed demon spitting fire at me and my father, relentlessly criticizing us for almost everything we did. I fought to remain patient; the few times I lost my temper only made things worse between us. Then one night, I had another dream:

I am in a prison cell, all alone, raging at the universe. I raise my arms into the air and scream out in frustration, "Why is all this happening to me?" Not expecting a response, I crumble to my knees. Then, although I can't see whom it belongs to, a genderless voice tenderly speaks out to me: "As you watch your mother deal with her illness, you are learning compassion. This isn't easy."

It was difficult to be compassionate when I took my mother's anger so personally, but the dream allowed me to see her behavior from an entirely different point of view. My mother was tormented by her fear of death. In the middle of the night she would wake up from nightmares, panicked that she was going to die. Once, in a dream, her parents came to visit her and asked her to join them. She pushed them away, furious at the offer. Suddenly I understood that her anger wasn't directed at me. Rather, she needed to remain as disgruntled as possible because lashing out was her only remaining lifeline. I knew that this wasn't a conscious decision on her part, but rather an instinctual reaction to her feelings of spiritual emptiness. Judaism had always been important to her. She had attended services on Friday nights and on all the Jewish holidays for most of her life; and doing that had given her solace. Since getting sick, however, she felt that God had abandoned her, devastated that God would have allowed her to become so ill. As she lost faith in the religion that had previously sustained her, anger was all she had. In order to survive, she was holding on to her rage; it was like the last ember in a dying hearth.

At the same time, however, pieces of her armor were cracking. Many nights she would melt into my arms and ask me to lay my hands on her to help her sleep. It had become a natural part of how we related, and she willingly participated. I was honored that she allowed me to help her. She didn't have to hide anymore, to keep up pretenses. She responded to my touch and had grown to trust me. Once, at her request, I sang her the same lullaby she sang to me when I was a little girl, and I watched her face grow younger. Not caring if other people knew what we were doing, she would relax like a child while I transmitted all the love I could summon through my hands, as she peacefully dozed off in my lap.

She told everyone proudly, "My daughter's a magician. I don't need sleeping pills when she comes to visit. Judith puts me into a trance with her hands."

Despite my mother's praise, I knew this was something we all can do. I had learned never to underestimate the power of love. When our family or friends are despairing or in pain, we don't have to sit by helplessly. Our love can be sustaining. True healing is put to the test in real life. This is when we can act, can apply everything we've been taught. For me, years of spiritual study were brought to bear as my mother lay dying. It was as though I'd been preparing for this moment all along.

When I sat with my mother, I often felt my grandmother's presence in the room. Three generations of women were gathered at my mother's deathbed.

Before this period, much of my energy had been tied up in grappling to find peace with my mother, in striving to make our relationship succeed. For the first time, I felt we had reached a resolution. All the barriers were gone. Even though, when I turned forty, I believed that I had come to terms with not having children, I now ached to have a child of my own. I wanted to pass on the gifts to keep the hereditary link unbroken.

My mother slipped into a coma late Christmas Day in 1992. As I was leaving her hospital room earlier that morning, she turned to me and whispered, "I love you, Judith." These were the last words she ever spoke. During the next week, when I went to the hospital each evening to watch over her, I knew we were irrevocably connected, clearly members of the same tribe. I became fascinated with the beauty of her body, her soft, pink belly rising and falling with each labored breath. As I looked at the horizontal cesarean-section scar above her womb, I imagined myself as a newborn infant being lifted out of her and into the world. Now the boundaries between us had become blurred. No tightening. No resistance. No more strife. We were so interconnected that it was hard for me to tell where she ended and I began.

My mother lay in a coma for ten days, but although she was wasting away, her vital signs remained stable. I had underestimated her tenacious hold on life; she would not let go of her

body. In the first week of the new year, my mother came to me
in a dream:

> We are standing on the roof garden of a two-story apart-
> ment building on Olympic Boulevard in Beverly Hills.
> My mother looks twenty years younger and is robust with
> energy. With a whimsical look, I ask her if she wants to
> fly. Without hesitation, she takes my hand and we lift off
> into the air miles above the city skyline, ascending toward
> the sun. She's amazed at how effortless our flight is. Cool
> wind rushes past our faces. We are both exhilarated.

I sat up in bed elated, but within minutes my mood darkened. The image of flying was an apt metaphor for her imminent
death. The message flashed before me like a huge multicolored
neon sign: My mother would be gone very soon. Any illusions
that I still had about her possible recovery vanished with that
dream. I had to accept the inevitability that even her unswerving determination and her bullheaded obstinacy didn't have the
power to ward off her death. Although the impending loss was
unbearable, I also knew there would be relief in the end of her
suffering, a freedom in the fight being over. It was time. I could
help.

Once at the hospital, with tears streaming down my cheeks, I
spoke to my mother, certain that she could hear me. "Mother,
you can't keep holding on. You must let go of your body. There's
nothing to be afraid of. Life doesn't end when you die. You just
go somewhere else. There'll be plenty for you to do there. You
don't have to worry about being separated from me. We'll contact each other. Our communication won't ever stop."

I knew she was in a coma too deep to allow for any physical
movement, and yet, impossible as it should have been, I felt her
gently squeeze my fingertips, letting me know that she had
heard me. I held her hand and went into meditation while she
lay in a fetal position on her side, breathing heavily. The entire

room pulsated with concentric waves of golden light, and I was filled with the profound and uncompromising love between a mother and daughter.

I was tempted to stay with her, but I didn't. I remembered when my beloved fourteen-year-old Labrador retriever was dying. Frantic, I called my mother from the animal hospital, and she rushed across town to meet me. When she arrived and saw me sitting in the kennel, holding my dog close, she advised me to say good-bye and leave. My mother believed that as long as I was in my dog's presence, she would struggle to hold on. I listened to her advice, and, difficult as it was, we both went home. My dog died soon afterward. Now I had to follow the same wise counsel that my mother had given me.

Taking one last look, making a small reverential bow in my mother's direction, I said a final good-bye and left the room. I walked to the parking structure in a trance, while an unexpected sense of calm washed over me. There were no loose ends between my mother and me, no insurmountable barriers to scale, no pressing issues to discuss. Driving from West Hollywood toward downtown, where I was scheduled to see patients in a residential drug-treatment center, I felt the fresh air rushing past my face. It had just rained, and I breathed in as if for the first time. A half hour later, I received a phone call from my father saying that my mother had died. I was filled with the grace of the moment, touched by how much faith she had in me. Despite her fear of death and her loss of belief in her religion, she had trusted me enough to give up control and pass on. She had leaped into the great abyss, motivated by the strength of our love.

For the three days following her death, I had no contact with my mother. I'd expected to sense her presence around me, but I didn't feel a thing. My father and I arranged the funeral, and the family flew in from Philadelphia. On the day of the burial, I hid an owl feather in the elastic waistband of my skirt and tossed it into the ground with the casket. I wanted to put something in the grave that I considered meaningful: This feather, in Native

American lore, is symbolic of the transformation from life to death. The owl, which is believed to be able to cross back and forth between the seen and the unseen, would help her with her passage.

That night, I had a dream in which she brought me a present:

> *We are standing on my balcony overlooking the ocean and my mother hands me a large, porous loofa sponge. "I want you to make sure you use this," she says. "It's the highest-quality loofa sponge available anywhere in the world." I am puzzled by this gesture, but I accept the sponge. My mother beams at me and disappears.*

Initially, I wasn't sure what to make of her present. Loofa sponges are used for rubbing off dead skin cells from the body. What was she trying to tell me? Then the answer came. In her own inimitable style, she was stressing how important it was for me to slough off and release the old in order to allow room for something new to replace it. She was making a plea that I not focus on her past pain and suffering, that I stop dwelling on the horror I'd felt watching her die. It was time for me to move on. She was encouraging me to embrace every moment of my life with the same enthusiasm with which she had lived her own.

I can't imagine how I could have survived the three-month period of my mother's dying without my intuitive dreams to guide me. I would have been lost without them. In my darkest days, when it seemed impossible to muster the energy to keep moving forward, these dreams lit up my path. I felt protected by them, heartened by their intelligence and compassion.

Such dreams respond to our deepest needs during times of crisis. An alarm is set off, calling on a wisdom within to direct us. The art is to listen, not to discount the information received, to follow its instructions. Through faith, intuition can intervene. Our inner resources are more bountiful than we envision. Even if we're alone, without the support of friends or family, the integrity of our spirit, the prescience we all possess, will come to our aid. Once we believe this, and recognize our strength, we gain courage to face whatever lies ahead.

To this day, I often feel my mother with me. One night, for instance, she came to my bedside, and while I lay suspended between sleep and wakefulness, I felt her stroke my hair with her hand. Her essence was like a subtle veil, one I could sense but could not reach out and touch. When I opened my eyes, she was gone.

On the Mother's Day following her death, I ran across an old photograph of my mother, taken while she was riding a camel in the Egyptian desert. I stared at her face, missing her very much, when suddenly I saw her wink at me. Startled, I ran into the next room to tell a friend. She laughed and said that earlier that morning she'd been looking at the same photograph and my mother had winked at her, too. This was just like my mother— to catch us by surprise and reassure us both that she was still there.

The great gift that came from my mother's death was that my father and I grew closer. While she was alive, my mother always took center stage and overshadowed our relationship. The love he and I had for each other ran deep, but never had a real chance to flower. It was waiting for the right time to emerge. After my mother died, my father and I began to really communicate for the first time. We talked on the phone daily, had dinner at least once a week, and shared the stuff of our lives. One aspect of this change was that he fully appreciated the woman I'd become, and relied on that. There was both trust and frankness.

Once my father told me that when my mother was pregnant, he saw an ultrasound of her belly in which he noticed that my head was almost exactly the same shape as his. When I was a child and insecure with my own identity, the fact that we looked so much alike had embarrassed me. My slender face, prominent forehead, olive complexion, and even some of my simple gestures—folding my hands in my lap when concentrating—were an exact image of his own. As my father spoke with such pride about our resemblance, I felt proud, too.

During a meditation, I had a vision in which we were walking down a dirt road in the canyons above Malibu and my father suddenly died. Instantly, his body disintegrated into dust but his heart was transformed into an exquisite statue of jade, so green that it could have come from the bottom of the sea. I took it with me on the journey home and treasured it. The new relationship I had begun with my father was that same precious jewel.

On Christmas Day of 1993, my mother had been dead for nearly a year. As on every Christmas before, I performed my ritual of feeding the seagulls loaves of bread by the ocean in front of my home. On this day, at least thirty of them swarmed around my head, squawking at one another and aggressively snatching chunks of bread from my hand. When the last of the bread was gone, I sat cross-legged in the sand while the birds landed on the ground and stood around me in a concentric circular formation. These throngs of white-breasted seagulls looking attentively into my eyes reminded me of angels, pure, white, and majestic. Then, fluttering their wings in unison, they rose high up into the azure sky until they became tiny black specks on the horizon.

I pictured the faces of the women in my family, some dead, some still here. Just like the gulls, we were all connected by a continuum. I felt particularly close to Melissa, my cousin Sindy's daughter. At age four, she had already demonstrated evidence of prescience. Melissa was more fortunate than I had been. If she needs us, Sindy, her grandmother Phyllis, and I will be there as role models to support and direct her without fear or reservation. When the time comes, perhaps she will do the same for her own daughter. Woman to woman, our intuitive tradition will be passed down. I walked back toward the warmth of my house, content in the knowledge that long after I have gone, the legacy will continue.

PART 2

Teachings

CHAPTER SEVEN

Preparing to See

In the beginner's mind there are many possibilities; in the expert's mind there are few.
—SHUNRYU SUZUKI, ROSHI

When I was nine, I dreamed that my grandfather, who had recently died, took me to see Jesus. There he was, larger than life, sitting on an enormous white stage in a glistening ballroom, the kind I'd seen on TV when the big bands of the 1940s performed. In my dream, I was so excited I could barely contain myself. My heart beating wildly, I rushed down the aisle and plunged into the warmth of his arms. As my grandfather looked on, Jesus embraced me. I snuggled into his lap, protected and safe, lulled by a chorus of distant angels. At this moment, I felt only love. Wanting for nothing, I remained in this state a long time.

Still enveloped by the sweetness, I awoke. It was nighttime. I couldn't have been up for more than a few minutes when the door of my bedroom swung open and my mother burst in. Sensing that something bad had happened, that I was sick or hurt, she'd come running.

"Are you all right?" she asked.

Sitting up in bed, I could still hear the angels singing. "I just saw Jesus," I told her. "I was with Grandpop, in my dream."

"Jesus?" she exclaimed. My mother shook her head and gave me a look I'd seen before, one of bemused tolerance, as if she didn't want to hurt my feelings by disagreeing. "I knew something was going on. I'm just glad to see you're fine." Smiling as she tucked me in, she gently whispered, "Your grandfather loves you very much. Now go to sleep."

My mother didn't make any more of my dream that night, but the next day she seemed to cringe when I started talking about how wonderful Jesus was. Exasperated, she sat me down and asked, "Where did you get this from? I've raised you to be a nice Jewish girl. All your friends are Jewish. We never taught you anything about Jesus." I'd just encountered this incredible being, but now I felt I had done something wrong and was treading in dangerous territory. I didn't understand. Why did my response to Jesus make me any less Jewish? I just saw him as a loving friend and guide.

Not surprisingly, I didn't mention this again to my mother or anyone else. But neither did I speak about the many other dreams throughout my childhood that communicated the same message of love, though with different characters and settings. I sensed that this entire domain was in some way off limits. As for Jesus, he appeared to me from time to time as only one part of this nocturnal continuum. I now consider him my first spiritual teacher and my first exposure to the love I later sought in working with Brugh Joy and others, and then discovered in my own meditations.

My early intuitive dreams, I have since realized, were preparing me to see. They were my initial encounter with the fact that the form our faith takes is less important than the love it imparts. Of course I couldn't articulate this as a child, but I did know that the goodness and rightness I felt were indisputable, even if I had to keep these dreams to myself. Years later, after a decade of meditating, searching, and studying with teachers from a variety of backgrounds, I was able to put into words this childhood knowing: The bedrock of spirituality is to learn about love.

When we approach intuition in this spirit, not as a means to accumulate power but as a vehicle for right action, clarity, and service, our intentions remain pristine. It is possible to be intuitive without any spiritual orientation: You could view this ability as the expression of a trainable, human skill. But to do so, you would be assigning it a very limited role. On the most basic level, intuition is a means of gathering specific information. It also possesses, however, a spiritual impulse that makes it a potent vehicle for healing, a poignant force readily contacted by our belief in the mystical, even if simply defined as love.

While growing up, I knew none of this. Frightened by my intuitive experiences, I had no context in which to place them, was afraid of my abilities for many years. Later, as I became an adult, my teachers imparted a message true for any and all wishing to open themselves up to seeing: To proceed, we must feel safe, we must know there is a net beneath us.

Clarifying and strengthening spiritual beliefs, I've found, is a way of providing that net. It may not be your way—and that's fine. But to prepare yourself to see, you'll need a path that is compassionate, and not based on power. My approach is through the spiritual, and I urge you to give this a try. It helps not to think of "spirituality" as some rigid concept with procedures and rules. The form of spirituality is a matter of choice—it can be religious in a traditional sense, or not. After all, through the ages spirit has had numerous faces and names: God, Goddess, Jesus, Buddha, Adonai, Tao, Father Sky, Mother Earth, or love. For some of us, however, it might be nameless, the quiet place inside. Whatever the form, through our connection with this sublime, compassionate presence our awareness begins to expand. We become more open, intuitively receptive. Our capacity to see is often born of an inner pilgrimage. The quest for spirit, our focused listening within, fine-tunes our sensitivities, bringing us greater insight.

By nature we are all seers, though our ability may remain latent. Also, the impetus to explore intuition can vary. For some it may be a choice, a gradual unfolding. For others, like myself, it may be thrust upon you, compelling you to begin. Suddenly you have a dream, a premonition, an overpowering hunch. Maybe you have never thought of yourself as intuitive, even doubted the reality of such things. Still, you can't argue with the clarity of your experience. You're at a crossroads, being pulled forward. Do you deny yourself? Go on with life as before? Impossible. Something tells you to stop guarding some rigid idea of who you are. For those so compelled, pursuing intuition is not a choice: It is a calling.

For one patient of mine, it came like a bolt out of the blue. Sophie thought she was crazy. She found me by flipping her television channels one Saturday night when I was on a public-access cable show. The topic of the show was intuitive dreams, and I was talking about how my mother had visited me soon after she died. It had only been a few months since her death, and I was still reeling from the shock. To speak of my mother on the air, though liberating, also made my loss more real. When Sophie heard me, she was driven to pick up the phone.

A Jewish immigrant in her early seventies, Sophie lived alone in a studio apartment in the Fairfax district, with Social Security benefits her only income. Her son had died of an accidental cocaine overdose one year before. Thus we shared a similar grief. Soon after her son's death, Sophie had fallen into a depression.

When she arrived for her first appointment, she explained why she had come. "I've been afraid to tell anyone," she said, "but every evening after dinner, my son sits across from me on a stool in the kitchen and keeps me company. He's just as real as you or me. I realize how strange this sounds, but when I heard the story about your mother, I thought you'd understand. My son's presence is comforting, but have I lost my mind?"

Since she was certain that both her daughters would be alarmed if she told them about her son's visitations, I was the only person she'd confided in. Being of a generation that didn't believe in psychiatry, Sophie had taken a big risk. "If I ever had a problem," she declared, "I'd always work it out on my own." This was a matter of pride, of not giving in to "weakness." And yet, she had a great need to make sense of her experience.

Bundled up in an old woolen coat and clutching her purse, Sophie sat poised on the edge of the couch. Though I saw how uneasy she was, I was touched by her determination to get to the truth. Most of all, I felt empathy for her isolation and self-doubt. She was an ordinary person with visions. That impressed me. No New Age convert or student of metaphysics, Sophie didn't think of herself as intuitive. Psychology was an alien language. I was the first psychiatrist she had ever seen.

Wanting to make Sophie more comfortable, I sat down beside her and offered her some tea. Gradually, as we talked, she began to open up, and then for over an hour spoke nonstop about herself. I learned she was a conservative Jew who regularly attended a synagogue in her neighborhood. She had received solace from prayer and the traditional Jewish rituals, but she was reluctant to tell her rabbi about the vision, afraid that he wouldn't understand.

Sophie had never had a vision before. She'd led a modest life. A strong-willed woman, she pulled herself up by her bootstraps whenever things got tough. There was nothing about her behavior to indicate that Sophie was or ever had been psychotic. Except for the overwhelming grief she felt, her mind was sharp and clear. Was Sophie hallucinating? Had she conjured up this image of her son out of loneliness? I didn't think so.

Because of the encounters with my mother, my profound belief in an afterlife, and the accounts I had heard over the years of dead relatives visiting patients and friends, I took Sophie's claim seriously. The description of her son was convincing and vivid; I was inclined to consider it real. Though he never materialized to me, I could feel his presence with us—a subtle veil of warmth, imbued with a focused intelligence, communicating love and concern for his mother. It was like standing silently in a room, eyes closed, with other persons nearby: Just because we can't see or hear them doesn't mean they're not there. When we are quiet, instincts finely tuned, we may sense them.

This was no imagining or picture that I reconstructed from Sophie's memories. During my medical training, I'd witnessed the identical thing time and again soon after a patient died: It was often possible to sense the dead intuitively. However, I also understand there's no way to prove or disprove this. It's simply a matter of belief. More important was the relevance this vision had for Sophie. Even if I hadn't considered it authentic, my approach would have been the same: to focus on the message of her experience.

Western medicine has traditionally been uncomfortable with visions, particularly those conjuring up the dead. Given this bias, it's not surprising that many physicians would have interpreted Sophie's vision as resulting from a biochemical imbalance set in motion by grief. In research studies, extreme stress has been shown to throw our neurotransmitters out of whack, resulting in pathological "symptoms," a tenet ingrained in the fabric of my medical training.

Although physiologically this may often be true, it doesn't tell the full story; it locks us into viewing intuition in a narrow way. Yes, when we're in crisis our systems react and change, yet that may be exactly the reason our awareness expands. Of course we will have discomfort, but so it is with growth. To see crises as opportunities, not just in psychological terms but as a gateway into intuition, is the key.

As a psychiatrist, I believe that we must acknowledge the integrity of our visions, to recognize them as a potential opening, so we may access a deeply resourceful part of ourselves. We don't have to lead bifurcated lives, splitting off our intuitive side. The price we pay is too high. By appreciating the full scope of our depths and capabilities, we can then strive for true emotional and spiritual health. Some of us are fortunate to have many such chances, but for Sophie this was the first. Her time had come and she was ready.

Sophie had harbored her secret for many months. It had been festering inside her, fueling her anxieties. When I assured her that I believed her experience was genuine, she grabbed my hand and kissed it. To be validated by even one other person when we're afraid we might be losing our mind restores our confidence. Then we can regroup and evaluate what's happening from a different angle, undistorted by fear.

There's a line from "The Covenant," by C. K. Williams, which has always spoken to me: "In my unlikeliest dreams, the dead are with me again, companions again, in an ordinary way." In this spirit, I neither overdramatized Sophie's situation nor did I minimize its significance. The essential question I asked myself was, How can I use this information to help Sophie find peace?

"If our loved ones feel they have unfinished business with us, their presence may linger after the body has gone," I said. "It's as if they have to make sure we're all right before they can leave. When you're ready, you must give your son permission to go."

It was easy for me to appreciate why Sophie had been unable to accomplish this right away. I would have done anything to keep my mother alive. Losing her had been inconceivable. It felt terribly unfair. Sophie's vision linked her to her son; in releasing him she would have to confront his death fully. I knew that situation well. But I also knew the strength that comes from listening to intuitive visions. It fortified my courage to move on so that I could share the legacy of love I had been given. I wanted to convey this to Sophie.

Her vision was the perfect vehicle. Through many conversations with her son, some of which took place in my office, Sophie slowly adjusted to his death. It was so abrupt; there had been no way to prepare. The vision gave Sophie time. Its message was always the same: Her son would be there as long as she needed him, until she could sort through her grief. In fact, his presence was often so strong I felt I knew him. Over the next few months, as Sophie resumed her life again—joining a seniors' group at her synagogue, making new friends—her son appeared less frequently. Finally, when she was ready to say good-bye to him, his visits stopped.

Intuitive experiences such as Sophie's are our birthright, and it's up to us to claim it. There's no elite to which this gift belongs—the seeds have been planted in everyone. To harvest them, we must first reprogram ourselves by envisioning the extent of our vastness, challenge anyone who insists on making us small. That we are limited as intuitive beings is a myth stemming from ignorance and false assumptions: Each one of us is multifaceted, radiant, and teeming with possibilities.

Imagine that you're gazing through a window onto a magnificent countryside. The view is unobstructed. For miles you're able to see green rolling hills, an expansive blue sky, hawks soaring past the sun, the outline of a distant village. The longer you look, the more there is to take in. There are exquisite details you might have missed out on, had that same window been clouded over. So it is with our intuitive sight. It can offer beauty and insight we may not even know is there. We have grown so accustomed to viewing the world through tarnished lenses that we've forgotten what it means to really see.

Whether you're a skeptic, simply curious, or already a believer, this journey is open for all. It doesn't matter if you've never had an intuitive experience or have been wary of such things. Once you are ready to take a second look, to open the door a crack and reevaluate, everything is possible. Because we so often create our own prisons, we also have the power to set ourselves free. All that is required is a willingness to suspend disbelief temporarily, daring to blow apart constraints that have held you back for so long. To awaken is an act of courage.

There's an integrity to the intuitive process that flows with a certain rhythm. Like a great river, it moves us along if we allow it. To be intuitive doesn't mean that we're enlightened or special. As we grow accustomed to seeing, it becomes completely natural, though our culture offers little support. Prescience is not something we can master in a day, a week, or even a year. Intimately related to the spiritual, it is a path that will take us as deep as we are ready to go. Our spiritual awareness keeps us honest, preventing our egos from ballooning out of control.

At the onset, you must approach intuition with the proper attitude: The power that comes with it can be very seductive, and should always be treated with the utmost respect. For that reason, one must find a mature teacher, both knowledgeable and humble, to guide the initial stages. After returning from Brugh Joy's conference, I was looking to meet someone locally, to establish regular contact and a consistent routine. My search for such a person began in fits and starts.

Over the following year I sampled a smorgasbord of gurus in Los Angeles, from a San Fernando ex-housewife who channeled an ancient entity bringing messages from the dead to an intuitive astrologer who catered to Hollywood stars. It was a colorful circus of diverse personalities and styles, some more palatable than others. But since for me they all lacked a certain depth, I wasn't motivated to study with anyone longer than a weekend.

One day, a friend suggested that I see a newly immigrated Malaysian man whose meditation methods had impressed her. I was intrigued, knowing from Brugh that meditation could deepen my spiritual practice and enhance intuition. The only problem was that by then I was becoming discouraged; I thought I'd exhausted the spiritual circuit and doubted that I would encounter anything new. But, certain that this particular friend was quick to see through metaphysical hype and hypocrisy, I decided to make an appointment.

A week later, in a modest fifties-style office building in downtown Santa Monica, I walked up a flight of creaky stairs and entered a sparsely decorated office with a single Formica desk and two worn armchairs. Sitting quietly in the corner was a man in his midforties, dressed in a simple gray cotton shirt and pants that might have come from Sears. He waited patiently for me to arrive, no hoopla or fanfare. When I looked carefully at him, suddenly all I could see were his eyes, two clear pools of light I'd known from somewhere before. Those eyes, which felt as if they'd always been gazing at me, could see my every hiding place, my faults and gifts alike. Ecstatic at the sight of him, I wanted to explode like a comet streaking across the sky. And all this before he uttered a word.

In the next hour, I poured out my life story, though he hadn't asked: The details just kept flowing out of my mouth as if from a spigot that wouldn't shut off. He listened in stillness, in complete respect, never once interrupting. When, finally, I was finished he spoke slowly and unassumingly in broken English about his background and meditation philosophy, making only a very few comments about me. In truth, it wasn't so much what he said but the radiance of his face. In his gentle, reserved way, he looked at me with so much love that I instinctively trusted him. I knew I had found my teacher.

I began attending a two-hour meditation class he taught Sunday mornings in the back room of an acupuncturist's office in Culver City. To my dismay, these were very frustrating sessions. I expected to find at least some sense of inner peace, but from the moment I closed my eyes all I felt was anxiety. The first few minutes of sitting were always the hardest. I'd fidget; my mind chattered incessantly. I couldn't calm down. Worse, there was the born-again Christian group next door, whose fervent hymns were as loud as if they were sitting in the room with us. How were we expected to meditate with such a racket going on? My teacher didn't look concerned. In fact, he seemed to be enjoying the music. But I was impatient, antsy. Aware of my discomfort, he smiled and advised, "Try not to let the singing disturb you. Keep on meditating. Eventually it will get easier." Since I respected him and he sounded so sure, I kept at it.

Before this, I had found it difficult to focus at home. Meditation wasn't as simple as just crossing your legs and closing your eyes. When writer and performer Spalding Gray told *Tricycle* magazine "I've been circling my meditation cushion for almost twenty years," I could totally relate to what he said. The most painful part was getting to the cushion in the first place. My teacher said, "It takes discipline to meditate. Do it for just five minutes a day." Easy enough, I thought. But I couldn't seem to pull it off. Carving out the time felt impossible. Full of good reasons why I couldn't sit, I always found something that stood in the way. I was too busy. The phone kept ringing. A neighbor needed me to move my car. I came up with a million "good" excuses. It wasn't that I didn't want to meditate, I just couldn't get myself to do it.

After about a month, suddenly, while meditating in class, something shifted. I don't know how or why. I hadn't really done anything different. With our neighbors belting out a particularly soulful "Rock of Ages," I tried to ignore my irritation and closed my eyes. As usual, my thoughts chimed in on cue and started blaring with the intensity of a loud radio in a tiny room. I guess I finally just tuned it all out. I'd hashed over the same conversations in my mind so many times, but now the relentless jabbering became like white noise. I couldn't hear it or the music anymore. Instead there was stillness, a feeling of tranquillity—my first taste of the comfort meditation could bring.

I could never have forced this. I just had to sit there faithfully week after week, when I didn't seem to be making any progress. Although I didn't realize it, I was moving ahead. Consistency was the secret. By showing up each Sunday, I was making my meditation a discipline. Surrounded by twenty other people, carried along by their energy and enthusiasm, I wasn't so easily distracted. Most important, I didn't let my restlessness stop me. Although subtle at first, a momentum was building: Once able to feel the peace that comes from meditation, I could more easily find it again.

By regularly quieting my mind, I grew accustomed to a new kind of inner listening. Beneath the incessant buzzing of my thoughts, I aimed always to return to the stillness. Far from being a void, it was alive, possessed an inherent vitality. In this state, intuition became more accessible, and not simply because of the lack of distractions. It was much more than that: The stillness seemed to have a language of its own. It would speak to me, tell me things during meditation and at other times. Issues I had been confused about would suddenly become clear: how to approach certain situations, deal with people, make decisions that felt right. Through the discipline of going inward and calming myself, my intuitive voice took form, became more consistent. Rather than a sporadic, random perception, it was evolving into a regular part of my life.

My teacher, a Taoist, believed in a universal intelligence—referred to as the Tao—upon which all spiritual paths converge. The purpose of meditating, he said, was to contact this force, get to know ourselves better, and strengthen our spiritual link. A by-product of meditation, though not its main goal, was a kindling of our intuitive awareness. It was a gift: We were never to blow it out of proportion or misuse it in any way.

And so, in this spirit, my meditation practice began. Initially I had to grow into it and go at my own pace. For the first few months, I meditated only two hours a week in class. Gradually, as I was able to do it on my own, the length of time I spent sitting increased. Now I make a point of meditating at least once a day. Early mornings are my favorite. Before reading the newspaper, answering phone calls, or preparing breakfast, I sit quietly for at least twenty minutes. This gets me off to a good start. Whenever I skip my morning meditation, I feel more frazzled and off center as the day goes on.

Meditation is the most powerful tool I have found to become more intuitively attuned. It allows us to cross over boundaries we may not know existed until we've moved beyond them. The reason many of you may not realize you're intuitive is that you have become conditioned to hearing only your mind. The intensity of your thoughts overrides everything else. Meditation gives you more options. Even if you have never thought of yourself as the "type" or have tried and been unsuccessful, when properly guided everyone can meditate.

I teach my patients to practice the same simple technique my teacher taught me. First, sit on a comfortable cushion, back upright, legs crossed. If sitting on a cushion is too uncomfortable, sit on a chair, making sure to keep your back straight. If you lie down it's too easy to fall asleep. With the palms of your hands resting together in the traditional prayer position, begin by making a reverential bow in honor of yourself and your spiritual source. Then, most important, start to breathe. Paying attention only to the rhythm of your in-breath and out-breath, notice the nuances of each inhalation and exhalation as the flow of air passes through your lungs and out past your nostrils and mouth. If thoughts come—and they will—note them but try not to get involved in them, and always return to the breath. In Yogic thought, this is the *prana,* our vital energy, the essence of life. Concentrating on it singly leads to the stillness as nothing else can.

You may be like me. I've always rebelled against regimentation of any kind. If someone tells me one way of doing something, I'm sure to do the opposite. I'm not saying that this is a commendable quality, but it's how I often feel. Respecting this about myself, I've chosen a method of meditating that suits my character. It's more free flowing, instinctual, without a lot of rules. But meditation is extremely personal. There are many excellent methods—including Zen, Vipassanna, Yoga, transcendental meditation—some more structured than others. It may help to experiment with a few. In the final analysis, how or where you meditate is less important than the outcome of the practice.

I know of a blackjack dealer in Reno who uses meditation to center himself amidst the chaos and confusion of the gambling casino. Inspired by the Hindu tradition, he's renamed himself Hanuman after the monkey god, recognized for being the devoted servant of Rama. During his breaks, he sits cross-legged beneath the glare of the bright lights, eyes closed, surrounded by the din of slot machines and people shouting. There he meditates as peacefully as he might on a mountain in Tibet. His practice has taught him to cope with external distractions and keeps him focused and astute.

To be able to meditate, no matter what the physical conditions, you must begin slowly. Meditation requires loyalty and perseverance. Initially, you can limit yourself to five minutes a day. Once you become more accustomed to sitting, gradually build up to twenty minutes over the next few weeks or months. You may stay at that level for a while. When you're ready, increase to a full hour. But don't worry if your mind is busy. It takes practice to sense the stillness, so try to be patient. If at first nothing much seems to be happening, you're not doing anything wrong. There's no rush. Just keep your attention focused on the breath as much as possible. Be gentle with yourself. Change takes time.

Intuition flourishes when you give it space to grow. Meditation can provide this. It is an organic process that allows prescience to mature gradually, in a healthy way. With time to assimilate this change, you will never be given more than you can handle. There's a natural tempo to opening that occurs if you don't force it before you're ready. Sometimes we may move ahead in leaps and bounds, at other times take only tiny steps forward, or even think that we're sliding backward. But however it may appear, this is an ongoing process of growth. Wisely prepare yourself to see. Make space for your own brilliance. Meditation can be your first step, a solid, well-grounded send-off to a truly amazing journey.

When I was a child, I had a fantasy that a space ship had dropped me off on Earth. I took comfort in believing that my actual home was far out in the stars on another planet, a place where I really belonged. Many nights, yearning to feel complete, I would sit up on the roof and gaze at the sky, searching, feeling an intangible presence just beyond reach. I hoped that if I stared out into space long enough I would make it my own.

Through meditation I later discovered what I had been looking for: a seamless continuity between myself and this very force. More than just offering an intuitive link, meditation brought my spirituality alive, wove into my life a sacred texture. A source of replenishment and solace, meditation amplified what was most holy to me and made it recognizable so that I could take it in.

But I wasn't able to achieve this overnight. Until I met my teacher in 1985, my meditation habits were irregular, without focus or form. I had tried meditating on the bed, propped up on a large silk pillow; in the living room twisted like a pretzel in the lotus position on the couch; and even in the bathtub at night soaking in deliciously warm water, surrounded by a circle of flickering votive candles. Still, I couldn't get it right. I felt like a restless old dog, shifting positions, never really settling into a comfortable one.

To solve this predicament, my teacher suggested that I set up an altar, a simple but ingenious idea that immediately intrigued me. He had pinpointed exactly what had been lacking. Rather than being haphazard about meditating, roaming from room to room, I needed a specific place where I could settle in. Meant to be a tribute to the Tao, our spiritual source, an altar is a physical touchstone joining us to it. In constructing one, my teacher had only a few instructions: It was to face the east (in the Taoist tradition, the birthplace of spiritual power); and I was to place a red candle on the right (symbol of knowledge), a white candle on the left (symbol of purity), and provide a container to burn incense. The rest my teacher would leave up to me.

Excited, I began right away. Rummaging around in my garage I found a small wooden table about two feet wide that I had used years before in my Venice apartment. Intentionally, I hadn't rushed out to buy a new table: I wanted one that already had part of me in it, reflected my history. So I brought it upstairs, dusted it off, and placed it on the far wall of my office at home, across from my computer. For a while I just looked at it, deciding what to do next. A few days later, while I was browsing in Bullock's, a roll of fabric jumped out at me. A beige background patterned with beautiful Asian women dressed in blue kimonos, it felt perfect. I got a piece large enough to cover the table's surface. With it in place, I added the objects my teacher recommended plus a small white porcelain statue of Quan Yin, the goddess of compassion. I was all set to go.

Little did I know the dynamic role my altar would play in both my meditation practice and my life. When my mother was dying, it was the place I sought at moments when I thought I couldn't go on. So many nights I slept next to it for the comfort it offered. Sometimes I would place on it a bouquet of colorful flowers or a bowl of fresh fruit—symbols of beauty and vibrancy I clung to in my need. Gazing at the radiant face of Quan Yin, often through a blur of tears, enabled me to remain focused on the truths I believed in, to forgive myself when I fell short, and to begin the next day anew.

When my life gets hectic, I know that I can return to my altar to rejuvenate myself. No matter how stressed out I am or how fast my mind is spinning, just sitting in stillness makes everything slow down. I meditate in front of it each day, though sometimes I'm drawn there in the middle of the night as well. If I am having trouble sleeping, it's the first place I head. Calming, a constant reminder of the power of faith, my altar helps me to relax so that I can rest comfortably again. I always leave feeling nourished, as if I had just drunk fresh water from a mountain stream.

One of my patients, Maggie, didn't enter psychotherapy to become intuitive, to meditate, or to learn about altars. She simply was having trouble with her boyfriend. Throughout her life, Maggie had had a series of relationships with dominant men. They had wanted to control her, and she'd relinquished her power to them, becoming passive and compliant, never speaking her own needs. Each time it was the same: She felt overlooked, undervalued. Now, after years of being single, she had once again met a guy who swept her away. They had been dating for only three months and already the relationship had become strained. The familiar pattern was repeating itself; she was beginning to have doubts.

Maggie, a media consultant, had been in lengthy psychoanalysis, so she had a sophisticated intellectual understanding of the unconscious factors that motivated her relationship choices.

Still, she was enslaved by her repetitive behavior. I knew that I needed to guide her in a different direction.

Maggie maintained two sets of friends. One group, including her present boyfriend, had fairly conservative beliefs, and they mocked anything that was considered "spiritual." The other, comprised of avid meditators, was devoted to pursuing a spiritual life. These were the people with whom Maggie felt most at home. Still, she limited her involvement with them because she was afraid of going overboard. Having studied meditation in the past, Maggie held back, reluctant to commit herself to a regular practice. Convinced that her conservative friends would condemn such an activity as "flaky" or "insubstantial," she never brought it up in their company.

For over two years, Maggie stayed on the fence, keeping her friends separate, leading a dual life. Looking at Maggie, I saw a reflection of myself ten years before: She was struggling with a similar split. I saw so much yearning and so much pain simmering just beneath the surface. I knew the massive amount of energy it took to keep these worlds separate. Always trying to please, to conform at any expense, even if it meant being untrue to yourself. I could also see that she was desperate to change but didn't know how. Her discomfort had finally grown so great that she was willing to try just about anything. I suggested that she set up an altar.

Out of touch with her intuition, uncentered, Maggie needed a designated place to regroup, a sacred spot in her home, formally defined, where she could learn to gather her power. That was the starting point. It is an easy action that any one of us can take if we feel confused or lost, needing to find ourselves again.

"An altar is a haven where you can go at any time to meditate and be alone," I explained. "It's your own private sanctuary . . . like a church or synagogue. But it doesn't have to be conventionally religious unless you want it to be. The important thing is that you sit quietly with yourself, find your intuitive voice, and begin to listen."

Maggie's face brightened. "An altar? A few of my friends who meditate have one. In fact, I almost set one up myself. But I was afraid other people would think it's weird. Especially my boyfriend. I didn't want to start a fight."

"Then pick an out-of-the-way location," I advised. "A back bedroom, office, even a hallway. Someplace where visitors don't usually go. An altar isn't meant to be a conversation piece. Actually, it's better not to discuss it with most people at all. No one should go there unless they're invited."

Maggie's altar needed to be a place where she felt unviolated, a nurturing retreat. Unfortunately, she didn't have many such places in her life. Most of the time she felt as if she were on a battlefield, dodging bullets. I knew the feeling. Life can become frantic, even when we don't intend it to be. Our altar is a refuge to come home to, where we can kick off our shoes, breathe deeply again, reconnect.

For me, the altar was just a beginning. I've come to see my entire physical environment as an intimate extension of my inner life. I try to create a sense of sacredness throughout my home. I live by the ocean. As I fall asleep I can hear waves crashing on the shore. During rainstorms, the impact of the wind and water rattles my sliding glass windows and shakes the frame of my bed, keeping me tapped into the wildness of nature. I need to look out at vistas. I long to see expanses of sky. The ocean sunlight filters through my bay windows into every room. Reflecting through crystals hanging from my ceiling, it projects dancing rainbows on the walls. A ceramic vase full of fresh flowers rests on my dining room table. Potted plants of all sizes and shapes are everywhere. A mammoth creeping Charley drapes two stories down over my balcony. Though it's important that my living area feel safe and spiritually inspiring, you don't need a palace—any space can be made sacred if the desire is there.

Seeming as if she'd been just waiting for permission, Maggie jumped at the chance to set up an altar. But first she had to reinvent what spirituality meant to her. Raised a Roman Catholic, she had rebelled against the restrictions of her childhood religion. Since then there had been a spiritual vacuum in her life. She worried that the objects on the altar resembled idols. Associating ritual only with Catholicism, she had to start over again from scratch.

Maggie's altar was simple: a small wooden bench, a round, white candle, and a crystal vase just large enough to hold a single rose. Altars can take a variety of shapes and forms. The objects we place on them should inspire us: statues, pictures, incense, fruit, flowers, candles, or any other symbols that hold special meaning. I encouraged Maggie to meditate in front of her altar daily, even when she didn't feel like it or if there were a million other things to do. Through this discipline, she learned how to direct her attention inward, over and over again, until it became habit. "Listen closely," I kept urging her, "until you can hear your intuitive voice again."

"How do I know what it sounds like?" she asked. "There are so many voices in my head. How can I tell them apart?" I reflected on my work at Mobius, how I trained myself to recognize the difference between what was logical or expected and what was intuitively true; the sense of rightness that's often present, a clarity, an immediacy, an unconflicted quality so resolute and impartial that the information received isn't open to debate. Explaining this to Maggie, I also advised her to be patient. "This voice is often quiet but steady. It might take some practice to hear."

In the beginning, Maggie was frustrated. The distracting dialogue in her mind was unrelenting. Whatever intuitive impulses she had were so faint that she could barely make them out. This is common for many of us. Our intellects have often been developed at a great expense: the annihilation of our instincts. To recover them, we must learn to listen in a keener way.

The power Maggie's altar held, and the dedication with which she approached it, made it an effective tool for change. Slowly, Maggie's intuition began to surface, at first small knowings, then larger ones. If she became confused, or slipped into old patterns with her boyfriend, she returned to her altar to consult her intuitive voice, just as she would a close friend. When she did, it told her the truth about things. It taught her to listen. It taught her to see.

If an altar appeals to you, it's an ideal way to create a peaceful environment in your home where you can meditate. Just knowing that you have a special place all your own, where you can be yourself without pretense or fear, can be amazingly reassuring. It provides a backup when everything else in life may be falling apart. Your altar can be a place of return: to your prescience, your inner knowledge, your mystical nature. It restores a sense of the sacred, propels your intuitive quest. A concrete, practical step available to us all, an altar can be a reminder of the sublime, an honoring of the great mystery.

Maggie is an example of someone who was curious about intuition. Jeff, however, came to me in a great deal of fear. He had always considered himself an intuitive person, but recently he had made two accurate intuitive predictions that had badly shaken him.

On one occasion, he dreamed that his sister had fallen seriously ill. Since he knew that her health was excellent, however, he didn't pay any attention to the dream. A week later, jogging in the park, she had a sudden heart attack and nearly died. Shortly after this, Jeff had a clear premonition that a close friend who was in financial trouble would lose his job. Within a month, the friend was unemployed. Foreseeing these events frightened Jeff, made him feel out of control. He was at his wits' end: He had never wanted to be intuitive. Why was he making these predictions now?

I met with Jeff, hoping to pinpoint what might have set them off. He walked in visibly shaken, a painfully polite, articulate businessman, impeccably dressed in a suit and tie. Everything about him cried out order: shoes shined to a T; hair blow-dried, not a strand out of place; a cellular phone and appointment book securely fastened in a brown leather satchel. He was organized— perhaps too well.

I found out he was a member of the Self-Realization Fellowship, a nondenominational church in the Pacific Palisades. Every Sunday, he and his wife would attend early morning services and then take a stroll around the parklike grounds. But over the past three months, their routine had changed. Instead of their walk, they stayed on for a two-hour group meditation in the main chapel. Each of Jeff's predictions had happened the next day. Jeff had never meditated before, let alone for such a long period of time; it was the obvious trigger. He had opened up too fast. Without intending to, by stilling his mind Jeff had become more intuitively receptive.

He was unprepared for this shift, finding any sort of change difficult. Obviously alarmed, he asked, "Why did I predict such upsetting things?"

I recalled my own experiences as a child, how distraught I had been about my early negative predictions, the heartache my mother went through. When not put in the proper context, seeming to come out of nowhere, prescience can be hard to assimilate. That's where I wanted to help—to dispel Jeff's fears, just as Thelma and Stephan had done for me.

"Many beginning intuitives feel exactly as you do," I said. "Disasters, deaths, and traumatic events are simply easier to pick up. It doesn't mean you're a bad person or there's something wrong. Crises of all kinds carry a stronger emotional charge and therefore transmit a louder intuitive signal."

If only I had known this before, so much of my confusion might have been avoided. It was a lesson hard learned, a fact basic to intuitive growth, information we can pass on to one another. There's no reason to take this intuitive journey alone. We can benefit from our shared knowledge, form a network, so no one needs to feel isolated anymore.

"Negative predictions come with the territory," I continued. "That's why children or new intuitives are more likely to pick up a head-on freeway collision with bodies strewn all over the road than to see the same car arriving safely at its destination. The same principle is true of appreciating the nuances of an intricate piece of music. To the untrained ear, the most dramatic aspects are what stand out. But eventually we can perceive an undercurrent of tones indistinguishable before."

No matter how logical or reassuring this sounded to me, Jeff didn't look consoled. He didn't want any part of being intuitive. He considered it an unwelcome responsibility. A creature of habit, he preferred what was already known and comfortable.

"If all my premonitions were positive," Jeff ventured, "it might be okay. Then they'd be easier to accept. But knowing about crises before they happen, particularly with people I love . . . no, that's not for me. It's much too painful. Even if I could warn them, I wouldn't want to be in that position."

Jeff was a private person, and he didn't like interfering with other people's affairs. Without the option to choose what he would or wouldn't see, for the time being he gave up meditating, and his premonitions ceased.

I had to respect Jeff's decision. He recognized his limitations and stuck to them. Nonetheless, I couldn't help feeling let down, as if I'd watched a space shuttle launched into the heavens and then seen it forced to turn back because of lack of fuel. Even so, I had to be careful not to become a cheerleader. My fear of intuition was behind me: I had earned the advantage of hindsight, had already reaped the rewards of this path and wanted to share them. But Jeff wasn't interested. Clearly, pursuing intuition is not for everyone.

I have a friend, a stunning blonde in her early seventies, a fearless adventurer and world traveler, always wanting to try something new. Although curious about intuition, she had never felt a real need for it. Still, not wanting to miss out on anything, she once asked me over a Thai dinner, "Do you think I should learn to be intuitive, too?" I smiled, knowing that this question was only her way of trying to please me.

I laughed. "No," I said, "unless you really want to, there's nothing to gain. It's never right to force it." She looked relieved, and we continued our meal. I had let her off the hook.

Even if you have a desire to be intuitive, the path may not always be clear. That's only natural. Difficulties can arise, but fear can be the greatest obstacle—of being called crazy, of getting out of control, of being misunderstood, of being wrong. Fear is insidious, but we can't let it stop us. Our society conditions us to be scared of intuition. If we dream of the future and it comes true, many of us have a knee-jerk tendency to think it "strange," or "disturbing," when our ability is natural, evidence of innate knowledge. We must undo our negative beliefs, no matter how ingrained. Recognizing that fear exists is the first step. But fear can burgeon, leeching out all inspiration, poisoning our dreams.

Some of your fear may be reality based. Too many individuals have exploited intuition as a means to control or manipulate, or for greed. Is it any wonder, then, that in much of Western culture the term *intuitive* has fallen into disrepute? Sensationalized by the press, scorned by traditional science, discounted by intellectuals, to again be considered holy, intuition must be redefined in human terms. It allows us to connect with one another more deeply, with empathy and respect, to join together as a collective force. Old stereotypes of intuitives as crystal-ball readers or carnival performers need to be left behind, replaced with our faces and names. We are the rightful bearers of this knowledge, the guardians at the gate.

At first it may be disconcerting to discover that we are vaster and more capable than we had ever imagined. Some of us may initially contract around this knowledge, needing time to feel safe enough to peek out from our hiding places and look around. After all, we're entering unmapped territory. Fear is bound to surface, but it doesn't have to force us to shut down.

The purpose of cultivating ourselves intuitively is to open. And then to open even more. With prescience, we come to know ourselves well, become more sensitive to friends and family. Better able to respond to their needs, we can be lovingly in harmony with our relationships. The choices we make become truly well-informed, based on our innermost desires, not on some artificial notion of who we are supposed to be.

Ignoring this part of ourselves can lead to depletion and depression. It's like trying to function on only two cylinders when we have a turbo-charged engine that can travel at lightning speeds. We putter along, make do, but suffer from the chronic drain, our energy reserves wasted.

So many patients have come to me in this state—tired and irritable. Out of touch with their intuitive voice, they strain to get through life by forcing decisions that really don't feel right. Their actions are dictated solely by what is visible: The quest for the invisible doesn't count. With no spiritual context, they have lost touch with the mystery. Yet we need not live in this state of disconnection. Recovering our intuitive voice provides the link.

By listening to it, we can cultivate the ability to hear, see, and feel, to become more acutely attuned to the nuances of our lives. We meet ourselves again, come face to face with our own shining. We've forgotten so much: the ravishing beings we are, the strength of our spirits, the wisdom we possess. All this needs to be reclaimed.

Intuition doesn't arrive fully formed or without effort. It thrives on our attention to subtleties, a refined interior focus. The difficulty is that many of us don't know how to reach deep enough to achieve this. We skim just above the surface, never quite taking the plunge. Along with meditation and altars, there is one more method to help prepare us to see: the use of ritual.

Ritual imparts a sacredness to our activities that may not be readily apparent. Ritual can give our lives a brightness, a vibrancy, a focus. Many of us take ritual for granted, forget how it shapes our relationships and lives. Imagine a world with no weddings, holiday festivities, birthday parties, or even funerals—our markers, our dearest touchstones unacknowledged and forgotten. How much we would be missing!

Just as ritual evokes the specialness of certain events, it also brings color and emphasis to our inner lives. By creating a forum to celebrate it, we specifically invite intuition in. When conducted with reverence and humility, ritual enables us to shift out of our conditioned patterns of viewing the world—to cultivate a respect and awe for the mystery that surrounds us.

I was introduced to the use of ritual at Brugh Joy's conference when I was beginning my psychiatric practice. We were scheduled to have an afternoon of healing. Fastidious preparations were being made; there were various rules to follow. I wondered what all the fuss was about. Everyone dressed in white, all forty of us silently filed into a huge candlelit meeting room. I cringed, thinking, What would my doctor friends say if they saw me now? Thank goodness they weren't there. Feeling more than a little foolish, and painfully self-conscious, I took my place beside one of the many wooden massage tables positioned around the room. When our turn came, we were to lie down so Brugh and the others could impart "energy" to us through their hands. The scene was set: Pachelbel's "Canon" played softly in the background, a tinge of sandalwood incense wafted through the air, colorful bouquets of flowers lined the floor. These were careful touches, aimed to convey a mood, to enhance the subtleties of what healing felt like firsthand.

Pretty soon, my awkwardness disappeared. The beauty of the room, the loving instinct this environment seemed to elicit in everyone, made my experience of healing all the more moving. It wasn't that I couldn't have felt this way in a less elaborate setting, but what ritual afforded many of us for the first time was a distraction-free structure made sacred by music, color, scents, and a group intention to heal. Particularly in the beginning we need all the help we can get to unmask our sensitivities. Ritual can hone them, eliminate static, enliven us so that we can more easily see.

Most important, our rituals need to be inspirational. It's pointless if they are unfeeling or rote. I have a friend who belongs to an orthodox religion. He prays five times each day, according to a format he passionately believes in. Recently he came to me, distressed that despite his prayers he couldn't feel the presence of God. Berating himself, he believed that he was doing something wrong. But instead of reevaluating the ritual and perhaps finding another that better suited him, he persisted in this same form. Devoted to his faith, he's still hoping to achieve a breakthrough.

The type of ritual we choose is extremely personal; it awakens a power dormant within. The efforts we make, either simple or intricate, assume meaning if we are sincere.

Another friend of mine was taught an endearing ritual by her grandmother. With the coming of spring, my friend's grandmother—now nearing ninety years old, and a painter—would brush her long gray hair and then toss the hair from the brush up into the air so the birds nearby could use it to make their nests. As my friend was growing up, every March she and her grandmother would do this together. Now in her forties, my friend has taught this honoring of spring and renewal, a connection to nature and new life, to her own daughter.

A ritual I learned from my teacher, which I perform twice monthly, is to pay tribute to the new and full phases of the moon. On those days, I eat vegetarian food, meditate longer, recite special prayers in front of my altar, and try to be particularly reverent. The purpose is to achieve balance and purification. A part of the Taoist tradition, this practice joins perfectly with my own beliefs.

Since I was a little girl I have been fascinated by the moon, sensed its mystery and power. Late into the night I used to stare at it, lying in bed, fine white light streaming through the cracks of my curtains. I loved to watch the moon gradually change form, growing from a barely perceptible sliver to a radiant orb that felt as if it shined right into my body. I could never separate myself from the moon. It has always been a part of me, molding my rhythms, drawing me up to the sky.

When my teacher spoke of the new moon as the initial phase of a cycle, a time when the flame is just being lit, and of the full moon as an epiphany, a culmination of forces reaching a peak, he put into words what I had long felt. Spiritual energy, he said, was particularly high at these times. Hence the reason to pause and pay tribute to them.

I should stress, however, that I recoil from taking part in ritual that feels false, no matter how powerful anyone claims it to be. But having found one that is true to my nature, I have made it a seamless extension of my spiritual life.

The practice of ritual has proved of great value for many of my patients. Providing a hands-on, action-oriented dimension to our work, it can bring insight to even the most murky dilemma. I'll conduct a ritual with someone in my office or I may encourage them to do this in solitude or in groups. When performed in nature, ritual is especially potent. The forest, desert, ocean, or mountains bring an excitement, a primal quality often less noticeable in the city.

Jenny, a gorgeous Hawaiian woman with long raven-black hair and warm brown eyes, was familiar with ritual, but she had lost track of it. Her father was trained as a kahuna, a holy man and healer, on the island of Kauai where she was raised. He passed on the secret teachings to his young daughter, but as she grew older the memories gradually fell away. Having lived a sheltered life, Jenny was hungry to experience more. At seventeen, when she graduated from high school, she left Kauai and moved to Manhattan to pursue a modeling career.

Signed by a top agency, she landed more jobs than she could handle and traveled the world on exotic photo shoots over the next few years. Money, fame, and prestige were hers and yet she was increasingly unhappy. Jenny's career had skyrocketed, her face had been on the cover of major fashion magazines, but something wasn't right. Modeling was becoming empty, yet she was afraid to leave it. Locked into a seductive lifestyle, adulated by the public and her friends, Jenny felt stuck and depressed.

For several months, in therapy, we discussed the pros and cons of Jenny's career, but she still hadn't made up her mind about what she would do. We were getting nowhere. It became evident that no amount of talking was going to help, despite Jenny's sensitivity, intelligence, and desire. I had reached this point before with certain patients. Seeing that she was immobilized, that it wasn't enough for her to understand the emotional and intellectual roots of her problem, I suggested she conduct a ritual. She remembered that her father had introduced her to this and was eager to give it a try.

We spent a full session exploring the specifics of what her ritual would be. What symbols were meaningful? Where would she like to perform it? With whom? The more concrete the details, the better the chance of imparting the potency to penetrate her block. Having grown up on the north shore of Kauai, she had a special feeling for the ocean and wanted her ritual to take place there.

This gave me an idea. "There's an ancient Celtic ceremony involving a circle of stones," I explained. A few years ago I'd learned of this from a friend and had used it myself. "You can perform the ritual at the beach. It's quite simple. Basically, you form a circle of stones and sit inside it until your answer comes. In Celtic mythology, stones hold a rich concentration of power, represent the living embodiment of Mother Earth. The circle is a configuration believed to contain mystical properties. It acts like a pressure cooker, focusing and containing energy. This could provide the boost you need."

This ritual appealed to Jenny. A few days later, on the morning of the next full moon, signifying the peak of a cycle, she drove her Volvo up the coast to a secluded beach north of Malibu. Wearing a long, flowing white cotton dress, she tied her hair back with multicolored beads in honor of the occasion. She brought with her some purple sage she had gathered from the Malibu hills, which in Native American tradition is associated with purification. Collecting a number of large stones from the shore, Jenny carefully set up the circle. In the center she placed a round ceramic container and burned the sage. Settling in, she sat cross-legged on a blanket, closed her eyes, and asked for guidance.

The next few hours she spent meditating and watching the ebb and flow of the waves. My instructions had been to allow the answer to surface rather than attempt to "figure it out." Although Jenny was doing everything right, nothing much was happening. But she waited, knowing that rituals have their own time frame. Even so, it was growing late. Doubts crept in, about the ritual and about her life in general. Did she have the strength to make a change? Jenny wasn't sure. The sun was setting; she was chilled. Despondent and restless, she was tempted to pack up her things. But she didn't. As she sat, somehow connected to the ancient knowledge of her father and everyone who had performed this ritual before, she understood the need to remain. A warm blanket wrapped around her shoulders, Jenny curled up and drifted off into a light sleep.

It was then, when she stopped trying so hard, that the answer came. In a flash she realized that she had to take a break. If just to get perspective, it would be worthwhile. Though logically she had come to this conclusion before, the strength of her intuition now compelled her to act. Her entire body softened in response. The rightness of the decision, though laced with a certain sadness, also carried a great sense of relief. Freeing as this was, Jenny knew better than to act rashly: It would take time for the insight to sink in.

Over the next few weeks Jenny and I waited to see if her resolve remained strong. I played devil's advocate, raising the objections I was sure her friends and colleagues would make. Jenny didn't waver, showing the same confidence I have seen in other patients following similar rituals. Having struggled to find a solution that makes sense, they aren't easily dissuaded. They are ready to put themselves on the line and trust their instincts at last. When Jenny was certain her mind was not going to change, she notified her agency that she was taking three months off.

For all of January, she returned home to visit her family on Kauai. Taking long walks on the beach with her father, she became reacquainted with the kahuna tradition. Something inside of her was sparked. She longed to learn more about healing. During that trip she decided to move back to the islands and enroll in college. Aware that other models would kill for her career,

Jenny acted on the courage of her beliefs. There were no guarantees that her plan would succeed, but she was determined to give it a chance.

Over the years Jenny and I have kept in touch. Now a doctoral student in psychology at the University of Hawaii, she plans to open a private practice on Oahu. Following her father's tradition, she is weaving her ethnic wisdom into her work. Jenny is pleased with the choice she made. The ritual of stones she performed on the beach made a breakthrough possible. When the moment came, she seized it. Despite all the pressure to continue modeling, she contacted a truer voice inside and followed her heart.

As it provides a structure, the beauty of ritual is the freedom it offers—freedom to explore what you really want from life, to define new directions, to clarify your visions and desires, even if you may not know what they are. It's a way to become centered, to stop giving away your power and to take responsibility for it. Implicit in all ritual is self-respect, as well as an honoring of a spiritual reality, however you define it, and faith that guidance is available. Such faith is essential for everyone who is preparing to see. Ritual helps instill this by illustrating time and again the depth of change that is possible when we act on what we know within.

To elicit guidance in our lives, we can also turn to prayer. It works no matter what your belief system, whether you appeal to a force outside yourself or to an inner wisdom. While meditation is an open-ended way of listening to spirit, prayer is a specific way of speaking to it. Through prayer comes clarity, and with it intuitive knowledge. Although life may not always go as we wish, the strength of our clarity, and the appreciation of the deeper meaning of certain events can carry us through.

When I was very young my mother taught me to recite two different prayers before I went to sleep: the Shema, an ancient Hebrew prayer stating, "Hear, O Israel: The Lord is our God, the Lord alone is One," and another in which I'd say, "Now I lay me down to sleep. I pray the Lord my soul to keep. Keep me safe throughout the night. May I see the morning light. God bless Daddy, Mommy, and Judi [my childhood nickname] for ever and ever. Amen." Burrowed beneath a mountain of covers, cozy and warm, I repeated both prayers without fail every night. They made me feel secure, connected to my Jewish roots and family. I should add, however, that I was motivated more by habit than devotion. It was something I did to be a "good girl," not because I was truly inspired.

For years, I underestimated the power of prayer. As a teenager, I resorted to it mainly when I wanted something or if I was in so much pain there was nowhere else to turn. Then, if I got what I requested or when the pain stopped, I promptly forgot what had helped me. In high school I would pray to have a boyfriend, to be "popular," or get a good grade on a math test. But looking back, I can now see that if all my prayers had been answered I would probably be in big trouble today. In some cases, unanswered prayers prove to be the blessing.

Through meditation and studying with my teacher I have come to view prayer differently. Once I had a direct experience of exactly what I was praying to—an unbounded love vaster than I had ever imagined—my faith strengthened. Previously, I was afraid that if I gave up my demands I wouldn't be heard, as if this intelligence were so limited it couldn't possibly respond to my needs without my specifically asking. Or that it had so many more pressing things to attend to. But sensing the infinite capacity of this love, I increasingly came to trust it.

Now, when I pray for myself or others, except in certain emergencies, I request only what is for the highest good, not presuming to know what that good might be. Though it is often tempting to specify "I want this" or "I want that," particularly if I'm in a lot of pain, I try to keep my prayers general rather than superimposing my own will onto them. The true elegance of prayer, I believe, is letting go of the results, confident that our needs will be met, maybe not in the exact form we had envisioned but ultimately in a better way. Scotch-taped to my refrigerator door as a reminder of the ideals that are important to me is the prayer of Saint Francis of Assisi, which I recite every morning before I begin my day. It says:

> *Lord, make me an instrument of Thy peace:*
> *where there is hatred, let me sow love;*
> *where there is injury, pardon;*
> *where there is doubt, faith;*
> *where there is despair, hope;*
> *where there is darkness, light;*
> *and where there is sadness, joy.*
>
> *Divine Master, grant that I may not so much seek to be*
> *   consoled as to console;*
> *to be understood as to understand;*
> *to be loved as to love;*
> *for it is in giving that we receive;*
> *in pardoning that we are pardoned;*
> *and it is in dying that we are born to eternal life.*

This simple prayer, which asks that we may be of service, imparts the basic philosophy of my spiritual practice. Promoting healing, prayer is thus my manner of addressing intuition. You may use this prayer or find another that appeals to you. Most important, choose one that stirs something deep inside, inspires you to be the kind of person you most want to be. The humility with which you approach prayer, not demanding results but remaining open to the answers, creates a spaciousness that allows intuition in. C. K. Williams, in a poem, has a beautiful way of describing this process: "I'd empty like a cup; that would be prayer, to empty, then fill with a substance other than myself." The emptiness is pregnant, the stillness full, intuition ever present when we pray.

Although I avoid stipulating outcomes in prayer, I regularly request guidance—to do the right thing, to know when to intervene or remain silent, to choose the most meaningful words to say when someone is stuck, to find inner peace or help others achieve it. A highly private and instinctual act, prayer can provide a direct line to intuition. By admitting that we don't know, we become willing to call on a greater force to assist us.

Matt was someone who greatly needed to be heard but felt that he'd been forsaken. A UCLA philosophy professor, a young fifty, dressed in well-worn Reeboks, a T-shirt, and jeans, he was cautious yet fascinated by intuition. A week after attending a lecture I gave on dreams he set up an appointment.

Matt had been raised a Baptist and had exhibited a strong religious faith while in his twenties. But then he fell into a depression in which he couldn't even get out of bed. He called on his religion to help, dragging himself to church on Sunday, barely having the energy to move, but his depression only got worse. After a few years of seeing psychiatrists, through a combination of medication and psychotherapy, he began to feel better. In the past, Matt had had a number of accurate premonitions. Now he'd come to me to learn more about them. But Matt wanted nothing to do with spirituality. That chapter of his life, he declared, was over.

Furious that his former beliefs had failed him, Matt rejected my suggestions that he pray or meditate. "You don't have to belong to a traditional religion," I said. "Discover your own way instead."

"Why should I?" he snapped. "Where was God when I needed him?"

For a solid month he aggressively voiced his protests. Empathizing with Matt's position, knowing how hard it was to begin again while he was still so consumed with anger, I just listened and gave him a lot of room. Matt's anger enlivened him. I felt goose bumps and appreciated this much-needed relief of tension, excited that Matt was letting loose. It wasn't the poisonous anger that some patients spew out with no intention of releasing it. This was a purifying rage, a sign that old defenses were melting. I had seen it in others many times before. Loss of faith is so devastating that it can become a wound that will not heal. People try to make do, deny or minimize the loss, or shield it with anger. But it is never really gone. Matt needed to vent his rage; beneath it lay a reservoir of pain he would have to confront if he continued therapy. Deep inside it lay the healing. Such a wound takes trust and time to reopen, and not everyone is willing to do this. But Matt was. In our work together, he dealt with his sense of betrayal, and eventually put much of it behind him. Only then could he redefine his spiritual views. He never felt comfortable using the term *God*. But in the context of seeking inner guidance and communicating with his higher self, Matt became willing to pray.

Together, in my office, we sat beside each other on the couch and closed our eyes. For me prayer is a joining of hearts and minds, all distancing gone. It is innately therapeutic, a humble act, that can prepare us to see.

"What should I do first?" Matt asked. He sounded uneasy. Because it had taken so much for him to come this far, I wanted to keep everything as straightforward as possible. "Simply pray to make contact with your higher self," I said. "Then listen for a response. It might be an image, a sense of knowing, or even a voice. The exact form doesn't matter. What's crucial is that you learn to recognize it. Let's just sit quietly together in prayer and see what happens."

A few minutes passed. As is often true, the response Matt received wasn't highly dramatic—no burning bush or voice of God. Rather, it was a subtle shift, a peaceful feeling that he could now return to. When we opened our eyes again, he knew that by taking this step old barriers had been broken down; a door had opened.

Matt began praying every day but not in the formal tradition of his church. He was finding his own style, was able to ask for direction and then listen to the guidance. In the past, he often had difficulty with decisions, depending on his friends and wife to advise him. Now he was training himself to make his own choices.

Early one morning Matt's son, who was in film school in New York, called to say he had a terrible stomachache. Sensing that something was seriously wrong, Matt prayed for guidance. Immediately, he knew he had to fly to New York right away. Both his wife and son felt he was overreacting, that it was probably nothing more than a flu. But he canceled his classes at UCLA, hopped on a plane, and was at his son's Greenwich Village apartment by evening. Shortly after arriving, his son's stomachache got so bad that Matt rushed him to the emergency room. Diagnosed with an acute case of appendicitis, his son had surgery that night. Because Matt had prayed and acted on the response, not dissuaded by anyone else's opinions, he was able to be at his son's side during this crucial time.

As a source of guidance, prayers have enormous worth, particularly during emergencies. There may be times when we feel compelled to pray, to send out a loud and clear SOS. We reach a crisis point with nowhere to turn. In these situations, we must speak our needs—pray with a specific intent. Instead of saying simply "Thy will be done" or reciting the Saint Francis prayer, we can request direct intervention as long as we aren't too explicit about what an acceptable response would be.

Recently, my father had a health scare. For months he had been experiencing excruciating lower back pain from arthritis. Stoic by nature, he kept this mostly to himself, but finally consulted an orthopedic surgeon, who recommended surgery—an extensive procedure that could require months of recuperation with no guarantee it would succeed. Nevertheless, my father saw it as his only hope and wanted to schedule surgery as soon as possible. I panicked, intuitively certain that surgery would only lead to trouble. But nothing I said to my father made any difference.

I didn't know what to do. It was like watching a train wreck about to happen and not being able to stop it. The person I loved most in the world was, I believed, in danger. Frantic, one morning I headed toward a rock jetty about a half mile down the beach from my house. It's a place where I've gone for years to think, or sometimes pray, and watch the sailboats glide out of the channel from the Marina into the open ocean. Sitting on a bench, I had a panoramic view of the Malibu coast, but nonetheless felt utterly alone. Gazing out on the still, blue water, the only thought I had was, I can't do this by myself. I need somebody to help me get through to my father. And so I prayed. Quietly weeping, trying not to draw attention to myself, I stayed glued to that spot for about a half hour. When I left, there was still no answer. But by then I'd relaxed, and was ready to begin work.

Immersed in my writing the rest of the afternoon, I forgot about the prayer. Then, toward five, the phone rang. It was my cousin Bobby, an orthopedic surgeon who lived in Ohio. I hadn't heard from him for over a year. The following week, he said, he was coming to L.A. for a medical convention and wanted to have dinner with me and my father. In all the confusion, I had never thought to ask my cousin for advice. My prayer had been answered, and so quickly. Bobby, an expert on the surgical treatment of backs, was one of the few people my father would listen to.

Thank God for Bobby's visit. As one doctor to another, he spoke to my father about the advantages and disadvantages of surgery. There were alternatives worth pursuing, he said. Of course I'd mentioned some of these to my father, although his surgeon had not, but my father could be stubborn. Yes, I was a doctor, but I was also his daughter. He needed to hear this from someone other than me. Bobby was perfect, a close relative and an orthopedic specialist. My father listened to and followed the advice that both Bobby and I urged on him—a course of medication that, as it turned out, saved him from major surgery—and his pain is now much improved. He is even back at Hillcrest Country Club again, at lunch and on the weekends, playing golf. I was grateful and touched that my prayer had been acknowledged.

Although we aren't guaranteed such direct response, the very act of prayer can be healing. It can instill faith, replenish our compassion when our well has run dry, provide stamina to survive even impossible circumstances. Try not to get locked into dictating the manner in which your prayers are answered. Help comes in a multitude of forms, some more obvious than others: a simple word from a friend or teacher, a dream, a message conveyed by a movie or book at just the right moment. By setting into motion our connection with the mystical, power flows where most needed. Our prayers send out an intuitive signal, a calling to heal.

When Grace, a patient who had recently immigrated from the Philippines, came down with bronchial pneumonia, I didn't know how to help. She was much too sick to have visitors or even talk on the phone. In our last conversation, Grace said, "Please pray for me," and I did. Later, she told me that during the two weeks when she was running a high fever, I often came to her in dreams. Grace appreciated the power of prayer, felt that my presence comforted her. I believe that through my prayers I was able to make contact with Grace, to lend her intuitive support from a distance until she was well again.

Prayer is a means of invoking wisdom, of strengthening our spiritual and intuitive link, of healing. It's never appropriate to pray for material gain—that would be a misuse of power. By asserting that love is the goal, however, we actualize the purpose of prayer, place intuition in proper perspective. Rich in meaning, elegant and pure, prayer is a resource that can prepare us all to see.

When prayer is used in combination with altar, ritual, and meditation, we are beginning to build an intuitive lifestyle. These tools beautifully complement each other and can be practiced individually or together. Rather than considering intuition as an isolated, mechanical skill, we can make it a cherished, integral part of our lives.

Starting this journey with a strong foundation, we're better able to navigate the road ahead. There's a magic in the beginning, a readiness, an anticipation. Just by taking the first steps forward, a chain reaction may take place. You meet exactly the right people at the right time who can guide you. Opportunities present themselves that are perfectly suited to your needs. A flow is established. However, the timing may differ for each of us; we must all proceed at our own pace.

If you're curious about intuition yet uncertain about what direction to take, this is a period to experiment and see how far you want to go. Expose yourself to different teachers. Hear what they have to say; digest it. Take what makes sense; discard the rest. It doesn't matter whether you've had an intuitive experience before. This could be the start.

Perhaps you've been skeptical but want to take a second look. It's important that you keep a critical eye, remain discerning. Unfortunately, intuitive fraud is rampant, and many people are too easily taken in or fall prey to deception. But also be careful not to let charlatans destroy what is worthy and true. There are fine jewels to be found, intuitives who are honest, talented, sincere. In your quest for truth, consider speaking to them before you write everyone off, then draw your own conclusions. Possibly something of value is awaiting you here, too.

Or you might be one of those people who immediately takes to intuition. It intrigues you, you're excited, there's not a moment to waste. Opening up is something you've been yearning for for a long time. Just remember, there's no urgency. Enthusiasm is wonderful, but as the great Tibetan saint Milarepa taught, "Hasten slowly." Give yourself moments to pause, to take stock, keeping your feet firmly planted on the ground. Remember your own strength; be wary of teachers who want to usurp your power or make claims about how much they know. Stay simple in your search.

What has drawn me most to intuition is its mystery. Ever changing and often elusive, the better I come to understand it the more there is to learn. The same is true of meditation, altar, ritual, and prayer. These aren't static techniques. Their power is fluid, transparent, always offering us something new. Windows through which we can glimpse truths, they reveal intuitive knowledge. By regularly utilizing these practices, we can acclimate to intuition and strengthen ourselves to avoid being blinded by the exquisite brightness of our new sight. Rather, we can bathe naked in the brilliance, extending our arms wide open to receive it all.

CHAPTER EIGHT

The Alchemy
of Dreams

Man is a genius when he is dreaming.
—AKIRA KUROSAWA

At different moments in my life, I am a psychiatrist, a lover, a friend, and a daughter, but at the core of my being I am most of all a dreamer. Whatever I'm doing, I hear my dreams echoing in a distant chamber, attuned to the rhythms of my body and the very substance of the earth. Dreams are my compass and my truth; they guide me and link me to the divine. They call out to me in an intimate whisper, always knowing how to find me. They speak my real name.

When my mother was five months pregnant with me, she required emergency surgery. Gigantic fibroid tumors had grown on the outside of her uterus, pressing inward, threatening to harm me. Something had to be done, and fast. But surgery could be complicated: The physical trauma of the procedure might result in bleeding or infection, or cause my mother to abort. Since my life was at stake, however, she had to risk it. She was put under general anesthesia and they operated.

Many years later, during a hypnotic regression session, I recalled this experience. So vivid was the interminable banging, the sound of metal grating against metal, the tearing of my mother's skin, that my ears buzzed from the intensity. This was my first awareness of being alive. I was awakened prematurely in a dark, claustrophobic space, with warm, salty fluid swishing past a strange form that felt like it was me—yet I didn't recognize myself. I struggled to escape from this alien place and return home, but I couldn't even begin to picture where that was. I was unable to break free; the deafening noise grew louder. I panicked and fell into a dream:

> I'm standing in front of a small clapboard farmhouse surrounded by green rolling hills. A robust blond woman with long braided hair, about thirty, cheerfully greets me. There is something strikingly familiar about her—the white organdy apron, her soothing voice and touch. I'm relieved to see her, certain I know her from somewhere else. I respond just as strongly to her husband and two teenage sons. These people feel like my real family; this is my home. We all talk and laugh for hours, easing the tension of my predicament.

In my prenatal dreams, this loving family continued to keep me company until I was born. Although I never learned who they were or where they came from, their presence was always sustaining. I ached to remain with them, but they advised that for the time being it was best I stay where I was. Reassuring me that I would be all right and that they loved me, these dear people, particularly the woman, talked me through the remainder of my often disturbing stay in the womb.

For me, these dreams are absolutely real; they are not metaphors, symbolic representations, or wish fulfillments. Currently, in fact, scientific evidence suggests that memory, dreaming, and REM sleep exist in utero. Also, research indicates that sensation can be remembered in a primitive form, and that the senses can function before they are completely matured anatomically. Brain life is thought to begin between twenty-eight and thirty-two weeks of gestation, but the hormone connected with memory traces is in operation by the forty-ninth day after conception, and the very first cells of the central nervous system appear at twenty-two days. Furthermore, at six weeks the internal ear has begun to develop; at eight weeks, the external ear has formed. Thus some scientists now argue that fetuses have the equipment to register the earliest intrauterine experiences, and that the memory of embryonic days can later be recovered. Though perhaps they would concede that I dreamed in the womb, they would surely have difficulties accepting that as a fetus I received visitations from another realm. Here, it comes down to a matter of belief. I can only tell you what I intuitively know to be true.

My before-birth dreams didn't stay with me throughout my childhood. In fact, it wasn't until I was an adult that I was able to recall them at all. I had to backtrack and retrieve my memories, to remind myself what happened at that time. If I hadn't done this, a huge piece of my personal history would have been erased—the family who cared for me, and the love and encouragement I received would have been blanked out. But reclaiming this information, I could now better understand my beginnings, chronicle the onset of my intuitive life, and appreciate the roots of my prescience. It all began, I realized, with my earliest dreams, when in the womb I was so abruptly awakened.

By tracing your own dreams, no matter how far in the past, you can fill in missing gaps in your life. This should come as no surprise to us: We spend about ninety minutes a night dreaming, and that is some five years in the course of a lifetime. Dreams are characteristic of our species; nearly every mammal has them. Though often fleeting, dreams hold compelling information—about your childhood, the present, the future, or even about other realms, which are easier to contact in this state. The great challenge, I believe, is to recover forgotten knowledge. By illuminating hidden memories you can find once again what you have lost.

For years I've been fascinated with why the deeper memory of who we are should be so elusive. Many afternoons, hiking in the canyons, I've watched red-tailed hawks gliding over the dry-lands and have sensed that at one time I could fly. Although reason tells me that here and now I can't, flying in fact seems more natural to me than walking. Images in dreams spark that certainty, bridge the chasm between who we're told we are and who we can be.

Perhaps there is some protective function to remembering slowly. If everything were to come back to us at once, maybe it would be too much. I once saw an intriguing Chinese film about reincarnation in which a woman refuses to drink the "serum of forgetfulness" before she is about to be reborn. Overwhelmed by the recollection of her former lives, she commits suicide.

It may be that we must recover our wisdom gracefully, let it emerge in its own time. Dreaming can facilitate this. A pristine state of awareness, it is a direct line to a place where alchemical gold abounds and nothing is devoid of meaning. Here, time and space are nonexistent; anything is possible. Specific guidance for living your life well lies in your dreams. Like a blank canvas, they provide a medium where both intuition and your unconscious can freely express themselves. You have only to listen.

To me, there is no such thing as a "bad" dream. Even the most terrifying nightmares, the kind where you wake up drenched in sweat, your heart pounding, are meant to be helpful. They point out areas in your psyche that need attention, and there is much to be learned from them. Emotionally intense, illuminating some of your worst fears, this kind of dream can be extremely cathartic. Once you face your demons and purge them, they no longer have the power to tyrannize you.

I once had such a nightmare when I hadn't been in a relationship for a long while and was feeling particularly vulnerable: With apparently deadly intent, two gangster types broke into my home. The man had slicked-back greasy hair; the woman was loud-mouthed and rude, blowing cigarette smoke in my face. They both strode into the living room, where I was sitting, as if they owned the house and me as well. Terrified of being killed, I froze, too intimidated to do anything to defend myself. But instead of physically harming me, in a jeering tone they announced, in unison, "Judith, you will never love or be loved by any man again." I awoke from the dream in tears.

This is an example of a nightmare that turned out to be of value. It was a reminder that my fears were once again getting the best of me; I knew enough not to take it literally. Instead I saw it as a message that an old, all-too-familiar and painful pattern had resurfaced—one of feeling abandoned, unloved, and alone—that required some of my sympathetic attention. Rather than writing it off as just a "bad dream," or berating myself for having such feelings, I acknowledged and readdressed my fear. Because I did so, it no longer threatened to surge out of control as fear tends to do when it remains unconscious. My dream apprised me of the obstacle I was facing so I could deal with it and move on.

Not all dreams are intuitive, and yet I believe that each one carries a personalized message that we need to hear. In one of Leonardo da Vinci's notebooks, he asks, "Why does an eye see a thing more clearly in dreams than the imagination does while awake?" The answer lies in the purity of the medium in which dreams express themselves. They speak truths that are unpolluted by the incessant rambling of our minds. With that interference gone, dreams provide a natural conduit for intuition With all channels open, we can receive information that was previously obscured.

Throughout the years, I've been a collector of dreams. I'll jump at any opportunity to hear one. I've recorded hundreds of my own dreams and heard many more from patients, family, and friends. There is a wise economy to the way dreams are constructed; not a single detail is wasted or too extravagant to include. To me, dreams are our truest signature: I can usually learn more about someone from a single dream than from an entire hour of talking.

Once I went out with a man, an accountant, who appeared extremely conservative and uptight. It was our first date, and I was sure we weren't going to get along. Trying to make conversation, I told him I worked a lot with dreams in my practice. His face lit up and he asked, "Can I tell you a recurring dream that I've had?" "Sure," I said smugly, certain it would validate my assumptions about him. I couldn't have been more wrong. In his dream, he told me, he was always faced with the same dilemma: His apartment was flooded and he didn't know what to do. Yet the solution he came up with impressed me. Putting on scuba gear, he learned to navigate underwater with such facility and ease that he was more comfortable than ever before.

As I understood it, the dream was a shining comment on his flexibility, the skill he had at solving problems, and his ability to acclimate to unexpected situations, all stellar qualities. After hearing the dream, I was curious to get to know him better. Although we never entered into a romantic relationship, he has become a trusted friend.

During my practice, I have come to see dreams as falling into two major categories: psychological and intuitive. Most dreams, in my experience, are the former, with themes aimed at identifying and sorting through unclear emotions. Intuitive dreams occur less frequently and are distinct in a variety of ways. Many times, for instance, you might experience intuitive dreams that have nothing to do with you at all. Or if they do reflect your inner conflicts, even if they're emotionally charged there is a neutral, matter-of-fact segment that stands out, imparting a message. Unlike psychological dreams, those that are intuitive can be oddly impersonal, marked by their remarkable crispness and clarity. Often I'm left feeling that I have been a witness, as if in a theater watching a movie.

Some intuitive dreams can offer guidance—you observe an event that reveals pertinent information; a person or simply a voice counsels you; the solution to a problem you've been struggling with suddenly becomes evident. Perhaps you may not even remember the details, but you wake up resolved about a previously confusing personal issue. Then there are also precognitive dreams, foreseeing the future. In these, the knowledge I'm receiving or the scenes I observe may be familiar or completely foreign to me. I typically stand apart from these events, detached, seemingly taking dictation from some outside force. Finally, yet another kind of intuitive dream is expressly meant to heal physically (while emotional healing can occur in all dreams). I may have conversations with people I've never met before who offer healing instructions about my patients, family, or me. Sometimes an actual physical healing takes place.

Differentiating these kinds of dreams, I'm still mapping the geography of an often confusing terrain, a geography that's ever changing, constantly revealing more to me. In reality, the different types overlap; their elements are interwoven. I'm always an explorer in this realm. What remains universally true is that the integrity of what dreams have to communicate is flawless: We can trust them.

PSYCHOLOGICAL DREAMS

James badly wanted to have an intuitive dream. Every night, after he organized the following day's work and responded to any unanswered phone calls, he would set a blank notebook strategically by his bed. Everything had to be just right for this sweet-natured businessman but true workaholic who approached his dreams with the same compulsiveness he did the rest of his life. Dropping off to sleep, he was determined that an intuitive dream would come, but each morning he would get up disappointed. Instead, about once a month he would have a recurring dream that wasn't intuitive at all.

It always took place in Atlantic City, on the beach near his childhood summer home. He is walking barefoot in the sand when the weather changes abruptly and a ferocious storm moves in. The landscape turns from golden to an ominous gray. Gusts of wind whip over the water as the waves grow larger and larger. Fighting against the wind, the water sucking him backward, James is about to drown. Each time the dream ends at this moment, and he wakes up, panicked and exhausted.

This same dream had been returning since he was a child, but recently it had become more frequent. James had never dealt with it before. "After all," he reasoned, "it's only a dream. Thank goodness it isn't real." A tough-minded financier, he prided himself on being self-sufficient, solving the critical problems at hand, and living in the present. Psychotherapy or dream analysis wasn't for him; he had come to me to learn how to become intuitive to help him with business decisions.

I'm always amazed to hear dreams with the power of the one James told, especially when the dreamer has little appreciation of its significance. Unknowingly, James laid himself bare and revealed his terror of an unidentified but haunting influence. Such fear is never without meaning. Encountering it for the first time can be one of the most exciting and transformative junctures in psychotherapy, through which enormous change may occur. But it is only a beginning.

James was naive. He expected intuition to be handed to him in a neatly wrapped package that he could simply open without looking any further into himself. But, as is true for many people, to become intuitive often requires that you do some searching introspection. When you have more pressing emotional issues to address, intuition may become obscured. This dream was imploring James to confront the source of the fear that had been overwhelming him for so long.

"Be careful not to jump ahead of yourself," I said. "Deal with the dream you've been given and see where it takes you."

James was skeptical. "I don't really believe in dreams," he said. "What good will it do me?"

"Well," I explained, "most of all, dreams send you messages. They can alert you to a part of yourself that may be shut off. Over the years, important memories can be forgotten, some of them traumatic. They tend to bind up energy so that it's not available for other things. Once you address these memories, energy can be freed. Of course, you'll feel much better in general, but there is also more room for intuition to come in."

James appeared to be absorbing my words slowly. Though not entirely convinced, he agreed to take a look at his dream.

"Dreams are like mirrors," I continued. "They can reflect some aspect of who you are now or else may focus on your past. The more emotion you have about them, the better. Even if you're frightened, stay with it. The strength of your feelings can lead us to the answer."

"Is there something I should do?" he asked. "How should we start?"

"First," I told him, "I'd like you to relive the entire dream while you're with me. Report every single detail. Take me right there with you. And stay aware of your impressions or feelings, no matter how unusual they seem. Try to relax and find a comfortable position to sit in. Then close your eyes and take a few deep, slow breaths."

I paused. Realizing that this was going to be new for James, I was prepared to let him ease into it at his own pace. That leap from ordinary consciousness into a dream state can feel awkward to a beginner, and especially to someone who is experiencing this transition for the first time. When you straddle two very different realities at once, the secret is to stay aware of both. You are totally immersed in your dream, yet simultaneously you witness and report what takes place—a balancing act you can refine with practice. Despite his skepticism and inexperience, James was a natural. In no time he was back on that same beach again, in the midst of the storm. As if the dream had just been waiting for him, he was compelled to plunge straight into his fear. This isn't always the right move, however: If emotions like fear are faced prematurely, some people get so overwhelmed they shut down. But I trusted his instincts and my own sense that he was ready, and I didn't intervene. Nervously clutching both hands together, James described his feelings.

"I'm so heavy. I want to get away but I can't. It's hard to move."

"Good," I encouraged him. "You're getting close to something. I know it's difficult, but stay in the dream. You've never taken it further than this. Let's see what happens."

"The waves are crashing all around me. I'm scared. The current is pulling me under. Water's coming into my mouth and nose. I'm choking." James's voice suddenly sounded small, desperate, like a young child's. That was the clue I had been waiting for. I followed it, a bridge back into time that could lead us to the origin of his fear.

"James, how old do you feel now?"

He winced. "It's strange," he said. "About eight, maybe even younger."

"All right. Now, try to make a shift. Let your image of the ocean go, and remember what it was like when you were eight. What happened then? Does anything stand out that upsets you?" A few moments passed, and the same child's voice returned.

"Oh God," he said, suddenly looking very pale. "I haven't thought about this for over twenty years. That was when my father was drinking. It was such an awful time. He'd sometimes punish me for no reason and then lock me in my room for hours. I would cry and cry but no one was there."

"Where was your mother? Wasn't she around?"

James let out a deep sigh. "I'm just not sure. When my father got mad, she'd disappear. I guess she was pretty afraid of him, too."

"Did he ever hurt you physically?"

"You mean did he ever break my bones?" James asked. "No . . . I don't think so. But he used to make me bend over and strap my buttocks and ankles with a thick leather belt. It would hurt so much. Sometimes I was black and blue for days. But it never got any worse than that. And he was like this for only about two years. When I was ten, he quit drinking for good. I remember that clearly because he and my mom would always argue about his drinking. It was a big deal for him to stop. Afterward, every-thing changed. He didn't hit me anymore. My father was nice again, back to his old self."

Placed in this context, much of James's behavior now made better sense. Workaholism was the perfect front for him to hide behind. Frantically busy all the time, rarely taking vacations, staying so numb that he didn't have to feel or delve into the past, he had the typical profile of an abused child. James's dream, however, provided the trigger for his recall. The terrify-ing waves symbolized the danger and helplessness he felt about his father. Only by articulating the circumstances of his abuse and then dealing with his feelings could James begin to heal.

It took many months to sort this all through. Our initial ses-sion was just the first step. The experience of child abuse needs to be approached delicately: Such memories can be devastating, and require time to sink in. But once James was willing to re-trace his steps, to face the reality of his father's actions and the impact they'd had on him, his recurring dream eventually stopped. Not surprisingly, he had his first intuitive dream soon afterward. James was being led to intuition even though it didn't come as directly as he had expected.

What fascinates me about psychological dreams is that many of them are common to us all. No matter how different we may appear to be, our inner struggles and needs are fundamentally similar. And so are the symbols our unconscious often uses to ex-press itself—at times the format or themes in our dreams are identical to those of many other people.

For instance, whether you are male or female, you may have dreamed either that you have given birth or watched someone give birth at a point when something in your life has been ful-filled: a project is completed, you start a new job, or come into your own in some way. Whatever the circumstances, a birth dream is an affirmation of your growth and achievements.

Or perhaps in a dream you triumph over impossible odds. There is a flood, landslide, or storm and you survive. You get the courage to leave an unhealthy relationship. You rebuild your home after it has been leveled. You beat your opponent in a strenuous game of sports. These dreams are a reflection of your inner strength, a message of encouragement to believe in yourself, an assurance that no matter how trying the situation, you can make it through.

Then there are those classic dreams—almost all of us have had them—in which your fears, anxieties, and insecurities surface. Do you recall the nerve-wracking scenario where you show up for an exam without anything to write with, or you arrive late and are locked out? The test is unbelievably difficult, yet you think you know the answers but can't even get in the door. Or how about the time you are chased by some horrifying pursuer? He's so close you can almost feel him breathing down your neck. But no matter how fast you run you can't seem to get away. Or the panic situation of driving your car down a steep grade and suddenly realizing that your brakes don't work? Frantically pumping them has no effect. The car's careening out of control but there's nothing you can do.

Recently, I had an anxiety dream at a point when I was feeling completely blocked in my writing, unsure about what new direction to take. In the dream, I'm shopping around for a new computer. Browsing in one of those chain stores that sell electronic equipment, I place my old computer down nearby on the floor. It holds all the material I've ever written on its hard drive, and I've foolishly made no backup disks. Absorbed in the new computers, I temporarily forget my old one. In that brief lapse, an unkempt, wild-eyed vagrant grabs it and goes tearing out of the store. Watching him, I'm so shocked that my heart practically stops. Years of hard work down the drain! I rush after him but it's too late. The man is gone.

This dream embodied some of my root anxieties: that I would never be able to write again, let alone in a fresh way, and that all the material I had written thus far would get lost. I strongly identified with the writer who was held hostage by his maniacal tormentor, brilliantly played by Kathy Bates, in the film *Misery*. Page by page, in front of his very eyes, she burns up the only copy of the novel he had been working on for the past several years. A comparable anguish for a writer I could not conceive.

I realized that this wasn't an intuitive dream because it too perfectly depicted my own inner dynamics (although the next day I did double-check to see if I'd backed up all my material—which I had). Rather, it was a message to have faith in my creativity, not to allow it to fall prey to my insecurities (represented by the thief), nor out of neglect (the drifting of my attention) to sacrifice what I had already attained in my writing in the search to try something new. Reflexively, I tend to resist the unfamiliar, though it may be for the better. The known, even if outmoded, just feels more comfortable to me. But this dream suggested the advantages of change (my interest in the new computers), as long as I honored and kept track of all my work.

The beauty of psychological dreams is that they help you recognize certain of your personality traits, some more productive than others, so you can take action and not become seduced by those that no longer serve you. Such dreams provide the ideal arena to uncover your hidden emotions. Fear, rage, and trauma can build up like toxins, often taking precedence over intuition. Until you get the message and take compassionate stock of yourself, they will endlessly play out in your dreams.

The patterning of our unconscious is perfect. It has infinite patience and knows exactly what we need, even if our rational minds don't agree. It also knows how to prioritize. As you discard the old, as you clean house, your intuitive instincts have more space to thrive. Of course it is possible to be intuitive and never do this. But for scrupulous development, and to use intuition for the highest good, you must strive for transparency. An impeccably tuned instrument is so much more precious than a neglected one, but it requires diligence and care. And you deserve the same. Although psychological dreams may not seem as glamorous as those that are intuitive, they help you to stay conscious of your motivations so that you have the most to offer. The soulfulness of being intuitive, for me, its greatest joy, is the giving of the gift in the most meticulous manner possible.

GUIDANCE DREAMS

*Fire is raging behind me. I'm in a fertile field, running
as fast as I can. Flames are devouring the land. I must
get away before they devour me. Now the fire is about to
overtake me; the heat is climbing up my back. The stench
of the smoke is nauseating and I can hardly breathe. Suddenly I hear an authoritative but oddly removed, genderless voice whisper, "Stop running. The fire can't hurt you
if you face it." Out of sheer exhaustion, I decide to take
this advice. The moment I turn around and look straight
into the fire, the flames disappear.*

This dream came to me at a time when I was very angry with a
colleague of mine. We had once been close, but when we started
running a clinic together our ideas clashed; tension was building
between us. Instead of addressing the problem, we were each
making heroic efforts to get along, but deep down I was
seething. Then came this dream.

The message was direct: Unless I confronted my anger—
which had grown so fierce that I had to use every ounce of self-
control not to explode when I was with him—the fertile field,
representing our once-thriving friendship and the success of the
clinic, would be ruined. But there was pride on both our parts.
We had taken some firm positions about certain policies, and we
each felt justified.

The dream, which graphically portrayed the intensity and potential destructiveness of my anger, was telling me that it was
both safe and essential to deal with this feeling, that the fire
couldn't hurt me once I did. I rarely get this furious with anyone. But at those times, my rage often seems all-encompassing.
I either bottle it up or try to smooth it over (even though I know
better), afraid that it will consume me. The instructive voice I
heard, whose detached but forceful tone was a tip-off that the

dream was intuitive, reminded me that this was a needless worry. I was being snagged by an old, unhealthy pattern, my tendency to stubbornly hold on to anger for too long when I think I'm right. Pointing out the futility of my position, the dream also depicted the mayhem it could reap.

This was a delicate situation. I knew how important it was to air our differences. But instead of waiting for him to make the first move, I decided to take the initiative. Tempted to resolve this whole mess right away, that morning I almost made an emergency call to his beeper. But something stopped me. Luckily, on an instinct, I first phoned my close friend Berenice, who studied meditation with me.

"It's amazing that you called," she said, cackling with laughter on the other end of the line. "Last night I had the clearest dream about you. We were both sitting in a room with our teacher, but he never spoke a word to you. Instead, he looked over at me and said, 'Tell Judith not to do anything now. She should let some time pass and allow everything to sink in.' I didn't have the faintest idea what he meant. Now it makes perfect sense."

The directness of Berenice's dream stunned me: I couldn't have asked for a more definite response to my dilemma. So despite my impatience to set things straight, I took a few days to cool off. This gave me a chance to vent my anger privately, so that when my colleague and I met I wouldn't inadvertently dump everything on him. Once I had strategized, and come up with some new solutions and defined areas where I was willing to be flexible, I invited him out to lunch.

"I realize that I've been stubborn lately," I admitted, "I want us to make a new beginning." My colleague's face, tense moments before, now relaxed.

"You know, you're right," he said. "You've been pretty hard to get along with . . . but so have I. Let's talk things through."

The impeccable timing and elegant interaction between my dream of the fire and my friend's dream of my teacher reaffirmed for me the strength and diversity of the guidance available to us all. You can actively seek it out. Whether you appeal to a beneficent force outside yourself or to an inherent inner wisdom, dreams can respond directly or through others to help you.

There is a profound mystery to dreams, a power that can work wonders in your life if you let it. You begin to expand your options by recognizing the refined interplay between the guidance received in dreams and your waking awareness. Just because you've reached a dead end intellectually doesn't mean the answer isn't there. Your mind has limits you need to respect. By looking to your dreams, possibilities can appear that you may not have considered.

You can do this in any situation. When my mother was dying, it was the guidance of dreams that gave me the strength and wisdom to get through. Just know that if you are having a difficult time, your dreams can give you wise advice. This is also true of less severe circumstances. Maybe you have reached a turning point; you want to make a change but aren't sure what to do. Or maybe you are thinking of switching jobs, entering a new relationship, making a geographical move. Dreams can clarify your choices.

Whenever I'm confused about something in my life and need direction, especially when I'm too emotionally involved with a situation to do a clear intuitive reading myself, I write a specific request on a piece of paper and then place it on a table beside my bed. This formalizes the process. In the morning, I record my dreams and look to them for the answer. If it doesn't come right away, I repeat my request each night until I'm satisfied. I recommend the same approach to my patients, and you can do it, too.

Ellen felt lost. A successful child psychologist who had recently turned fifty, she'd been in private practice for over twenty years and had grown dissatisfied with her work. After reviewing possible alternatives, she found nothing that appealed to her. Ellen came to me as a patient, following a year of soul searching, afraid that it was too late to make a change, feeling trapped and depressed. Since she had always been an avid dreamer, I suggested that she turn to her dreams for guidance.

Though Ellen was familiar with analyzing her dreams, she had never actually asked them for advice, or thought of herself as intuitive. If dreams offered help, she gladly listened. But this happened infrequently; for her they weren't a consistently dependable source. Now, every evening before she went to sleep, she began jotting down one simple request: *Please help me find a meaningful direction in my career.* For a few weeks we went over her dreams. It seemed that she was getting no answers. Nonetheless, a strange pattern started to unfold. Apparently unrelated, tagged onto each dream, would be an unusual phrase, whimsical language such as "the pink brontosaurus," "an upside-down sky" or "a gleaming strand of purple pearls."

These phrases had a luminous quality that popped right out at me, made the hairs on the back of my neck stand up. My reaction told me that we were on to something. But I still didn't quite know what it meant. "Keep a list of these phrases," I said. "We'll take a look at it together and see what we come up with." The result was over five pages of expressions that sounded as if they came out of Dr. Seuss.

"Does this have any significance for you?" I asked.

"Only that I've always been fascinated by unusual words," Ellen said. "When I was a teenager I used to collect them, pin them up on my refrigerator door, and repeat certain ones aloud just to make myself laugh." A wave of goose flesh rippled up my arms. I suddenly understood. The dreams were instructing Ellen to write.

Looking brighter than I'd ever seen her, she loved the idea. That same afternoon, she rushed home, picked up a pen, and started putting her thoughts down on paper. Quirky, offbeat expressions such as those in her dreams flooded onto the page. She couldn't get them down fast enough. Combining her skill as a child psychologist and her flair for words, she began to weave together stories, which later became a delightful children's book. This was a perfect creative outlet. Ellen's guidance dreams uncovered an untapped talent that brought her great joy. Rejuvenated by her writing, her clinical work also took on a new life. It wasn't necessary for Ellen to change her profession, she just needed a counterpoint to complement it.

Ellen was proof that you don't have to have any previous intuitive experience to receive guidance dreams. Although their messages aren't always spelled out, if you stay aware of what they are trying to communicate, the clues are always there. As with Ellen's dream, the answers may be enormously creative. The more attuned you become to deciphering them, the easier it gets.

When you're analyzing guidance dreams, there are some specific intuitive clues to look for. Certain material zings with energy and grabs your attention. It may be only a single word or image, or perhaps an entire segment. Thoroughly search your dream for such sections. Then write them down to see how they are related to your original question. Always stay aware of your body's responses—a sudden wave of goose bumps, a chill, the hair on your neck standing up, a flushing of your face, sweating or a quickening of heartbeat or breath. This is your body's way of telling you that you're on the right track. Sometimes when the answer is more obvious, you can experience an immediate "Ah-ha!" feeling, as though a bright light has suddenly been flipped on in a room. (Of course, these varied responses can help you pick out essential segments in all types of dreams.) But no matter how distinct the message, it's up to you to listen.

I have a friend who wanted to open up a small coffeehouse and bookstore in Venice Beach, but he wasn't sure the timing was right. "Why don't you ask for guidance in a dream?" I said. He thought that was a terrific suggestion and proceeded to write down his dreams for the next several nights. He couldn't recall exact details, but each morning he was left with the sinking feeling that entering a business now would be a big mistake.

Though extremely intuitive, this friend could also be bull-headed, and he went ahead with his plans anyway. Every stage of the process, beginning with getting a loan, turned out to be painful and frustrating. Ultimately, he had to close his store after only eight months because he wasn't making it financially.

Like my friend, I also learned the hard way to take my intuitions seriously. Years before, when I hadn't heeded my premonition about my patient Christine's suicide attempt, there were almost tragic results after she overdosed on the pills I'd prescribed. During the several weeks of her coma, I had much time to think about what happened. That was the turning point, reawakening me to the importance of intuition and the price I would pay for disregarding it. Now if I'm stuck and don't know what direction to take with a patient, I head straight to my dreams—the strongest intuitive connection I have—or they come to me spontaneously.

The advice I receive from dreams doesn't have to be earth shattering to be valuable. For instance, the other night I dreamed that a schizophrenic woman I was especially fond of, whom I'd been treating since I first opened my practice, abruptly went off her medications. In the past, whenever she had done this on her own, the results had always been disastrous. About once a year I'd receive a phone call from some emergency room in the middle of the night, saying that she was blatantly psychotic and needed to be hospitalized. I didn't want this painful and demoralizing pattern to repeat itself. Although I had no other reason to believe that anything was wrong, I still called her the next day to check it out. My dream, unfortunately, had been accurate. Once again she had run out of her medication and failed to renew the prescription. Luckily I succeeded in convincing her to go to the pharmacy and resume treatment. Spurred on by my dream, I was able to intervene immediately and spare her psychiatric hospitalization.

Just as I was alerted to contact my patient, your guidance dreams also can often be red flags warning you of danger. Even if you haven't formally developed your intuitive abilities, at certain times of need an internal alarm system goes off to protect you. Guidance dreams can specifically tell you how and when to avoid being harmed.

A few years ago, my friend Lisa was traveling with several friends in an old VW van from Taos, New Mexico, back to California. At midnight, fatigued from driving twelve hours, they pulled over somewhere in the northern Arizona desert and set up camp. The sky was crystal clear, the moon full, the air crisp and cool. They each crawled into their sleeping bags on the desert floor.

As soon as Lisa fell asleep, she dreamed she saw a pair of bright headlights coming toward her down a winding desert trail. A four-wheel-drive jeep pulled up next to her and a ranger in full government uniform got out. In a serious tone, he advised, "You and your friends had better get back into your van. A huge dust storm is about to come through this area. It isn't safe to stay outdoors." Lisa didn't see anything unusual about his visit and thanked him for the tip. He said good-bye, climbed back into his jeep, and drove away.

When Lisa woke up, the night was perfectly still and there was no sign of a storm approaching. But she had always been interested in dreams and knew enough to pay attention to them. She immediately woke her friends and, despite their grumbling, managed to gather them into the van. A few hours later the van began to rock back and forth in winds of over fifty miles an hour, and spiral currents of dust and sand whipped through the desert until dawn. The flying debris was so thickly caked on the windshield that it was impossible for them to see out, but thanks to Lisa's dream they were all safe.

Guidance dreams such as these aren't unique to our culture. The Aboriginals of Australia have considered them sacred for over fifty thousand years. In their vision of life, time has two dimensions: our everyday reality and a spiritual plane known as the Dreamtime. When tribal members are ill or in trouble, selected persons may send healing messages or warnings through their dreams. In other instances, Dreamtime ceremonies are performed by shamans and through them ancient teachings are relayed. The Aboriginals view such guidance as so completely natural that they use it to determine tribal law.

In the Australian film *The Last Wave,* a lawyer takes on the defense of a group of tribal Aboriginals accused of murder. Although they are unwilling to reveal to him the circumstances surrounding the crime, the lawyer begins to receive the needed information in his dreams. The problem is that he doesn't know how to decipher them. Frustrated at his clients' silence, he turns to one of the men and asks, "Don't you know how much trouble you're in?" Coolly, the tribal member looks back at him with shining black eyes and responds, "No, man. You're the one who's in trouble. You've forgotten the meaning of your dreams."

Native Americans also honor their dreams. Their vision-quest ritual, a solitary or group journey into nature, is an appeal for a revelatory dream or vision for the purpose of healing, solving a problem, finding a guide, or facilitating a rite of passage, such as a boy passing from puberty to manhood. Vision quests are intentionally rugged and often involve fasting for many days or sleeping on the ground unprotected, sometimes naked, even during rainstorms or freezing weather. Exposed to the elements, the body quickly becomes exhausted. In this weakened state, however, the mind is less chaotic and thus more susceptible to dreams. Only after the vision has made itself known is the quest considered successful.

In our culture, dreaming has become a lost art that needs to be revived. By listening to your dreams, you can receive instructions on how best to maneuver through life's obstacles. They are a deep, instinctual response to your innermost conflicts and needs. Over the years, I have trained myself to pay close attention to dreams, and so can you. They aren't distributed only to a gifted few. The secret lies in your own belief. Once you take the first step and allow for that possibility, guidance will be waiting for you.

PRECOGNITIVE DREAMS

In some dreams you can receive specific guidance about the future, though the message may be presented to you in various forms. To recognize such precognitive dreams, there are a number of clues. Often the imagery is startlingly vivid: You watch an event unfold that might be totally unrelated to you, or you're given information about your own future, or you wake up knowing details about events that haven't yet occurred. You may be given information clarifying times, dates, places, or the direction your life is going to take. More than a simple road map, precognitive dreams can be a precursor of blessings to come or offer underlying meaning about more difficult times. Though you may be given a preview of a totally unfamiliar situation involving unknown persons, most likely you will have precognitive dreams about yourself or those you love. This is especially true of mothers and their children.

In the fall of 1989, I witnessed such an intuitive bond between a mother, her son, and a dolphin named Bee. At the time, I was having severe neck pain from a bulging cervical disc. My friend Stephan Schwartz of Mobius told me about a pilot program in the Florida Keys that was proving quite successful. Patients with a variety of illnesses swam with the dolphins in an open marine park. As a result of this contact, their symptoms improved. Since I had gotten very little relief from traditional medical treatments and had always been fascinated by dolphins, I leaped at the opportunity. Late in October, I boarded a plane to the Florida Keys, heading for a week-long workshop at the Dolphin Research Center (DRC).

During my stay, I met participants in some of the other programs being conducted there. Among them was a dental hy-
gienist, Cathy, from Enid, Oklahoma. She had brought her
three-year-old son, Deane-Paul, who was born with Down's
syndrome, a form of mental retardation. Even so, he was active
and strong. He ran around with tremendous energy, and exuded
a wonderful life force. Cathy had heard about psychologist
David Nathanson's work enlisting dolphins to teach language
skills to handicapped and emotionally disabled children.

One afternoon, while Cathy, Deane-Paul, and I ate lunch, she
told me about a dream she'd had a month before becoming pregnant. In the dream, she was on a beach in the Caribbean, standing at the shoreline. Suddenly she spotted a pod of nine sleek,
blue-gray wild dolphins swimming between a pair of enormous
monoliths, heading toward her. As they came close, one of the
larger females offered its baby to Cathy, saying, "Please take care
of it for me." As Cathy held the tiny dolphin in her arms, she
watched the pod dive back into the sparkling turquoise water
and disappear.

The dream confused her. She had been to the ocean only once
since she was a little girl, and although she always appreciated
the beauty of dolphins, she had never spent any time with them.
Despite the vividness and matter-of-fact, almost predestined,
quality of the dream, the dolphin's message seemed so unlikely
that Cathy didn't give it much credence. Already the mother of
two young girls, she hadn't planned to have any more children.

A month later, despite using birth control, she unexpectedly
became pregnant with Deane-Paul. From the beginning, he was
lovingly welcomed into her home. Despite Cathy's efforts to
teach him to speak, however, he didn't utter a single word the
first three years of his life. Then one day, Cathy took her kids on
an outing to the zoo. When they stopped at the dolphin pool,
Deane-Paul's face instantly lit up: At the very sight of them, he
became more animated than she'd ever seen him, as if they had
woken him up. Not long afterward she heard about the dolphin

program at the DRC. Inspired by the dream, she decided to enroll her son.

As I spent time with the dolphins, I found that there was something therapeutic about being close to them, about touching the baby-soft texture of their skin and hearing their extraterrestrial sounds. They radiated a joy and goodness that flowed generously from their bodies into mine. The pain in my neck began easing up almost immediately. By the end of the week, I no longer needed to wear my cervical collar for support.

In between my own swims, I would see Deane-Paul, a tiny blond-haired boy with a huge orange life preserver around his waist, frolicking and taking lessons in the pool with a dolphin named Bee. She was a friend to him, an untiring companion who carried story-boards in her mouth week after week, with large words printed on them. David Nathanson, an enormously loving teddy bear of a man with a marvelous sense of humor, would pronounce the words aloud and Deane-Paul would repeat them as his vocabulary grew. Watching, I realized he was not only learning to communicate verbally—I saw that his spirit was coming alive, too.

Deane-Paul and his mother shared a bedroom in an apartment located close to the DRC. One night he woke up, and Cathy couldn't quiet him down; she had never seen him so distraught. He kept crying, "Oh my Bee, oh my Bee," and tried to run out of the house. Eventually he sat curled up beside the front door, calling out to her until dawn. The next morning they received the news: Bee had died during the night.

The love between Deane-Paul and Bee had allowed him to intuit her death in a dream. At first, he fell into a depression, grieving. But his work didn't stop after her death. The relationships he had established with other dolphins helped to sustain him through a very difficult period, although his rapport with them was never as strong as with Bee. And the fact that Bee often came to him in his dreams, where they swam through the clouds together, eased the transition. Deane-Paul's initially intense bonding with Bee had begun his metamorphosis from a mute, withdrawn child into an active little boy who shortly afterward attended kindergarten at a public school and has a vocabulary that is steadily improving.

Cathy's life has also changed. She has learned that prescience is a precious instinct that can be relied upon. It forewarned her of the birth of her son and outlined the direction of his healing. In her dream, she took responsibility for a child; in her life she has helped him to flourish. Cathy hopes to set up a program similar to the DRC that benefits other learning disabled children.

As with Cathy, precognitive dreams can set you on a particular path, serve as a beacon of light on a darkened highway. But glimpsing the future doesn't mean that you don't play an active part in it. Or that you can just sit back and think, Oh well, it's going to happen anyway, I don't have to do a thing. Your dreams are not excuses to become lazy or negligent. Rather, they provide general guidelines for you to follow.

Although some precognitive dreams will become reality regardless of what you do, many merely present possibilities. The ultimate responsibility for your future is yours. At twenty, when I was directed in a dream to become a psychiatrist, I had to go through medical school and a residency program to realize it. If I hadn't done my part, there would have been no impetus for the vision to materialize. As always, you play the largest part in determining what happens in your life; each choice can effect a different outcome. Dreams involving your future don't do the work for you. In the final analysis, you're in partnership with your dreams, and must take the necessary action to bring them to fruition.

Although there are certain messages that we read as metaphors, some dreams can caution us about danger, and it would behoove us to take them literally. They appear out of the blue, tend to be quite specific, and are often unrelated to our feelings or expectations. When we follow their instructions, we are given an edge, an added protection. By sensing danger we often have the power to avoid it.

This was the case with my friend Dennis, who was leaving one morning for a business meeting in New York. Dennis wasn't afraid of flying, so when he dreamed his plane was going to crash he was alarmed. At the airport, while buying his ticket, his anxiety kept building. By the time he was in line to board, his fear was so great that he couldn't get on the plane. It took off without him and later experienced mechanical difficulties. Although there was no crash, the pilot had to make an emergency landing in the Midwest and several passengers were injured.

Sometimes, however, a dream can warn you of danger but you are unable to avert it. On a number of occasions, right before an earthquake hit Los Angeles, I've dreamed about it. I can distinctly feel the earth trembling, hear my sliding glass doors rattling violently in their frames, get physically thrown off balance. I realize at the time that an earthquake is taking place, yet I still remain cool, unaffected, as if I'm a witness to the event, not an active participant—an indication that the dream is intuitive rather than a sign that I'm feeling unsteady about some aspect of my life. The difficulty is that my dream can occur from one to ten days before the actual event. Nor can I always tell the severity of the quake. So although I know it's coming, short of leaving the city for the entire period, there is nothing much I can do other than making sure that my food and water supplies are well stocked.

Similarly, a psychiatrist friend of mine had a dream in which Ronald Reagan, then president, got shot. In it she witnessed the entire scene: the face of the gunman, the location where the shooting took place, and that Reagan survived. "The dream was so real," my friend later told me, "as if I were really there." Shortly afterward, the assassination attempt on Reagan's life actually occurred. Ultimately, my friend was powerless to affect the outcome of the shooting she foresaw.

You don't necessarily play an active role in every precognitive dream, nor are they always directed to you personally. As you become more intuitively astute, certain information just automatically comes through. You are simply a receiver, able to pick up what is about to happen on a collective level as well as in your own life. Such precognitive dreams provide a quick news flash, forewarning you of a future event. There is no need to feel guilty or responsible if you can't prevent what is about to take place. It may not be within your power to act on this knowledge, although in certain circumstances it may help you to become better prepared. Nonetheless, I consider all precognitive dreams a blessing, evidence of the depth of connection we can have with ourselves and the world around us.

In my practice, I have often been guided by them. Shortly after I began working as an intuitive at Mobius in 1984, I had my first precognitive dream involving a future patient. It was about a man named Al whom I'd met at a Christmas party a few days before. In it, a voice announced, in the same genderless calm voice present in many of my intuitive dreams, "Al is going to contact you for an appointment." This surprised me because we had only chatted briefly that night; I had no idea that he was even looking for a therapist. I was both amazed and delighted when within a week Al called.

Over the years, I have had identical dreams about other patients, many of whom I have never met or even heard of before. The format and message of the dream is consistent, only the name changing, and I am always excited when I have one. Without exception, these relationships have a meant-to-be quality and turn out particularly well. There is a special chemistry between us from the start, a compatibility and trust that allows therapy to take off. Dreams such as these are signs to me that I am supposed to work with somebody, for just a few months or for many years. Whatever the length of time, the result is consistently positive, healing for us both. No matter how booked up my schedule is, I always make room to see patients whom I intuitively learn of in this way.

I tend to have precognitive dreams about the patients I feel closest to or have known for a long time. Familiar with their rhythms, I can sense when something is off, dream about them when they're in need. Once, while on a meditation retreat in the

Smoky Mountains with my teacher, I went back to my room to take an afternoon nap. Dead tired from our demanding schedule, I fell into a deep sleep and dreamed that I saw a patient, a recovering alcoholic I had been working with for over two years, huddled in a chair, weeping. A detached observer, I watched her sinking further into despair as the image held strong, even after I woke up. Although I had another psychiatrist covering for me, I felt compelled to give this woman a call. Something important was up that couldn't wait—I had to act. I was glad that I did. It turned out that her boyfriend had just stormed out of the house after they'd had a heated fight. Distraught, she was about to sacrifice five years of hard-earned sobriety and take a drink. But thankfully, she talked her feelings out with me. As a result of my dream, I was able to intervene at a critical moment and point her in a healthier direction.

Precognitive dreams can reflect and enhance the intimacy of all relationships, including those in psychotherapy. My work with patients isn't limited to the hour or two that I spend with them in my office each week. A viable inner connection is established, a channel opened between us, an overall intuitive tie.

Not long ago I had a dream in which an exceptionally healthy patient of mine took me aside and nonchalantly announced, "I want you to know that I have cancer." As if this wasn't unusual, I politely replied, "Thank you for telling me." My emotional neutrality, however, so typical of intuitive dreams, vanished the moment I awoke. I was shocked by this news and I didn't want to believe it. After all, this man was a nonsmoker, jogged ten miles a day, ate a low-fat diet and had energy to burn. Hoping I was wrong, I filed the dream and waited. To my dismay, at our next appointment he told me that during a routine physical exam a suspicious spot on his X ray had been discovered and it had turned out to be malignant.

The strength of our bond allowed me to learn beforehand about his cancer. It's interesting that, at the time, this man didn't realize he had lung cancer, yet in the dream he was the one who notified me. I believe that some part of him actually did know and wanted to communicate it. And so he did, because of our intuitive rapport. This dream wasn't about reversing his cancer. It was more a tribute to the trust we had established.

When you care about someone, it's natural to have precognitive dreams about them. Implicit in intuitive relationships is that you become intuitively privy to very personal things, some of them quite painful. This is both an honor and a responsibility. As a therapist, I want to know the whole story. It helps me to stay alert to what my patients are going through so that I can be there for them in a complete way.

You don't have to be a swami with a turban on your head to dream of the future. Everyone can do it. But first you may have to redefine some of your ideas about the world. One is that from an intuitive standpoint, time is relative. In precognitive dreams, as well as other intuitive states, past, present, and future blur together in a continuum. Time is not arranged in distinct, orderly segments as it appears to be from the perspective of our waking minds. A comment that Albert Einstein once made about time leaves a strong impression on me: "For us believing physicists the distinction between past, present, and future is only an illusion, even if a stubborn one." When I focus intuitively or have a precognitive dream, it feels as though I'm tuning in to a collective bank in which all information, regardless of its time frame, is stored. Once I got used to this, accessing the future no longer seemed so unusual.

The greater reward that precognitive dreams offer is to allow us to stay in greater harmony with our own lives. It's as if the volume is turned up on an exquisite symphony playing just below our conscious level of awareness. For a moment we can begin to appreciate what Walt Whitman speaks about in "Song of Myself": "I and this mystery here we stand. . . . Apart from the pulling and hauling stands what I am." Precognitive dreams reveal elements of our future, and sing our own songs back to us. By listening, we can again begin to dance in rhythm as we were meant to, moving in step with the sacred.

HEALING DREAMS

I hate being sick, though I'm one of those lucky people who only occasionally have to see a doctor. But for over six months I had been having recurring severe sinus infections. Each trip to the ear, nose, and throat specialist would end up with my having my sinuses drained, a ten-day course of antibiotics, a few weeks of feeling better, and then my symptoms would return. Since I wasn't responding to the therapy, my doctor suggested a series of complicated nasal X-rays and an MRI scan to see if there was a blockage requiring surgery. Not wanting the expense or trauma of the tests, I kept putting them off, but I got tired of being sick so much and finally gave in.

The night before the scheduled X-rays, I had a dream:

> *I'm lying in a medical office on a flat wooden table, my body covered by only a white cotton sheet. I feel totally at peace, almost euphoric. I don't think of questioning where I am or what is happening. There are a number of thin silver needles inserted about an eighth of an inch into my skin, over various parts of my head and sinuses. In the next room I can see my mother smiling, looking youthful and healthy, giving me a go-ahead signal with her hands. Relieved by her presence, I know I'm in the right place. An acupuncturist stands beside me, assuring me that these treatments will make me feel better.*

This dream specifically told me what to do. Although I had considered acupuncture before and sensed that it would help, my life was already so busy it seemed like too large a time commitment to take on. Hoping that antibiotics would be a quick fix, I waited. In fact, I knew of a wonderful acupuncturist whom a friend of mine had been raving about for years. Now, on the advice of the dream, and especially because I had gotten my mother's okay, I canceled the medical tests and set up an appointment. Over the next three months I went in for acupuncture twice a week, and my recurrent sinus infections stopped. This simple solution enabled me to avoid possible surgery, ultimately saved time and expense, and eliminated a great deal of unnecessary annoyance.

This was a dream that facilitated my healing. Prompted by my extreme dislike of the tests, it showed me a way out. I was grateful for how succinct it was, leaving little room in my mind for interpretation. I was also convinced by my feeling of total relaxation, verging on bliss, as if I were wrapped in a warm cocoon. It was identical to those heavenly experiences I've had when someone gifted works on me energetically with their hands. These feelings of well-being are easily recognizable signs of healing that we can look for in our dreams. I believe that my recovery began in this dream; the acupuncturist I later sought out simply took over.

There is a healing instinct within us that can manifest itself in our dreams. Though this can occur on an emotional level, my focus here is on the physical, which I haven't emphasized before. When you are asleep you open yourself up to healing forces. I am not saying that you have two sets of powers—one when you're asleep and another when you're awake. But in dreams, your resistances and inhibitions fall away; things can happen that you don't ordinarily give yourself permission to experience.

Whether you believe that healing dreams come directly from the divine, or view them as an expression of your higher self (I no longer make a distinction), just know that if you become ill, your dreams can be with you every step of the process—from the initial diagnostic phase and all through treatment. They may even enable you to find a cure. In the same way that you can actively solicit guidance in other dreams, you can also request direction about healing. Or, as in my case, it may simply be offered to you.

Dreams give you instructions about how to heal and may at times also be greatly reassuring. This is particularly true if you have a life-threatening illness, when many questions and uncer-

tainties arise. Periods between checkups are often the most difficult. Fears crop up that can devastate you if you let them. Healing dreams monitor the pulse of your recovery by relaying to
you intuitive information that feels so genuinely authentic it has
the power to quell such fears.

Robert had been diagnosed with colon cancer two years before
he started psychotherapy with me. He had undergone a partial
large bowel resection, but had not required a colostomy. His surgeon, a sensitive woman and well respected in her field, reassured
Robert that the malignancy had been completely removed. Although his prognosis was excellent, he still worried. He abhorred
hospitals and never wanted to see the inside of another one again.
The follow-up battery of X-rays and body scans he had to go
through every six months terrified him. Each time it was the
same: The week before each checkup was the worst. Now, with
another meeting with his oncologist only days away, he had come
to my office riddled with fear. Nothing I tried—meditation,
guided imagery, or hypnosis—worked. I felt powerless to console
him.

A few nights before this appointment, however, Robert had a
dream in which he was undergoing surgery at UCLA Hospital,
where he had originally been operated on. Perfectly alert and unafraid, he watched his surgeon make a painless incision with a
scalpel down the center of his abdomen. Next, she removed
Robert's entire colon and ran her fingers over it to show him that
it was healthy and tumor-free. Then she passed it to him to hold as
he marveled at the vibrant, glistening pink colon tissue. An extraordinary event that surely would have shocked him had he been
awake, in the intuitive dream state none of this seemed unusual.

"You mean I'm really okay?" he asked his surgeon in the
dream.

"See for yourself," she responded. "The tumor is gone."

Robert, a soft-spoken computer analyst at Caltech, had never
had a dream like this before, didn't believe in the metaphysical.
Respecting his views, I didn't push it. But intuition, he felt, was
different. This he could relate to: Feminine intuition was a com-

mon thing; he and other people he knew had hunches and often acted on them. But intuition? No, according to Robert; that was just too far out. Possessing a sharp analytical mind, he could have easily dismissed the dream since it had no rational basis. But when he awoke, it had been so dazzlingly lifelike that he could have sworn it actually happened. Nor could he argue with his own sense of relief.

Uptight to begin with, Robert had become almost phobic about his cancer returning. This dream changed that, instilled a new faith that he had finally overcome his illness. When he told me what he had seen, I knew that it wasn't just wishful thinking. There are times when you want something so badly that your dreams respond and fulfill those desires. Merely fantasies designed by your subconscious, these dreams aren't intuitive, nor are they based on fact. Robert's dream, however, was different. The clarity with which he described the surgery, the acuteness of each detail, his extreme sense of well-being throughout, and the authenticity his experience had for him all rang true to me.

After Robert's next checkup, all his tests came back normal, and he was given a clean bill of health. For the first time since he had been diagnosed, he stopped worrying. His dream comforted him far more than any kind of therapeutic intervention I had been able to make. Robert was still anxious about his life. But he was no longer obsessed about his illness recurring, and our work deepened. Over the past four years, Robert has remained cancer-free.

It's easy to be consoled by dreams that bring you good news, but what about those that show you things you don't want to see? You may be tempted to downplay unsettling information, to write it off by saying, "Don't worry, it's only a dream." Although some premonitions can be painful to accept, they're actually special gifts. If you detect an illness in the early stages or seek treatment soon enough to prevent its spread or complications, you may avoid undue suffering. In some cases, these healing dreams could even save your life.

A close colleague of mine once recounted such a dream, told to him by a retired army colonel. In it, the colonel is being shown a home by a real estate broker. The upstairs is sparkling clean and beautifully decorated, but the downstairs is a mess, with the stench of urine emanating from all the rooms. Apologetically the broker tells him, "I'm afraid I can't sell you this house. It will have to be condemned unless the first floor is fixed." Disappointed, he agrees.

The colonel knew enough to discuss the dream with my colleague, an expert in dream analysis, and together they realized that this could be a warning—the colonel might have a problem in his urinary tract. They came to this both from their sense of the dream as a foreshadowing and from the imagery: the overwhelming disarray in the downstairs of his house representing the lower part of his body, coupled with the unmistakable odor of urine. The colonel decided to go see his physician to check it out. Skeptical, his doctor humored him and performed a routine urinalysis, and was surprised to find minute traces of blood present, which were later determined to be caused by a bladder tumor that required surgery.

A few weeks after the tumor was removed, the colonel had a second dream, and in it he returns to the same house. This time both floors are sweet-smelling, immaculate. The broker happily notes the improvement and announces, "Now this house is ready to be put back on the market!" The colonel considered this a message that his bladder had healed; later he received confirmation that the cancer was gone, and he has had no further urinary difficulties.

Unfortunately, you may often miss such healing dreams because they are metaphorical and require proper interpretation. In conventional analytic terms you could attribute them to your attempt to resolve unconscious conflicts rather than as a call for you to heal physically. In part this is true; dreams have many layers. But from an intuitive perspective, analysis alone doesn't tell you the whole story: Sometimes you have a dream in which you foresee your finger is hurt. And it might be just that simple, no hidden psychological meaning. Your finger is going to need care. The dream could be a straightforward message, not a metaphor, that requires no further interpretation. It is important, therefore, to view dreams at their various levels.

In ancient Greece, during the period of the Temple of Aesculapius, healing dreams were highly valued. Typically, if you were ill, you'd be brought to the temple and put up in a dormitory with other patients until you had a dream. This was a sign that you were ready. At that point, you'd meet with the healers, known as "therapeuti," and treatment for your illness would be developed on the basis of your dream.

For Native Americans the dream state is more real than the physical world, and contains leads for solving problems. When tribal members fall ill, they look to the shaman for help. A spiritual healer and dreamer of the tribe, he's able to traverse both the seen and unseen realms. Through the use of medicinal plants, prayers, drumming, ritual, and dreams, the shaman becomes a transparent channel for receiving and implementing healing knowledge. Considered an authentic voice of spirit, these instructions are then precisely followed.

As significant as dreams are that guide you to healing, there are those that themselves have the power to do the healing. Sometimes the change may be subtle: A kink in your neck is gone, a headache relieved, or maybe a dark mood has lifted. You might not even remember the dream, but the next day you indisputably feel better. Then there are those rare, dramatic examples such as the one my dear friend Linda told me.

When Linda was a freshman psychology student at the University of Humanistic Studies in San Diego, she enrolled in an introductory class on dreams. All students were asked to bring in a few current examples of their own dreams for analysis. Linda had always been an avid dreamer, but under the pressure of the assignment she couldn't remember a single one, and was afraid she might fail the class.

At about the same time, she developed a lipoma, a benign fatty tumor, at the base of her spine. In one month it had enlarged almost to the size of a billiard ball, causing her considerable pain. She worked as an assistant to her physician, and he recommended that she have the tumor surgically removed right away. But Linda kept putting it off, hoping to avoid both the stress of the operation and the toxic side effects of general anesthesia.

The lipoma worsened, causing her so much agony that during class she had to support her back with an inflatable beach chair while sitting propped up on a pillow. Still she resisted surgery. One night, while struggling to complete a term paper, Linda began to cry. Then she prayed. "I can't concentrate or do my work. I'm in too much pain. Please help me." Exhausted, she stopped writing and fell asleep.

That night, she dreamed she was alone, lying flat on her back in bed. Through closed eyes, she saw a distinct image of a three-foot hypodermic syringe beside her. Seemingly on its own, the tip of the needle punctured the right side of her neck and penetrated the entire length of her spinal cord, down to where the lipoma was lodged. Though enduring excruciating pain, she was unable to move, not having voluntary control of her body. Only after the syringe began sucking out a pale white, watery liquid from the lipoma did her discomfort cease. Completely aware of what had taken place, yet witnessing it intuitively as an observer, Linda remained asleep until morning.

When she awoke, she recalled everything and rushed straight to a full-length mirror. Standing directly in front of it, examining her back from every conceivable angle, she could see no sign of the lipoma. With her fingertips she poked and probed her spine for any remnants of the bulging lump. It had completely vanished.

This happened at a time when Linda had just begun to meditate and study the Hindu tradition. She had heard accounts of dramatic cures, but her teacher had warned her not to get distracted by such things. Although amazed by her experience, she followed his advice. Rather than blowing her dream out of proportion, she gratefully accepted the healing but didn't give it undue focus. She was able to consider the incident as a direct confirmation that other dimensions could be tapped into that could bring about actual physical change.

Linda was lucky that her university was nontraditional. Because she was studying transpersonal psychology, a discipline that acknowledges the spiritual realities, her professor explained that she'd had a healing dream. He didn't overanalyze it or impose any contrived interpretation. Nor did he ascribe to Linda any superhuman qualities. But fully realizing how rare and precious these dreams are, he was able to recognize it as an act of grace.

A few days later, Linda returned to her doctor, wanting her back reexamined to make sure that everything was all right. Seeing no evidence of the lipoma, he raised his eyebrows and shot Linda a befuddled look. "Isn't this interesting," he remarked. "I guess you don't need surgery after all." That was all he said. As if nothing odd had happened, he then scribbled a note on her chart, instructed her to get dressed, and went on, business as usual.

Instinctively, she knew not to mention the dream to him, afraid that he might be threatened or put her down. Not wanting to jeopardize their working relationship, she felt the dream was much better left alone. Linda's spiritual beliefs were so new; she needed support, not criticism, until she became more self-assured. She viewed this dream as a reminder that a vital and active transcendent influence exists. It reinforced her faith to move forward and signaled her readiness to pursue a career as a therapist and, eventually, a healer.

All of us are capable of dreams that heal the body. But will we make use of them? There are many people who are completely closed to the possibility. Then there's another group—most of us—who will experience more subtle, common versions of healing dreams once we begin to trust that such physical change can occur. Perhaps someone simply touches you lovingly in a dream and the next day you wake rejuvenated, your minor ailments gone. Or you drift off to sleep and find yourself lying on a white sand beach basking in the sun, and are relieved in the morning to see that your cold has disappeared. Finally, there are those people like Linda, whose experiences show us the possibility of the seemingly miraculous. Don't be disappointed if you never undergo such radical cures. Linda is an extremely gifted, intuitive healer; she has made the spiritual her whole life's work. But also don't decide that this kind of healing through dreams is impossible and give up on your potential. Allow yourself to believe—even though in this case, as in so many others where intuition is involved, old ideas die hard. Attend to your dreams. Give yourself a chance to learn from them.

Despite the tremendous advances of medical science, there is much that it still can't explain. While sleep can help the physical body, dreams can rejuvenate the spirit. When deprived of dreams, people have been shown to become emotionally unstable, confused, even psychotic. Our dreams recharge us. I believe they contain mystical properties: Unencumbered by your body, you are freer, lighter in substance, can even fly if you wish. When you dream, you're more receptive and sensitive than at any other time in your life. You merge with a benevolent intelligence that touches you, and in some special circumstances it even heals. With your ordinary defenses down, your armor cracks apart so you can open to the larger voices calling out to be heard.

DREAM JOURNALS

The real art of dreaming is in remembering our dreams. Once we record the details in a journal they can no longer slip away. I can't count how many times I have been lying in bed half asleep in the middle of the night, certain I'll never forget this extraordinary dream I just had—but the next day it's totally gone. Dreams are by nature ephemeral. By keeping a journal, we can bear witness to the intangible, commit our dreams to concrete form. When we do this, we are serving as holy scribes and translators, just as Thomas Moore says in *Care of the Soul:* "Our notebooks are our private gospels and sutras, our holy books." Dream journals allow us to honor our inner lives, are a living testament to our personal odysseys.

I still have piles of my old dream journals, with worn bindings and faded pages dating back to the early sixties, stacked high on my closet shelves. Reviewing them, I can recall exactly what was going on in my life at the time of each dream. Keeping a regular diary has never appealed to me because what happens in dreams is usually much more fascinating to me than even my most compelling daytime activities.

While I sleep, I'm no longer weighted down by the physical and am free to explore different realms. This is when I am at my most vulnerable, so it's vital that my surroundings be quiet and safe. Because being awakened abruptly from a dream feels wrenching—as if I've been yanked out of a room in the middle of a conversation with someone—I do everything in my power to prevent it. I have a strong nesting instinct and like to create a snug environment for my dreaming. This is why when I travel, adjusting to a strange hotel room, no matter how luxurious, is often difficult for me. My dreams, as a result, tend to be erratic and sketchy, harder to recall. The familiarity of my bedroom, the softness of my pillow, the warmth of my down comforter, make it easier for me to settle into a peaceful sleep.

Every morning, whether I'm traveling or at home, I spend at least a few minutes retrieving my dreams from the previous night and writing them down. Before I'm fully alert, I lie still, with my eyes closed, collecting my dream images. This is such an automatic part of my morning routine that I rarely even think about it. The tricky part is recording a dream that surfaces in the middle of the night. If I get up long enough to turn on the bedside lamp and enter the dream into my journal, I can have trouble falling back to sleep. I have tried to program myself to hold on to the dream until the next day by fixing its details in my mind, but this doesn't always work. Sometimes I compromise by scribbling down a key word or phrase, using a small penlight to see, hoping I'll be able to make sense of it in the morning. But since for me dreams are too important to miss, on these occasions—they occur only every few weeks—I usually decide to wake up completely and, if necessary, sacrifice the sleep.

If you also have trouble going back to sleep you might try a voice-activated tape recorder. I have friends who find this method less disruptive than having to write something down. Keep the machine close so without even opening your eyes or turning on a light you can tape your dreams. Then simply transcribe them in the morning. Recorders aren't an ideal substitute for a journal, though. For you to refer easily to your dreams they need to be organized chronologically and written down.

Some nights I remember as many as five vivid dreams; on others I retrieve none. Each of us has his or her own unique pattern. There are cycles to our dreams, a natural ebb and flow. During winter, a time of dormancy and the coldest, darkest season of the year, I'm less physically astute and my dreams are more difficult to recall. I can often sense them hovering in the distance, beyond an invisible boundary. The harder I try to grasp on to them, however, the more elusive they become. Since dreams are so important to me, I feel at a loss without them, as if I've gone partially blind. But even when I'm in a dormant part of my cycle or have no awareness of my dreams, there are effective ways of stimulating these memories.

Mark couldn't remember his dreams. A talented literary agent who worshiped creativity, he thought that he was missing out on something and came to me to find it. Every morning his wife would launch into a detailed account of her dreams of the night before, which sounded like a Steven Spielberg adventure movie. When Mark woke up, his mind was completely blank. I suggested that he start a dream journal.

"How can I keep a journal when I don't even dream?" he asked.

"The point of starting a journal," I told him, "is to honor your intentions, to give yourself permission to dream. It doesn't matter how much you remember. Just date it and write it down. A line, a color, a shape, a few key words, a fragment. Any clues that give you something to work with. Don't worry about how unimportant they might seem. Just record them immediately, before you do anything else, so they don't get lost."

"But how do I begin?" Mark needed a concrete plan.

"Before you go to sleep, shut your eyes and ask for a dream. Something inside of you will hear it and respond."

"What if nothing happens and I don't dream at all?"

"Don't give up," I encouraged him. "It might take a while. Just keep at it and you will."

Mark took this as a challenge. He was eager to start. Rather than randomly writing on loose scraps of paper or including his dream images in already used notebooks, at my suggestion he bought a hardbound journal. It's important to have a special designated place to log them. This journal was off limits to his wife, and she respected that. It became his confidential diary, exclusively devoted to recording his dreams, a forum for them to speak.

Each night, Mark would make his request and then drift off, hoping for the best. For the first week, he couldn't recall a single thing; the journal remained empty. Puzzled, I asked him about his sleep habits. He told me he was one of those people who put their heads on the pillow, go right to sleep, and in the morning jump straight out of bed like a bullet. By six Mark would be glued to the phone, making his early New York calls.

"You're getting up so fast you're losing your dreams," I said. "Rest there for a while with your eyes shut. See what comes. The secret is to prolong what's known as the hypnogogic state, the period between sleep and waking. It's a magical time when you're consciously aware of your dream images but are still not quite alert."

"Is there anything I should specifically do?"

"Simply lie relaxed and still," I said. "Images will form. Gently focus on them and watch where they take you. You don't have to force anything. Try to remain a detached observer. The images will pull you along. At first they may seem disconnected or fleeting. But eventually a scenario will emerge. It's like watching the replay of a movie. You can actually see your dreams enacted all over again. The difference is that now you're actively witnessing them and can choose at any point to open your eyes and write them down."

Fighting his instincts, Mark didn't leap out of bed anymore. He was doing everything right but still got no results. Finally, after a few weeks, he became aware of some snapshot-like dream images. One day he was surprised to see a face flash before him—his favorite grandmother, who had died when he was nine. Excited, he didn't wait for what came next and noted it in his journal. Another time, he saw an image of himself as a young boy holding a small cocker spaniel, his beloved childhood dog. Watching it closely, it led him into a dream in which he and the dog were lost in some strange town far away from home. At first these images and dreams seemed disjointed, but he persisted, diligently recording each entry. Over the next few months, the isolated pictures began to connect and reveal the loneliness and loss Mark suffered as a child after his grandmother died. Recalling this, he was now able to express the grief he never allowed himself to feel before.

Mark didn't dream in epic proportions as his wife did, but he had found his own natural style, analogous to the simple elegance of a Japanese haiku poem. Some people's dreams are like seventy-millimeter Technicolor movies. Others recall only fragments or single scenes. The form, dramatic quality, or length is not where the value lies. The act of recovering the information and your ability to utilize it are what determine the worth of the images.

From a purely psychological perspective dream journals are a priceless archive. With your dreams down on paper you can unearth important events in your life that you'd forgotten about, as Mark did. Or you can piece together unconscious negative patterns in yourself so you can take the necessary action to change. You are able to monitor your own growth in dreams, gauging the progress you make in your journal, acknowledging the healing that occurs.

For years a patient of mine kept dreaming that she was back in college at Berkeley in the sixties, wandering through the campus desperately trying to locate something she'd lost. No matter how hard she searched, she never found it. Now in her late forties, a divorced high-school math teacher who led a fairly quiet life, she yearned for the freedom and sense of adventure she once had in school. These dreams were telling her that she had left a cherished part of herself behind and needed to reclaim it. Once she actively took steps to create that same freedom in her present life—becoming more politically active, taking vocal stands on social issues, and expanding her circle of friends—the dream became less frequent and finally stopped. It was last mentioned in her journal over a year ago.

In keeping a dream journal, we not only chronicle the patterns of our unconscious, we can also begin to pinpoint and make use of our intuitive dreams. Our journals play a dynamic role. They house the intuitive guidance we request to live our lives well so the knowledge we gain can't be lost, misinterpreted, or forgotten. They're a living testament to the healing we receive in dreams, so that we can remember and make full use of this healing. Containing concrete evidence of our future predictions, our journals enable us to correlate our dreams with an actual event when it takes place. By logging our dreams, we can often tell at once which are accurate and practically apply this newly identified intuitive material.

Several years ago, my boyfriend left me for another woman. I was crushed. I would have done anything to make the relationship succeed. I kept thinking to myself, I wish we'd get back together again, as if repeating it like a mantra would make it come true. I was working myself into a frenzy, but he wasn't interested in coming back. I knew that it was best to be apart because I wanted a committed relationship and he didn't, but I was obsessed. One evening I asked for a dream to show me a way out of this mess.

At three o'clock one morning, in the midst of a huge thunderstorm, I awoke with a seven-digit West Hollywood phone number rolling around in my head. I was dead tired, but since I rarely picked up numbers intuitively in my dreams, I knew I needed to jot this one down. I switched on the overhead light, reached for my journal, and noted it.

The following morning I dialed the number with no idea what I would do if someone answered. After two rings, a woman picked up the phone and said, "Together Again Productions. Can I help you?"

I thought this was some kind of a joke. "Excuse me," I asked, "can you tell me what your company does?"

In a perfunctory tone, she replied, "We're a television production company. We make 'Movies of the Week.'"

Barely able to keep from laughing, I said, "Sorry, I must have the wrong number," and hung up the phone.

Although my boyfriend and I never did get back together again, the dream interjected a touch of cosmic humor. Having received an unexpected response to my request, I took it as a personal message to lighten up, to stop taking everything so seriously. This was the gentle nudge I needed to remind me to go on with my life. If I hadn't made the effort to transcribe the phone number, I would have missed out.

Once we document our dreams, it may be obvious which are actually intuitive, or it may take weeks, months, or even years to confirm. For instance, in the early eighties I had a dream that I was director of a medical clinic. The building, which I could see vividly, was actually one I had often passed on Wilshire Boulevard in Santa Monica, a one-story faded pink stucco structure built in the fifties, at that time leased to an acupuncture college. The dream was so clear that it felt intuitive to me, but there was nothing to suggest my connection to the building. I noted the specifics in my journal, dated the entry, and labeled it with a special star, as I do with all dreams that I suspect are intuitive. You may also do this to organize your journal better and save time trying to locate a dream. In this instance, it was seven years later that, to my great surprise, I found myself about to start running a substance-abuse recovery clinic in the very same building.

A journal is an ideal way to keep track of your intuitive dreams. Although you may have a hunch that a dream is intuitive, if it isn't validated right away, there's a tendency for you to forget about it. This is less likely if you write it down. Then when the incident you dreamed of later takes place, you can review your notes and determine which elements were "on" or "off." Your dream journals provide you with reinforcing feedback, so essential to the cultivation of intuition, giving you confidence to develop and grow.

To start your own dream journal, I suggest that you go out to your favorite bookstore and browse through the journal section. There are many kinds that you can purchase: leather, linen, colorful cotton prints, some with pictures of dolphins, foxes, or bears on the cover, others decorated with star maps or pressed flowers or gorgeous nature scenes. Pick out the one that most appeals and inspires you to write down your dreams. Place it right beside your bed with a pen attached so that you can conveniently reach it when you wake up. Keep with it a small penlight or voice-activated tape player if you have to record a dream during the night. This is your private notebook, which no one else should touch. You need to feel safe to record every uncensored nuance of your dreams—even the most embarrassing, awkward, and revealing segments. It would be pointless to omit these portions out of fear that you'll offend or shock someone else. This journal is just for you. No one should read it unless you explicitly give permission. Also, cherish the time you spend retrieving your dreams. Those few moments in the morning, while you lie suspended between sleep and waking, are sacred. Protect them from interruptions. In this state, you are in direct communication with both the seen and unseen realms.

Remembering dreams is unearthing that which is underground, giving it breath and life. When our dreams and the everyday world merge, there's a seamless continuity of experience, dissolving the illusions of division and separateness. Once this is achieved, we begin to speak a new language that translates into many aspects of our lives. We feel an ease, a communion with intuition that allows it to settle, to make a nest for itself. No longer an occasional guest, intuition has taken its rightful place in our homes.

CHAPTER NINE

Intuitive Experiences in Everyday Life

Recognize what is right before your eyes, and what is hidden will be revealed to you.
—THE GOSPEL ACCORDING TO THOMAS

It was a typical busy Saturday, the time I set aside each week for shopping and chores. Already I had been to the car wash and hardware store; now I was browsing for a birthday gift for my father. Main Street in Santa Monica is one of my favorite places. I love the scent of jasmine, lavender, and vanilla wafting from the shops, the smiling faces of people strolling by, the heat of the sun baking my bare shoulders.

As I roamed from store to store engrossed in my search, suddenly, out of the blue, I thought of Barbara, my best girlfriend in grade school. I hadn't seen her in years. We were joined at the hip while growing up, did everything together—she was even with me the night in Seal Beach, right in front of her family's summer home, when I first got kissed by a boy. But at fourteen, as I started using drugs and became a full-fledged hippie, Barbara and I drifted apart. One of the last times we spent together, we took a walk in our neighborhood in Westwood, and—I think just to please me—because I was smoking a cigarette she lit one up, too.

Yet there I was, over twenty years later, not just thinking of her but flooded with images of my friend. Warmed by these memories, my shopping finally complete, I walked over to the Rose Cafe for a snack. As I stepped through the door, scanning the bustling space for a table, I spotted a familiar face. A beautiful woman now, but looking much the same: It was Barbara.

"Judi, is that you?" she exclaimed, calling me by my childhood name. I sat down with her, thrilled, and we began to bring each other up to date. Learning that I was a psychiatrist, Barbara beamed quietly, happy for my success. "And what about you?" I asked. I'd heard she was a photographer. "Well," she said, pausing for a moment, "our timing is unbelievable. . . . I'm getting married tomorrow."

I had to catch my breath. There had been so much love between us as young girls. For our paths to be crossing at such a significant moment sent a chill running through me. Growing up, we'd always been there for each other, present at the milestones of our lives. I hugged Barbara, whispered "Congratulations," but soon it was time for her to go. As we parted, I knew from the deepest inner authority, that meeting Barbara was no mere accident. It was two old friends again being drawn together, if only for a moment, a merging of past and present; just how intuition often intervenes in everyday life.

In ancient Celtic mythology, the Isle of Avalon is a mystical place of extraordinary power where intuition reigns. In *The Mists of Avalon,* Marion Zimmer Bradley tells us, "There was a time when a traveller, if he had the will and knew only a few of the secrets, could send his barge out into the Summer Sea and arrive . . . at the Holy Isle of Avalon; for at that time the gates between the worlds drifted within the mists, and were open, one to another, as the traveller thought and willed." According to the myth, because so many people lost faith in intuition and no longer acknowledged the influence of the Unknown, the mists grew so dense that Avalon became unreachable and lost forever.

In the same way, our own mystical nature has become obscured. It's actually there for each of us; its apparent disappearance is simply an illusion. Like the ancient traveler, we're blinded by the mists of fear, self-centeredness, and lack of faith. We've forsaken the mystery. And even if we were willing to make the effort to retrieve it, where would we look? The good news is, we can stop searching; intuition is ever present in our day-to-day lives.

Intuition may touch your life dramatically, though more often in so mundane a fashion that such simplicity may cause you to overlook it. You can write off some instances as chance collisions of people, places, and time. But suppose you alter your focus a bit. Suppose you view such random-seeming occurrences—known as synchronicities—as inspired coincidences, signs that something other than the haphazard is at work. There is magic in doing this, an acknowledgment that a greater force is moving through our lives, linking us all together.

Perhaps you have experienced déjà vu, the sense of having been somewhere or known someone before. There is no logical basis for your feelings, but they are so real you could swear that they're true. At another time you may intuitively pick up an event as it is actually happening. This is intuition—different from precognition, which is when you accurately predict an event before it occurs. Finally, if you've ever been labeled "overly sensitive" and seem to take on other people's moods or even feel their physical symptoms, you have encountered intuitive empathy—a common yet overlooked expression of prescience.

In our modern world we're moving at such a rapid pace we miss seeing the extraordinary in the little things. But it's right there, between the lines, where the mystery lies, the place where we'll find the key to the parting of the mists.

SYNCHRONICITY

Have you ever experienced perfect timing, a moment when everything just seems to fall into place? For a brief interim, you step out of the random chaos and find that all forces are aligned, with nothing preplanned, and yet all is in order. Events come together with such exactitude that it feels you've been launched onto a preordained course. You can't stop thinking about someone and you run into them on the street; a person you've just met offers you the perfect job; you miss your plane and on the next flight you sit next to someone with whom you fall in love. This is synchronicity, a state of grace.

Once, attending a doctors' staff meeting at Cedars-Sinai Medical Center, I met a surgeon named Michael. Immaculately dressed in a three-piece suit, tanned and handsome, he asked me out to lunch. In the Hamburger Hamlet at the edge of the Sunset Strip, we engaged in small talk for a while. He appeared quite straightlaced, speaking about his prestigious country club, golf on the weekends, Wednesday night poker. He was a nice enough guy, but not my type. Except for being physicians, we didn't seem to have much in common.

Usually when a date isn't going well, I try to ease out of it gracefully and as quickly as possible. But this was different. Although my first impulse was to eat fast and then politely leave, I couldn't say exactly why, but I found myself talking about my spiritual beliefs. Then, abruptly, the conversation turned to death—the words just flowed out of my mouth. Whenever this had happened to me in the past, there always turned out to be a good explanation. Thus, even though it felt strange to be conversing this way with someone I knew so little about, I decided to trust it.

Michael, I learned, had never talked in detail about death to anyone before, but on this particular afternoon he couldn't hear enough about my description of an afterlife, how the spirit is eternal, how death is not an end but simply a transition into other dimensions as real as our own lives. For two hours we sat in huge fanbacked wicker chairs in a restaurant that looked like it belonged on *Gilligan's Island* while he listened, transfixed, urging me to continue whenever I slowed down.

Throughout lunch, I kept thinking, This is one of the weirdest dates I've ever had. Not that I was uncomfortable with the subject matter, but there was just something unsettling about the way it was happening. I kept having the urge to change the conversation to something more commonplace: medicine, film, the weather. But the piercing immediacy in Michael's eyes, his hunger to absorb it all even though he claimed no spiritual leanings of his own, were cues that something important was up. Although the reason wasn't clear, it was obvious that Michael badly needed to hear about death.

We finally said our good-byes and walked out to our cars. As I headed west on Melrose toward my office in Century City, I wondered, What just happened? Why did such a profound topic arise with someone I hardly knew? Before I had a chance to come to any conclusions, my beeper went off. I had an emergency admission at the hospital, had to get over there right away. The rest of my afternoon flew by. By the time I finished seeing patients, it was late evening and the lunch conversation had receded into the background, out of my conscious thoughts.

A month later, a friend called to tell me that Michael had been killed in a freak motorcycle accident on the Ventura Freeway. For a moment I was stunned. Michael dead? It seemed impossible. He had his whole life ahead of him. People like Michael get married, have children, lead charmed lives. They aren't supposed to die young.

Images of Michael haunted me the rest of the day. Although we had only met twice, I felt I'd known him a long time. Suddenly the seemingly offbeat direction of our conversation at lunch made sense. There was some unconscious part of Michael that had intuited his impending death, yearned to know everything he could about it. I'd been the messenger.

Michael's early death was tragic. And yet, death is a part of life: It seemed inescapable that there was a certain rightness to my conversation with Michael. I felt privileged to have been witness to such a turning point, glad I hadn't run from it. Neither of us had seen the larger picture, the far-reaching implications of our talk, yet I had sensed that something important was happening. Now it was evident that a synchronous event had positioned Michael and me together at a critical point in his life.

Intuition often intercedes in the most subtle ways. Since I hadn't foreseen Michael's death, I didn't have the option to tell him about it even if I had thought it appropriate. (Nor would such a warning have guaranteed that his death could be prevented.) Being intuitive doesn't mean I'm superwoman with the power to alter the future. Or that I know everything about a person at any given point in time. Usually, unless I'm specifically tuning in to someone with a particular question in mind, I receive only what's needed for the moment. I have come to respect that. In Michael's case, I felt consoled, seeing how interrelated we all are, aware that in some small way I could help someone prepare for what was to come.

Fortunately, I'd known enough not to impose my will on our meeting. You may find yourself in a similar position. Remember a time when a situation just didn't seem to fit. Perhaps you felt that a crucial piece of the picture was missing, but you couldn't quite articulate what it was. It could have been a man who looked and acted like an old boyfriend asking you out on a date. Because the similarities were so striking, you decided to accept. Or maybe you ran into a woman you hadn't seen for years. Even though you may not have been close to her, you felt the urge to have a long talk in which something important to you was revealed.

The secret is to go with the mystery. When a situation doesn't make immediate sense, a larger overall message may appear if you let it unfold naturally. This doesn't mean you should place yourself in circumstances that are potentially destructive. You need to stay alert, use your head, know when to walk away. But you must also try not to discount or underestimate the implications of synchronous events. In some instances, the relevance is instantly obvious; in others, as with Michael, it takes time. We have to trust the divine ordering of our lives.

Synchronicities are an expression of our intuitive rapport with the world around us. I am thrilled whenever they occur, and I look to them for guidance. Synchronicities delight me, reaffirm that I'm on the right track. Though I believe that everything in life has meaning, synchronicities are a direct acknowledgment of our prescience; they highlight our collective link. Whenever patients come to me wanting to be intuitive, I advise them to pay careful attention to and record synchronous events to appreciate how frequent they are. This makes intuition more real. I've trained myself to notice synchronicities, and I encourage you to do the same. So many can be lost if you aren't specifically watching.

Once when I was driving up Sunset Boulevard to a friend's house in Laurel Canyon, I happened to turn my head and look into the car next to me. Startled, I did a double take: I was sure the woman at the wheel was a patient of mine, Jane. Though I waved at her, however, she sped right by me without response, and I then realized it wasn't Jane at all, just someone who bore a close resemblance. Such cases of mistaken identity, I've learned, especially if my confusion is so marked, often have special significance and are synchronicities. In this incident, my attention was drawn to Jane, so I knew to tune in to her intuitively and find out what was going on. Right away, I sensed her despair. I tried to reach her that night but she wasn't home. The next day, when Jane came in for her scheduled appointment, she was frantic, having just discovered that she'd been fired from a teaching job she loved.

You'll come across signs of synchronicities everywhere. The trick is just to stay aware. The stronger your reaction is to even small clues, the better the chance they are intuitively meaningful. Suppose you're driving to the market one afternoon and notice that the license plate on the car in front of you has your brother's name on it. Immediately this grabs your attention. You haven't seen him for a while, wonder how he's been. Twenty minutes later, just as you're loading your groceries into the trunk, he drives up beside you. Or maybe a portrait of a close friend crashes to the floor, its frame shattering. The next day you learn that she'd been in a car accident that very afternoon. Or a particular song keeps going through your mind that reminds you of an old girlfriend—you were crazy about her, haven't heard from her in a year—and when you go to the mailbox, what do you discover? She's written you a letter. The key is to recognize these connections. Go out of your way to emphasize intuition all around you.

Some synchronous meetings are serendipitous and can be harbingers of good fortune. When you take advantage of these golden moments, your life can change for the better. Such opportunities don't only crop up during important business meetings, extravagant parties, or special events. If you stay on the lookout, they won't slip through your fingers. Synchronicities are enmeshed in the fabric of the ordinary. They can happen to you when you least expect them: in the Laundromat, at the car wash, in line at the bank.

Patty had come to see me because of an ongoing sense of restlessness and depression. "It's not that my life is terrible," she said in our first session, almost apologetically. "I have a good job I've been at for over ten years. Being a librarian is okay, but something is definitely missing."

Secretly, she told me, she'd long had a dream: She wanted to run a small café serving healthy, low-fat, but delicious cooking, using all freshly grown ingredients. She could actually picture the tables, the curtains, the blue vase of flowers on the counter where she would serve tea. Vivid as it was, however, her dream seemed too much to try to realize. Though she was an excellent cook, loved to invite her friends over for festive dinner parties, and was known for her inventive recipes, she had no restaurant training, little money saved, and few business contacts.

Still, Patty's dream wasn't totally unrealistic. If it had been, I would have expressed my concerns. At least I wanted to help her explore. Too many people get stuck in jobs they hate or that give them no real satisfaction. They long to escape but can't see the way. "First," I advised Patty, "allow for the possibility that your dream can come true. Your belief is essential. Then," I continued, "look for signs everywhere that can guide you. Pay attention to coincidences—and notice if opportunities present themselves. When you're receptive, they can often be put right in front of you."

Patty had never approached life like this before. She confessed that she wasn't totally convinced, but, intrigued, she agreed to experiment. This didn't mean, however, that she would just sit back and wait for something to come to her. She began by creating a few special pasta dishes that she persuaded some local delis and restaurants to carry. Though Patty's food was selling well, it was also clear she'd have to expand to make a profit. But how?

In this period, she attended an alumni function honoring a famous graduate of her university. When the event was over, a friend of one of her old college roommates mentioned that he needed a ride to the airport. Since it was on her way, Patty volunteered to give him a lift. As they drove, Patty asked what line of work he was in. "I own a string of restaurants in the Phoenix area," the man answered. One thing led to another, and Patty began sharing her ideas with him. His interest was immediately piqued. As a result of this conversation she made a new friend who later provided her with the advice, support, and contacts she needed to begin taking steps toward opening her own café.

By training herself to look for synchronicities, Patty didn't miss out on this one. Previously she couldn't even imagine her dream coming true, let alone that someone would be placed in her path to help. Too shy to speak up, she might have let this same situation pass her by. But now, more confident about her own goals and receptive to such "coincidences," Patty knew how to make the most of this conversation. She was at the right place at the right time. But it was more than that. Patty had created the proper mind-set to recognize a synchronicity as it occurred. This simple shift in attitude allowed Patty to open herself to an incredible opportunity.

As you become more alert, you will encounter a variety of synchronicities in your life with many different purposes. Just as certain synchronous events can highlight circumstances that may benefit you—in relationships, career decisions, or any important choices you're trying to make—others can keep you out of danger. In some instances, instead of being drawn toward something, you may be directed away from it—and later discover it was a situation that could have harmed you. Without effort of your own, factors beyond your control align themselves in your favor. When this happens, it's a blessing, plain and simple, and you need to accept it as such.

I have a patient who at the last minute was asked to help with her eight-year-old daughter's school camping trip. It was to take place about one hundred miles away in Ojai the following day. That Sunday night she and her husband jumped into their Land Rover, left their home in Santa Monica, and headed up Highway 1, along the coast. Early the next morning, January 17, 1994, the big Los Angeles earthquake hit—a walloping 6.8 on the Richter scale. My patient's neighborhood was one of the most devastated. The damage to their home was horrendous: sliding glass doors shattered, a gigantic wooden beam in their bedroom ceiling dangerously split apart, massive cracks gouging practically every wall. Because my patient and her husband were synchronistically called out of town, they escaped almost certain physical injury.

Synchronicity was a favorite topic of the Swiss psychiatrist Carl Jung. He defined it as "a meaningful coincidence of outer and inner events that are not causally related." He spoke of a collective unconscious, a universal pool of knowledge, independent of culture, belonging to us all. It's the basis, he believed, of what the ancients call the "sympathy for all things," and it is my conviction that synchronicity stems from this commonality. We're all swimming in the same waters, riding the same waves, can feel the reverberation of one another's movements.

Many of you view yourselves as isolated islands, but you are more tied to others than you think. Acknowledging this common thread is yet another way for you to awaken and lead a richer life. It can remind you of the global interconnection we all have, helping you to feel less alone, dissolving artificial barriers.

Of course, synchronicities can occur with total strangers, but for me they happen most with people I love—little everyday things that are a touching reflection of our closeness and never cease to warm my heart. We don't even have to live in the same city or talk a lot: Our intuitive bond is always there. For example, my friend Jack lives in upstate New York, and we see each other only a few times a year. Recently, he told me, he was on vacation in Boulder, Colorado, browsing in a used-book store, and I suddenly popped into his mind. Nothing particularly unusual—just things we had done together in the past, conversations we'd had. An avid science fiction fan, he went to that section and, still thinking of me, reached for a book that appealed to him—*A Wrinkle in Time,* by Madeleine L'Engle. When he opened to the title page, he was amazed to discover my name—Judi Orloff—handwritten and dated November 1961, when I was ten. As a child, I always made it a point to write my name in all my books in case they ever got lost. When after high school I moved out of my parents' home, I donated stacks of these old books to Goodwill. Somehow, twenty years later, one of them ended up in Boulder and my friend had come upon it.

When Jack mentioned this, tears came to my eyes. The intimacy of this synchronicity, affirming the strength of our friendship, endeared him to me all the more. How could such an incident have ever been planned? That Jack would be in this particular bookstore at exactly the right time to discover one of my favorite childhood mementos triggered a rush of feelings in me. Most tender, though, was the incontrovertible sense that we are all bound together by such love. If we only look for it, the evidence is everywhere.

The smallest of synchronicities, when you view them from this perspective, have meaning, if only to reinforce the understanding that we are all related to one another in some way. Although some synchronicities may affect you more than others, all have value. Whether or not I fully grasp its import at the time, I have come to see each synchronous moment as possessing rare and perfect harmony—like the accuracy of a bull's-eye, the precision of a hole in one, the impeccable sequence of a royal flush. Synchronicity is a sign that we are intuitively attuned, not only to our immediate friends and family, but also to the greater collective.

DÉJÀ VU

My friend Rachel was on her way to be interviewed for a position as a counselor at a residential drug and alcohol treatment center. As she got closer to her destination, a dangerous area of downtown Los Angeles, she found herself in a neighborhood full of crack dealers, hookers, and gangs. Driving along in her Mustang, windows rolled up and the doors locked, she had serious second thoughts about working in such a community. But the instant she made a right-hand turn off Alvarado Street onto Lake, something changed. She could have sworn that she'd been there before. Not only did she seem to recognize the street, but she also knew the exact layout of the ramshackle Victorian house she was about to enter for the first time.

When she walked into the house, it was exactly as she had pictured it. The stairway winding up to the second floor, the sensation of the worn nylon upholstery of the office couch against her skin, the faded pictures on the wall, even the miniature collie in the backyard had a strange familiarity. Suddenly the situation took on a new light. There was a rightness to it, an absolute inevitability that was undeniable.

During the interview with the director of the program, a tough, streetwise woman with soft, brown eyes, Rachel felt that she was with family. This was the beginning of a productive three-year position, setting her career in a totally different and exciting direction. For most of her life, she'd been sequestered in the affluent world of West Los Angeles, but this recovery house with twenty sober addicts and alcoholics, some recently released from prison, became her second home.

Rachel had registered similar instant recognitions before, but they had never felt this compelling. Over the preceding few months she'd been lost, unable to commit herself to jobs that were offered, questioning whether or not she even wanted to stay in L.A. With this new recognition, however, Rachel had been set back on course. A sense of relief washed over her as she knew with certainty that this was where she was meant to be. The deterioration and shabbiness of the physical environment were immediately less important; what mattered were the sense of purpose she felt from the first moment she arrived and the strength of her instinct that she belonged and was safe.

This common form of intuitive experience, déjà vu, has happened to many of us. It may be instantaneous or it can creep up on us with time. The expression is from the French for "already seen." When it occurs, it seems to spark our memory of a place where we've already been, a person we've already met, an act we've already performed. It's a signal to pay special attention to what is taking place, perhaps to receive a specific lesson or to complete what is not yet finished.

There are many theories to explain déjà vu: a memory of a dream, a precognition, a coincidental overlapping of events, or even a past-life experience in which we rekindle ancient alliances. In the final analysis, it doesn't matter how we choose to define it. What matters is that it draws us closer to the mystical. Déjà vu is an offering, an opportunity for additional knowledge about ourselves and others.

If I'm experiencing déjà vu, I immediately stop and take notice. These moments may be overwhelmingly clear, or they can be elusive, come in a quick flash and then be gone. To slow down the experience, I try to observe everything about it. I listen carefully to what's being said, see how it might relate to me, stay aware of what I can learn or how I can contribute positively to the situation. When particular memories, images, or feelings are evoked, I allow them to work through me, watch where they lead. Careful not to overanalyze the situation, I make an extra effort to remain intuitively open during these times and absorb it all.

During my psychiatric residency, I rented an apartment on the boardwalk in Venice. I loved being there. Its funky architecture, the fresh ocean air, the breathtaking sunsets, the rich mix of people—it satisfied all my needs. But when I started a private practice and my income increased, I was advised by my accountant for tax purposes to buy a place. For a long time I resisted the idea, but finally I gave in. My criterion was simple: I just wanted to live by the beach. Easy enough, I thought. But nothing I saw felt right. Frustrated, I was just about ready to give up when a real estate broker called about a new listing. I was tired and braced for disappointment, but halfheartedly I agreed to meet her anyway. The minute I walked into the place, I instantly knew I'd entered my home. It was strikingly familiar and inviting, as if I had actually lived there before. With nearly every nook and corner recognizable, I didn't need anyone to show me around. The physical surroundings were beautiful, but it was more than that. Intuitively, it felt like the house and I were being reunited—it was calling out to me, welcoming me back. How could I not trust my response? Two months later I moved in, adjusted to the change easily, though getting cozy in a new home had often taken me a long while, and have happily lived there ever since.

Be on the lookout for occurrences of déjà vu in your daily life. They may be easy to miss or overlook. You might have had one and thought, Isn't this interesting or strange, but didn't make any more of it than that. Instances of déjà vu are intuitive moments when a door cracks open, an especially critical point that invites you to observe in detail and probe the situation in front of you. Don't let this experience go unremarked. Discuss it with someone you know who would understand so that you can get their input, too. Bringing a déjà vu experience out into the open energizes it, acknowledges its significance, gives you a chance to take a thoughtful look at what it means.

Writing of a trip to Africa, Carl Jung described an unmistakable feeling of déjà vu when he viewed a slim black man leaning on a long spear looking down at his train as it made a turn around a steep cliff on the way to Nairobi. In *Memories, Dreams and Reflections,* he writes, "I had the feeling that I had already experienced this moment and had always known this world which was separated from me only by distance in time. It was as if I were this moment returning to the land of my youth and as if I knew that dark-skinned man who had been waiting for me for five thousand years." Although this world and this man were something alien to him and outside his present experience, Jung saw the whole thing as perfectly natural, and somehow he wasn't at all surprised by it. He called this a recognition of what was "immemorially known."

In Western culture, we are brought up to consider anyone who isn't an immediate member of our circle of friends and family as a stranger. Yet at times you meet people you feel you've known for years. The usual formalities of etiquette seem unnecessary. You can talk to them about anything and they understand. You laugh easily together, perhaps share the same jokes. An offhand remark, the tone of their voice, the way they take their coffee, all seem commonplace. It isn't that they remind you of someone else or that their personal qualities are endearing. You relate to them not as strangers, but as people with whom you have shared history; you are members of the same tribe.

This has been the basis for the most significant and enduring relationships in my life. Within the first few minutes of meeting someone I am certain if we're going to be close friends. The feeling that I've known them at some other time or place, that ours is a reunion rather than an introduction is always there. At the beginning, there's a gut-level connectedness and ease between us not present with other acquaintances or friends.

Though I've learned to rely on my instincts about this, at times it's hard for others to understand. Particularly about guys I date. "He's such a nice person, why don't you give him a chance?" I've heard from well-meaning family members and friends. Logically, I knew they were right and, for a period, doubted myself. After all, I very much wanted to be in a relationship. Maybe I was somehow sabotaging my dearest wish. So I tested it out, spent time with men who had extremely fine qualities but with whom I didn't feel that instant connection. Without fail, it never worked out. Every major relationship I've ever had with a man has started with a feeling of déjà vu.

I'm not suggesting that you don't pursue relationships that interest you, or that they won't be successful if the déjà vu component isn't there. When you have a strong positive feeling, honor it. If you have a neutral feeling, you may want to explore. But also take notice if you experience déjà vu. This is different from electric chemistry, a strong physical attraction, or even an instant rapport. Although those aspects may be present, déjà vu is the sense that you've actually known this person before. You can't force it or pretend it's there—the experience stands on its own. Observe for yourself how this type of relationship differs from others. Use déjà vu as a cue that something very special is going on, and investigate the intuitive aspects of your bond.

A patient of mine, Carol, an interior designer, knew that she was going to marry her husband the first day they met. It had been three years since a harrowing divorce ending an unhappy first marriage. Carol was still recovering, and definitely wasn't looking to get involved with anyone new. Her life was finally settled again, and she liked it that way. She figured that when the time was right, she would get into a relationship. But there was no rush.

Then, at a friend's party, she spotted Tom. Something about the way he smiled, the glint of his sleek, silver hair, his voice, and the sinewy shape of his hands was so familiar that she was certain she had known him before. After they talked, it was obvious their paths had never crossed, but he had the same feelings. Following their first lunch date, they became inseparable.

"It's remarkable, the way we related," Carol told me. "From the first moment we were comfortable with each other. Little things—his smell, touch, even the way he said my name immediately seemed second nature to me. At times, we even instinctively know each other's habits and tastes. Like the other day, Tom sent me lilacs when he had no idea how much I loved them. Or when I played him an obscure Billie Holiday song last week and found out he had the same recording. I can be myself around him. More so than with any man I've gone out with. It's so wonderful that it's hard to get used to!"

A few weeks after meeting Tom, Carol announced to me that they were getting married. I felt torn. On the one hand, I thought it probably would have been safer for them to wait a while and get to know each other better. Yet I also respected that Carol was highly intuitive and trusted her feelings about Tom. She wasn't an impulsive person. Besides, everything she said made me believe this experience was a déjà vu. She and Tom had an intimacy from the start, the kind that usually develops in couples after they've been together for many years. Both Tom and Carol agreed that there was an inevitability about their meeting, a predestined quality, as if they'd just been waiting for this moment all their lives.

Three months later they were married. Over the years, their romance has only grown, their initial closeness and understanding continuing to carry them through the inevitable ups and downs of a marriage. Soon they will celebrate their tenth wedding anniversary.

Relationships that begin with déjà vu may happen more quickly than others. But even those that take off like a whirlwind tend to retain a certain groundedness and substance. There's an organic, unpressured rhythm to the way they unfold, seemingly possessing a life of their own. These are the graced relationships, feeling more like a reunion than a union. They still require commitment and effort, but the couples I know who have "recognized" each other in this way have all remained together.

This is not to say that a déjà vu experience with someone means you're going to marry them. It could be that you'll enter into a short-term relationship that especially helps you to grow or begin a long-lasting trusted friendship. Whatever the outcome, déjà vu is a sign that something extraordinary is occurring and to take heed.

Not all déjà vu experiences are positive. You may run into a person you're sure you've known before and every cell in your body screams out, "Stay away!" which is something definitely worth listening to! Different from other intuitive impressions, there's a past history here that resonates. You may not be able to pinpoint the exact nature of your connection, but you must stand firm and respect your feelings.

This happened to a friend of mine, an entertainment attorney who had no previous experience with déjà vu. Expert at his job, he's a sweet person, the type who gets along with everyone. At a business meeting, however, he spotted another attorney from behind. He had never met the man, but instantly loathed him. "I can't explain it," he told me. "It was as if I knew everything about that guy before I even saw his face. Like somehow we'd been involved with each other's dealings before, even though we hadn't. One thing I was sure of: He's not to be trusted." On the basis of his déjà vu, he stayed clear of this man, not wanting even the slightest contact. About six months later, he was amazed to see this same lawyer's picture plastered on the front page of the business section of the *Los Angeles Times*. Notorious now, he had apparently masterminded some financial scandal in which he'd embezzled millions of dollars in corporate funds.

Whether your reaction to a déjà vu experience is positive or negative, the possibility of having one is inherent in partnerships of all kinds, particularly the more intimate ones. It can occur in your business, friendships, and family, often leading to pivotal outcomes that affect the direction of your life.

Finding a spiritual teacher can also feel fated, much like finding a mate. One of my strongest feelings of déjà vu happened when I first met the man who was to become my teacher. The moment I laid eyes on him I was sure he was the one. Suddenly I understood what I'd been searching for so long: There my teacher sat, right in front of me. This whole scene was so dazzlingly familiar it felt we'd been together a thousand times before. More than just an old friend, I instinctively knew him to be my spiritual guide, the person who ultimately understood me best of all. On that day, a journey began that has continued for the last ten years.

There are situations in life that are glitches in time, when the rules bend and the mystery takes hold, enchanted moments that sparkle with ethereal light. These are déjà vu. They can take place anywhere, at any time, and with anyone. You're traveling for the very first time in a foreign country and come upon a winding cobblestone street in a village. Odd as it may seem, you instantly feel as if you've lived there before. Or perhaps you're in a restaurant and sense an inexplicable kinship with a woman sitting in the back corner booth. Don't let these possibilities pass you by. Take notice, rely on your instincts, and investigate. There's no way of predicting where one of them might lead or what it will teach you. Identifying intuition is only the first step. Summoning the courage to take a chance and act on it, to have faith in what is not yet visible, will make the experience your own.

CLAIRVOYANCE

On the evening of April 29, 1992, while taking a shower, I had a vision of a horrifying scene. I was standing in the center of a

bustling city. Overhead, a giant, seventy-foot loaded revolver
was aimed down toward the ground. All at once, city sounds
were blotted out by a thunderous blast. The gun fired a deadly
spray of bullets, ricocheting off nearby office buildings into the
crowd. There was chaos—the sound of glass shattering, people
screaming, the stench of smoke. A few bystanders lay wounded,
drenched in blood on the sidewalk. I shuddered from the violent
force of the explosion, but survived unharmed.

My first inclination was to take this vision personally. What
was I so angry about that might have triggered such a destructive sight? I couldn't come up with anything. No arguments
with friends or family. No conflicts at work. No excessive inner
turmoil. This was a cue to me that what I'd seen wasn't related
to my own state of mind but was intuitive—and I had no idea
what it meant. Though riveted by the vision's clarity, all I could
do was wait and find out. As I dried myself, I was aware that it
wasn't unusual for me to see such vivid imagery in the shower.
It's often there like magic the moment I step in, as if I'm entering an intuitive telephone booth. I have experienced many of my
most compelling premonitions in the shower. Free of tension
and unpressured, with hot water drenching my body, all kinds of
pictures (not exclusively intuitive) pop up spontaneously and
then disappear. But this one was particularly graphic and stuck
in my mind.

Minutes later, when I flipped on the TV to watch the six
o'clock news, I understood. The Rodney King verdicts had been
announced that afternoon: In south central Los Angeles, hundreds of fires blazed as angry demonstrators torched buildings,
looted local stores, and assaulted passersby. Heavy gunfire flared,
and a thick layer of brown smoke hovered above the skyline.

My eyes glued to the newscast, I was appalled by the apoca-
lyptic turn the city had taken. Nonetheless, the violent nature of
my vision had focused me, put me on alert. I was better prepared
to deal with the tumult, wasn't caught off guard as I might have
been. Although I hadn't identified my vision as explicitly clairvoyant (it's sometimes difficult for me to tell if an intuitive im-

pression is current or will take time to materialize), it had lessened the initial shock, made it easier to stay centered despite the madness that was gripping Los Angeles.

Clairvoyance means "clear seeing." Though often used as a synonym for intuitive, there's a distinction. Clairvoyance is not seeing into the future, but hones in on events taking place in the present, whether right next door or all the way across the globe. It can keep you in touch with the pulse of your community. The more highly charged a situation, the clearer it is for you to perceive intuitively. This is why social and political unrest can serve as a trigger for clairvoyance. The riots are a perfect example. Such upheaval on so grand a scale makes for an especially loud and strong intuitive signal analogous to cranking up the volume full blast on a radio. While I luxuriated in the shower, at my most relaxed and receptive, the riots escalated. I was primed to pick them up. The more intense the emotional and physical impact of any incident, the more it gets amplified on an intuitive level, like a hot news flash.

The potential to be clairvoyant is in all of us—it's not limited to professional intuitives or enlightened spiritual masters. Although often left dormant, clairvoyance is a human skill that, with the proper direction, will rise to the surface. In certain instances, as with my experience of the riots, it may occur spontaneously. But you can train yourself to be clairvoyant, make it a discipline.

The first step is to become conscious of your feelings. Begin to live in your entire body, not just your mind. So many of us walk around obsessing maniacally, numb from the neck down. It's no wonder that intuitive insights can seem alien. But if you really define in a fresh way what each emotion feels like—anger, fear, sadness, joy—you'll be much more ready to notice precisely how your body responds. Know your feelings inside out in their most exaggerated form so if they're more subtle to pick up clairvoyantly you won't miss them. Your body acts as an intuitive receiver, often first registering impressions deep within its very core.

To sense these changes, you will need to still your mind. When it's jammed with thoughts, intuition can be blocked out. Try to plan at least ten minutes each day to sit calmly, uninterrupted. Practicing silence, whether through meditation, yoga, contemplative walks by the ocean, or even a soak in a warm bath, frees up space. This quiet time, while you aren't doing anything but just "being," conditions your mind to open to a myriad of impressions, only some of them intuitive.

The key to cultivating clairvoyance is to work at it sincerely. Even if you have never had a single intuitive experience, you can put yourself into training. There's a simple exercise I teach my patients—I use it myself whenever I tune in to someone clairvoyantly—and you may want to try it, too.

First, make sure you're physically comfortable and free from interruptions. Turn off the phone. Shut the door. Be certain that no one else will walk in and break your concentration. Next, take a few full, deep breaths, relax your body, set aside your concerns of the day, and drift into a meditative state. There is no rush. Spend as long as you like to settle in.

Now, choose a friend you're particularly close to and begin to focus on her first name passively. Pick someone who is easily reachable, who you know will be candid later when you ask for feedback on your reading. Hold this name gently in your mind. Try to think of nothing else. Visualize only her. In the beginning, it's helpful to pose definite questions—start with the general and gradually work your way to the specific. For instance, you can simply ask yourself how she is feeling today. Open to the fullness of each sensation that arises. Don't force anything or resort to logic. Impressions will come. Perhaps an invigorating wave of energy will sweep over you. Or you may feel incredibly irritable out of the blue. Scan every inch of your body for even the slightest changes. Do you have a stomachache? Nausea? Are you depressed? Have your shoulder muscles tightened into a painful knot? Don't hold on to any feelings for too long. Allow them to flow organically. Sense these variations within every cell.

When you're ready you can go into more detail. Once again, you begin by formulating a very specific question. Where is your friend right now? What's she wearing? What's she thinking? Is she alone or are there other people there? Specifically break down every element. Ask each question separately and allow sufficient time for the answers to unfold. You may pick up only snatches of scenes, solitary images—or maybe you'll even watch an entire scenario play out. Release any previous expectations; let yourself be surprised. Clairvoyance can be like seeing for the very first time. There's something sacred about it, tuning in so closely to another human being or event that you can actually merge with that experience.

Clairvoyant impressions often come in snapshot-like flashes, the images, smells, tastes, sounds, and textures vivid but fleeting. They're typically presented to you in a series rather than as any single, fully formed picture. For example, if you're tuning in to a friend's present location, you may first see the stunning profile of a towering snow-capped peak, then a second scene below it of a single-story rustic log cabin perched above a dry creekbed. But you must wait for the third image to reveal your friend, sitting outside knitting in an antique willow rocking chair, alone on the front porch. These impressions may be elegantly detailed and fit together like intricate pieces of a puzzle that might not make sense right away. You may feel a sense of urgency about them, see an unusually striking sight, have a palpable sensation. Listen to the nuances of your reactions, noticing when something feels "off," "on," or unusual. Jot down all your impressions. Otherwise they too easily fade.

When the reading is finished, call your friend as soon as possible to check out these impressions with her. This gives you direct feedback about your accuracy. When you make mistakes, don't be discouraged. This is the way you grow. The mistakes I've made over the years have been just as valuable to me as my "hits." If I'm off about something, I try to figure out why. So many times I've overlooked or discounted images because they seemed meaningless at the moment, only to discover how cor-

rect they were later. From this I've learned that it's vital to remain neutral, to report everything and not overanalyze or make
arbitrary judgments about what I see. Feedback is central to developing as an intuitive. It can validate our perceptions and
allow clairvoyance to mature.

The process I've described—tuning in, giving yourself permission to go wild and allow your impressions to take form,
no matter how outrageous, then getting feedback on your
reading—is the basic formula for refining clairvoyance. Use it
to illuminate any circumstance that is confusing to you. Clairvoyance is a gift to be treated respectfully. With practice, it
can come to feel so second nature to you that it naturally in-
termingles with all aspects of your life.

A patient of mine, Dana, was an energetic and ambitious production assistant at a major film company in Hollywood. Lately,
though, she was beginning to wonder if she was losing her
mind. At work, nothing she did seemed right. Her boss, an executive producer, snapped at her constantly and, it seemed, for
no apparent reason. He had always been a joy to work for, but recently something had changed. Dana was afraid that she was one
step away from being fired. On the surface, none of this made
sense. Since Dana was good at her job, and had never had problems with her boss before, I advised her to look at the situation
intuitively.

Dana was no intuitive novice. For the past year, as part of psychotherapy, I had helped her develop her intuitive skills. By now
she felt comfortable doing readings on her own. I suggested that
she set aside a half hour to focus on her boss. "Even if you get all
the information you need in the first few minutes," I said, "it's a
good idea to allow for more than enough open-ended time." Sitting in her favorite brown suede armchair in the den while her
three-year-old daughter was away at preschool, she meditated
quietly and began to tune in to her boss's name. Trusting that

whatever impressions she received would be related to her answer, she knew not to interpret them until she was done.

Within minutes, she noticed an annoying pressure in her forehead, which gradually built until her head felt as if it would explode. The throbbing was relentless. Dana wasn't prone to headaches, and never appreciated how excruciating one could be. But she went with the pain, didn't succumb to the temptation to open her eyes and cut the reading short. Inwardly she stayed focused and asked, "How is this headache related to my boss?" For a while nothing came. Then suddenly she saw a single, sharp image of him looking dreadfully ill. He was at the drinking fountain right outside his office. He leaned over, swallowed a tiny red pill. At once the situation become clear. It had never occurred to Dana before that her boss might be sick, that this could explain his erratic behavior.

With a little bit of asking around at work, Dana found out that she'd been right. Her boss, she learned from a co-worker, had been suffering from horrible headaches for months. Only recently had he broken down and seen a doctor. The diagnosis was high blood pressure, for which he was now taking medication. With this information, the elements of Dana's reading now came together: the pill, the headache, the sense that he wasn't well. This put a whole new slant on things. Dana decided not to take his moods personally and to see what happened when he felt better. Her strategy paid off. Not long after, he visibly brightened, stopped lashing out at her, and became the easygoing guy he'd been before.

Clairvoyance, as a discipline, can be learned, but at times it may also come to your aid when you least expect it. The more pressing the problem you're trying to solve, the more passionately you care about it, the more readily it will be engaged. When you are wide awake all night long wrestling with a complicated decision, you can unconsciously send out a distress signal and elicit a response. Just as you're convinced that you've reached a dead end, the answer spontaneously comes.

A colleague of mine, a well-respected pediatrician who had no belief in intuition, jokingly mentioned to me what he described as a "daydream." He was sitting in the doctors' dining room at Cedars-Sinai eating lunch, totally absorbed in a newspaper article about the governor's plans to reduce the deficit. In a brief lapse that couldn't have lasted more than a few seconds, he inexplicably pictured the governor telling him that now was the perfect time to refinance his house. The truth of the matter was, he had felt pressured about money for quite a while. For over six months he'd been relentlessly scouring the local banks for the right loan, with no success. He had exhausted all potential lenders and was about to give up—until he was startled by this unsolicited message.

The whole thing seemed absurd to him. Even if he had believed in the intuitive—which he didn't—of all the messages to come through, why this one? It was so mundane. But what if it was true? He really didn't think his daydream would pan out; it was such a long shot, yet he couldn't resist the urge to check on it. "What do I have to lose?" he grumbled, making one last call to his bank. As it happened, on that very day, a new type of loan had become available, perfectly suited to his financial needs. When I gently prodded him, asking, "Do you have faith in intuition now?" he just shrugged.

"It was a lucky guess. That's all." He smiled at me as if we shared a forbidden secret. He wouldn't admit it, but I knew he had been affected by the chain of events, that something inside him had shifted.

Sometimes, however, there are situations when more is at stake than a home loan. One Saturday afternoon, a patient's mother made an emergency call to me, panicked with an overwhelming feeling that her nineteen-year-old daughter Katie was in trouble. She'd left a number of messages on her answering machine, but Katie hadn't returned her calls. Lately Katie had seemed depressed, disturbingly distant, but refused to talk about it. Her mother didn't want to intrude on her life, but she was consumed with worry. "What should I do?" she asked. "Is it okay to drive over to Katie's apartment?" I knew what a hard time Katie had been having, was concerned about her myself. Still, my allegiance was to my patient, protecting her confidentiality, not violating a trust. But sensing the truth of her mother's instincts, knowing how crucial it was to follow such feelings, without revealing any specifics I simply encouraged her to believe in her hunch and go.

When Katie's mother rang the doorbell and got no answer, she let herself in with her own set of keys. At first it looked as if nobody was home. Then she spotted her daughter collapsed on the bed unconscious, an empty container of sleeping pills and a half-finished bottle of vodka beside her. As she took in this horrific sight, her own heart nearly stopped. Had Katie not been rushed to the hospital, there's a good chance that she would have died.

Clairvoyance can serve as a basic survival mechanism by sending out a series of red alerts. I have heard many stories of parents who instinctively knew when their children were sick or in need, although separated by thousands of miles. Clairvoyance is at its peak when you love someone; you're bound to them by an invisible intuitive web. If something is wrong you can sense it. This connection enlivens clairvoyance, enables you to receive signals much like a radio tower. The more open you are, the subtler the signals you're able to detect, the stronger your wherewithal to avert potentially dangerous circumstances.

For every major decision in my life, I bring to bear a combination of logic and intuition. They complement each other beautifully. If I'm about to take on a new project, explore a different direction in my career, make an investment, plan a vacation, or enter into an intimate relationship, I try to look at what I may take on from every conceivable angle. The facts of any situation are important to me, but if they don't check out intuitively, no matter how alluring the proposition, I will invariably turn it down.

For readings to be dependable, I must remain neutral, but this isn't always easy. If I am too emotionally involved with the person or situation I'm focusing on, it's nearly impossible to set my feelings aside. Whenever I want something badly or am overly invested in the outcome, I can't stay detached enough to get an accurate take on it. My own desires and expectations muddy the picture. There's no way that I am going to be able to see clearly.

One night I got into a horrendous argument with my boyfriend. Out of nowhere, it just blew up in our faces. He got incensed about some remark I'd made but was too upset to talk about it. I was left in the dark, and the more I pursued the subject the angrier he became. Before I knew it he had grabbed his denim jacket and stormed out the door. Well, I felt as if I had committed the crime of the century, but had no idea what it was. Worse, there's nothing more maddening to me than being shut out. Unfortunately, I couldn't do much about it at that moment, so I attempted to tune in to the cause of his anger clairvoyantly. Good luck! How could I have expected to be neutral about such a volatile event? I was far too angry and hurt even to attempt to do a reading. It was ridiculous. I couldn't get enough distance from my own feelings even to begin to sense his.

To use clairvoyance you must recognize your capabilities and limitations. Although clairvoyance is not a magic bullet or an infallible instrument, it does offer you a more penetrating vision, a chance to make smarter choices, to respond more sensitively to others. Whether you study with a skilled teacher or begin to train yourself, the spirit with which this is undertaken must always be for the purpose of love: living it, communicating it, spreading it around. Then perhaps, with this knowledge, you can pause and take a deeper breath, find true solace in the wisdom you have gained.

INTUITIVE EMPATHY

Have you ever found yourself chatting with someone at a party who seems perfectly nice, and then you suddenly notice that your energy has been drained? How about that time you went to a light movie feeling fine and left sullen and depressed? In each case, there's a good chance that you were picking up the moods of the people just a few feet away. Or perhaps there have been times when the guy who sits next to you at work is in such a sparkling mood that his exuberance is contagious. You feel incredibly happy but wonder why. These are instances of intuitive empathy, which many of us have, often without realizing it.

Empathy comes naturally when you're sensitive to somebody else's emotions or ideas. A good friend gets married and you celebrate her happiness. A business associate loses his job after his company goes bankrupt, and you, too, are shaken up. Your sister is diagnosed with cancer and you feel her fear and pain. When you respond to another person with a generosity of spirit, it's a sign that you're an open-hearted loving human being who truly cares.

Intuitive empathy, however, goes further. It's the capacity to merge with someone else and, for a moment, see the world through their eyes, to sense the world through their feelings. Intuitive empaths are so uncannily attuned that they can feel what's going on inside others both emotionally and physically as if it were happening to them. If you're such a person it may be impossible for you to distinguish these sensations from your own, leaving you doubting yourself.

Not limited by the same boundaries as other people, empaths all too often feel more than they ever bargained for. Also, since empathy can become automatic, ingrained in your habits, you may not appreciate its impact on your life. Of all the intuitive phenomena, it may be the most overlooked and misunderstood. Frequently confusing and disorienting when unidentified, empathy can become a gift once you discover how to adapt to it. Unfortunately, because empaths suffer from so many symptoms other than their own, they're too easily written off as hypochondriacs by physicians who are puzzled by their complaints.

Murray, a good example of such an empath, doesn't date. He can't. In the sixth grade, without realizing what it was, he experienced intuitive empathy for the first time. In each of his classes, he was assigned a seat next to Laura because their last names started with the same letter of the alphabet. Laura suffered from terrible stomachaches. So did Murray, but only if he was around her. When he reported these stomachaches to his parents, they sent him to a pediatrician for a medical checkup. Nothing was found. His parents and teachers didn't know what to make of his complaints. It took Murray to figure it out. Once, when Laura was absent for over a week, Murray noticed that his stomach felt fine. With exceptional insight for a boy his age, he concluded that his symptoms somehow must have been related to her. As an experiment, he asked his teacher to change his seat—and from that day on the stomachaches never returned. But though Murray was sharp enough to realize that Laura's distress was influencing him, he never did solve his more essential problem: how to use his empathy in a positive way without being overcome by other people's feelings. Since empathic symptoms are most exaggerated around their source, the more intimate Murray is with someone, the more overwhelmed he gets. This makes dating next to impossible.

I too was an empathic child, but unlike Murray I didn't know that my feelings were related to anyone else's. When I was told I didn't have a "thick enough skin" or I was "too sensitive" and needed to toughen up, I bought it. My friends couldn't wait for the weekends to hit the shopping malls or to go to parties, but I was never as up for it as they were. Since at times I felt overloaded in large groups of people (I could never predict when), ordinary pleasurable activities could turn into a nightmare for me. At these moments, I would try to clamp down hard and block everything out, afraid that if I weakened my guard the intensity might blow me to pieces. I was a gigantic sponge, unknowingly absorbing the pains and emotions of people around me, often without even the thinnest membrane between us. I could be sitting on a bus and suddenly get a dull ache in my lower back, never guessing that it was coming from the elderly man sitting beside me. Or I might be in the checkout line in the market, standing too close to a woman who was sad, and not know why I felt like crying.

I had become a human chameleon, a condition ingeniously portrayed in Woody Allen's *Zelig*. In this film, Zelig has such a weak identity that in order to be liked he actually turns into whomever he talks with. During the film, he becomes a Nazi SS officer, a Chinese laundry man, a Hassidic rabbi, a mariachi singer in Mexico, and an obese fellow tipping the scales at 250 pounds.

It wasn't until I started working in Thelma's lab that I spoke with other intuitive empaths, many of whom were healers. I was stunned to find out that there was a name for what I'd been feeling, and that such ability could be put to good use. For so long, it had felt like a third arm I didn't know what to do with. But empathy was second nature to these healers. They were so accepting and nonchalant about it that for the first time in my experience it didn't seem strange.

One afternoon I had lunch with a wonderful woman with a waist-long gray braid who was in her early eighties. She had been an intuitive empath since childhood. A psychotherapist and healer with a thriving practice, she used her talent to diagnose patients by sensing their ailments in her own body. Even so, the symptoms she picked up didn't stick to her. Through meditation, she had learned how to become empathically attuned to another person's physical and emotional state but not take them on.

"How do you do it?" I asked her, fascinated.

"I simply see myself as a channel," she said. "I let the feelings flow through me without overidentifying with them."

This sounded reasonable at the time, but it has taken years to really understand and apply what she meant. An astute therapist once pointed out that the qualities I absorbed from other people were the ones I wasn't clear about in myself. Take anger, for instance, which sometimes creeps up on me unnoticed, or may simmer just beneath the surface. If, however, I remain oblivious for too long, my intuitive empathy lets me know by kicking in full force. Then I not only sense other people's anger more keenly, I also attract it: Everyone around me now seems angry about something, and the negativity registers in me. But once I resolve the source of my own anger, the "hook" is gone, thus I no longer pick up these feelings as readily in others or empathically take them on.

Magic? Not really. The most basic principle of intuitive empathy, the secret for you to disengage from a barrage of unwanted emotions, is to remain as conscious of your motivations as possible. Don't allow depression, fear, anger, and resentment to build, thus unwittingly magnetizing them toward you. The clearer you are emotionally, the less problematic empathy becomes. The difference is that when you're at a restaurant and a disturbing wave of angst comes your way from the man in the next booth, it won't glom onto you and sap your energy. The energy drain comes only if your buttons are pushed. As long as you don't resist or engage the angst in any way, you're able simply to notice it and say "Ah-ha. Isn't this interesting"—and then let it pass right on by.

But what about physical symptoms? How can you avoid taking these on? This is a little different. It's true that if you're prone to migraines you'll also tend to notice them empathically in others, can probably spot them coming a mile away. This generally applies to any physical vulnerability you have. And yet you may also pick up many ailments that you have never personally experienced. The art is to learn how to detach from them.

Meditation can help. Your body will be your guide. By centering yourself through the daily discipline of sitting, you can learn to become a neutral witness to your sensations. If you feel a slight pain in your back, notice it coming and going like clouds drifting in the sky. Don't resist or overemphasize it. Simply observe. The point is to get distance from the pain while still remaining aware of it, as if watching a movie. This gives you the flexibility to choose whether or not to engage the feeling. It may take you a while to catch on, but give yourself time. By not latching on to the pain or tensing up, it becomes more fluid, softer, may even disappear. There's great freedom in this.

My friend Hayden didn't even realize she was being zapped by intuitive empathy until her husband pointed it out. Hayden is one of the kindest people I know, unselfishly supportive of friends and family. She loves to give, but there was a downside. When speaking with someone who was anxious, depressed, or suffering physical pain, Hayden noticed, she'd also start feeling the same way. Drained, she often needed hours to shake off the discomfort.

Hayden's husband, very sensitive himself, was concerned. He suggested that she might be picking up people's feelings through intuitive empathy. Recognizing this to be true, Hayden could begin to deal with it. She treasured being empathic—it allowed her to love with all her heart, to be present to the fullest. She didn't want to give that up. But to preserve her energy, she could no longer shoulder everybody else's worries. It wasn't good for her or them. Hayden solved this dilemma by reenvisioning her style of giving. Besides meditation, a strategic change in attitude can allow you to detach. Hayden knew intellectually that she wasn't responsible for other people's pain, nor could she fix them. But though she had tried to act on this understanding before, now, given her predicament, she really had to live it. For Hayden, this was the key. It gave her permission to back off a little, to be just as caring but from a more centered place so that she could use her empathy well and enjoy it.

In my work, empathy gives me a head start on what my patients are feeling and allows me to track them, not only mentally but in my own body. When I open the door to the waiting room to greet a patient, I can often sense how she's doing before she even says a word. It's as if invisible tendrils are protruding from her body all the way over to me. We touch each other, though not physically. So delicate is this sensation, that it reminds me of how a butterfly feels, wings still fluttering imperceptibly when it alights on the palm of my hand.

The heightened sensitivity that goes along with being an intuitive empath can be a mixed blessing. Some people never get to the good part because it seems almost too much to bear. I believe that many agoraphobics are terrified of leaving their homes because they're actually undiagnosed intuitive empaths. They can't tolerate crowds, and will go to any lengths to avoid them. Being on busy streets, in hectic department stores, in jammed elevators, or packed like sardines in an airplane is overwhelming, so much so that they must get out, and fast. Surrounded by throngs of people, there's just too much intuitive stimulation. That's why they feel safer at home, driven into isolation simply to survive.

But not all intuitive empathy is this extreme. More commonly, it appears in our everyday lives in subtler ways. I'm friendly with an elderly Jewish couple, Bertha and Saul, who have been married for over fifty years. Constant companions, they're so close it's as if they live in each other's skin. Sometimes this drives them crazy. Their rhythms have so blended that they are a single unit and respond to each other viscerally. If he gets a pain in his hip, she feels it. "What's the matter with you?" she asks him without his uttering a word. Then there are times when Saul detects a recognizable pang in his heart and says to his wife, "Don't deny it, Bertha. You're longing for your sister to call." "You're such a know-it-all," she snaps back, annoyed by how easily he can see right through her. Because they've lived together for so many years, they've become as one.

This also happens with many parents and children. A patient of mine who had a five-week-old baby boy woke up in the middle of the night, her throat constricted, gasping for breath. As a new mother, before even thinking of herself, her first instinct was to check on her baby. Panicked, she rushed into the nursery and discovered that her son had a terrible cough, was burning up with fever. The moment my patient identified the problem, her normal breathing returned, as is sometimes true of intuitive empathy, and she immediately placed an emergency call to her pediatrician. Empathically developing her son's symptoms turned out to be a godsend. It grabbed her attention, enabled her to act quickly and get him the treatment he needed right away.

My friend Liz was so empathically linked to her cousin, who was in Cedars-Sinai hospice dying of AIDS, that she felt his highs and lows as if they were her own. It wasn't that she tried to do this. They were simply that close. Raised in the same neighborhood in nearby Hancock Park, they were inseparable as children. Before he got sick they talked at least once a day and told each other everything. She had been at his side for each beat of the illness, sharing it all, down to the smallest details. Whether she was at the hospital or across town, at moments she would get nauseated, dizzy, or depressed just as he did. Toward the end, she also experienced waves of unusual peace. Of course, this wasn't always comfortable for Liz. But she viewed such intense response as a sign of their deep affection and wouldn't have wanted it any other way. Love is like that, she realized—this was its true beauty. Their mutual connection allowed Liz to fully be there for her cousin when he needed her, to participate lovingly in his death.

The communal state of intuitive empathy feels more natural to me than the arbitrary walls and self-imposed prison cells we construct to isolate ourselves from one another. When you first begin to recognize empathy in yourself, you may need help acclimating. Don't hesitate to consult someone who is knowledgeable about the challenges involved. This may be a therapist, a skilled intuitive, a meditation teacher, or a healer—it's best if they have had some direct experience in this area themselves. Once you're no longer frightened by intuitive empathy, you can view it as a seamless extension of love with the potential to unite us all. Its very existence suggests a oneness, a brotherhood and a sisterhood that each of us can embrace. A deeper compassion arises in you along with an appreciation for our similarities.

I believe there is an invisible network connecting all sentient beings. But it lies dormant until intuition acts as a generator to activate and enliven it. Our everyday lives provide a potent backdrop, a laboratory of sorts in which we can experiment with a plethora of possibilities. A light touch, a sense of play, and an abiding respect will invite intuition in and show us the lay of the land. Intuition needs to be neither exaggerated nor diminished, but rather recast in the context of the modern world so that we may integrate it. We must recognize it in the much-discounted miracles of simple things in our daily life. Then a marriage between the mystical and the ordinary will part the veils of the mists, so that Avalon may once again exist—not as an enchanted remote isle, but alive and pulsing in our streets and in our hearts.

CHAPTER TEN

The Well-Balanced Intuitive

Humility is the surest sign of strength.
—THOMAS MERTON

Rows of glaring hot lights made everything in the television studio seem unreal. I was sitting in the audience next to a woman whose sister claimed that she'd been cursed by a witch, waiting my turn to appear on a talk show focusing on intuitive fraud. Already onstage were the cursed woman, a well-dressed attorney's wife; her current intuitive, a flamboyant bleached blonde with an excess of cleavage; and a 300-pound man—also a clairvoyant—who owned an intuitive phone line that doubled as a sex line during off-hours.

I was mortified. When I agreed to appear on the show I had imagined a panel of regular people, each of us describing the potential for fraud. Not this circus! Worse, I was to appear last as the so-called expert, commenting on what each person had said, tying the show together. Recognizing the awful spot I was in, the cursed woman's sister squeezed my hand sympathetically and sighed, saying, "Honey, good luck."

Until that moment, even with all the work I had done, my exposure to intuitives who were such blatant caricatures was minimal. It mattered less to me at this point whether they were authentic or not. What really upset me was the flaky, off-the-wall stereotype they projected, one major reason why reputable people mistrust intuitives. Of course looks aren't everything, but in this particular area they communicate a lot.

The well-balanced intuitive doesn't wear long white robes or carry a crystal ball. She doesn't grab your palm in the middle of the supermarket and insist on giving you a reading. Nor does she blurt out unsolicited information. She's an ordinary person; the most remarkable thing about her is that she appears unremarkable. Her power is internalized, integrated. She doesn't have to flaunt it. As she uses her gift discerningly, radiating an understated sense of calm, we see before us someone with no need to glorify herself, someone who is profoundly simple.

The identity of intuition has, sadly, been tarnished. It must be rehumanized, its integrity reestablished. The essence of holiness in the intuitive has to be restored. There is a film I love, *Resurrection,* that follows the life of a woman who passes through various stages of acceptance that she is an intuitive healer. Although for a time she is pulled into publicly demonstrating her power to the masses, she eventually opts to use it in a more humble fashion. In the movie's final scene, she is the proprietor of a gas station in an isolated stretch of California desert. When a young cancer-stricken boy happens to pass through one day, she embraces him without saying a word, secretly and silently healing him. She does it not out of a need for recognition or applause, but from humility and a pure desire to help.

It is not only because of frauds, however, that the general public often views intuition in a poor light. Consider the position of traditional medicine: If you look at the *Diagnostic and Statistical Manual IV* (DSM), the Bible of the American Psychiatric Association, you'll see that clairvoyance is equated with psychosis. It is referred to only as a symptom of a mental disorder, a biochemical instability that needs to be wiped out by powerful antipsychotic drugs like Thorazine. There is nothing positive, healthy, or sound about it. Unfortunately, the overall sentiment among most mainstream physicians is that intuition is nonexistent, a sham, or a disease.

I think that such medical attitudes are shortsighted. Though many psychotics are convinced that they can read your thoughts or predict the future, in a well-balanced person intuition can be learned or is a natural evolution of spiritual growth. Not only was I never taught this, but until the DSM was revised in 1994, I hadn't heard of the topic of spirituality being officially addressed in psychiatric circles at all. Now everything that pertains to it is lumped into a four-line category called "Other Conditions That May Be a Focus of Clinical Attention" and limited to situations that involve the loss or questioning of faith. No specific mention of intuition is ever made. Even now, only a minority of psychiatrists will acknowledge it, and fewer still view the intuitive as a gift.

During my training, patients were either psychotic, needing medication, or they weren't. The boundaries were well defined. It's no wonder, then, that in the mid-1980s psychiatry was looking like a spiritual wasteland to me. I had gone the psychotherapy and medication route, seen its advantages and drawbacks, but longed for more. I was hungry to find ways to include intuition and spirituality in my practice, but there were no good models for this that I knew of. Then I heard about the Spiritual Emergence Network (SEN), a teaching and referral center just outside San Francisco founded by Stanislav Grof, a psychiatrist, and his wife, Christina. The SEN made an important distinction between mental illness and spiritual emergency. The premise of the SEN was that certain personal crises can lead to spiritual expansion. Volunteers and staff generally referred callers from all over the world to health professionals—psychiatrists, psychologists, and licensed therapists—who were clinically trained and also experienced in dealing with intuition. This was exactly the compassionate, smart, responsible alternative I'd been seeking, no psychic phone line or flaky opportunists. It was a godsend to know that such a group existed, an "expanded model of mental health care to help people in crisis by using scientific and spiritual methods." I contacted them and immediately volunteered to be the Los Angeles regional coordinator.

Through the SEN I received calls from all sorts of people, from housewives to CEOs, many of whom were having powerful mystical and intuitive experiences. I heard panic in their voices. Often afraid of going crazy, they needed great courage to reach out. They were all too aware of what traditional psychiatry had to offer, and were terrified. Heavy-duty drugs, electroshock therapy, or even intensive psychotherapy were naturally no consolation to them. At the SEN, I learned not to feed into their fears but to help them find a spiritual context, to appreciate their struggles in a new light—not in terms of dysfunction, but as an entry into something far greater. I saw that when these people were supported rather than judged by conventional standards, their crises could evolve naturally, sometimes resulting in tremendous breakthroughs. This could lead to a truer appreciation of intuition in their lives—and on occasion a real talent was awakened.

Soon after I started, the SEN referred a Latino woman, Theresa, to me. An advertising executive who had hardly slept for ten days, each night Theresa wept uncontrollably, frenetically pacing, wringing her hands, groaning. She had never felt like this before, was horrified to be losing all control. Raised in a tiny village in rural Guatemala, for most of her life Theresa had held strong beliefs in sorcery and herbal cures. Trained as a *curandera,* or medicine woman, she had been shown how to use her intuitive dreams and visions to heal. As a result she was wary of conventional psychiatry.

At twenty, after moving to Los Angeles, she stopped practicing her native traditions. She badly wanted to be a success and nothing was going to jeopardize that. In the conservative, high-powered business world, her spiritual ideas would only make her appear strange. Instead, she shortened her name to Teri and dressed to kill, as if she had memorized every single word Dale Carnegie had ever written. She conveniently lost sight of the old ways and for eight years climbed the corporate ladder, becoming recognized as one of the top women in her field. Then one night she had an unexpected vision. When she came to see me, she was still straining to keep up her professional façade, but there were dark circles under her eyes.

"You'll probably want to commit me," she finally blurted out. "I had the most horrendous vision. Last Monday I woke up in the middle of the night and there was my oldest sister standing right in the corner of my room. She had a gaping hole in her chest the size of a basketball. A flood of white light was gushing through it. I was petrified. I knew she was going to die."

That night Theresa tossed restlessly until dawn. She loved her sister but was furious that this vision had intruded into her now completely Westernized life. Later that day she received a call from Guatemala. It was her sister—she had just been diagnosed with lung cancer. Theresa had tried to put her past aside, but it had caught up with her and could no longer be ignored.

I was certain that Theresa was not psychotic. Rather, the premonition had caused her anxiety to skyrocket. Unprepared for these two worlds suddenly to collide, she had tried to split off her visionary part, but it had insistently broken through. Right away, I understood what a gigantic clash this had created in her. My role would be to help Theresa reunite these two aspects of herself.

"That can't be done," she argued. "Either I'm a *curandera* or a businesswoman. The two don't mix." My heart went out to Theresa. It was like hearing an echo of myself just a few years before. I knew what I had to do: I told Theresa my story—how I struggled with the same intuitive split and overcame it. If I had stayed more removed, this point would have lost much of its power. My approach was similar to that of twelve-step programs: I presented myself as someone who's been there, sharing the ups and downs of the journey. At first Theresa was suspicious. How could we be so similar? In fact, the first few months we worked together, she thought I was merely humoring her. Though she heard my words, she didn't really believe me.

My challenge was to help Theresa view her intuitive abilities in a new way. For her to become a modern-day seer, her antiquated stereotype of the village witch had to go. As we talked through her fears and old ideas, her past no longer a secret, the anxiety she had suffered slowly faded away. But still our work proceeded in baby steps, until eventually she was ready to use my office as a safe place to try to open up intuitively.

One day she announced that she wanted to do a reading. This was the moment I had been waiting for. At that session and many times later she gave me readings about my life, and I gave her feedback about their accuracy. This meant I had to be prepared to reveal information that could be extremely intimate. There was no point in denying what Theresa correctly picked up just because it was too private. That would defeat the whole purpose. Being this personal with a patient always requires a judgement call. But I sensed that Theresa could handle it.

I remember the time she said, "I see an image of you with your feet cut off. You can't seem to get your balance." At the moment, she couldn't have been more right. That entire day had been ghastly: A friend struggling not to drink was once again out cold in a hospital chemical-dependency unit; my VW's battery went dead while I was visiting her; and because of having to rent another car, I was late for an appointment with a patient, who left before I could arrive. I openly shared this with Theresa, not to belabor my frustration but to help her translate the metaphor of her vision.

At another session, Theresa asked, "Do you know an elderly man who's having breathing problems? He has a very round face and a great sense of humor." I placed him immediately. This was my father's best friend, a perennial joker in his early eighties. He had been hospitalized at Cedars-Sinai the day before, in the ICU with a dangerously high fever from acute pneumonia. I gave Theresa feedback to let her know she was right. Little by little, through exercises like these, her confidence grew. I felt as if I were training a prize fighter who'd been out of the ring for many years. Though rusty and unsure, with practice she comfortably grew into her prescience, learning to wear it like a loose garment—not just with me, but in the business world, with her family, and especially while her sister was ill.

Theresa was an intelligent, open-minded, high-functioning person who just happened to be in the middle of a crisis, a perfect example of someone overwhelmed by a spiritual emergency. While at the SEN I was struck by how many people fit this description. They were seeing visions, hearing voices, and often feared for their sanity. But to categorize their symptoms as psychotic and write them off merely as a sign of mental illness would have been a terrible disservice. Without the right kind of help, the emergence of intuition as a spiritual turning point would surely have been missed.

Despite my love for this approach, there were of course times when it just wasn't appropriate, especially when it came to the chronically mentally ill. As much as I believed in the intentions of the SEN, with some patients I got terribly frustrated. As regional coordinator, most troubling was the barrage of calls I received from blatantly psychotic people who were convinced they were intuitive: the burned-out manic-depressive who'd been in and out of the mental institutions for years, the schizophrenic on Thorazine who swore that the FBI was out to get him. The most hopeless and forsaken of the chronically mentally ill came to me, hoping I would validate their special powers, something no psychiatrist had done before.

This put me in an awkward position. Much as I wanted to be encouraging, with patients whose psychosis had become entrenched it was impossible for me to separate it from intuition. In good conscience, I could only work with them using traditional medical techniques. They were struggling—to get a job, live on their own, eat right, take care of personal hygiene. The last thing they needed was to dwell on the metaphysical. Even those rare few who I thought showed some evidence of intuitive ability were too emotionally unstable to risk pursuing it: For me to have emphasized intuition would have only aggravated their psychoses.

So there I was, professing to be intuitive, offering to bring out intuition in others, yet refusing to help them. They couldn't fathom my reasons, often felt betrayed by what they perceived as hypocrisy and lack of support. It was demoralizing to be pigeon-holed as yet another unsympathetic psychiatrist, even worse than the others because I was misrepresenting myself. I had to fight my urge to give in to them. But I knew better. I also had ethical and legal obligations: If someone felt homicidal, I had to notify the police; if someone felt acutely suicidal and had no family to give supervision, I was bound to call in either the police or a psychiatric emergency team. My responsibility was to protect the individual.

No matter how difficult it was, I sometimes had to watch patients like these walk out my office door, believing me to be one of the bad guys. I would send them to county facilities, give lists of programs and referrals to therapists by making the first call, if necessary suggesting the names of shelters for the homeless. Some did take me up on my efforts and tried to turn their lives around. Others, however, felt that I was just another doctor who had let them down. I could feel their pain that I wasn't providing what they wanted.

In psychosis intuition often gets distorted. Certain people have a basic biochemical imbalance in their brains, which causes some internal wires to get crossed. I'll be sitting in my office listening to a perfectly sincere woman professing how intuitive she is—she can read my thoughts, she claims—and I know for a certainty that she's wrong. No matter how careful I am in saying this to such people, however, they just can't hear it. I get the feeling that they're reaching out in the right direction, but get tricked by a false façade, fall through a trapdoor and become lost. The truth they allegedly see is usually disjointed, foreign to the world we know. Many ordinary psychotics cling to the belief that they are intuitive as if it were the last life raft on a sinking ship. Nothing I say or do can change their minds. When I try to focus them in a different direction, they simply won't give it up. It's as if being intuitive will somehow legitimize who they are, endow their lives with dignity and meaning.

One patient, "Solarus," a.k.a. Steve, raised in a conservative Jewish family in Brooklyn, spent two years in a Turkish prison, convicted of possessing marijuana. If his parents hadn't made a deal with the Turkish government, he could have been sentenced to death. Steve spent many months in solitary confinement, brutally abused by his captors. His bleak prison cell contained nothing more than a bare wooden sleeping bench. There were no windows, no light. The mistreatment and deprivation made him crack. During that time, he began "channeling" an entity called the "Sun Spirits," who convinced him that he was on a mission to save the world. Adamant that they were protecting him, he believed he was their messenger.

After being released from prison, Steve holed up in an apartment in a sleazy section of Hollywood. He rarely went out, refused to bathe, and raved incessantly about the Sun Spirits. His parents were at their wits' end, and sent him to me about a year after he returned from Turkey. He agreed to come in only because I was intuitive and would therefore understand.

Desperate to be believed, Steve arrived intent upon proving that what he was experiencing was real. He looked so vulnerable. I had a strong impulse to comfort him; his entire identity was at risk. He reminded me of a child who had gone astray, starving for validation. But I had to be careful not to get hooked in because of similar feelings I had while growing up. To be helpful, I knew I had to remain objective.

Steve channeled the Sun Spirits for me, but nothing about them felt authentic. When the voices came through him, they were often critical and cruel. "You're ugly and fat," they would snap. "It's pathetic that at twenty-six you can't even support yourself." Then in the next breath they would proclaim, "Love is everything. We've chosen you to spread the word." I felt compassion for Steve, appreciated the hell he'd been through. It was a miracle he had made it out of prison alive. I didn't want to take the rug out from under him, yet I had to be honest. His demonstration didn't convey the wholesome, true feeling of a genuine intuitive experience. There was a psychotic flavor to it, a bizarre, condemning tone that rang false. The Sun Spirits seemed more a reflection of Steve's disowned feelings, mainly negative. It was clear that in order to cope with and survive the trauma of prison, a part of his personality had splintered off.

This was definitely not what Steve wanted to hear. He had big plans to market himself, to get his message across to the public by going on the spiritual lecture circuit. In fact, he had found an adoring girlfriend who considered him an enlightened being and was planning to accompany him on the road. Because I wasn't willing to agree that his channeling was intuitive, I could make no impact on Steve. He never returned to see me. The last his family heard of him, he was with his girlfriend somewhere in the Midwest, penniless, trying to attract a following.

From working with Steve and many others like him, I developed a feel for when it's appropriate to encourage intuition and when it isn't. Timing is critical. Most important, you must first start with a solid emotional base. Otherwise, exploring intuition may only make matters worse. This is especially true if you try to force an opening when you're not ready. Overdoing spiritual workshops or consulting teachers excessively may place too much pressure on you, so much so that in your zealousness to progress, you get frustrated or burned out. Then, too, there's the glaring example of overeager people with visionary aspirations ending up floridly psychotic on hallucinogenic drugs. Over the years, I've seen too many of them land in emergency rooms, strapped to a gurney with hard leather restraints, bound at the ankles and wrists, being shot up with Thorazine to bring them down. Just as a tree needs to have its roots firmly planted in the earth so as not to get blown away, your foundation must also be sturdy. Only then will there be no danger that you'll get overwhelmed. With patience, intuition can evolve organically.

One of the healthy, positive routes you can bring to intuition—and perhaps the most powerful—is creative expression.

There's something inherently balancing about it when you're swept up in the flow. At these times, you're giving birth to what is most true in you, not solely from the standpoint of the intellect but from your deepest recesses. Overthinking kills creativity, as it does intuition. The magic comes when you give up mental control and allow a greater force to take hold. In this groove you can be showered with original ideas and intuitive insights. All systems alert, you're so ripe for inspiration that it floods right through you.

My friend Janus, a screenwriter, rarely thinks about being intuitive. But she is. Early one morning, she was awakened by a dream in which the plot of an involved story was perfectly laid out. It was about a crooked evangelist who's afraid he has performed a legitimate miracle when a young boy is healed by his touch. Janus sprung out of bed and rushed into the kitchen where her husband was drinking tea. When she told the dream to him, he was enthusiastic: "Write it down," he said, "it's a terrific idea." Immediately she flipped on her computer. When the story actually seemed to write itself, she knew she had a hot script. Janus's husband, a producer, eventually sold it—and it was made into the film *Leap of Faith,* starring Steve Martin.

Janus frequently dreams her story lines. To her, it's the most natural thing in the world. "The most magical moments in my work are when I step out of the way," she says. "Dreams are the ultimate means to do this." Whenever she faces a problem in her writing, she consciously puts herself into the troublesome scene as she drifts off to sleep. An observer in her own dream, she watches the action and the motivation of the characters play out. This gives her a running start on finding a solution. I know many writers who routinely use similar techniques.

Robert Louis Stevenson, for example, drew on his dreams for the classic thriller *Dr. Jekyll and Mr. Hyde,* the story of a prominent doctor who is transformed into a serial killer. I was fascinated when I first read Stevenson's account of his creative process: "I had long been trying to write a story on this subject, to find a body, a vehicle, for that strong sense of man's double being which must at times come in upon and overwhelm the mind of all thinking creatures. . . . For two days I went about wracking my brains for a plot of any sort; and on the second night I dreamed the scene at the window and a scene afterwards split in two, in which Hyde, pursued for some crime, took the powder and underwent the change in the presence of his pursuers. All the rest was made awake and consciously."

From his description, I knew that Stevenson had tapped into an intuitive source. My feeling was confirmed when he spoke of the amazing "Little People." They instructed him beat by beat what each section of a story would be, even keeping an eye on the needs of the literary marketplace. Stevenson saw his conscious self as the "Little People's" agent, transcribing their ideas verbatim.

To me, this is the epitome of intuitive creativity. Every time I hear about artists who are directed through dreams, voices, or visions I am moved. An extraordinary fluidity and layers of possibility exist in these states. The intensity of the creative process, the surrender required to get to the really good stuff inside, is exactly what fuels intuition. Stevenson's approach made great art because he was able to travel to inner places most people never have access to. It wasn't something he tediously labored over. The very spirit of his work carried him there.

When you immerse yourself in creative projects, whether or not you think of what you're doing as intuitive, you place yourself in an intuitively supercharged state. Passionately focused on your work, you set your intellect aside and shift out of ordinary awareness. Once in a creative rhythm, a wellspring of colors, sounds, and images appears. You, as the artist, simply take dictation. The painter Joan Miró worked in just this way: Rather than interpreting his dreams, he replicated them intact, in brilliant colors on canvas.

Of course, you won't be constantly racing ahead at full speed. Just as intuition ebbs and flows, so do rhythms and cycles of creativity. When we go through those frustrating days or even months when it seems like nothing much is happening, it's futile to force it. There is no way to hurry a rose to bloom. These are breathing spells, intervals of gestation, moments when we must relax and allow the wisdom we have gained to incubate gently. The poet Rilke describes the artist's path when he says, after the storms of spring, summer comes "only to those who are patient, who are there as though eternity lay before them."

It's easy to lose sight of this. Sometimes when I write I find myself tense and laboring at the computer, muscles tight, jaw clenched, getting nowhere fast. I'm trying too hard, need some time off, perhaps to hop into my car and drive up the coast. With the top down, my hair wild in the breeze, my spirit can soar again. While I'm listening to a tape of Muddy Waters—I'm crazy about the blues—collecting seashells on the beach, watching kids bobbing up and down on the Santa Monica Pier merry-go-round, or thinking about nothing in particular, fresh ideas have the space to float in.

Then there are those graced periods when my writing is effortless, intuition flowing so abundantly I can hardly catch it all. Entire days can fly by when I even forget to eat. I keep notepads stashed near my bed, by the bathtub, on the passenger seat of the car. I won't hesitate to pull over by the side of the road, stop a conversation in midstream, or wake up in the middle of the night to get down my ideas. These are exhilarated moments of being in sync, when the energy I've gathered during the dormant phase comes into fruition.

I believe that all forms of creative and intuitive expression originate from an infinitely fertile spiritual source. In the same way that artists create, visionaries peer into the invisible. The painter Paul Klee recognized this when he said, "Art does not reproduce the visible. It makes visible." To me, the shared challenge of both intuitives and artists is to translate the intangible into material form. This can take the shape of a novel, a painting, a song, or may come through as a prediction about the future. The kind of information we pick up depends on our intention. Any creative endeavor can provide a medium to help intuition grow.

I have a patient, Molly, a painter who is proof of this. For my birthday, she once gave me one of her watercolors, a painting of a grove of deep green California oaks nestled high atop a chaparral-dotted Malibu crest. I have it hanging on my office wall. It's more than just beautiful: It actually seems to manufacture light. The otherworldly colors are vibrantly braided within each brushstroke; a fine golden hue flickers right through. The first time I saw it, I instantly sensed its power.

During creative spurts Molly possesses the same quality of presence and openness that I've been privileged to feel during my best readings. For her, there is no time more joyous. "I don't even have to think about what I'm doing," she says, "I feel energized. Ideas seem to shoot through me right onto the canvas." This is an intuitive state; it feeds Molly's art and in turn is fed by it.

Like Molly, I always know when I'm really on. Then, doing a reading has the freedom and expansiveness of riding a horse bareback across a sunlit flowered field. There's a depth of sight and effortlessness that takes over when I can let go just enough to surrender. This is the real thrill of the intuitive, the same vital energy fueling creative flow. Without it my prescience would surely be diminished, the artist reduced to mere technician, a tiny speck of light compared to a radiant orb.

I am in awe of how infinitely creative intuition can be. One day at lunch a friend excitedly told me about a Brazilian psychologist and visionary, Luis Gasparetto, whom she had just witnessed. "He has no formal artistic training," she said, "but he claims that a number of the great masters—Renoir, Picasso, Modigliani, Van Gogh, and others—intuitively express themselves through him. He whips out drawings in no time that look like the originals." I wanted to see for myself. Unfortunately, that was his last Los Angeles engagement scheduled for a while, so it wasn't possible. Curious, I tracked down a videotape of that night and scrutinized him to see if he was for real or somehow faking it. I'm a tough audience when it comes to these things. The integrity of intuition is just too important to me; I won't diminish this gift by accepting "magic" or trickery.

Lying back on my bed, I switched on the tape. Gasparetto, a youthful man of about forty, barely spoke a word the whole time. His eyes shut, listening to classical music at full blast, he used both his hands and feet simultaneously to produce as many as four drawings in a matter of minutes, all similar enough to the style of the great masters that an untrained eye might easily confuse the two. Reaching for tubes of paint, never once looking at them, he later remarked, "I choose the colors by instinct. I sense them in my body, feel them in my skin." Without ever using any brushes, he squeezes the paint onto a canvas, applying pressure with his fingers, the heel of his hand, his knuckles, and his feet, furiously spreading it around, sometimes even working upside down. It is truly an astonishing sight: He moves at such speed, and his limbs are so finely coordinated, that he looks more like an automaton than a human being.

I do not know if this man is actually channeling the great masters, as he says he does. I believe, however, that he is extremely open to the creative flow and that his intuitive connection with the style of certain artists allows him to impressively reproduce their paintings. In this he is quite gifted. I saw in Gasparetto a refined demonstration of intuition and the creative working together in harmony.

Unfortunately, I've also run into gifted people who don't always use their power well. I've seen genuine intuitive ability mixed with a lack of maturity and discernment. This is a lethal combination. Motivated by gigantic egos, seduced by an insatiable need to control, these individuals lose their sense of balance and their priorities. Too many times I've known of people like this who prey on the innocence and naïveté of vulnerable seekers. I get furious whenever I hear of someone voluntarily handing over her power to irresponsible teachers who greedily snatch it up.

I met such a man recently. A friend of mine called late at night to rave about a Peruvian shaman, a wondrous healer he felt I just had to see. The shaman would only be in town for a few days; my friend could arrange an appointment. I usually don't consult healers other than my own spiritual teacher; I prefer to stay focused on one path. But because of my curiosity, the fact that I'd had some annoying stomach trouble lately that could really use help, and my friend's insistence, I agreed to check him out.

The signs were ominous from the beginning. The shaman charged an exorbitant fee for his services—to be paid strictly in cash—and made claims of fantastic cures. My friend argued, "He's better than Carlos Castaneda's Don Juan. What difference does money make if he's for real?" The whole thing didn't feel right. But after all this time and study, there was still a part of me that wished for a miraculous cure-all, a healer who could wave his magic wand and make everything okay.

Right after breakfast one morning, I drove to a Brentwood home straight out of *Architectural Digest* where the sessions were being held. This man was in such demand that people were herded into the living room, waiting their turn. I felt odd, disturbingly like a child. Here we were, by all appearances a group of successful professionals, turning to him to fix us. It was sad, absurd, and naively hopeful all at the same time. Finally, after two hours, when everyone else had gone, my name was called. I was led into a private room in the back, as if entering an inner sanctum. The shaman looked so authentic that he could have been hired by central casting. A bone-thin, hunched over Mayan in his late sixties, he spoke no English. The woman who sponsored his trip to the United States served as his translator. This is going to be good, I thought.

After greeting me, nodding his head, he then uttered some words in Spanish. The translator asked, "What are your symptoms?"

"Lately I've felt these waves of anxiety," I said candidly. "I haven't been sleeping well, and my stomach's been killing me."

Never once looking me in the eyes, the shaman picked up a small mirror and ran it up and down the underside of both my forearms. He pinched the skin on my wrists. Then, staring grimly at the floor, he shook his head and mumbled something under his breath in Spanish. The only word I recognized was *loco,* and the rest didn't sound much better.

"What did he say?" I asked, panic beginning to overtake me.

The translator hesitated, as if not wanting to break the bad news. "He apologizes but he can't do anything for you."

"What are you talking about?" I managed to squeak out.

"I hate to tell you this," the translator said, "but there's no hope. Soon your stomach will get so bad you won't be able to eat. You'll grow thinner and weaker. Eventually you'll just waste away and die."

I was shocked. For a few horrible seconds, half of me believed him, deferring to this man as if he were an all-knowing sage. I felt about an inch high, terrified that I already had one foot in the grave. "Isn't there anything more you can advise?" I asked. The shaman turned his back to me, as if irritated, and replied he'd have to consult his dreams. The translator looked at me with such pity it made my skin crawl, and solemnly whispered, "I'm so sorry."

Suddenly, the melodrama of it all shook me to my senses. I felt like I was playing a leading role in a B movie. Why was I listening to this man? He was using fear tactics to hook me in and I, a trained psychiatrist and intuitive with years of solid spiritual practice behind me, was taking the bait. The entire scene had been one giant setup. Of course, the obvious next question I was expected to ask was "How much more would it cost for you to look in your dreams?" But, thank God, I didn't. Grateful that my presence of mind had returned, I knew that nothing he'd said was true. The spell now broken, I was furious, and blasted them: "You mean to say you've known me only five minutes, condemn me to suffering a horrible death, and then send me off completely stripped of hope! How can you be so irresponsible? Even if you are right, where is your compassion?"

I left, marveling at how ready I'd been to sacrifice my power to a complete stranger, sucked in by the awe of his followers. Such blind devotion should have been a tip-off. Just because someone claims to be a great shaman doesn't mean he is. Unfortunately, I later discovered that at least a couple of people fell for almost exactly the same line that this man handed me and ended up doling out ungodly sums of money to be healed. The irony is that some actually felt better. Whether they were simply suggestible or this man had some real skill, I don't know. What I do know for certain, however, is that controlling people through fear is unconscionable, a red flag that an intuitive is unbalanced, and should be avoided.

Meeting this man was a harsh reminder of the dangers of so-called healers who are domineering and motivated by greed rather than compassion. Because I was going through a hard time and wanted immediate relief, I was susceptible to being tricked. No matter how knowledgeable we are, we may be tempted to go to any lengths to get well. But sustained healing can take place only when a teacher ignites resources we already have within, not if he professes to do it for us, creating a false dependency.

I am also angered by charismatic intuitives and spiritual teachers who exploit students sexually, promising an inside track to spiritual advancement. Some of these "gurus" may even believe it themselves; they have no remorse.

Once, out of curiosity I attended a talk given by a popular but controversial spiritual teacher based in Los Angeles. By this time he was infamous for having sex with his female students, but still the lecture hall was packed. I saw at once that he was incredibly funny, attractive, and radiated a charismatic appeal. Actually, he was too charming; I was immediately put off. Nonetheless, I recognized from his responses to the audience's questions that he was a stunningly sharp clairvoyant with an astute understanding of how energy moved. Seductive, full of himself, and talented: a deadly mix.

Soon after that night, accounts of his flagrant sexual escapades with students appeared in the press. Promised enlightenment, many women had gone along with him, not because they wanted sex, but as an act of unconditional surrender to their guru. He would buy them jewelry and fine gifts, wine and dine them at expensive hotels—then move on to another conquest. Not surprisingly, these women felt abandoned, abused, outraged. Many had given him large donations they couldn't afford, had sacrificed their jobs, even their families. Finally they got fed up and left the group, often struggling to rebuild their lives from scratch. His following scattered, and with the press on his back, this man eventually was run out of town.

It is never necessary to have sex with our teachers in order to grow spiritually. Even the ancient mystical discipline of Tantra, which focuses on sexuality as a vehicle for transcendence, is never forced upon anyone. If a teacher ever insists that sex with him—or her—is the only way to enlightenment, run in the opposite direction as fast as you can.

In my own life, as a therapist and intuitive, I've strived to be clear about sexuality, maintaining firm boundaries with people I'm reading. Looking into someone's life so closely, particularly if I don't know them well, can breed an instant intimacy that may be easily misinterpreted. Once I was introduced to a man on a remote-viewing project I was doing. Thrilled to learn I was an intuitive, he asked to come to my office for a reading. This was not unusual—I often give readings to people I work with—so I gladly agreed. But from then on, he began laying it on too thick about how incredibly wise I was, blushing like a smitten schoolboy: He'd clearly developed a crush on me. I was flattered, but I knew it wasn't real. He had the unmistakable glazed look of someone all too eager to relinquish his own power and project onto me an elevated status that had no bearing on who I was. Realizing how unhealthy it would be to feed into this, I gently explained what I thought was happening and put a stop to the whole thing.

I've seen many intuitives and spiritual teachers fall into the trap of getting sexually involved with their students. It's a predictable challenge, and needs to be anticipated before serious damage occurs. Some teachers deal with it by becoming celibate. Others reach a crossroads where their integrity is tested—and many fail. Catered to by adoring students, they succumb. In the best of circumstances, they admit their indiscretions, sincerely learning from their mistakes. But a malignant few remain power hungry, ravenously feeding on attention like sharks but losing sight of their real purpose.

Intuitives and spiritual teachers are human beings. No matter how wise, they all have obstacles to overcome. Beware of those who are eager to impress, encourage dependency, or charge outrageous amounts for their services. The most artful intuitives and healers I've known, ones with authentic maturity, are straightforward and humble, and they charge reasonable fees. They don't coerce by fear and have nothing to prove. A true healer's skill lies in kindling your power.

A holy bond is formed in any healing relationship. Whenever I'm working with someone in therapy, it's always more than just the two of us involved. A third entity is born: the spirit of the therapy itself, an expanding spark with an inherent intelligence and character. It's a compass that marks the way, clarifying my job if I listen.

My office hours usually go nonstop from nine to five. For most of the day, I'm intuitively wide open. I feel like a telephone operator on a gigantic switchboard, handling a rush of incoming calls. Listening to my patients both intuitively and with my intellect, I simultaneously track a myriad of images and sensations along with their words. Logic often lays the groundwork, intuition filling in missing gaps, color, and detail. I'm hyperalert, my body alive, but at the same time I'm detached, witnessing the session as an observer. I rarely know what I'm going to say until the moment I say it. Very little I do in therapy is preplanned. Trusting the direction the session is taking, I try not to exert undue control or superimpose my own agenda.

When I first began weaving intuition into my work, I was afraid I wasn't doing enough if I simply allowed myself to be guided. In medical school I had been programmed to be ever vigilant, to scrutinize every situation, take full charge. Unless I shouldered the entire load, I was convinced, I'd be cheating, cutting corners. Thus I often ended up trying too hard when it wasn't necessary. At night I would drag my body home exhausted, limp as a rag doll. I didn't have the slightest idea how to conserve my strength.

Now whenever my energy is depleted, I know to back off. The tougher sessions especially begin to exact a toll. To avoid this I pause for meditation breaks, intuitively disengaging throughout the day. Reconnecting with my spiritual source feels like standing beneath a waterfall, being bathed in pristine water. It's my shield and protection, easing the heaviness, infusing the light once more. Only then can I be fully present in my work.

Sometimes my role is simply to mirror intuition in someone else. But I have to be careful. Too often, patients expect me to give magic answers. They make me into an authority figure, disempowering themselves by believing they can't be intuitive as well. Time and again I try to confront that illusion, realizing how destructive it is. But even in people who know better, this impulse is amazingly tenacious.

One of my patients, Sam, a computer whiz at a local think tank, hounded me constantly. Naively in awe of anything intuitive, he imagined me to be all-knowing. Even worse, he craved solutions to his problems without making an effort himself, which got on my nerves. "Can't you just tell me this one thing," he'd persist, grilling me about his problem of the day. Had I allowed it, Sam would have been willing to defer to me completely. It never dawned on him that he could do this himself. "Why don't you give it a shot?" I urged when he once again demanded a reading. Sam resisted, citing all the usual excuses: "I don't know what I'm doing. What if I'm wrong? Only special people are intuitive." Nonsense. Because I was fond of Sam, knew how capable he was, I stood firm.

Finally we struck a deal. He'd initially risk a reading himself, then I would follow with mine. We began by practicing. Typically I'd repeat a name of someone I knew well and then "send" it to him. He'd relate his impressions, right or wrong, and I'd respond with feedback. As we proceeded this way, intuitive images came to Sam more freely, and he began putting pictures and feelings together like pieces of a puzzle. The insights he gained from this method later helped him to deal with dilemmas he had been pressing me to read. There's no substitute for jumping right in and doing the work.

I have no hard-and-fast rules governing when to give a direct intuitive response. It's a matter of discretion: The timing has to feel right. If someone is an ardent disbeliever, out of respect I steer clear of the issue unless an interest is expressed. Nor, as I've said, do I stress this point in the emotionally unstable, who might misinterpret the information. Then there are people like Sam, obsessively enamored of intuition, who need to view it more realistically. The same is true for those who wrongly turn to it to overmanage their lives. "Let's tune in to the whole week," one patient of mine frequently asks, expecting a blow-by-blow accounting of the next seven days' events. I don't encourage this, however. For critical issues, maybe. But first she must do a reading herself. Then I'll chime in. I believe that the joy of life is in discovery, not in plotting out our every move. Even if that were possible.

To me, the best use of intuition is when I can help define a problem, allowing a person to apply such knowledge constructively. With someone who is well grounded and doesn't over-glorify intuition or abuse it, I'm more apt to be direct. Also, if I sense that real danger is involved—for example, the time when a patient came to me alarmed his plane was going to crash and I intuitively agreed—I will be forthright.

Joan, a movie producer and long-term patient, had been listless for over a month. In the middle of shooting a film, she could barely keep up with the harrowing schedule. Usually overflowing with energy, she found her fatigue so debilitating that she called from location and asked me to tune in. This wasn't like Joan, who rarely sought intuitive help. I knew it was important. Picturing her body's afterimage, I intuitively scanned it, the way a Geiger counter picks up radiation, to detect if anything was wrong. This is where my medical knowledge really comes in: Sweeping across from head to toe, I visualize each organ, individually cross-checking my responses to see if there's a glitch. If something isn't right it stands out, lighting up, its texture and consistency altered, a feeling similar to running your hand over silky fabric and coming to a tiny irregular knot. Focusing on Joan's blood, I sensed it was thin, some vital element missing. Since Joan's production schedule was so hectic, it was almost impossible for her to make time to see a doctor. But when I told her what I saw, she arranged an appointment. Though her health was otherwise fine, the doctor discovered that Joan had a severe case of anemia.

During intuitive readings, I don't reveal anything without considering the implications. Always I ask myself, Will this information be helpful? Even with people like Joan, when I believe it will be, I'm still careful about my presentation. There are so many ways to go wrong. I know of a well-meaning intuitive who was asked by a single mother to do a reading of her newborn daughter. Intuition revealed the possibility that the child would be learning disabled. On hearing this, the mother looked as if she had been run over by a truck. This was the last thing she wanted to know. As a forecast of the future, even if true, all it accomplished was to plant fear in her—in this case no useful purpose was served. Though another mother might have wanted this knowledge, it was still a judgment call. The balance between when or when not to speak out can be incredibly delicate.

I find this to be particularly critical in potentially life-threatening circumstances. Dropping a bomb on someone that they have cancer or AIDS can often cause more harm than good. Then there's also the chance that my perceptions are inaccurate. Readings are not infallible. In such situations, I tend to err on the conservative side, stressing the gravity of my concerns without getting specific. I point people in the right direction by strongly urging them to get checked out medically, but they must take it from there.

In some instances, it's inappropriate to do a reading at all. Just as I would never walk through somebody's front door without an invitation, I never look into someone intuitively unless there's an opening. When I try to tune in and it feels like I'm hitting a brick wall, I know to back off. An invisible force field repels me. Even if someone has requested a reading, something inside them is resisting. Images I pick up don't congeal, or they blur like a fading watercolor. Other times I just draw a blank, or feel there's nothing substantial to grab on to. Any attempt to push through such protective barricades would be an invasion of privacy.

Intuitive balance entails communicating what you know with respect, being discriminating but also trusting your heart to guide you when to act. Confidence doesn't come overnight, but when you make the effort to balance your intuitive gifts, you gain both energy and stability. At home with your prescience, you are now free to enter new realms, at the same time still well grounded. Like a martial-arts master, you stand poised and centered, intuitively in tune wherever you are.

Not that this means you can't be at ease, free of pretense, a part of the ordinary, daily world, in any situation. Some of my most impressive intuitive insights have come to me while driving, shopping, walking by the ocean, or even sitting on the swings at Venice Beach. I often go there when I'm stuck and need to figure things out. Facing the boardwalk, hands gripping the cool chain links, I push off barefoot from the sand. Swinging high, I take in the fabulous pageant of people passing just a few feet away: couples jogging in matching skin-tight magenta shorts; a group of young black boys gyrating to a rap tape; futuristic-looking roller skaters who could have stepped straight out of *Bladerunner*. As I continue to swing, my mind clears, intuitive images rush by. Answers occur to me as naturally as if I were on an isolated mountain peak. In the midst of this whirlwind of activity, there's a special sweetness in knowing I can be completely at one with it all.

CHAPTER ELEVEN

The Spiritual Path
of Intuition

Seeing into darkness is clarity . . .
Use your own light
and return to the source of light.
—TAO TE CHING
(TRANS. BY STEPHEN MITCHELL)

The afternoon sky is a deep azure, so tranquil and pure I rise up in spirit, hovering high above the earth. Caressed by a soft summer breeze, I gaze down at a lush expanse of fertile undulating hills. Nestled there is the quaint East German village of Weimar. The scene is idyllic. Hearing my cousin Irene's voice yelling, "Judith, hurry up," I return to earth, taking in one last look . . . before I meet the horror that awaits me only a few steps away.

It's the summer of 1991. I am walking down a barren concrete path, about to enter the death camp at Buchenwald. A chillingly sinister contrast to the peaceful landscape above. Staring up at the looming stone guard tower, I can make out every bare inch of its still-intact metal gun mounts. Swallowing hard, I strain to keep my composure, but the ground itself seems to be tugging at my feet like quicksand. There is no past or future, only this moment. I feel the ghosts of the dead everywhere.

I had just arrived in Germany the day before. Even at the Frankfurt airport the sound of German echoing through the loudspeakers was eerily unnerving. Rationally, I knew the Holocaust had happened over fifty years ago. But I was both a Jewish woman and an intuitive; an inner instinct responded. The threat of annihilation pierced through to my core. The German men and women I talked to couldn't have been friendlier. I was well aware of that, yet still a part of me feared that if I made one wrong move I would be found out and seized. Until then, persecution of an entire people was a terror I had only vaguely identified with when my mother had expressed it while I was growing up. Now I understood her feelings better.

On a train to Bavaria to join Irene, I shared sweet rolls and coffee with a woman doctor from Nuremberg I had just met, chatting away with her as if nothing were wrong. But as I looked out the window at the fairy-tale countryside speckled with castles and meadows of wildflowers, I cringed, intuitively sensing the history of this picture-perfect setting imprinted like a malignant afterimage.

Something compelled me to visit a concentration camp. I couldn't not go. I was curious—curious to see for myself what one was really like, not just to shed light on my Jewish past but to really register the malevolent extremes humans are capable of if unchecked. I wasn't sure how or why, but somehow this knowing was going to make me feel more whole.

Now here I was with Irene, an English teacher at an American military base in Germany, her new BMW parked in the visitors' lot a million miles away. And hell, bounded by a sea of barbed wire, stretching out before us. The camp has been preserved down to the smallest detail, just as it looked in the war. The point, of course, is to remember.

Shivering though the day is warm, we pass through the arch beneath the ominous tower. A stifling grayness descends. We tour the grounds, entering the crematorium, the gas chamber hideously disguised as a shower room, and the building where the "medical" experimentation took place. Climbing the winding stairway, we enter the prisoners' barracks, stark and airless. Disturbingly sparse handfuls of straw cover multileveled wooden platforms where human beings slept three to a bed, hundreds to a room.

I sense their presence. They are prowling the camp, brushing against me. I'm starting to feel vaguely nauseated, numb. My breathing turns shallow, barely perceptible. I notice myself becoming suspiciously calm, frozen inside. I get this way whenever I'm really scared. Yet the truth that is calling out to me far surpasses my fear.

Drawn to better understand the meaning of the darkness, I instinctively go off on my own—an old carryover from childhood, to retreat within whenever I feel overwhelmed. Fighting an impulse to cut off the experience, I sit on the remains of a rectangular cement foundation at the far end of the camp. It was at this spot that the public executions were carried out. Ironically, despite the eeriness of the setting, I feel safest alone. I close my eyes to meditate, not knowing where it will take me. My light cotton blouse feels as though it could be ripped off at any moment by the sheer accumulation of so much inhumane violence committed here and still present now. I cross my arms around my chest, holding it tight.

As I quiet myself in meditation, I can intuitively feel the echo of the atrocities that occurred in this place, leaving my body leaden and chilled. I see every detail of the camp vibrating at tremendous speed. Transfixed, I marvel as the intensity of the motion strips away the surface of everything in sight, revealing a pervasive blanket of darkness beneath. It is a toxic, gritty film pulsating ever so slightly, infiltrating the scene, leaching every last molecule of vitality and tainting the very air I breathe. At the same time, I'm deluged by voices and images of people I believe were captive here. It's happening so fast I can't hold on to any of the words. The darkness is insinuating itself on me. I'm lost in it; nothing I've encountered previously begins to compare with this nightmare. I feel my sense of self weakening. Fortunately, I recognize in a flash of insight the stranglehold the darkness has on me: All I can think about is getting away from this place. Jolted out of my meditation, I open my eyes, grasping onto the wall's cold cement blocks with both hands. I need to touch something solid and firm to reassure me that I'm okay. I stand up, my legs still unsteady beneath me. I hurry back through the archway under the guard tower and leave.

The memory of the camp haunted me the rest of my trip through Eastern Europe and for weeks following my return home. I felt lethargic and depressed, aching all over as if coming down with the flu. But I wasn't physically ill—I just felt utterly defeated by the darkness. It seemed so ferocious, so incomparable in its destructive force. Not that I hadn't been aware of this darkness before. It had been trailing me my entire life, just in lesser forms. When I was a child, it was the boogeyman, the clattering of the wooden shutters against my window on a windy night, or the spookiness of being all alone in a big, empty house. It lurked in shadowy corners, intimidating me at a distance but never fully showing its face. I'd always counted on the ultimate triumph of love over evil, but now my faith was shaken. Love didn't seem to have a fighting chance.

Soon after getting back to Los Angeles, I climbed one of the highest peaks of Malibu Creek State Park, overlooking the ocean, to get some perspective. The earth was warm from the morning sun, and I found a smooth, rounded boulder on which to meditate. This land, held sacred by the Chumash tribe, is where I feel most secure. The V-shaped canyons sheltering me in their arms like a mother, the grand old oaks venerating a silent wisdom, and the earth carpeted with golden mustard, all delighted me. There was peace here, always waiting to be found.

Sitting cross-legged, in an old pair of jeans I love so much, I breathed in deeply and began to meditate. Within minutes, however, I found myself transported back to Buchenwald. I was completely disoriented; it took every ounce of restraint I had to stay present. Not this again, I thought, sinking at the sight. Still, there it was: that terrible darkness, outstretched before me, in complete view. But this time I didn't bolt away. Comforted by the safety of the canyon, I cautiously sneaked a closer look. Here on familiar turf, courage was easier to summon. To my surprise, I recognized a dimension I'd missed while at the camp: The faintest glow of light flickered through every structure, even the ground itself, building the more I focused on it. Single-mindedly I watched, thinking of nothing else, feeling a mounting sense of love. Right before my eyes, it appeared to be birthing itself, light bearing light in a breathtaking spectacle. Pure, luminous, penetrating even the blackest crevices, it extended far beyond the electrified barbed-wire fences and into the sky.

In the face of such magnificence, my fear fell away. I drank it in, memorizing every nuance so I'd never forget or again feel so desolate. Reconnecting with this light, I felt as though I'd found once more my dearest love. I realized it had been there all the time. Consumed by fear, however, I just hadn't looked far enough to see it. Rigid before, my body softened, a flood of energy rushing through me. I breathed easily for the first time in weeks, smelled the aroma of pungent sage and rosemary growing in patches on the canyon slopes. Dwarfed by the enormity of this radiance, the darkness seemed minuscule, and yet the two were intimately linked. It looked as if the light were holding the darkness deep within its belly, sharing the same blood supply. In that moment, I began to grasp what I later better understood: that even in the worst depravity, the light can still exist. It is only our fear that blinds us to it.

I cannot, of course, claim the unspeakable experiences at Buchenwald as my own. Nor do I want in any way to diminish the misery there by making too facile a connection to my own fortunate life. Nonetheless, my visit to Buchenwald had the effect of compelling me to start exploring the meaning of darkness in the world. It was the first step of an ongoing process. Such issues are more easily stated than resolved, but I keep searching for greater clarity.

The psychiatrist Viktor Frankl, one of my heroes, has guided my thinking. In *Man's Search for Meaning,* he courageously portrays the years he spent as a prisoner in Auschwitz:

> *In spite of all the enforced physical and mental primitiveness of the life in a concentration camp, it was possible for spiritual life to deepen. . . . Only in this way can we explain the apparent paradox that some prisoners of a less hardy makeup often seemed to survive camp life better than those of a robust nature. The salvation of man is through love and in love. I understood how a man who has nothing left in this world may still know bliss, be it only for a brief moment, in the contemplation of his beloved. For the first time in my life I was able to understand the meaning of the words, "The angels are lost in the perpetual contemplation of an infinite glory."*

Though I've been spared what Frankl confronted, I've come to believe that the spiritual path of the intuitive is to face both the dark and the light—not to sever a portion of life and see only what pleases us. Many people may initially recoil at the idea that we all contain a spectrum of dark and light with the potential to act out both. But we must be warriors, alert to the multiple forces in and around us. Thus we must search deep inside to identify and topple our fiercest demons. And then heal that part of ourselves. At the same time, we must tend what is most admirable within, embracing our truest strengths. All for the purpose of edging closer to the source of light from which we have come.

Our ultimate goal is to become more awake. To appreciate from all angles the stunning complexity of who we are. Consider also that even in the most dire of circumstances, there exists a possibility for magnificence and connection to spirit. As Frankl suggests, we can create a life founded on love anywhere. Spirituality means connecting with our hearts and a higher power; intuition can help open ourselves to do this. However, it's not the only way; to borrow an expression from the writer Raymond Carver, it's just "another path to the waterfall." But as your prescience matures, you become more of a transparent vehicle, able to experience multiple layers of reality that deepen your spiritual appreciation. A channel opens, your armor falls away, love is easier to feel and it can move you.

Spirituality is not an abstract concept from an intuitive perspective. It's always right before you—manifested through dreams, visions, and intuitions—but you must make it come alive. Live it, breathe it, recognize it even in the minutiae of your life. As you do, you discover we're not just two-dimensional beings bounded by our skin. People in India recognize this in the sweetness of their greeting to each other, saying, *"Nameste,"* "I respect the spirit within you," instead of "Hello." This spirit is in us all, intuitively unmistakable and vast. The poet Kabir describes it so well:

> *There is a Secret One inside us;*
> *the planets and all the galaxies*
> *pass through his hands like beads.*
> *This is a string of beads one should look at with luminous eyes.*
> (Trans. by Robert Bly)

Our prescience provides this. The advantage to being intuitive is not simply to see more but to make sense of what we see. When everything comes together and even seemingly disconnected pieces click into place, it satisfies our most inquisitive impulses. Our ultimate reward as intuitive people, however, if we are also spiritually open, is to be able to glimpse the incredible light I encountered at Buchenwald—which, by the way, is everywhere. For me, feeling such love for even a few minutes a day is finding heaven on earth. Nothing is more healing.

My trip to Buchenwald and the intuitive insight I gained are precious to me. With the power of love reaffirmed, I came away more able to find it in any circumstance, no matter how extreme. By viewing every experience as a gift, life has become more fulfilling and a lot less painful. On the most frozen, iciest of slopes, if you look closely enough, there will always be the tiniest of flowers. This is the great wonder. The most demanding spiritual challenge is to search for the light in any situation, even when things seem to be utterly unfair. A hard lesson, certainly. But one well learned.

Searching for the light may be difficult because we tend to be mesmerized by darkness. Our fear of it eclipses the light. Such fear is so primal and firmly embedded that it's powerfully reflected in how we react to the forces of nature. I've never seen an author capture this more masterfully than Annie Dillard in her story "Solar Eclipse":

> *People on all the hillsides, including, I think, myself, screamed when the black body of the moon detached from the sky and rolled over the sun. But something else was happening at that same instant, and it was this, I believe, which made us scream: The second before the sun went out we saw a wall of dark shadow come speeding at us. We no sooner saw it than it was upon us, like thunder. It roared up the valley. It slammed our hill and knocked us out. It was the monstrous swift shadow cone of the moon. . . . It rolled at you across the land at 1,800 miles an hour, hauling darkness like plague behind it. . . . We saw the wall of shadow coming, and screamed before it hit.*

Darkness comes in all forms, from without and within. Yet I believe that when we become conscious of our darker side we're less likely to be seduced by it—this awareness helps us not to get sucked in. By confronting our anger, hurt, fear, and resentments, we can refine our spirits like a finely polished diamond. As Gandhi says, "We must be the change." Coming to terms with our own darkness can help us find peace. It's not only liberating for us, it can also profoundly affect how other people behave in our presence.

Late one summer afternoon I was driving my white VW Rabbit, heading for Chinatown to meet a friend for dinner. Even though I was passing through a seedy neighborhood, the weather was so sticky and hot that I had unwisely rolled all the windows down. When I stopped at a red light, an enormous man, large enough to play defensive tackle for the Raiders, suddenly darted from the corner bus stop and rushed toward me. I saw him leap up onto the hood of my car and felt a gigantic thud as he began to bounce up and down as if on a trampoline. It all happened so fast I didn't have time to get scared. Before I had a chance to close my window, he stuck his arm through it and grabbed for my head. I was sure he was going to strike me. Instead, his rage evaporated. He gently cupped my face in his hands. Gazing straight into my eyes, he smiled so sweetly, like a baby, that I couldn't help but smile back. Then, as abruptly as he'd appeared, he dodged through traffic mumbling to himself, returned to the crowded bus stop, and sat down. When the light turned green, I continued on, disbelieving, but grateful I was still in one piece.

That man was quite capable of hurting me, but he didn't, and I kept asking myself why. As I replayed the scene in my head over the next couple of days, I came to understand. For one thing, I couldn't look more nonthreatening; I don't go through life giving off a lot of fear or expecting at any moment to be attacked—qualities that, according to self-defense classes, count for a lot. But on an energy level, I believe the answer goes deeper. We all radiate an energy field that extends way beyond the body, an "aura," which is partially a reflection of our emotional state. Others can often feel it, even if they don't identify it as such. Anger in particular is easy to sense. In certain situations, when people walk around dangerously close to the edge like the man I encountered, it can set them off.

This is where the work I'd done on myself really served me. Because I make a concerted effort to deal with my more difficult emotions and then let them go, there was less of a buildup for this man to zero in on intuitively. Instead, at a subtle energy level, he responded to a more peaceful part of me and smiled instead of tearing my head off (though probably none of this was conscious on his part). Sometimes violence cannot be stopped no matter what we do. But the more peaceful we are, the better chance we have of bringing out the peace in those around us.

It's all too tempting to project our darker sides onto something outside ourselves. After all, the bad guys who make the eleven o'clock news are easy targets. Their actions are so glaring they're hard to identify with. But it also happens in a less obvious way. As a psychiatrist, I see people who project all the time. The qualities they most resist in themselves are the ones they project onto others. For instance, I once treated an extremely successful dentist who was a pathological liar, but he'd come to me complaining that everyone else was cheating him. His beliefs were so fixed, I barely made a dent in them. Even after being convicted of fraud, he swore he was framed and trusted no one.

Projection is a primitive, unconscious instinct learned in childhood. It takes years of effort to unlearn. Even the other day when I stubbed my toe on a doorjamb, my first inclination was to blame the door rather than admit my own clumsiness. Projection distorts our view of the world and prevents us from understanding each other and ourselves. But being intuitive demands clarity, so that we can see beyond our own projections. Only then can we appreciate people and situations as they actually are, not how we imagine them. The commitment that comes with being on a spiritual path impels us to clean up our acts at every opportunity.

For two years I was a medical consultant at a residential alcohol and drug recovery program for Jewish criminal offenders. As part of our outreach services, several counselors and I visited a high-security men's prison in Chino to celebrate Passover with some of the inmates. The other women knew the ins and outs of the prison system, had come here on many occasions, but this was my first time. I was eager to experience what a prison was like from the inside—to get a better feel for the men in our program. But my interest went beyond that: I wanted to learn more about freedom, and sensed that somehow these men could teach me.

To get from the front entrance of the facility to the compound where the seder was being held, we were escorted through the enormous yard by a group of heavily armed guards who could have been clones of Arnold Schwarzenegger. Walled off on all sides were hundreds of uniformed men robotically smoking cigarettes, all jammed together in an outdoor concrete area the size of three city blocks.

As we walked by, we became the main attraction. I felt invaded by the men, their eyes devouring us like we were raw meat as they taunted us with catcalls. I had the sensation that we were passing through a sea of "hungry ghosts," the lost souls that Vietnamese Zen master Thich Nhat Hahn talks about, those who can never be fulfilled. They were sitting ducks for everything that was terrible in the world to be projected smack onto them. I knew better, but I felt threatened, and silently judged them, too. Yet I couldn't stop staring at the swarm of anonymous faces pulling me in. My friends' voices sounded far away, muffled. For a few moments, I must have fallen into a trance, because there again I could intuitively see the darkness that had infested Buchenwald, only present to a lesser degree. It was spewing out from the men's hair, their breath, their skin— slinking across ledges of buildings, creeping up closer toward me. No light in sight. Why couldn't I see it? Because of my experience at the concentration camp, I questioned myself. I knew something inside me had shut off.

What a relief it was to arrive safely inside at our destination. Thank God for the familiar. The rabbi, wrapped in a blue and white prayer shawl, his yarmulke pinned to the little hair he had left, the Torah safely nearby . . . the baskets piled high with matzohs and plates of gefilte fish about to be served. Now I could catch my breath. Waiting for the seder to begin, the inmate seated beside me started to strike up a conversation. A tattooed, muscle-bound man with long, curly, black hair, he immediately got mileage out of my obvious discomfort.

"Never been to a prison before, huh?"

"Nope," I managed to get out.

"Well, I've been in the joint for over ten years."

"What for?" I inquired politely, trying to seem like this was no big deal.

"I'm a bank robber," he boasted. "Big time."

"Oh really," I cooed, wanting to appear duly impressed. He just shook his head back and forth, grinning. I felt like such a fool. Then, with a twinkle in his eyes, he said, "You see those ugly gorillas out there." He pointed gleefully to the crowded yard. "Well, they could eat a little girl like you up in one big bite." The whole thing seemed so absurd, both of us burst out laughing. The ice was broken.

During dinner, I found him to be an extraordinary man. "It took being in prison to get my spiritual life to open up," he told me. A voracious reader, he deftly quoted the Buddha, Krishnamurti, Ramana Maharshi, his mentors. Their pictures were taped to the walls of his cell. He was a daily meditator, devoted to his practice—more so than many people I knew. But most impressive was his outrageous humor, the lightness with which he approached life. I never detected a hint of feeling sorry for himself. Amazingly, under dreadful conditions, he'd been able to heal.

When the seder ended, the guards safely escorted us back through the yard to the front exit. The physical scene hadn't changed—the same hordes of men, the same cigarette smoke, the same taunts—but now my take on it was different. Intuitively, the darkness I saw was no longer one-dimensional. Its denseness had broken up, revealing an underlayer of phosphores-

cent pinpoints—each one no larger than a grain of sand—as if a
pitch-black night sky was now sprinkled with glittering stars.
The very atoms and molecules of everyone and everything
seemed to be radiating, piercing the entire environment like
lasers. It was a loving light, so soothing I just wanted to bask in
it. Once I had a single bare speck to hold on to, a focal point, I
looked on as offshoots multiplied, growing brighter and
brighter. It was a very strange sight, awesome. I was watching
hardened criminals lurking around, lit up like lightbulbs, and
they didn't even realize it.

My dinner partner unknowingly had been the key. Talking
with him had deflated my fear because he so strikingly defied
my projections. The light in him sparked my ability to see.
True, many of the inmates were intimidating—for good reason.
And on an intuitive level, a visible darkness surrounded them
that to me was quite real. The distortion was that it was all I
saw. I'd been so afraid and angry at how invaded I felt that my
projections went wild. The minute I started to withdraw them,
to look beyond outward appearances at our similarities and common failings, the light that had always been present was able to
shine through. My myopic vision of the prison shattered; the
ball of frozen tension inside me burst along with it. I felt free.
Now I grasped the larger picture, not just a fraction of it. I realized that given other circumstances I too might be propelled to
commit criminal acts. I'd never held up a liquor store, joined a
gang, or been busted for drugs, but could appreciate the desperation that leads to such behavior. We all feel anger, disappointment, despair. Beyond the question of how tough an
environment we come from, and the real hazards of poverty, for
instance, the essential difference is that some of us are better at
controlling our emotions and don't act them out destructively.
Once I stopped condemning the inmates and viewed them with
a little more compassion, I was liberated from my projections.
The darkness didn't consume me.

The spiritual path of intuition is to acknowledge our projections so they don't get in our way. It takes mindfulness and

courage for us to stop and say, "Hey, wait a minute. I must've gotten hooked by a projection. Let me take a closer look." Believe me, this changes things a lot. Once we begin to see external reality as a potent mirror reflecting what's going on inside us, we no longer separate the inside from the outside, or "us" from "them." This is an important lesson for anyone, but for an intuitive doing a reading, being projection-free is like shooting a picture with the lens wide open, light pouring in.

Spirituality is a lifelong pursuit. You don't reach a quick epiphany, get struck enlightened, and suddenly arrive. As Stephen Mitchell writes, at times spiritual transformation can be like "cleaning the heart with a piece of steel wool," with clarity always the goal. While reading his book *The Gospel According to Jesus,* I was especially impressed by the story of the spiritual journey of Chao-Chou, a Zen monk from the T'ang Dynasty. Achieving enlightenment when only seventeen years old, he still chose to remain with his teacher for another forty years. He did this out of love, but also to heighten his insight further and purify his character. Other monks left to teach at a much earlier age. But Chao-Chou was matchless in his excellence and patience. Finally, at age eighty, he felt ready to teach. Chao-Chou proposed a humble philosophy: "If I meet a hundred-year-old man and I have something to teach him, I will teach; if I meet an eight-year-old boy and he has something to teach me, I will learn." Remarkably, he taught until his death at age 120.

Chao-Chou can be a model for us all. You don't have to be shut away in a far-off monastery to live a spiritual life, even though our world has many more distractions. Like his, our task is both to solidify our connection with a higher power through techniques such as meditation or prayer, and to make love a priority in how we think and behave. When living this way, for example, it becomes a lot harder to hold a grudge when a boss treats you in a manner that seems unfair, or to announce rashly, "I'll never speak to you again," if a friend inadvertently hurts your feelings. This doesn't mean that we're instantly transformed into saints. It's just that now, more spiritually aware, we gravitate toward loving solutions.

There's a sacredness to being human. This was brought home to me in a vivid dream I had about my mother at a time when I was intently involved with my writing—my most powerful meditation—although frustrated by how emotionally demanding it felt. My mother had been dead for about a year when she came to me and said in her adamant style: "You have no idea how lucky you are to feel so passionately. That's the great joy of being on earth. Where I am things are different. The same intensity isn't there." I awoke saddened by her longing but also got her message loud and clear: It's a great gift to be human, to have real passions that we can go all out for. On a deeper level the dream also reminded me that we must honor the whole experience of life as sacred, not divide ourselves into neat little categories, designating what is spiritual and what is not. Such a split is an illusion.

In the film *Wings of Desire,* an angel falls in love with a beautiful trapeze artist. At the end, he sacrifices his wings in order to be with her. But this kind of sacrifice is not necessary for us. We can be as divine as we want, right here on earth. Nothing's stopping us. We're the template for where love begins. It's a chain reaction. The more we love and accept ourselves, the more we're able to love and accept other people. To achieve this for even a millisecond is to know the meaning of holiness.

Over a decade ago, when I returned from my first conference with Brugh Joy, love was rushing through me like a great river. I thought it would never cease. I was sure I'd found the answer. Now, at last, my life would be changed. With the best of intentions I drove straight from the seclusion of the high desert to join my parents for lunch at a ritzy country club they belonged to in Beverly Hills, a place that had previously set my hair on end because I felt so utterly out of place. With all this love in my heart that September afternoon, I assumed things had to be different. Not so. Within minutes I became just as much of a miserable outcast as I'd been before. The truth was, I didn't really feel I belonged in many places because I wasn't comfortable in my own skin. Finding this comfort was my spiritual task. The route there was through my insecurities, in search of an authentic voice. Not, I learned, by beating myself up, but by gently and patiently penetrating the fears that were stopping me.

The enormous outpouring of energy I experienced at Brugh's didn't last forever. Nor was it meant to. It was simply a taste of what was possible if I was willing to carry on that work in myself. The more we incorporate love in our lives, the closer we get to heaven. I don't view heaven as some otherworldly, unreachable realm. It is here right before us, intermingled with our humanness, waiting to be found.

Often, when you begin a spiritual path—especially when you're working with a teacher—the focused energy can be so potent it breaks down inner barriers that seemed impenetrable. You're free to feel such a heightened awareness of love that it may spark an intuitive opening, a double whammy that is mind-blowing, to say the least. In this state, you may see brilliant lights around people like the halos crowning saints in Byzantine icons. Even your dog, your plants, the pots and pans in your kitchen exude it. Literally everything glows. Or you feel a oneness with the universe that can bring incredible joy. These are called peak experiences. Though dramatic and truly illuminating, they're not the be-all and end-all; rather, they are simply one marker among many on the path.

In 1986 I spent two weeks on the north shore of the island of Kauai, participating in a women's workshop on spirituality. After meditating intensely with the group before a three-day period of silence and fasting, I walked through a lush jungle down to the water's edge, to watch the sunset. The evening was warm and moist. A light wind blew through my short cotton dress as I rested my back on the trunk of a fragrant plumaria tree. I got lost in the swaying movements of its leaves and deep violet flowers. They looked like feathers and seemed to be gesturing to me. To my surprise, I began to feel sexually aroused. Waves of heat started pulsing through the bark and into my body, flowing up my spine to my scalp—then down to my genitals and feet. It was absolute bliss. I kept the slope of my back glued to the trunk, afraid if I dared move or analyze what was happening, it would stop. For once, thank God, my mind cooperated. The sexual intensity mounted slowly and then faster until my entire body exploded into an orgasm.

When it was over, I rested on the cool ground beneath the tree, gazing at a canopy of glittering stars. Logically I knew this entire incident was outrageous. But the odd thing was how natural it all seemed. I felt soft like a baby. My harsh edges had been smoothed out, every inch of me vibrating and alive. Since becoming a doctor, I'd spent so much time thinking on my feet, making tough decisions fast, I often forgot I even had a body. I had become so civilized and proper, obsessively intent on doing "the right thing," that I'd sacrificed my wilder spirit. But now it was back.

Previously I had always depended on a man to bring out my wildness and sexuality. In a relationship, I could be passionate and playful; when I was single, I somehow felt less feminine and lacked a certain warmth. I didn't see that I possessed my own vital sexuality, independent of anyone else. On this particular evening, however, as I witnessed every tree, every blossom, every rock, and the earth itself, radiating sensuality, I realized that it was also inside me. I felt womanly and full, in touch with that part that could run naked on the beach without shame, howl in the light of the full moon.

And yet, compelling as this moment had been, I knew from my teacher not to dwell on it. Peak intuitive experiences are transitory. There are hundreds of different kinds that come and go the more deeply your practice continues. If you focus on them for too long, you can get sidetracked by their beauty and lose sight of what lies ahead. I'll never forget what took place on the beach in Kauai. Even today I can't help but look at leaves fluttering in the breeze and smile. Still, I know it's as dangerous to lose myself to the light as to the darkness. I took what I learned from that night and moved on.

Unfortunately it's quite easy to be seduced. A friend of mine had been meditating only a few months when he began having some pyrotechnic visions, each more striking than the last. He'd be gazing down at his body while floating high above it; fantastic light shows with purple strobes would burst from the center of his forehead; a band of mischievous orange-robed monks with shaved heads would be rolling in laughter as their images flew by during meditation. Off and on for days this flashy show continued; my friend was getting pretty impressed with himself. Then suddenly it all stopped. Upset that he was losing ground, he went to his spiritual teacher, believing that in some way he'd failed. His teacher listened patiently, unconcerned, and then reassured him, saying, "All experiences have value. Just keep meditating."

By this he meant you should not cling to any experience, no matter how dramatic, because it removes us from the present—that the secret is to endow even the simplest moments with meaning, see each one as divine. Peak experiences are merely the glitterati of the journey, not necessarily a sign of spiritual attainment. Notice them, learn what you can, but don't become too enticed. In *A Gradual Awakening,* Stephen Levine says, "Enlightenment is freedom, the thought of enlightenment is prison." The instant you get enamored with how evolved you think you are, your ego gets snagged and you get thrown off course.

I once knew a workshop junkie who bounced from teacher to teacher just to get a hit of the energy. He never stuck around long enough, however, to do the real work. With his saccharine glow and perpetual glazed smile I could spot him coming from a mile away. When he sporadically dropped in on my teacher's classes, he'd make a beeline for me, giving me a big hug—which was all right because I was glad to see him—but there was always a forced quality, as if he was trying too hard. He looked undeniably blissed out, too much so. Authentic spirituality embodies a range of experience, not just feeding off the high points. As author and teacher Ram Dass says, "If you get phony-

holy, it will end up kicking you in the butt." The most spiritual
of acts is to be genuinely human at every moment.

We have no idea when spiritual insights will come. Our times
of struggle can be just as pivotal as when we're feeling really
connected. All we can do is work toward being intuitively open,
no matter what's happening. Life will do the rest. The point is
not to sit around just waiting to become enlightened. The richness of our emotions, the very events of our lives, provide a potent springboard from which to grow. So often, at my lowest
points, when I feel like I just can't go on, an intuitive realization
or vision restores me. The effect is instantly healing, and I come
back to myself.

One night I pulled into the Saint John's Hospital garage,
about to see a patient who'd just nearly overdosed on cocaine. I
wound up the crowded concrete ramps until I found a parking
spot; this was the last place I wanted to be. Tired and depressed
(my mother had just fallen ill), I didn't have one ounce of energy
left over to give to anyone. Yet there I was, in the front seat of
my car, wriggling out of my jeans into a more "professional"
outfit, transforming into "the doctor" once more. I couldn't have
felt less spiritual. My body, a leaden weight, just sat there. For
one brief moment I crossed my arms over the steering wheel, lay
my head down to rest. Before I knew it I drifted into a vision.

I was standing in the midst of the clearest, never-ending sky
with a being who knew me inside out and loved me completely.
He wasn't human, visually no more than a stick figure you'd see
in a child's drawing. Yet somehow I was certain there was no one
more important to me than he. We were in a huge place, infinite
in all directions, the earth a tiny speck below. In a split second
he showed me a detailed replay of my life, every person, every
place, every event. I saw that no matter how important any of it
seemed, it was a mere blip compared to the vastness now surrounding me. Exhilarated, I felt my perspective shift. There
were no beginnings, no end, just a oneness to which we are all
linked. In my depression I'd lost sight of this. But with such a
joyous reminder I was freed from my smaller frame of mind.

It would be wonderful if I could have kept this vision alive forever. But no matter how inspiring and true, visions by nature tend to fade. Our challenge is to recall and savor them, making them part of our life so they stick. There's no limited supply. Being intuitive allows us to create room for new ones constantly. And visions build on each other. For example, the vision I had at Saint John's didn't stand by itself. Its theme of oneness had come to me many times before, underlying the basis of my own spiritual beliefs: We are all interrelated in a gigantic cosmic net. My prescience helps me to remember.

As you bring intuition into finer focus, you have the freedom to appreciate the extraordinary beauty of spirit and feel its oneness. Once you have a personal experience of this, you'll get a radically different slant on the world, sensing an organic connection to all of life—as I see it, the very reason we pursue a spiritual path in the first place. Search for this oneness in your dreams, meditations, during readings, or while simply walking by the ocean or hiking in the woods. No reminder is too small.

Our connection to one another and to the entire universe exists everywhere. But certain locations in the world are magical; they're intuitive treasure troves that evoke even more of a connection. These places seem to buzz with energy and activate us, sacred sites such as Machu Picchu, Stonehenge, the Great Pyramids in Egypt, or the colossal stone monoliths on Easter Island. The history of the land seems to be embedded in the soil, the landscape, and the architecture, preserving the memory of what happened there as concisely as if it had been stored on microchips. When you're intuitively open, you can join with the ancient quality of the land, hear its voice, sense the enormity of its spirit.

A few years ago I visited the Wailing Wall in Jerusalem, a place so holy that people of many religions make pilgrimages there from all over the world. For the Jewish people, this wall is especially sacred. It's all that remains of the ancestral temple that was destroyed in A.D. 70, when the Jews were forced into exile. Traditionally, Jews have journeyed there to shed tears and mourn the original loss of their homeland. The wall is not merely a historical marker, however; many Jews regard it as a physical touchstone to a greater sanctity.

As I slowly approached the women's side of the wall, I felt I was being drawn into the vortex of a tornado. At least a hundred women, heads covered with shawls in muted colors, were wailing at the top of their lungs. I felt besieged by their outpouring of grief. I wanted to run from it, yet I just stood there. As usual when overloaded, my first response was to go numb. Mechanically, I lifted my arm and placed my neatly folded prayer into a crack between two mammoth golden-brown stones, as was the custom. Then, as if a switch had been flipped, my feelings returned, but magnified, larger than life. Like a hypnotic incantation, the moaning and wailing of the other women lured me in. I hadn't intended to cry, but soon tears filled my eyes. I was startled; I'd been feeling fine. I was sure I had nothing to cry about.

Uncontrollably, my body began to tremble as a wave of sadness hit me. So many personal losses came back at once: memories of smaller disappointments, my grandfather's death, relationships I'd worked so hard on that failed. And my weeping didn't stop there. Gathering momentum, I cried not only for myself but for my family and friends, for all the troubles and injustices in the world that came to mind. Finally, I cried just to cry. In a tremendous release, I completely let loose. It was a cleansing, purifying catharsis, as the despair washed through me and became something more. My cries and the wailing of every woman at the wall blended together with all that had come before us, merging into a single sound. I was immersed in a whirlpool of grief, not just my own, but a larger grief that seemed to be arising from the heart of the collective.

As if coming out of a trance, I noticed the sky growing dark. I could hear the evening prayers of the Muslims echoing mournfully throughout the city from a central mosque nearby. I looked up at a clock tower, stunned to see that two hours had passed when I'd only planned to stay a few minutes. The old city of Jerusalem glistened, the last rays of sunlight reflecting off the winding cobblestone streets. I walked briskly back to my hotel. Exhausted, I couldn't wait to jump into a steaming hot bath. But I was also exuberant: Beneath all that grief at the wall, I'd felt a collective oneness, an ecstatic and merciful unifying force. At that point, I'd only been meditating a year and had gotten just glimpses of it. But now there it was—right before me, glorious as could be.

It took many months for what happened to sink in fully. Yes, I was somehow catapulted into a profound feeling of connection. But how did I get there? I needed to know. Slowing everything down, examining it in stages, I came to appreciate more than ever that the Wailing Wall itself was sitting on a powder keg of energy—amplified over the centuries by every person who'd ever come to grieve. Even those who don't think of themselves as intuitive can't help but feel its pull. I'd no idea how tremendous it would be and within minutes had been launched into a hyper-alert intuitive state. First, without intending to, I began to cry. But that was just the starting point, one layer that soon melded into another. Surrendering to my sadness, I let it carry me as it grew in intensity, until its very force lifted me from my own emotions to an experience of collective grief. I could never in a million years have willed this to happen. And then, not resisting the frenzy of this collective grief, I felt it evolve into a sublime oneness. I knew we all were of a single heart, the ancient memory of love binding us through time.

Love has a way of moving us beyond the artificial boundaries we've created. It's the uniting ingredient, no matter what path we choose, transcending religious differences. Just because we adhere to a particular faith doesn't have to limit us from appreciating the good in them all. Without love, we are spiritually adrift. The world can appear impoverished, fraught with an endless series of insoluble problems. Separation from love is the primary cause of our pain. With love, we have the courage to take our difficulties in stride and turn them into demonstrations of faith.

As intuition ripens, we become better equipped to perceive love, not only in ourselves but in our family, friends, and even in the darkest places on earth. Whether we've just won the lottery or lost our job, we're ultimately being challenged to become more compassionate, large-hearted people. Then we can live as fully as we were meant to, not being so hard on ourselves or feeling victimized by every bump in the road. When seen through loving eyes, our lives begin to take on a different cast, to exude a new vitality and meaning. The aim becomes, as Raymond Carver suggests in the poem "Late Fragment," "To call myself beloved and feel myself beloved on the earth."

To be intuitive means so much more than being able to see into the future. It can be our entry into a full-bodied spiritual life, where love abides and everything has a purpose. From the very start we may sense this, but with refined prescience it's like standing in a moonlit room as vague shapes and shadows gradually materialize into recognizable forms. Every step of the spiritual journey, no matter how small or when we begin, leads us closer to the intuitive wisdom of our hearts and to love. We can't help but grow stronger. Love gives us the power to transform any seeming calamity into an asset and source of comfort. It's a magical tincture that enables us to spin straw into gold, to become alchemists for a more bountiful and enlightened future.

CHAPTER TWELVE

Honoring the Gift

Watching the moon
at dawn,
solitary, mid-sky,
I knew myself completely:
no part left out.
        —IZUMI SHIKIBU
         (974–1034)

The story I have told you about my life—how I struggled with my intuitive abilities as a child, lost them during medical training, then found them again—has been of my awakening. Over time, I have learned to honor the great gift I was given. At first, however, it didn't feel like such a gift. I was often totally discombobulated by it, half the time worried that there was something terribly wrong with me. What saved me were the angels who appeared along the way—mentors and teachers who had traveled this path before and shared their wisdom with me. This made all the difference.

Once a source of real confusion and fear, intuition has now become my greatest passion. My drive to make sense of it and put it to good use has made me the person I am now. Had such knowledge been handed to me on a silver platter, who knows how things might have been? Easier, in some sense, I'm sure. But circumstances were different when I was growing up: For many years I had no place to turn for counsel.

Today, you have more choices. My hope is that my experiences can guide you on your journey, so you won't feel as lost as I did. The times dictated there'd be little support for me as I fought to find my authentic voice, and because of this I have come to consider it all the more precious—my life's blood, my strength. I am never going to lose it again. Looking back, however, I wouldn't change a thing. Even the hardest parts. Intuition was a gift I had to grow into.

By no means am I alone. There are so many of us out there, no longer willing to be silent, ashamed, or secretive about our visions, at last gathering the courage to speak our own truth. I was once more struck by how loud this mass outcry has grown when I was recently invited to appear as an expert on a popular network TV morning show about the paranormal. To prepare for the taping, I was sent a huge pile of letters to read. The producers had been deluged by mail from viewers who sounded like clones of the earlier me. The questions asked, the concerns expressed, were so familiar I could have written these letters myself. I was overwhelmed, touched by the isolation these people were feeling, their heartfelt desire to be understood.

Vickie F. from Charlevoix, Michigan (population 3,100), wrote about being intuitive: *All through school I had friends who thought I was weird so I learned to suppress the feelings. Can anyone help me?* From Big Springs, a west Texas oil town, Theresa said, *I get the heebie-jeebies when I go to someone's home or feel the violence or the warmth there. Either I've lost my mind or I'm extremely intuitive. I'm writing this letter to you because I don't know where to turn.* And from the tiny fishing community of Homer, Alaska, Vickie G. echoed the experience I had when I was nine: *My grandfather came to me to say good-bye on the night he died. I will never forget it. I was so afraid people would think I was nuts.*

These women, and three others, were chosen to be guests on the show and flown in from out-of-the-way places where they had no resources to call on. They were completely on their own. And I thought I had it bad! The idea of such sensitive people, so geographically remote, with no healthy intuitive role models in sight was mind-boggling to me. I felt instant empathy for them. I was in an ideal position to help. What an incredible opportunity for me to recirculate all the knowledge I'd been given. This is just what the journey is about. To create a chain among us, each person sharing what we know with another and passing it on.

The afternoon of the taping we all arrived a few hours early, at the producers' request, and met backstage. Seven women, including myself, from backgrounds as diverse as you could imagine, sat together in a windowless studio waiting room with a lavish buffet to snack on. One by one, they began to recount their stories to me—some with reluctance, some unable to get the details out fast enough—as if gathered together around the warmth of a village fire. I was moved, amazed. Each seemed to be speaking the others' experience. We were all of one mind. None of them had ever publicly reached out before. Even some of their friends and closest family members didn't have a clue that they were intuitive. I was barraged with questions: "Why do I make predictions in the first place?" "Should I tell people about them?" "How did I know that my cousin was going to die? Could I have prevented it?" "Do you ever get used to this?" "Are you scared?"

As I shared my story, I watched them slowly relax. A strength of mine is that my fear of intuition is behind me and I can communicate this with confidence. Also, the fact that I'm a psychiatrist lends me a credibility I wouldn't have without the degree. In Western culture, particularly, an M.D. is a symbol of authority that can really work for me in such a still-unaccepted area. Clearly the members of the group, although befuddled by their abilities, were quite sane.

By far what troubled them the most was that they kept intuitively picking up tragedies before they occurred: deaths, accidents, illness, particularly in those closest to them. But so many
times their attempts to warn loved ones or avert disaster were
thwarted. "Some people won't believe a word I say," declared
Theresa. "They just don't want to hear it." Even for those who did
believe, warnings often weren't enough to prevent the disaster.

The main message I wanted to communicate was twofold: Beginning intuitives are notorious for getting only negative images simply because on an intuitive level these images are the
loudest, so emotionally charged. But with training it's common
to open up to a constellation of impressions and receive positive
information, too. In addition, just because you see a vision doesn't
necessarily mean that you have the power or responsibility to do
something about it. Intervening may or may not be possible.
Understandably, I knew this point would be difficult for them
to accept—the impulse to want to spare people unhappiness or
trauma is always there—yet by acknowledging our limitations
my aim was to ease their guilt. I felt privileged to be in a position to interject hope where there was none before.

The experiences of these women remind us that visions, intuitive knowings, and dreams are not alien to our nature. Mistak-
enly, we identify them as something other than ourselves, but in a
profound sense they are as life sustaining as every breath we take.

On the most practical level, intuition allows me to communicate with the important people in my life, including my patients,
in such an elegant, multilayered way that I can understand them
better—deepening all my relationships. Further, by sensing their
energy I feel who they are more completely and in turn may sensitively respond to their needs. My father, for example, was not one
to talk a lot about feelings. But whether I was in his presence or
not, because of our intuitive link, I knew in my bones when he was
upset and could register waves of joy when he was happy. The same
is true of my closest friends. They are a part of me, intimately connected, our souls actively intertwined. It's much tougher to feel
lonely because as an intuitive I'm never really all alone.

So many riches would be stripped from my life if these abilities faded—like first being able to take in dazzling colors and then suddenly being left with only black-and-white. The intuitive messages I receive daily are gratifying down to the cellular level. The guidance itself is a blessing, but beyond the actual information I pick up, by tuning in I fuel the connection with my spiritual source, continually adding fresh kindling to the fire and tapping directly into primal energy. Every nuance of my being is touched by it. It feeds me.

When you first become introduced to the heightened awareness of spirit that often comes with intuitive experiences, it can take your breath away. The freedom you feel, the love flowing out of your heart—its absolute gorgeousness—sends shivers up and down your spine. Though such intensity is usually short-lived, the true bonus of being this open is bringing the wisdom you've glimpsed to bear in everyday life. You might not have ever known you had so much love inside. And now you do. It's waiting, ready to be called forth at any moment—even in the most mundane situations.

Reach beyond the current world in which you live. Use this book as a map to a world inaccessible to most people. You can access it. At any moment you can connect with a life of love and understanding. On the outside you need to change very little; what counts most is the shift you make in your own thinking. First you must want to travel this path. There is no rush. Open your heart, allow yourself to dream, let your spirit soar. Envision a grander sense of what is possible.

Take any step as a beginning. The resources available (especially in large cities) are more plentiful than ever before. Bookstores and libraries are magical places. Just reading about intuition or spirituality can lead to a breakthrough, ignite a curiosity that inspires you to go on. I practically live in the metaphysical bookstore near my house, sitting on a stool for hours leafing through what's new. However, if you come from a rural community, treasure troves like these are not always so easy to find. I was astounded to hear from one of the women I appeared on television with that she has to travel over sixty miles to find a shop that carries such reading material. The small bookstore in her town won't stock these titles because they're considered "strange" and of questionable value. I was sadly reminded of how stuck in the Dark Ages some places are, how far we still have to go. For this reason I've included in the back of this book a list of resources for you to contact, including a guide for further reading.

If you want to go on, to explore one step further, the surest route I know to intuition is through meditation. It lets you tone down the static in your mind, amplifying your intuitive voice. Stick to the basics: Ritual, prayer, and setting up an altar can move you in this direction, too. Your approach may be as simple as you like. Experiment. Keep your eyes open for lectures and workshops, anything that appeals to you. I can't count how many different events I've attended that have filled in yet another missing piece of the puzzle. It's good to investigate a variety of teachers and learn from those you respect. My own teacher has been the single most powerful influence on my spiritual and intuitive growth. Build a circle of friends who wholeheartedly support your path. None of us can do this alone. We need one another.

Keep fertilizing the ground. Every concrete action you take prepares you to be intuitive, not just at the moment, but as a way of life, setting the stage to know things in a different way. All of us have our own special talents. Intuition comes through in many forms: visions, dreams, knowings, sounds. The more quiet time you spend with yourself, the better acquainted you'll become with each variation. You'll gravitate toward the one that feels most natural. For me, it's dreams. I look forward to them— I can depend on their lucidity. It's in my dream state where I'm completely at home. For you it may be doing intuitive readings, sensing energy, healing with your hands. Try everything. Discover what your calling is.

I hope you will take this journey. It's studded with challenges, constantly transforming. There's no ceiling to what we can learn. Follow your inner voice, straight to the center of things—

see with all the passion and power that lies bubbling within you, and let loose. My wish is that you identify with at least a thread of my story and take off from there.

Even now the world is changing. So many people I encounter are painfully aware of something missing in their lives. No amount of material gain can fill it. They yearn to be able to connect with a deeper meaning and wholeness. As a result of this need, many are seeking spiritual answers. Intuition can be one way in—and gradually it's becoming more accepted. Twenty or thirty years ago it would have been unheard of to have a daily talk show about the paranormal on network TV. Yet today not only is the media making more of an effort to take the subject seriously, but people from all over are growing brave enough to declare their intuitive experiences.

Increasingly, it's accepted practice for police departments to use intuitives to aid criminal investigations; high-profile business leaders are recognizing how indispensable their intuition is to their work; health professionals are turning to their own intuitive abilities to diagnose and heal. Little by little, the change is happening. Intuition is a creative influence that enlivens every element of life, spurring you on not only to live more fully but to flourish. You can be a part of the change, starting most importantly in your own heart and home.

What better place to set this in motion than within your family? For example, you and your spouse may be going through a rough time financially, but when you tune in you clearly see that within a matter of months the situation will work itself out. This spares you both a needless period of worry and anxiety, taking your relationship out of the pressure cooker. Intuition can enhance how your family interacts: By intuiting their feelings, looking beyond surface motivations, and foreseeing the larger picture, you can approach them more constructively with love.

As a mother, my friend Susan's intuitive instincts came into play even before the moment of conception. One evening, as she was busy cooking for a dinner party at her home, her mind on a million other things, she was suddenly overwhelmed by an extraordinary intuitive sensation. "A soul was pushing in on me, as if announcing itself," she said. "There was an absolute urgency. I knew it was asking to be born." Over the years Susan and her husband had learned to listen to her intuitions. Later that night, when their guests had left, she told him what happened. They had been married for several years and had talked about having children, but until now the moment never felt right. Though wavering before, on the strength of Susan's feeling and their genuine desire for a child, they decided to give it a try.

Once they did, everything fell into place. Not long after, Susan woke up one morning positive that this was the day she was going to become pregnant. "It was too much," Susan said. "As we were making love, I was certain of the exact instant I conceived." Sure enough, a few weeks later she found out she was pregnant, confirming what she'd already sensed to be true. Susan was delighted, but she really wasn't surprised.

During her pregnancy she set a precedent by establishing an intuitive relationship with her child in the womb. Intuitively she picked up that she was carrying a boy, plus information about his looks and personality, which later proved to be accurate. Meditating each day to align herself with her baby, she established a close rapport early on that continued after his birth.

When her son was very young, at times Susan would intuitively check in on him at school. Her aim was not to be intrusive, scrutinizing every little detail (even if she could), but simply to get a general idea whether or not he was okay. Susan was no snoop; she respected her son's privacy. For her, intuition served mainly as an alarm. In the same way, many mothers sense if their kids are in trouble but don't consider themselves intuitive. I believe that such sensitivity is an organic extension of the maternal bond, as is the healing power of touch. Susan, for instance, would hold her son when he was ill, sending energy through her hands, to help heal his symptoms and calm his distress. This was totally natural to her, and, as he grew older, she communicated the same naturalness to him.

Imagine what the world would be like if children were praised and encouraged to voice their intuitive abilities instead of being stigmatized, discounted, or judged. Imagine a whole generation growing up more balanced and happy, expressing their gift, not being pressured into pretending to be something they're not. I would have given anything for that freedom. You can offer this to your child. Allow them the room to improvise and play with intuition without the fear of a restrictive muzzle being clamped down on them. I have seen the most beautiful light come over children's faces when their parents give them permission to explore intuitively. It's wonderful to watch as a brand-new universe unfolds right before their eyes. Even if you have never been intuitive yourself and don't know what to do if your child is, there are places to turn, several of which you'll find listed at the back of this book. There are people you can contact—therapists, intuitives, and healers—who can answer questions, allay your fears, show you how to nurture this quality in your child.

I recently became acquainted with a mother, Laura, who was at her wits' end. Her ten-year-old daughter had been seeing what she believed to be "auras" and "tiny balls of light traveling at high rates of speed." Laura told me, "She sees them all the time—at home, at school, in the car, at the mall, everywhere she goes. She noticed them around a teacher at school, around our family dog, around a flag, and even around herself." For two years, Kate had been having these visions and they frightened her. At night they were the most intense, so much so that she developed a terror of the dark. "Her father and I thought it was a childhood fear," Laura said. "But after two years our patience was wearing thin."

Laura had no experience with intuition. Even so, though she wasn't sure, she sensed that Kate's ability was a gift—but was worried by the anxiety that accompanied it. Most of all she yearned to understand so that she could be supportive of her daughter no matter what. When I met Kate and Laura, I recognized right away that they sincerely wanted guidance. Their faces were as beautiful as cameos, although both seemed shell-shocked by the strain of the last few years. Laura had only one personal agenda, to find out how to help her daughter, the ideal attitude for doing some real good. It impressed me that she was willing to let go of her misconceptions, eager to hear what I had to say. Kate was a freckled, brown-eyed, darling girl, smart as could be, who more than anything wanted to know: Is what's happening to me bad?

I sat down with mother and daughter, reassuring them that Kate's abilities were much like having a highly developed sense of sight or sound. This was hard for Kate to absorb, given her fear, and she was still filled with questions, especially about the colors she saw. "What does red mean?" she asked. "How come some people have purple all around them and others have more green?" "No one knows for sure," I told Kate, "but down through the ages mystics who can see colors as you do have agreed on certain things. For example, when someone gives off a lot of green, they tend to be loving and come from their hearts; yellow means that they're logical and intellectual; red is the color of anger, pain, or passion; purple tends to be the color of intuition, often linked with creativity." I emphasized that there was nothing strange or bizarre about her visions and that they could be a big asset to her as she grew up.

Kate and Laura had such a backlog of worry that I realized it would take more time than we could spend together that day to make a significant dent in it. Unfortunately, they were about to return to their home in Montana. But it was a solid beginning, their first direct exposure to another intuitive, a frame of reference to make sense of what was happening. Laura felt particularly relieved to be pointed in a positive direction. Though doing her best under the circumstances, she had been essentially all alone, floundering. Once, Laura even confided, as a desperate measure when they moved to a new city, she had naively requested that Kate promise to leave her fears behind. Of course, the well-intentioned plan had backfired. Kate's fears only escalated by being kept in.

I wasn't surprised. From my experience as an intuitive child, I knew that Kate's anxiety stemmed from being right on the edge of another dimension. What frightened her was the unknown. I was also certain that once she integrated and used intuition in her life, her fear would fall away. There's no sense in trying to squash these abilities; suppressing them just creates a whole new series of problems. Fear doesn't disappear—it just shows up in other forms, like being afraid of the dark, of other people, of leaving the house. I urged Kate and her mother to contact a healing center in their area so that they would have the opportunity to work with people who had successfully dealt with this fear and could support Kate through it. Only then could Kate enjoy her gift and make it her own.

My friend Stephan Schwartz told a story I loved about the time he was invited to give a talk to kids on intuition and body energies at an innovative summer camp in Virginia. In his own matter-of-fact style, he spoke of the same kinds of colors Kate saw and how we are all made up of energy that can be intuitively perceived by some people. When he finished, a group of nine- and ten-year-olds swarmed around him, each one excitedly exclaiming, "I can do that, too!" As he listened further, though, he learned that this ability also scared them. Right then and there, Stephan decided to work with the kids to show them that seeing colors was perfectly natural and nothing to be afraid of. Over the next few weeks, he designed games to dispel their fears and make the whole thing fun. Taking turns, they would look at one another's energy, determine what color it was that day, and then ask that person how they were feeling. With practice, they began to match up colors and emotions. Pretty soon, sensing energy became second nature to these kids, no longer scary at all.

You can play similar games with your own kids. For example, sit across from each other, eyes closed, and alternate roles, intuitively sending and receiving. Keep it light, laugh as much as you can, create an atmosphere to explore. If you're the sender, pick a sharply defined image like an orange, a specific number, or the face of a person you both know well and passively concentrate on it. Ask your children, as the receivers, to relay the col-

ors, textures, sensations, or pictures they pick up. Then give
them feedback on where they are right or wrong, highlighting
the positives. You can try another approach when you and your
kids are in the car. While stopped at a traffic light, ask them to
focus and predict the exact moment the light will change. Make
sure they know that it doesn't matter if they're right or wrong.
This is simply an exercise in tuning in that allows them to practice. Or try Stephan's game when you're out shopping. If your
children can see colors around people, encourage them to tell
you what they look like, not making too big a deal out of it, yet
at the same time acknowledging that their perceptions are real.
Kids raised this way are less likely to consider intuition weird or
special. They'll appreciate it for what it is: an innate ability
many people have.

To be an enlightened parent demands more than merely
being tolerant of intuition. It means that you fully embrace it, as
you would any other talent in your child's life. Even if intuition
is new to you, or you've never had a single experience of this
kind yourself, it's vital that you believe in and support these sensitivities in your children. When kids grow up with the security
of being totally accepted for who they are, they naturally feel
empowered and respond in turn with love. Nurturing the best
in one another, your family can then become a microcosm of
peace, contributing to a more harmonious society.

The peace and goodness within people are of inestimable
value. Nowhere is this more dramatically shown than in the
tale of Sodom and Gomorrah, told in the book of Genesis. The
story goes that God agreed to Abraham's request that these
crime-riddled cities be saved if just ten good men could be
found residing there. Although not even ten could be found and
Sodom and Gomorrah were destroyed, what is striking to me is
the precept that the goodness of a few people could have saved
the cities; the positive consciousness of ten would have been sufficient not only to overcome the corruption of many but, in
some cases, to change the world.

We must begin with the love in our own hearts. In ever-
expanding circles, we may then extend it to our family and friends,

out into the workplace, and finally the world. Once we realize how interconnected we all are, we see that the integrity of our actions in every aspect of life makes a difference to the whole. Consider this: Beyond the personal sphere, an area where each one of us can exert a positive influence on a broader number of people is in our careers, no matter if we wait tables in a diner or head a multinational corporation. Well-motivated, pure intentions combined with the increased sensitivity to others that the intuitive brings can infuse any kind of work with a higher level of meaning.

I am delighted to see a growing number of businesses recognizing the value of intuition and regularly putting it into practice. Not surprisingly, however, reputable businesspeople tend to shy away from the term *psychic* (the loaded stereotype of the Gypsy fortune teller still hovers so near), sticking instead to the safely neutral *intuition,* whose connotations are more down to earth. I know of attorneys who admit to using intuition in their negotiations; scores of high-level executives turn to it for help in management and decision making, financial forecasting, and detecting problematic situations before they occur. There are over 1,000 consultants in the United States alone who are hired by top-notch companies to conduct intuitive training programs for their employees. Even the Graduate School of Business at Stanford University offers a course in which intuition is taught as a strategic skill. Trammel Crow, one of the country's most influential real estate developers, gets right to the heart of the matter: "I believe that business leaders take some positions and make some decisions transcendentally. Not magically. Intuitively."

I was also impressed by the Intuition Network, an organization comprised of thousands of people in business, government, science, and health who are committed to integrating intuition into their work, their personal lives, and the world. Relying on inner resources is their main priority. What excites me most about this group is that they are not just theorizing anymore: They are emissaries, putting their convictions into action, carrying intuitive wisdom out onto the front lines, teaching conferences and seminars, conducting training programs for businesses both large and small. They would have been laughed out of existence a mere thirty years ago, or at least ignored. Today, individuals in the group apply intuition to every kind of work imaginable.

I was especially intrigued by the work of one woman who was employed by the National Forest Service in the Northwest. Traveling into the lush national forest areas of Washington, Oregon, and Idaho, her job, as an intuitive consultant, was to promote better understanding between government managers and Native American tribal members regarding land-use policies. Before her work began, both sides were diametrically opposed; there was a huge communication breakdown. At a four-day retreat aimed at resolving this deadlock—which included sweat lodges, powwows, and many hours of charged group interchanges—she helped park managers penetrate their rigidity and not only hear the words of the tribal presenters, but also sense their deeper thoughts and feelings to find better solutions. When the retreat was over, Native Americans and Forest Service officials alike felt as if they had truly been heard and reached a mutual compromise. To me, this is the epitome of how the intuitive and the rational mind can complement each other, creating harmony in a previously irreconcilable situation.

The intuitive techniques available to you in your work are exactly the same as those you may use in your personal life. The arena is different, that's all, underlining just how adaptable and multifaceted these tools are: intuitive readings, dreams, looking for synchronicities, meditation, listening closely to your body, visualizations, and sensing energy. Each one is powerful, mysterious, but within your reach. When you bring them to bear in your work they can provide a bridge between the practical and the sacred, reinforcing your inner resolve about what is appropriate and right.

Peter, a talent agent in his midthirties, had been a patient of mine for over a year. Early on, he had expressed an interest in using intuition in his work and now he'd become pretty good at it: Seeking out answers in dreams was his specialty. At one session, he told me about a roadblock he'd just run up against in a heated film negotiation he was immersed in, one of the biggest in his career. Nothing about the contract had been simple, but up until this point he felt on top of it. Right before our session, though, the studio had taken an outlandish stand on terms. Peter, enraged, was tempted to walk away from the whole deal. Knowing how much was at stake, I urged him not to respond rashly, but instead to ask a dream for guidance. Still fuming, he hesitantly agreed.

That night, after requesting to be shown what to do, Peter dreamed that he saw the studio executive floating blithely by in a hot air balloon. Without a care in the world, this man launched a puny papier-mâché helicopter into the sky. On the ground, dressed in military regalia and flanked by an armed regiment, Peter retaliated with heavy artillery; not realizing that the chopper was merely paper, he attempted to blow it to bits. He missed each time. Worse, the shots boomeranged back at him, inflicting near-fatal damage to his troops.

Peter awoke, certain that he had received a message: The dream was telling him that the executive's ploy had no substance, inventively getting this across with a humorous pictorial pun that made us both smile. No doubt about it, as far as the dream was concerned, the man was full of hot air. Not only that, his helicopter was totally harmless. To top it off, Peter was issued a warning: If he was bent on playing hardball by striking back with an equally preposterous proposal or out of spite, even letting the deal go, he would just end up hurting himself and his client. Moderation, not overkill, was called for here. Peter got the point. With this guidance, he continued on, tactfully not overreacting to the studio's antics, and made an enormously successful deal for his client. I was pleased that Peter didn't act on impulse but had learned enough to set aside his outrage and seek a truer solution in his dreams.

Intuitive insights can be instrumental not just in negotiations but also in sparking technical breakthroughs or inspiring the birth of new products. I recently read an elegant account of a semiconductor research engineer's discovery, a classic example of how a waking image can spur creative thought. Newly arrived from Taiwan, he was entranced by seeing his first snowfall. The way the snow landed on the tops of cars but failed to cling to their sides immediately gave him an idea for improving the silicon microchips he was developing. Using the snowfall as a model, he ingeniously reconfigured the inner structure of the silicon wafers, thus radically increasing the chip's performance speed. Though I know practically nothing about engineering, I was dazzled that nature could provide such a potent intuitive catalyst for an important technical advance, not to mention how utterly receptive this man was to it.

When you're intuitively attuned to your environment, ready at any moment to attend to cues, your work can be transformed into an amazingly rich tapestry of input and output, action and response. It's dynamic. At an inner level, so much movement is constantly going on, a panoply of discovery. Dr. Jonas Salk captures the essence of this magic: "It is always with excitement that I wake up in the morning wondering what my intuition will toss me like gifts from the sea."

These gifts, these messages, can shed light on all work matters, including choosing the right career. Or sensing on a gut level when one is a poor fit—even though it may look perfect on paper. Or helping you to decide when the time is right to move on. You don't have to waste years in unfulfilling jobs that take you nowhere. You deserve to go full throttle into a career that brings you the most joy. But how do you find it? Let's say you just know you're in the wrong position, but you don't have a clue what to do. You wait and wait, lightning doesn't strike, nothing changes. Then what?

The simplest move is to start keeping a journal of dreams, inspiring images, thoughts, and brainstorms. Just continue posing the question, What direction should I follow? and wait for a response to guide you. I guarantee you that, with patience, the answer will come. But don't stop here. Take advantage of the entire array of intuitive approaches I've discussed. Just making the decision to listen to your intuition shifts things. This is terrain that hotel magnate Conrad Hilton was wisely familiar with: "When I have a problem and have done all I can to figure it out, I keep listening in a sort of inside silence till something clicks and I feel a right answer." Trust such a response in yourself, not as an oddity or fluke but as an essential facet of your working life.

The same intuitive principles that operate so beautifully in your own career can translate into an overall global business atmosphere as well. Currently, of necessity, there's a mounting awareness that the systems of the earth are interconnected. If you hurt one, you hurt the other. Intuition never fails to remind us at the most primal level that our interrelatedness is undeniable. For that reason, the segment of the business community that values intuition is a hopeful sign of things to come. They've got a head start on a fundamental truth: Simply on the basis of survival, businesses must begin to work in partnership and choose projects that are life affirming, taking into account our dealings in global terms.

We have come full circle. Our earliest ancestors passed on a rich intuitive heritage: prophets, oracles, shamans, healers make up a vital portion of our history. Yet as the Age of Exploration took off and science became revered, what had been considered natural for so many thousands of years was then labeled superstitious nonsense or condemned as the work of the devil. Seers were deemed to be witches and burned at the stake for their so-called crimes. Later, industry and technology—focused always on rational explanation—drove more nails in the coffin of intuition. But now, at the edge of the twenty-first century, there is an increasing movement of people who realize how much of our soul we've sacrificed. That split just isn't necessary. Envision a future where all of our analytical accomplishments and the intuitive work hand in hand—realizing the best of both worlds. That's where I believe we're headed.

To me, nowhere does this fit seem more well suited than in medicine. When I received my medical degree I took the Hippocratic Oath, swearing by "Apollo the physician, and Aesculapius, and Hygeia, and Panacea, and all the gods and goddesses, that, according to my ability and judgment, I will keep this Oath . . . and with purity and holiness I will pass my life and

practice my art." Despite the staggering, life-saving technological advances of modern medicine, we must remember that it was
born of a spiritual tradition from which intuition organically
stems. Many of us don't think of medicine as having spiritual
roots. But the time-honored words of this oath remind us of how
luminous a presence its sacred underpinnings really are. Over
the centuries, however, we've lost our bearings.

For many of my years as a psychiatrist, hospitals were practically my second home. I have great respect for all that's good
about them, yet I know, too, that many changes need to be made
before we reach the enlightened, all-embracing future I hope for.
We can learn so much from other cultures. In China, for instance, since ancient times traditional physicians have been
trained that everyone contains spiritual energy; they acknowledge and work with it when treating the whole person. Today,
throughout much of China, patients have choices—there's a
blending of disciplines. In numerous well-known teaching hospitals, Western and Chinese medicine productively coexist—
waiting rooms are typically packed, on one side dispensing
modern pharmaceuticals, on the other herbs. It is a truly heartening sight.

An acupuncturist I know, Dao, a doctor and teacher of traditional Chinese medicine in Los Angeles, encourages his students
to develop spiritually, intuitively, and physically to become
well-balanced practitioners. Remarkably, Dao comes from
thirty-eight generations of Chinese medical doctors. I listened,
fascinated, as he told me the story of his father, so technically
skilled and intuitively astute that he was referred to as Shen
Zeng, the Divine Needle. A sight Dao will never forget is the
first time he watched his father diagnose a patient's condition
before he even laid eyes on her by simply listening to the sound
of the woman's walk: the signature of a true master.

China hasn't cornered the market, though, on intuitive diagnosis or intuitive healing. In my travels in England, I was pleas-
antly surprised to see that healers are beginning to be given
their proper due. Their work is spreading, slowly but surely
commanding the respect it deserves. Some healers are right at

the hub of the action: They staff coronary care units and cancer wards, using energetic healing with their hands to help treat disease and ease pain. Others are employed by physicians in their offices. Also impressive to me is that the National Health Service has even been known to pay for their services, a sign that finally healers are emerging as a force to be reckoned with. In fact, they've actually formed their own professional organizations, accrediting members only after they've served approved apprenticeships and demonstrate a level of intuitive excellence.

Even Prince Charles and other members of the Royal Family are well known for the support they give to alternative medicine. So widespread is their endorsement that when a friend of mine went to buy a homeopathic flu remedy in London, the bottle was stamped BY APPOINTMENT TO HER MAJESTY, QUEEN ELIZABETH II, indicating that the Queen had been a patron. There's an aura of sponsorship for nontraditional health care in England that makes me optimistic.

How wonderful it would be if healing and intuition were approached in that same spirit in the United States. Not that we've been without progress. The newly established Office of Alternative Medicine at the National Institutes of Health (NIH), in its embryonic stages, is looking at everything from diet and nutrition to mind-body control to energetic therapies. Already a Mind-Body Intervention Panel is examining the effectiveness of spiritual healing and the medical uses of prayer. The fact that a government agency could be behind this is nothing less than a miracle to me.

Of all the projects funded at the NIH, those centering on therapeutic touch, an offshoot of laying on of hands, have especially caught my eye. Developed by a nurse, Dolores Krieger, therapeutic touch is the most widely practiced form of energetic healing in the United States, employed by over 30,000 nurses and other health-care givers. Picture the healer as a conduit—hands held a few inches from your body, directing energy like a radiant sun into every pore—the love, the warmth rushing into you, reviving your energy, making you come alive.

The similarities between this type of healing and what I've learned from my own teachers are undeniable to me.

In your own life, you can take actions that allow you to become intuitively in harmony with your own body, keeping tabs on how you're feeling physically as well as energetically. Get to know your body, the subtle changes it goes through. Familiarize yourself with when it feels "on" or "off." Listen to information about your health when it comes through in dreams or intuitions; even specifically request it. Then when you need medical advice, you can speak with authority about your inner workings, be in partnership with your physician, and assume an active role in your care. Whenever possible seek out primary M.D.s who are sensitive to many approaches. They don't need to be full-fledged believers in intuition —it would be ideal if they were—but at the least they need to respect your input and take it seriously.

You may be fortunate enough to have in your area one of the handful of physicians who are breaking ground, bringing the intuitive out of the closet, putting it to work. I know of a highly regarded gynecologist whose office staff includes an intuitive healer. Her job is to make intuitive diagnoses as part of the initial exam to get an earlier read on a patient's condition. Just as I have done in my practice, she empathically merges with a patient's body, finely focusing on each organ, zeroing in on the source of illness—sometimes pinning down a diagnosis before any actual physical signs turn up. If needed, and often by request, she also does healing with her hands.

Intuitive diagnosis is not an unfathomable mystery. It's an approach that medical schools could teach as part of the standard curriculum. In addition to listening to a patient's heart and lungs, or palpating the outline of a liver, students can be shown how to sense these organs intuitively as well. My own training as a physician primed me to be an intuitive. One of the great miracles of medical school was being able to see and feel the anatomy of the human body. As a student "scrubbing in" on major surgeries, I had the wondrous experience of watching a heart connected to a labyrinth of blood vessels beating in a patient's chest; of touching a uterus, ovaries, kidneys, and lungs—a privilege each of us should have, if we desire it, simply as an initiation into what it means to be human. It's so odd to me that most people walk around without the foggiest notion of what we look like inside. Emblazoned in my memory is the energy of each organ, its smooth, moist texture, its even, overall warmth and glistening color. When I intuitively tune in, these varied frequencies, with ongoing practice, have now become easier for me to sense.

My dream is that physicians will explore intuitive diagnosis together—it's not infallible and still very new—so that combined with healing we can broaden our clinical expertise. When our education in the workings of the body and mind, a sacred teaching of its own, is wedded to a root intuition we all possess, our work is bound to benefit. People always say to me, "I can't believe that you're a psychiatrist and an intuitive! What an unusual mix." It doesn't have to be this unusual, however. Just think of it: What could be more natural than a doctor with intuitive insight who can heal not only with medicine but with energy? We could be rallying all our forces, making the most out of what we have to give.

Beyond technology, beyond the grandest achievements of the intellectual mind, our bodies and spirits are aching to be healed, physically as well as spiritually. This demands that medicine evolve, breathe with our spirits as they continually grow more vast. It's time to honor the knowledge of our bodies that we glean from being intuitive, and to seek an inner stillness that can sustain us. Medicine must be able to keep pace with the needs of the human heart. However, it will always fall short until it embraces the fundamental essence of healing: that we long to love and be loved, to feel and know the nature of our divine source. When science and spirituality finally join forces, medicine will achieve its full power. And doctors, by reviving their own spirits, will become true healers once again.

As a civilization we can no longer afford to silence intuition. Our success is indelibly linked to staying in close touch with our inner instincts, with what we intuitively know to be true, not diminishing the value of our intellect, but enriching it. Otherwise, we run the risk of reenacting over and over again the tragic legend of Cassandra, the prophetess cursed by Apollo so that her visions would never be believed. Even when she foretold the destruction of Troy, her words fell on deaf ears. In our world, we must not allow this to happen. To be a seer is to be deserving of the highest esteem.

For me there's a strength that has come from being intuitive. It's not fragile or tenuous, wilting when I need it most. The more my faith in my intuitive instincts matured, the more they assumed a natural authority that far overshadows even the circles of fear I've been known to run around myself. Just recently I appreciated anew how this clarity is a saving grace, restoring my sense of perspective. For the past few years I had been putting together an intuitive research project with a woman who was perfect for the job. In fact, Catherine and I had grown quite close. I couldn't have asked for anyone more skilled or devoted, and I had no reason to doubt that she would see the project through to the end. Even so, six months ago I dreamed that Catherine and I were intently discussing the project in a beautiful Manhattan hotel room overlooking Central Park. All of a sudden, another woman's voice enthusiastically called out from a back bedroom, "I really love the work you're doing." I never once saw her face, and I was sure we hadn't met, but I knew that she was going to play a critical role in the project, perhaps even be Catherine's replacement—a notion way too overwhelming to deal with at the time. I put it on the back burner.

Months later, Catherine announced that she'd been offered a job she'd be crazy to turn down and was moving out of L.A. My heart sank. I was happy for her, but terrified that the project would fall apart, devastated by the loss of her support. In the past I would have been consumed with fear, feeling utterly defeated. But now I didn't fall into that trap; I remembered the dream and didn't panic. For weeks I was left on my own, but the peace of mind my dream offered kept me afloat until one day I received a call: A friend of Catherine's, newly relocated from New York, was on the line. She was bright, energetic, just as excited about the project as Catherine had been. Instantly we connected; our work together to finish the project has begun. Once again I seem to have been blessed with the right person at the right time.

Why this experience is valuable to me and what I hope to impart to you is that being intuitive doesn't mean that we're free from doubts and fears. It's just that with faith our intuitive convictions take on more power. The balance changes; our knowings become so potent that they counter the negativity that threatens to knock us off base. On the one hand I might be thinking, Oh my God, I'm going to be abandoned. Yet a stronger feeling, an exhilaration, ripples through me, signaling that something good, perhaps even better, is ahead. When this happens, I go with my intuition. There's no contest. No matter what messages we receive, they're guideposts intended for our growth, a thread between us.

The ties that bind. If there's one thing that never ceases to amaze me in my work and in talking to people nearly everywhere I go—from the woman at the dry cleaners to parking attendants to clinical psychologists—it's that practically everyone with the tiniest hint of permission, has an intuitive story to tell. There's a longing I've witnessed in so many people to reconnect with their visionary side. This burst of intuitive electricity, surging through us as a collective, is only one sign of openings upon openings yet to come. We all possess extraordinary capacities: The reality is that we can see forward into the future, back into the past, and can accurately intuit the present. Wondrous, yes— but only the tip of the iceberg. Being intuitive allows us to move through time fluently, provides an ever-widening portal through which we can view the divine.

The highest purpose of our lives, as I see it, is to give and receive love. We're reminded of this regularly in churches and synagogues, and we try to do our best to be good people. But many of us have not yet had a direct, convincing experience of the divine. Intuition can make it real. It can remove the intangible barrier that keeps love from us, unveiling the mystery.

The divine is right before our eyes, but so often we can't recognize it—the great riddle of the universe. Ordinarily we walk
around in the world unawakened, painfully divided from the holiness in our lives. To feel the divine firsthand, it helps for us to
learn how to become sensitive to the subtle energies in our
body—intuitive and heart energies especially—and do everything we can to enliven them so they can grow. Then the range
of what we're able to sense intuitively gets bumped up a few
notches and the divine is magnified. Stilling yourself daily in
meditation, for instance, with the specific intention of contacting the divine is like depositing pennies in a bank. Each time
you meditate, your energy builds. At the start you may feel
nothing, but gradually you pass over an invisible threshold; before you know it, you have the experience.

Any way you fine-tune your sensitivities—focusing on the
beauty around you, getting your energy balanced by a healer or
teacher, giving and receiving love at every possible turn—moves
you closer to the divine. It could happen one night when you're
gazing up at the stars as you have a thousand times before. Suddenly you'll really see: You become entranced by their pale,
shimmering light; a shift occurs and now the night sky appears
more beautiful than you ever could have imagined—perfect, in-
escapably holy. You're in awe, appreciating the divine perhaps
for the very first time.

The point of our journey, the harvest of intuition, is this direct
knowing of the divine. With a tender hand, it carries us over the
abyss that separates us from an enlightened future. Even in our
troubled world today, there's hope, which is nurtured by our love,
our acts of kindness, our longing to reach out to the light. By
doing this, we're preparing the foundation for the transition yet to
come. With intuition at our side, sensing the reality of the divine
that is always with us, we have a faithful reminder that a loving
world is not just an elusive fantasy: it's within our power to
achieve.

Love creates a circuit between people. Once we're able to offer
ourselves love, it begins to overflow and we treat others with
more care. Giving love inherently feels good—there's no food on

earth so sustaining. By helping others we also help ourselves. This is our healing. Love flows through us as we reach out and become its messenger. We don't need to make any grand gestures. Often, in the simplest of actions, we find something to give. A word of encouragement, a smile, or a pointed question at exactly the right time is all that's required.

When intuition and love are commingled, when we take the time to find our spiritual source, we are finally meeting ourselves and ministering to our hearts. What was latent within us comes alive. The depth of our spirit is limitless. We must trust where it leads us, to the center of our being, holding fast through darkness and light. As Rilke, in his wisdom, advises a young poet, "Go into yourself and see how deep the place is from which your life flows." This is both the starting point of our journey and the ultimate epiphany. There is no end.

This path is far from solitary. We walk it together, sustaining one another, forging a new way. One by one, each of us is igniting a pure, steady inner light. We're becoming a luminous sea of candles flickering in what before was only shadow. Already change is here, bringing with it the promise of collective spiritual and intuitive awakening, beginning to liberate us from old fears and misconceptions. The force welling up inside us cannot be stopped. It's as if all of humankind's previous actions have been priming us for the coming era.

The change is not a silent one. It has a distinct sound. Late at night, if I listen carefully, I can hear the stirrings of a gentle wind emanating from the earth's core. It is warm and soothing, penetrates every crevice of our world. I can feel it rising in my blood and bones, as exacting as a laser beam, as soft and round as the memory of my mother's womb. It is blowing through each of us. All of mankind will be touched; it is only a matter of time.

Afterword

Writing this book has been a journey toward my own freedom. For so many years, as a psychiatrist and an intuitive, I felt exiled in two different worlds. Both parts of myself are equally dear to me, the currents of each running deep. During my years of medical training I cultivated a great respect for the rational mind. I also touch a realm that many people have yet to see, as real to me as the earth beneath my feet. I've struggled to heal the split between these two worlds. My spirit wouldn't stand for anything less.

My quest to become whole is unusual only in not having been acknowledged as a common path. We are all visionaries. Even if you don't think of yourself as intuitive, our prescience lies latent, a shared legacy we each have the right to claim. That any of us have ever been forced to suppress our intuitive experiences is a travesty, the toxic fallout from a form of ignorance I'm fighting to dispel. I hope my life may be a template so your path can be easier, so that many of the stumbling blocks I faced can be avoided or, at the very least, anticipated. The wonder I've felt at discovering the versatility and expansiveness of the spirit is awaiting you, too.

My path was intricate, often like a maze. I needed a decade to establish my center: ten full years of swinging back and forth like a pendulum to understand that this split was an illusion. It's not that intuition resides in one realm and the rest of the life we lead in another. The barrier between the conscious and the unconscious is a lot more permeable than we think. These two apparently separate domains can be organically meshed. The secret lies in the vastness of our beings, our capacity to unite what on the outside seem like opposite extremes. We don't have to make a sacrifice, choosing to live out just one side of ourselves. There is a saner common ground. We can embody it all.

Through the Northridge earthquake, the Altadena and Malibu fires and the recent floods, for nearly two years I continued writing *Second Sight*. Despite these disasters and the lingering chaos they caused, still each day I felt I was slowly inching closer to myself. My tendency for many years was to take refuge in anonymity, never wanting to attract too much attention, wary that in doing so I would somehow come to harm. Expressing my true voice—not in a whisper but with outright assurance—never felt safe to me. Maybe it's because I was raised by a mother of such intensity and strength that I got used to living in her shadow. It let me off the hook; there was a comfort zone there. But as I came into my own as an intuitive woman, I hungered more and more to put into words the yearnings of my deepest heart. This book has been my salvation, revealing the secrets I've kept to myself for such a long time. So many of my emotions are laid bare here. It has made me strong. This has been my healing.

For me, the beauty of being intuitive is moving closer to the wisdom of our own hearts. Though it can be simply a means of information gathering, I've found its highest value is in penetrating the layers of reality that reveal the interconnectedness of all things. My hope is that by turning inward, by pursuing an intuitive path, you begin to feel a connection with yourself, with others and with the world around you, but most important with spirit. Then our pangs of loneliness and longing can finally be eased; the exile from ourselves is over. At last we've come home.

When I look at my life, the evolution of growing into my intuitive abilities, I see a persistent image. I'm standing next to a massive block of unformed stone, steadily chiseling away. I know the rock is sacred. I know I must keep working, no matter how long it takes. There's enormous joy in this. And devotion, a willingness to return day after day, even though my progress may at times be hard to discern. The rock becomes more radiant as I work. Its angles, curves, and crevices are infinite.

What this image evokes in me, and what I kept coming back to in my own mind over and over while writing *Second Sight,* is freedom. The freedom I've felt liberating my authentic intuitive voice, not having to pretend to be small anymore or conform to someone else's notion of who I should be. The freedom to soar as high and dive as deep as my spirit will take me, to forcefully and with pride speak my own truth. And so I feel blessed. With all my heart I wish the same freedom for you.

Guide for Further Reading

Broughton, Richard. *Parapsychology: The Controversial Science.* New York: Ballantine Books, 1992.

Bruyere, Rosalyn. *Wheels of Light.* New York: Simon and Schuster, 1994.

Crichton, Michael. *Travels.* New York: Alfred A. Knopf, 1988.

Dossey, Larry, M.D. *Healing Words.* San Francisco: Harper- Collins, 1993.

Garrett, Eileen J. *My Life.* Salem, NH: Ayer Company, 1986.

Grof, Stanislav, M.D. *The Holotropic Mind: The Three Levels of Human Consciousness and How They Shape Our Lives.* San Francisco: HarperCollins, 1992.

―――, and Christina Grof. *Spiritual Emergency: When Personal Transformation Becomes a Crisis.* Los Angeles: Jeremy Tarcher, 1990.

Joy, Brugh, M.D. *Joy's Way: A Map for the Transformational Journey.* Los Angeles: Jeremy Tarcher, 1979.

Krieger, Dolores. *The Therapeutic Touch: How to Use Your Hands to Help or Heal.* New York: Simon and Schuster, 1992.

Le Shan, Lawrence. *How to Meditate: A Guide to Self-Discovery.* New York: Bantam Books, 1974.

Levine, Stephen. *A Gradual Awakening.* New York: Doubleday, 1979.

―――. *Guided Meditations, Explorations and Healings.* New York: Anchor Doubleday, 1991.

Mishlove, Jeffrey. *The Roots of Consciousness.* Revised 2nd ed. Tulsa, OK: Council Oak Books, 1993.

Moyers, Bill. *Healing and the Mind.* New York: Doubleday, 1993.

Murphy, Michael. *The Future of the Body: Explorations into the Further Evolution of Human Nature.* New York: Putnam/Jeremy Tarcher, 1992.

Ostrander, Sheila, and Lynn Schroeder. *Intuitive Discoveries Behind the Iron Curtain.* New York: Prentice-Hall, 1970.

Rhine, J. B. *ESP after Sixty Years.* Boston: Brandon Publishing Company, n.d.

Targ, Russell, and Keith Harary. *The Mind Race: Understanding and Using Intuitive Ability.* New York: Villard Books, 1984.

―――, and Harold Putoff. *Mind-Reach: Scientists Look at Intuitive Ability.* New York: Dell, 1977.

Resources

Spiritual Emergence Network
   c/o Association for Transpersonal
   Psychology
   P.O. Box 50187
   Palo Alto, CA 94303
   415-453-1106
   www.spiritualemergence.info

The Intuition Network
   475 Gate 5 Road, Suite 300
   Sausalito, CA 94965
   415-331-5650

The Institute of Noetic Sciences
   101 San Antonio Road
   Petaluma, CA 94952
   707-775-3500
   www.noetic.org

The International Society for the
Study of Subtle Energies and Energy
Medicine (ISSSEEM)
   356 Goldco Circle
   Golden, CO 80401
   303-278-2228

Spirit Rock Meditation Center
   P.O. Box 909
   Woodacre, CA 94973
   415-488-0164

Esalen Institute
   Big Sur, CA 93920
   408-667-3000
   www.esalen.org

The John E. Fetzer Institute
   1292 West KL Avenue
   Kalamazoo, MI 49009
   616-375-2000

The Institute of Transpersonal
Psychology
   1069 East Meadow Circle
   Palo Alto, CA 94303
   650-493-4430
   www.itp.edu

National Institutes of Health
Office of Alternative Medicine
   6120 Executive Blvd, Suite 450
   Rockville, MD 20892 9904
   301-402-2466

The Association for Comprehensive
Energy Psychology (ACEP)
   303 Park Avenue South, Box
   1051
   New York, NY 10010-3657
   619-861-2237
   www.energypsych.org

Acknowledgments

There are so many people whose encouragement empowered me to write this book:

Stephen Mitchell, writer and guide, and Vicki Chang, healer, friends there since the beginning.

Michael Katz, literary agent, midwife for both the vision and delivery of this project; without his insight and devotion, it would never have been born.

My extraordinary editors: Colleen Kapklein, whose enthusiasm and skill did so much to bring the manuscript to completion; and Nanscy Neiman-LeGette, whose loving care shaped and developed it.

Richard Pine, my angel of a literary agent.

Shaye Areheart, publisher, friend, and champion of my work.

The amazing team at Three Rivers Press: Philip Patrick, Kate Kennedy, Jay Sones, and Dyana Messina.

Stephan Schwartz, mentor and sounding board, pioneer, generous giver of time and wisdom.

For their dedicated participation and patience in helping to define and map out the book, I'm grateful to Thomas Farber, Paula Cizmar, and Andrea Cagan.

Many others have also made vital contributions, and I want to acknowledge the assistance of Hal Bennett, Diana Baroni, Jonathan Cott, Burnard LeGette, Daniel Kaufman, Mark Kuo, Thelma Moss, Jeffrey Mishlove, Daoshing Ni, Mark E. Pollack, Terry Schoonhoven, Hayden Schwartz, Barry Taff, and Jollyn West.

My abiding appreciation to my family and friends for their soul support: Mila Aranda, Barbara Baird, Ann Buck, Janus Cercone, Janis Clapoff, Melissa Friedman, Linda Garbett, Berenice Glass, Michael Manheim, Richard Metzner, Mignon McCarthy, Dean Orloff, Theodore Orloff, Phyllis Ostrum-Paul, Sindy Paul, Marc Seltzer, Chris Snyder, Elizabeth and Nate Snyder, and Leong Tan.

Finally, I want to express gratitude to my patients, from whom I've continued to learn so very much as we travel together on the path.

About the Author

Judith Orloff, M.D., is a board-certified psychiatrist and assistant clinical professor of psychiatry at UCLA. She is also author of the bestsellers *Emotional Freedom, Positive Energy*, and *Dr. Judith Orloff's Guide to Intuitive Healing*. Dr. Orloff is an international lecturer and workshop leader on the relationship between medicine, intuition, and emotional freedom. Her work has been featured on CNN, PBS, and NPR and has appeared in *USA Today, O Magazine*, and *Self*. Dr. Orloff is the creator of YouTube's Intuition and Emotional Freedom Channel at www.youtube.com/judithorloffmd. She lives by the ocean in Los Angeles, California.

For information on Dr. Judith Orloff's books and workshop schedule, visit DrJudithOrloff.com or send inquiries to:

Judith Orloff, M.D.
2080 Century Park East, Suite 1811
Los Angeles, CA 90067

Also by Dr. Judith Orloff

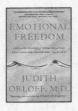

Emotional Freedom
Liberate Yourself from Negative Emotions and Transform Your Life
$24.95 HARDCOVER (CANADA: $27.95)
978-0-307-33818-1

Positive Energy
*10 Extraordinary Prescriptions for Transforming Fatigue, Stress,
and Fear into Vibrance, Strength, and Love*
$14.95 PAPER (CANADA: $18.95)
978-1-4000-8216-2

Dr. Judith Orloff's Guide to Intuitive Healing
5 Steps to Physical, Emotional, and Sexual Wellness
$14.95 PAPER (CANADA: $21.00)
978-0-8129-3098-6

Available wherever books are sold